C Programmer's Toolkit

2nd Edition

Jack Purdum

PROGRAMMING
SERIES

C Programmer's Toolkit, 2nd Edition

©1992 by Que® Corporation

Library of Congress Catalog No.: 91-61729

ISBN: 0-88022-788-5

93 92   8 7 6 5 4 3 2

Interpretation of the printing code: the rightmost double-digit number is the year of the book's printing; the rightmost single-digit number, the number of the book's printing. For example, a printing code of 91-1 shows that the first printing of the book occurred in 1991.

To my dad, John W. Purdum

Publisher
Richard K. Swadley

Publishing Manager
Joseph Wikert

Managing Editor
Neweleen Trebnik

Production Editor
Cheri Clark

Copy Editor
Gayle Johnson

Editorial Assistants
San Dee Phillips
Molly Carmody

Technical Editor
Tim Moore

Cover Design
Dan Armstrong

Book Design
Scott Cook

Production Coordinator
Mary Beth Wakefield

Production
Claudia Bell
Brad Chinn
Michelle Cleary
Mark Enochs
Sandy Grieshop
Denny Hager
Audra Hershman
Phil Kitchel
Bob LaRoche
Laurie Lee
Ann Owen
Tad Ringo
Linda Seifert
Bruce D. Steed
Phil Worthington

Indexer
Jeanne Clark

Composed in ITC Garamond and Macmillan Digital
by Que Corporation

Dr. Purdum received his B.A. degree from Muskingum College and M.A. and Ph.D. degrees from Ohio State University. He was a university professor for 18 years before becoming president of Ecosoft, a software house that specializes in microcomputer software. Dr. Purdum has received many teaching and research awards, including a National Science Foundation grant to study microcomputers in education. He has published a number of professional articles; a BASIC programming text; and magazine articles in *BYTE, Personal Computing, Interface Age,* and *Computer Language.* He also has authored several other C programming books.

CONTENT OVERVIEW

TABLE OF CONTENTS ▼

It's been almost three years since I began writing the *C Programmer's Toolkit*. A lot has changed in those three years. Systems are generally faster now, with 80286 and 80386 being the dominant systems. MS-DOS still is the operating system of choice, but Microsoft's Windows is gaining support. The days of the non-IBM-compatible machine also seem to have passed. Most programmers now can assume that video memory, MS-DOS, and other elements of the system behave in a predictable manner.

Another significant change is that the number of compiler vendors has been reduced substantially. When the first edition of this book was written, there were two dozen C compiler vendors for the PC. Now that number has been reduced to about a half-dozen. Of those, the market is dominated by the Borland and Microsoft C compilers.

Although other vendors exist in the C compiler market (for example, Watcom, Zortech, and Metaware), the second edition of this book concentrates on code for the Borland and Microsoft C compilers. In those instances in which the source code for a function differs between the two compilers, we will draw your attention to those differences. Because most other vendors support a standard library with functions similar to Borland and Microsoft, the reader should have little difficulty compiling the functions for other compilers.

The most significant change in this edition of the text is the addition of two new chapters. The first of these new chapters develops a character-based windowing system. This chapter explains how character-based windowing functions are written, and it develops code for alert and dialog boxes. The second new chapter is an application that uses many of the functions found throughout this text, particularly the windowing functions. Although the application is quite useful on its own, the real value of the chapter is showing how the functions presented in this text can be combined into a large application.

In addition to the people acknowledged in the first edition, I would like to thank the many readers who have made comments and suggestions on the book. Many of the improvements in this edition are the result of their efforts.

Jack Purdum
Indianapolis, 1991

PREFACE TO THE FIRST EDITION

The definition of the C language by the X3J11 committee of the American National Standards Institute (ANSI) is now finished. Not only are the syntactic rules of C defined, but so are the contents of a "minimal" standard C library. The functions provided in the standard C library, for the most part, are those functions that you can expect to find as part of any ANSI-compliant C compiler. As such, virtually all of the library is as machine-inspecific as possible.

The benefit of such a standard library definition is that you have some assurance of the core functions that can be used regardless of the hardware or operating system being used. If you write programs that only use these standard library functions, the problems associated with porting your code to another environment will be significantly reduced.

On the downside, if you use only those functions in the standard C library, you may miss some of the advantages offered by both the operating system and the hardware elements that are available to the programmer.

The *C Programmer's Toolkit* attempts to provide functions that are *not* part of the standard C library, but that should prove useful to you in your programming efforts. The functions provided in this book can be grouped into three broad catagories. The first group of functions draws upon the resources provided as part of MS-DOS (for example, interrupt calls to the operating system). A second group of functions is based on known elements of the hardware associated with MS-DOS machines (for example, direct writing to screen memory). The third group of functions is generic in that they can be used on any system that provides an ANSI C compiler (for example, the statistical and financial routines presented in Chapter 9).

The first two classes of functions are specific to MS-DOS and IBM PC and compatible machines. If you are writing C code for some other environment, chances are pretty good that the code could be modified for that system. The third class of functions should be portable to virtually any system.

For those of you writing for MS-DOS and PC compatibles, the source code for all of the functions and programs described in this text is included on the disk bound in the back of the book. If you want to use these functions, you should compile them with your favorite compiler and (preferably) use a librarian to create a Microsoft-compatible library file (for example, *.LIB). If you do not have a librarian, you can link in each support function as a separate object module (for example, an *.OBJ file).

As usual, many people have contributed to this book in one way or another. Specifically, I am indebted to Chris Devoney, Carl Landau, Tim Leslie, and David Reed for their help. I would also like to thank Allen Wyatt, who served as technical editor, and others at Que for their efforts to make this a better book. To all of them, my sincere thanks.

Jack Purdum
Indianapolis, 1989

TRADEMARK ACKNOWLEDGMENTS ▼

Que Corporation has made every attempt to supply trademark information about company names, products, and services mentioned in this book. Trademarks indicated below were derived from various sources. Que Corporation cannot attest to the accuracy of this information.

ANSI is a registered trademark of American National Standards Institute.

UNIX System V is a registered trademark of AT&T.

Turbo C and Borland C++ are registered trademarks of Borland International, Inc.

Eco-C88 is a trademark of Ecosoft, Inc.

IBM is a registered trademark of International Business Machines Corporation.

WordStar is a registered trademark of MicroPro International Corporation.

Microsoft, MS-DOS, QuickC, and Windows are registered trademarks of Microsoft Corporation.

THUMB TAB INDEX

Introduction

This introduction discusses what we hope to accomplish in this book and how we will accomplish it. We also will lay out some of the conventions and ground rules for using this book, plus some ideas to help you get the most from this book. Finally, we also argue why you might want to read the entire book, even though you think that your interest lies in one specific area only.

The Goals of This Book

This book's primary goal is to provide you with C functions that will be useful in your programming activities. Although a number of commercially available libraries offer functions similar to many presented here, there are several advantages to using this book. First, the book explains how each function works, giving you a broader understanding of each function and how the C language is used with your system. Second, this book/disk set provides the source code for each function. Having both the source code and an understanding of how things work will make it easier for you to modify or extend the functions. Having the source code also means that you can move most of the functions to other environments if necessary.

Many functions presented in this book will be new additions to your programming arsenal; you would not find them in a standard C library. Most are not found in the proposed C standard library as defined in the ANSI (American National Standards Institute) X3J11 report. There are exceptions, such as the chapter on searching, sorting, and parsing, but there usually is little reason for you to write these functions because they are defined in the ANSI standard C library. You must, however, develop various support functions to make a standard library function (such as sort()) work properly. This book will show you how to write support that takes advantage of those specialized standard library functions.

Clearly, many C compilers provide more library functions than are defined in the ANSI standard library. Some of these functions will be discussed in this text. Still, there are advantages to presenting them here. First, you will have the source code to those functions when it may not be available otherwise. Second, and perhaps more important, you will understand how those functions work. Many of the screen functions presented in Chapter 1, "Screen Functions," for example, are available in commercial libraries. But once you learn the additional material covered in Chapter 1, you should be able to write almost any interrupt routine you want using MS-DOS. Further, this text shows you how C functions work; you can use this knowledge to write new functions that are similar to, yet different from, those presented here. You should not think it unnecessary when reading about a function that you already know and may have used. Instead, think of it as a learning experience that will expand your own programming abilities.

Another of this book's goals is to develop a design philosophy that makes it easier to write functions that are reusable in different programming tasks. If you think about it, `printf()`, `fgets()`, `qsort()`, and other functions are widely used because they can cope with a variety of programming tasks. Invariably, the secret to writing such flexible functions is knowing that they can work with abstract data structures. That is, a function does not have to know about the underlying data structures being processed. It may require a certain *type* of data, but whether that piece of data is a basic C data type or a member of a complex structure makes no difference to the function itself. Of course, you cannot always write functions for abstract data structures, but the text will show you ways to make your functions as flexible as possible.

Finally, this book will help you improve your programming skills in two ways: You will learn new programming techniques as you go along, and—more important—you will learn what makes a function generic and how to prevent limiting your work to a specific task. After all, the more you can reuse existing code, the less work you will have in future tasks.

Hardware-Compiler Specifics

As important as generic functions are, it is impossible to make all functions portable to all environments. Each hardware system has its own set of "magic numbers" that make no sense in a different hardware (or software) environment. This is especially true for I/O ports, screen locations, interrupts, and related constraints that the programmer must view as constants. Yet, to present a polished program, you must take advantage of such hardware constants. Therefore, many of the functions presented in this book are specific to the IBM PC system family running PC DOS or MS-DOS. (From now on, "PC" will be used to refer to any IBM PC or compatible.)

Not all the functions presented in this book, however, are system specific. For example, virtually all functions that discuss string manipulation, searching, and sorting can be implemented on any machine. Further, many of the functions concerning numerical methods, time, and date are applicable to all systems. Many individual C functions can be moved to other systems with minimal effort.

Another consideration is the specifics of the compiler itself. There are more than a dozen C compilers available for the PC, each slightly different from the others. For example, even though printf() is a standard C library function, not all compilers support the same conversions (for example, %p may not be available). In other cases, header files that contain system-specific information have different names. There are also different names for functions that perform the same task. For example, opendir() and readdir() for one compiler do the same thing as findfirst() and findnext() for another compiler. Such duplication of tasks under different function names cannot be avoided because the functions are not standardized (that is, they are system specific and not part of the ANSI standard library). Because they are specific to a given environment, however, these functions will add polish to your programs because they do exploit the hardware-software support resources of the system. If there is a difference between function names, those differences are pointed out in the text so that you can compile the programs with different compilers.

The compilers used to test the code presented in this book are Borland's Turbo C, Ecosoft's Eco-C88, and Microsoft's Quick C. Most other commercial C compilers will perform much like these three compilers. The text that accompanies each function will point out potential areas of conflict if any exist.

How To Use This Book

Each chapter discusses one general area of coverage. If your interest is in string processing, you can turn immediately to that chapter and begin reading. There is, however, a reason for the sequencing of chapters. For example, if you want to center a string on the screen in color, you should be familiar with the function that enables you to print text in color before using the function that centers the string. In this sense, many of the functions discussed in later chapters use functions developed in earlier chapters.

Even if you want to concentrate on just one functional area, I would still suggest that you make a quick pass through the entire book before jumping to your area of special interest, for two reasons. First is the chapter sequencing mentioned earlier. You will have a better understanding of the function in question if you know how all support functions work. The second reason for reading the entire book is that you never know when the "flat forehead effect" will occur. I wonder how many times I've been reading a book on one subject when, suddenly, something in the text turns on a light and I find the answer to a (seemingly) unrelated problem. I slap my hand to my forehead and say, "Why didn't I think of that before?" Who knows? The answer to one of your problems might come to you unexpectedly, triggered by the discussion of an unrelated topic.

Chapter Organization

Each chapter starts with an overview of the functions it presents. Often, different functions use similar techniques. The screen functions in Chapter 1, "Screen Functions," are a good example. The general use of interrupts is discussed at the beginning of the chapter. The function discussion then focuses on the important aspects of the function itself. If an element is common to several functions (for example, "magic numbers" or port and memory addresses), that element is covered in the beginning of the chapter.

Each chapter also details many of the problems you might encounter by using one type of compiler as opposed to another. For example, one compiler might use malloc.h as its memory allocation header file whereas another uses memory.h. If several functions must use one of these header files covered in the chapter, these differences will be noted early in the chapter instead of being repeated in the discussion of each function. Therefore, the purpose of the discussion at the start of each chapter is to point out differences that are "consistent" among compilers.

The remainder of each chapter is a presentation of the function's source code and a description of how the function works. Some functions are so simple that the discussion may only be explained adequately. Regardless of the description's length, it will include enough material to leave you with a thorough understanding of the function in question.

Conventions Used in This Book

To simplify your reading, a number of conventions are used in this book. First, C keywords and function and variable names are written in a different typeface. This makes it easier to distinguish the keyword for from the text word "for" as well as to distinguish function and variable names that might otherwise be confused with normal text. In addition, function names are followed by parentheses, such as main(). This makes it easier to tell a function from a variable name.

Second, the C code that appears in this text can assume one of the following three forms:

- a listing

- a code fragment

- a program

A listing (for example, listing 1.2) is a complete C function. A code fragment (for example, code fragment 1.2) is simply several C statements presented to illustrate a point in the text. A program (for example, program 1.2) contains C source code with a main() in it.

If a program is typed in and compiled, and the necessary functions are linked in, it will run. A code fragment rarely contains enough statements in it even to be compiled. (Data definitions are often missing in code-fragment examples.) A listing can be compiled, but not run because it does not contain a main() in it.

Some Assumptions About You

This book assumes that you already know the syntax rules for the C programming language. If this is not the case, you should consider reading an introductory C programming book before reading this one. (An unbiased suggestion would be this author's *C Programming Guide*, 3rd Edition, published by Que Corporation.)

It is assumed that you have access to a PC-type computer and C compiler. If you do not have a C compiler, it would be to your advantage to select one of the three mentioned earlier. If you already have a compiler for your system, chances are pretty good that the code presented in this text will work with it with little or no change. You also might want to purchase a librarian. A librarian enables you to combine individual object files

(*.OBJ) into a library file (*.lib) for use by a linker. This is easier than linking each object file at link time. Some compilers include a librarian; others do not. The Ecosoft librarian is relatively inexpensive, and it works with any compiler that can produce a standard OBJ output file.

Some Tips for Getting the Most from This Book

It is good practice to experiment with a function as you read about it. If you read this material while curled up in your favorite armchair and put off using it until the next day, you won't get as much learning value from it as you would by reading about and using the function at the same time. By all means, "read and do" at the same time.

Finally, the source code for each function can be found on the disk that accompanies this text. This should save you time when you experiment with the functions. The source code is presented in the chapter subdirectories on the disk. Each file name corresponds as closely as possible to the source name as it appears in the text. That is, if you want to look at the source code for the center() function presented in Chapter 2, "String Processing," you could examine it with the command (assuming the disk is in drive A):

```
A>type chap3\center.c
```

Each function's source code is found by using the book chapter as the subdirectory and the function name as the primary file name followed by the letter *c* for the extension of the file name. The subdirectories are simply the chapter numbers (for example, chap3).

Sometimes a function name has too many letters to be used as the file name on the disk. For example, the function name invert_mat() is shortened to invert_m.c on the disk. This is necessary because MS-DOS allows a maximum of eight characters in the primary file name. This should not pose a serious problem, however, because the relationship between the full function name and the shorter file name should be obvious.

In fact, the conflict between function and file names indirectly leads us to our first design consideration:

Make the function name long enough to convey its primary task, but short enough that it is not laborious to type.

Using the preceding example, we could have shortened the function name to inv_m(), but it is not nearly as descriptive as invert_mat(). We could have used invert_matrix(), but invert_mat() is probably long enough to jog our memories even months after our last use of the function. If the name reveals the function's task at a glance, and if the name contains fewer than 10 characters, you have named the function well.

A programmer's life is full of compromises and trade-offs. Choosing between short and long function names is one of the easier trade-offs to resolve, because it usually boils down to personal preference. You will discover, however, that more serious compromises need to be addressed.

Another useful design philosophy is based on the "KISS" principle—Keep It Simple, Stupid. Almost every function presented in this text can be written several different ways. Indeed, your code can be written so cleverly that you must relearn it whenever you want to use it. To avoid this, you always should look for the simplest and most direct way to code your functions. Generally, code that is easily understood is also easily maintained. In C programming, you will learn that a few short steps often will take you a long way.

Of course, an elegant solution might be more efficient in terms of memory usage or speed, but often the gains are so small that they simply can't outweigh the beauty of a clean, simple approach to the problem. Obviously, you will choose the design philosophy you want to follow, but you would be wise to consider the trade-offs carefully.

Now, let's begin putting together your toolkit of C functions.

CHAPTER 1

Screen Functions

In this chapter, you will learn how to use the PC's resources to perform different screen functions. The functions can be grouped into those that affect:

- The entire screen

- One or more of the screen's lines

- The cursor and its position

- The screen's attributes

- The screen mode and page

A Basic Design Choice

You can perform most screen functions in two ways: by writing directly to the segment of (video) memory used for the PC's screen output, or by using the facilities provided by MS-DOS to write to the screen.

Direct Memory Writes: Pros and Cons

The greatest advantage of writing directly to video memory is that it is very fast. Indeed, speed is the only real advantage of writing directly to video memory. Complications can arise, however, when you use this direct-writing method.

To perform a direct write to video memory, you must know where the video memory is located in the system's memory address space. The complications arise because the video memory's base address differs, depending on the type of video display being used. The video memory address for a Color Graphics Adapter (CGA), for example, is different from the video memory address for a Monochrome Display Adapter (MDA). Even worse, some early systems that claimed "PC compatibility" had video memory in different memory locations regardless of the video adapter.

Fortunately, most of the systems in use today are "PC compatible." Of the many video modes supported by the PC, the text mode is relatively standard, regardless of whether the output device is an MDA, CGA, EGA, or VGA display. Because it is a simple task to determine where the start of video memory is for these devices, most of the functions presented in this book concentrate on character-based video. This results in a relatively portable set of functions across the many PC-based video displays. Even so, there still are aspects about video memory that require you to pay close attention to details.

Even if the video memory's base address is found, the segmented memory architecture of the Intel 8086-80386 family of CPU chips requires the use of four-byte pointers to access video memory. The 640 kilobytes of memory that MS-DOS can access are broken down into 64K chunks called *segments*. The way these segments are used also affects the way programs are written.

In many programming situations, you need only one memory segment for program code and one memory segment for the data used in the program. If you have ever heard someone mention a "small model" C compiler, that person was referring to a compiler that uses only two memory segments for program development: one code segment and one data segment. Several important consequences result from using a small-model compiler. Because there is only one data segment, any data pointer must be only large enough to act as an offset within the 64K address space. This offset, therefore, needs to be only 16 bits (2 raised to the 16th power is 64K).

By comparison, a "large model" compiler, which must access more than one data segment, needs not only the 16 bits for the offset part of the address within a segment, but also another 16 bits for the segment address itself. As a result, the pointer for a large-model compiler typically uses 32 bits for pointer manipulation. Moving from a small- to a large-model compiler results in some slowdown in pointer manipulation.

Direct writes to video memory increase the speed, but at the cost of a more complex code, possible incompatibility with earlier PC systems, and the possibility of having to use four-byte pointers.

To help overcome the four-byte pointer manipulation problem, some compiler vendors have released versions that support a "mixed" model. Microsoft, for example, has Release 2.0 of Quick C, and Borland has Turbo C. In a mixed model, you can mix two- and four-byte pointers in the same program. This means that pointers that must accommodate a segment-offset address can be made four bytes in size and that those that will be used in the same segment can be two bytes in size. These compilers support the reserved word "near" to signify a two-byte pointer, and "far" for a four-byte pointer.

If your compiler supports mixed-model pointers, always use near pointers whenever possible. This will ensure that the pointer manipulation is performed as efficiently as possible. Use four-byte pointers only when you have no other choice, such as when addressing video memory directly. The default pointer size for mixed-model compilers is a near (two-byte) pointer.

If your compiler does not support the mixed model, any functions that use the direct memory access techniques presented at the end of this chapter will need to be compiled with a memory model that supports four-byte pointers. In most cases, the faster screen I/O speed will offset any possible loss due to larger pointer sizes.

Using BIOS Resources: Pros and Cons

The advantage of using *BIOS* (Basic Input/Output System) resources for screen functions is that video memory location and compatibility problems are not considerations. Virtually all the screen functions perform their tasks through the use of software interrupts for the BIOS services defined for MS-DOS. The result is code that is simple to understand, easy to maintain, and portable to all MS-DOS machines. Nothing beyond the BIOS calls (such as device drivers like ANSI.SYS) is required to accomplish the tasks. BIOS resources also eliminate the problems posed by a large-model compiler.

The disadvantage of using BIOS resources is that you sacrifice the speed provided by direct memory writes. This loss of speed occurs because BIOS calls often execute more code than is necessary to accomplish the task at hand. This is particularly true when the task is simply writing a character to the screen.

Making a Choice

This book will acquaint you with both methods of accessing the video display so that you can select which technique to use for your particular programming tasks. After a brief discussion of where things are in memory on an MS-DOS machine, this chapter presents several functions that show you how to use software interrupt routines. The chapter closes with a discussion of how to perform direct writes to video memory and gives a generalized function for formatting output to video memory.

MS-DOS in a Nutshell

Reduced to its simplest form, MS-DOS is made up of three fundamental parts:

- The BIOS

- The DOS kernel

- The command processor

The BIOS is responsible for the rudimentary input and output of the system, including the video display, keyboard, line printer, disk I/O, and date and time services. The major responsibility of the DOS kernel is memory and file management. The command processor is the part most visible to the user. It accepts directives from the user (such as DIR and COPY) and causes them to be executed. The most common command processor, which is supplied with MS-DOS, is known as COMMAND.COM; other command processors (often called *shells*) are available, however.

The command processor is capable of processing three types of commands from the user: commands that are either *internal* or *external* to the command processor, and *batch files*. Using COMMAND.COM as an example, commands such as DIR and COPY are contained "within" COMMAND.COM and can be executed directly. External commands, such as CHKDSK, must be loaded into memory by COMMAND.COM before they can be processed. Batch files simply are commands that can be interpreted by COMMAND.COM; they are either internal or external to COMMAND.COM.

The memory map shown in figure 1.1 will help you visualize where the different parts of MS-DOS reside after you first turn on the system.

Fig. 1.1. A typical memory map for MS-DOS.

0x0000	Interrupt vectors
0x0400	BIOS
	DOS kernel
	Device drivers
	COMMAND.COM (resident)
	Program area (TPA)
0xA0000	Display memory
0xC8000	Additional BIOS services
0xCC000	
0xE0000	
0xFFFFF	Reserved for BIOS

As you can see, the programs you write eventually end up in the Transient Program Area (TPA) of memory. To make the TPA as large as possible, only part of COMMAND.COM is kept in memory at all times; the remainder of COMMAND.COM is swapped in and out of memory as needed. Notice also that the area of memory reserved for the video display begins at 0xa0000. This is consistent with the normal MS-DOS limit of having 640K of memory, even though memory (video memory, for example) must exist outside this limit.

This chapter will show you how to access some of the services available to you through the BIOS and how to write directly to the video memory for increased I/O speed. First, some of the BIOS routines will be looked at.

Using Software Interrupt Routines

One MS-DOS resource is the BIOS. Normally, BIOS services are contained in read-only memory (ROM), hence the term *ROM BIOS*. To use the services of the BIOS, you need only to set up BIOS arguments properly and call the proper BIOS interrupt number. The BIOS interrupt affecting the video service routines is interrupt 0x10h (read as "10 hexadecimal"), which is called the *video interrupt*. (For more information on all BIOS services, you can refer to Terry Dettman's *DOS Programmer's Reference*, an excellent resource available from Que Corporation.)

Function Numbers

Many of the BIOS interrupt services perform only one task. Interrupt 0x00h, for example, is the divide-by-zero service routine. The video interrupt, on the other hand, provides more than a dozen video service routines. Because the different video services all are part of interrupt 0x10h, you need a way to distinguish between them. The result is something called a *function number*, which tells the BIOS the specific video service routine you want to use. Therefore, if function 0x01h is the function that sets the cursor type, you would say, "Interrupt 0x10h, function 0x01h is the video interrupt for setting the cursor." All the screen functions presented in this chapter build on the various functions associated with the 0x10h video interrupt services of BIOS.

With this in mind, all you need to learn is how to pass the proper information to BIOS to accomplish the task at hand.

Calling an Interrupt

To call a BIOS interrupt, you must load the CPU registers with specific information necessary for the BIOS services to perform their task. To do this, you need a convenient means of loading a set of "pseudoregisters" with the information required by the real CPU registers. Fortunately, this process is accomplished easily with a portion of the dos.h header file (see code fragment 1.1).

Code Fragment 1.1. XREG *and* HREG *structures for* dos.h *header file.*

```
struct   XREG{
   unsigned   ax,bx,cx,dx,si,di;
};
struct   HREG{
   char   al,ah,bl,bh,cl,ch,dl,dh;
};
union   REGS   {
  struct   XREG   x;
  struct   HREG   h;
};
```

All C compilers use the structure declarations shown in code fragment 1.1. Note that the structure named XREG emulates *16-bit* CPU registers, and HREG emulates *8-bit* registers. Finally, REGS is a union capable of holding either the XREG or the HREG structure. (The actual storage requirement for REGS is 12 bytes, the size required by XREG.)

In a function, the definition

```
union REGS ireg;
```

creates a union named ireg of type REGS. Because it is a union, its contents can be treated as if they were 16-bit or 8-bit registers. If, for example, you need to stuff five hex into the (16-bit) ax register, you might use

```
ireg.x.ax = 0x05;
```

If you need to stuff the same information into the 8-bit al register, you could use

```
ireg.h.al = 0x05h;
```

Because ireg is a union of type REGS, you can use either the XREG or the HREG structure, as long as you carefully keep track of the union's contents at all times.

Most of this book's interrupt calls use the REGS union for loading the register with the information needed to use properly the BIOS interrupt services. The specifics of how REGS is used will become clear as the screen functions are described.

Finding Out About the Screen—*getvmode( )*, *getvcols( ), getvdev( )*

If you plan to do a lot with the video screen, it will help to know something about the environment you are using. In other words, what kind of video display are you facing? The functions presented in this section use BIOS interrupt routines to find information about the screen being used.

A programmer never should assume anything about the screen's status. For example, some programs (especially some public domain software) leave the screen in a 40x25 color text mode after the program ends. If your program starts by addressing the cursor at row 12, column 60 of the screen, all kinds of things might happen. Play it safe and find out about your environment before you use it.

The Get Video Mode—*getvmode( )*

The source code for getvmode() is presented in listing 1.1.

Listing 1.1. Get video display mode.

```
/*****
                        getvmode()

    This function determines the display mode for the video device.

    Argument list:    void

    Return value:     int     the display mode, the value of which has
                              the following meanings:

    0   40x25 BW text, color card      8   160x200 16-color PCjr graphics
    1   40x25 color text               9   320x200 16-color PCjr      "
    2   80x25 BW text                 10   640x200 4-color PCjr        "
    3   80x25 color                   13   320x200 16-color EGA        "
    4   320x200 4-color graphics      14   640x200 16-color EGA        "
    5   320x200 4-color graphics      15   640x350 monochrome
```

6	640x200 2-color graphics	16	640x350 4 or 16-color
		17	640x480 VGA 2-color graphics
7	monochrome text	18	640x480 VGA 16-color "
		19	320x200 VGA 256-color "

```
*****/

#include <dos.h>

int getvmode(void)
{
   union REGS ireg;

   ireg.h.ah = 0x0f;           /* Function 0x0f gets video mode */

   int86(0x10, &ireg, &ireg);
   return (ireg.h.al);
}
```

The purpose of getvmode() is to announce the type of video display device being used. As is typical of most interrupt 0x10h calls, the function number for the video interrupt is loaded into the ah member of the h structure. This structure is stored in the ireg union, which is of type REGS, as discussed earlier.

Because the ah member is the only one that needs to be loaded, you now can use the int86() function to call the BIOS interrupt routine. The prototype for int86() is

```
int86(int intno, union REGS *ireg, union REGS *oreg);
```

in which:

intno   is the interrupt number of the service being called

ireg   is a pointer to input register information needed by the interrupt

oreg   is the register information returned from the interrupt service routine

Therefore, the line

```
int86(0x10, &ireg, &ireg);
```

tells you that you are calling interrupt 0x10h (that is, the first function argument), and that the necessary register input information is found in ireg (for example, the second argument, ireg.h.ah, holds the function number), and that any return information from the interrupt will be placed in ireg.

The input and output unions both are ireg because there is no need to preserve the information in ireg after the int86() function call. Allocating another REGS variable is not necessary. All you are interested in is the value that the BIOS interrupt routine places in the al member of the structure. You can let ireg do double duty by using it to pass on the necessary "setup" information for the interrupt, and to hold the information returned from the interrupt.

Because interrupt 0x10h, function 0x0fh returns the type of video mode in the al member of the structure, the line

```
return (ireg.h.al);
```

returns the contents of the AL register that corresponds to the video display mode currently in use. The interpretation of the integer value was detailed in the function header in listing 1.1. If the return value is 3, for example, then the current display mode is an 80x25 color text screen.

Get Video Columns—*getvcols( )*

The getvmode() function tells you the current display mode but requires your program to "look up" the interpretation of the return value from the call. If you call getvmode(), you probably will test the return value to determine what to do next. For example, you might have something similar to the code in code fragment 1.2.

Code Fragment 1.2. *Typical mode decoding logic.*

```
int cols, mode;

    mode = getvmode();

    switch (mode) {
       case 0:
       case 1:
         cols = 40;
         break;
```

```
     case 2:
     case 3:
     case 4:
     case 5:
     case 6:
     case 7:
       cols = 80;
       break;
     default:
       cols = 0;
       break;
   }
```

This code is common because often you need to know only whether you are working with 40 or 80 columns of text. The getvcols() function removes the support logic needed to decipher the number of columns available from your program and moves it into the library function.

This step-saving approach is another element of a design philosophy for writing a library function or any other tool:

Whenever possible, remove repetitive code from the program and place it in a library function.

Indeed, this philosophy is the whole idea behind a standard library. To illustrate, imagine how tiresome it would be if you had to type the source code for printf() into every program. By placing the code in a library function, you not only save typing time but also reduce debugging time necessitated by logic and typing errors.

The getvcols() function is illustrated in listing 1.2.

Listing 1.2. *Get video columns.*

```
/*****
                         getvcols()

    This function determines the number of columns being used
  by the video display via interrupt 0x10, function 0x0f. Most
  compilers require including the dos.h header file. Several
  other library routines call this function, such as ereol(),
  erabos(), and so on.

  Argument list:    void
```

continues

Listing 1.2. *continued*

```
    Return value:    int      the number of columns currently being used
                              by the video display (40 or 80). 0 is for
                              graphics mode.

*****/

#include <dos.h>

int getvcols(void)
{
   union REGS ireg;

   ireg.h.ah = 0x0f;

   int86(0x10, &ireg, &ireg);
   if (ireg.h.al < 2)
      return 40;              /* 40-column mode */

   if (ireg.h.al > 3 && ireg.h.al != 7)
      return 0;               /* Return 0 for any graphics mode */
   else
      return 80;              /* 80-column mode */
}
```

The beginning of getvcols() is identical to getvmode(), except that you examine ireg.h.al to determine the number of columns available on the display.

If you decipher the return value from getvmode(), you will find more information. But if you are interested only in the number of available screen columns, using getvcols() eliminates the need to decode the return value from getvmode().

Get Video Device—*getvdev()*

Note that getvcols() and getvmode() return values that depend on the screen mode's current status. If you are using an EGA display and you type **MODE BW40** on the command line, both getvcols() and getvmode() suggest that you have only a 40-column screen with which to work. The getvdev()

function returns a value that tells you what the screen is *capable* of rather than its current status as dependent on the mode's status. This function is illustrated in listing 1.3.

Listing 1.3. *Get video device—color or monochrome.*

```
/*****
                                getvdev()

     This function determines whether the video supports color.
   Note that the return value is not affected by the MS-DOS
   "mode" command. Bits 4 and 5 determine video status. If 4 and
   5 are on, it is a monochrome card.

     Argument list:    void

     Return value:     int        1  =  monochrome
                                  2  =  color
*****/

#include <dos.h>

#define VMASK   0x30           /* Bit mask for testing      */
#define VPORT   0x410          /* Port for equipment status */

int getvdev(void)
{
   int i;

   i = peek(VPORT, 0x00);      /* This assumes OFFSET, SEGMENT */
   i = i & VMASK;
   if (i > 32)
      return 1;                          /* Monochrome */
   else
      return 2;                          /* Color */
}
```

If your compiler does not have a peek() function, change the first three lines of getvdev() to:

```
int *i;
i = (int *) VPORT;
i = i & gaVMASK;
```

Either form accomplishes the same task.

Pitfall Plaguing *peek( )*

Different compilers might handle the getvdev() function in somewhat different ways. The order of the arguments used by the peek() function might not be the same as that shown in listing 1.3. The code given earlier in this chapter shows the argument order as memory offset (VPORT) followed by the segment address (0x00). Other compilers (Turbo C, for example) reverse these two arguments so that the segment address appears before the offset. Turbo C presents things the way humans think about memory addressing, and Eco-C88 presents the arguments in a computer-oriented fashion. As long as you are aware that such differences exist, you easily can modify the arguments' order to suit your compiler's requirements.

Bit positions 4 and 5, found at VPORT (0x410h), determine the type of display device being used. These bits are interpreted as follows:

Bit 5	Bit 4	Device
0	1	40x25 color
1	0	80x25 color
1	1	80x25 monochrome

Remember that the mode command's status does not affect the value found in bits 4 and 5. As a result, you can test the return values to see whether color is supported. If getvdev() returns 2 (color) and getvcols() returns 80, it is safe to assume that 80x25 color information can be displayed on the screen.

Choices, Choices, Choices

As a programmer, you usually have choices about the way a given task is done. For example, listing 1.3 uses the peek() function to determine whether the video device supports color. There are, however, other ways to determine the same information. Listing 1.4 shows how to use an interrupt to determine whether the display supports color text.

Listing 1.4. *Using the equipment status word interrupt.*

```
/*****
                              getvdev1()

    This function determines whether the video supports color. In
    this function, bits 4 and 5 have the following interpretation:

                   01      40x25 color
                   10      80x25 color
                   11      80x25 monochrome



    Argument list:    void

    Return value:     int        1 = 40x25 color
                                  2 = 80x25 color
                                  3 = 80x25 monochrome


*****/

#include <dos.h>


int getvdev1(void)
{
   union REGS ireg;

   int86(0x11, &ireg, &ireg);
   return ( (ireg.x.ax & 0x30) >> 4);
}
```

Interrupt 0x11 gets the equipment status word for the system. The interpretation of the bits is shown in table 1.1.

Table 1.1. *Equipment status word.*

Bits	Interpretation
0	Disk drive installed (1 = yes)
1	Math coprocessor installed (1 = yes)
2-3	System board RAM
	00 = 16K

continues

Table 1.1. *continued*

Bits	Interpretation
	01 = 32K
	10 = 48K
	11 = 64K
	(On PS/2s, bit 2 is a pointing device and bit 3 is not used)
4-5	Video mode
	01 = 40x25 color
	10 = 80x25 color
	11 = 80x25 monochrome
6-7	Number of disk drive (one offset, so that 00 = 1 drive, 01 = 2, etc.)
8	Not used
9-11	Number of serial cards
12	Game adapter (not used on PS/2)
13	Internal modem (PS/2 only)
14-15	Number of printers attached

In listing 1.4, you bit-shift the value in AX to get the video mode before returning from the function. It should be obvious that interrupt 0x11 can give you much more information than simply the video mode.

Finally, listing 1.5 shows another way you can determine the initial video mode.

Listing 1.5. *Using video mode byte.*

```
/*****

                            getvdev2()

   This function determines whether the video supports color. In
this function, the video mode is read directly from system memory.
The byte at memory address 0x0040:0049 (segment:offset) stores the
video mode. The interpretation of the return value is as shown in
the function header in listing 1.1.



Argument list:     void

Return value:      int        video mode number (see listing
                              1.1 for interpretation)

*****/
```

```
int getvdev2(void)
{
   unsigned char far *ptr;

   ptr = (unsigned char far *) 0x00400049;

   return (int) *ptr;
}
```

This example simply uses a *far* character pointer to examine the memory location where the video mode is stored. The cast to a four-byte pointer is needed to avoid warnings from the compiler when the mixed model is used.

As shown in listings 1.3, 1.4, and 1.5, you can choose how you determine the video mode. Similar alternatives exist for many other interrupt routines. Now the question becomes "Which code should I use in my programs?" The answer depends on the specific needs of your program. If your program expects to call a function many times, speed differences might be important. If you are programming microwave ovens, code size may be the limiting factor. You must decide what factors are most important.

You can get some idea of the speed differences among listings 1.3 through 1.5 simply by looking at the code. Because listing 1.5 has no other function calls in it, you would expect it to be the fastest. The other two listings both have function calls in them, but listing 1.4 also involves some bit masking and shifting. Therefore, you might expect listing 1.4 to be the slowest of the three methods. Table 1.2 shows the relative timings for the three methods.

Table 1.2. *Relative timings for the video mode functions.*

Function Listing	Relative Time (Fastest = 1.0)
Listing 1.3	14.0
Listing 1.4	2.0
Listing 1.5	1.0

As suspected, the pointer version (listing 1.5) is the fastest, and listing 1.3 takes about 14 times longer to execute. What table 1.2 does not show, however, is that it took 30,000 iterations of the various function calls on a 33Mhz 80386 machine to get the timings high enough to interpret them.

Even then, listing 1.3 took less than .8 of a second to perform 30,000 iterations of the function. Therefore, if your program calls the function only once, it probably doesn't matter which version you use.

You often are confronted with choices similar to those suggested in listings 1.3 through 1.5. As a general rule, pointers provide the fastest solution to a given task. Likewise, the fewer the number of function calls within a function, the faster the execution speed of the function.

Changing the Video Mode— *setvmode( )*

As your computing needs change, or if your program is to run on different machines, you might need to modify the video mode. The setvmode() function (see listing 1.6) enables you to do this.

Listing 1.6. Set video mode.

```
/*****
                              setvmode()

      This function sets the display mode for the video device.

      Argument list:    int mode    The list of possible values
                                    includes the following:

      0   40x25 BW text, color card     8   160x200 16-color PCjr
                                            graphics

      1   40x25 color text              9   320x200 16-color PCjr
                                            graphics

      2   80x25 BW text                10   640x200 4-color PCjr
                                            graphics

      3   80x25 color                  13   320x200 16-color EGA
                                            graphics

      4   320x200 4-color graphics     14   640x200 16-color EGA
                                            graphics

      5   320x200 4-color graphics     15   640x350 monochrome EGA
                                            graphics
```

```
   6  640x200 2-color graphics        16  640x350 4- or 16-color
                                                  EGA graphics
   7  monochrome text

   Return value:     void

*****/

#include <dos.h>

void setvmode(int mode)
{
   union REGS ireg;

   ireg.h.ah = 0x00;                   /* Function 0 */
   ireg.h.al = mode;

   int86(0x10, &ireg, &ireg);
}
```

As shown in listing 1.6, function 0x00 enables you to set the video mode to one of 15 different values. This program is the same as the "mode" command in MS-DOS, but the argument is a numeric value passed to the function (mode). No checking is done on the argument to verify its value. (If you want, you can add code to check that a valid argument is contained in mode.) The call to interrupt 0x10 then sets the video mode to match the mode argument.

Using the Screen—*cursor( )*, *scroll( )*

Now that you can tell what type of video device you are facing, you can begin developing functions that enable you to work with the screen. The first of these functions is cursor(), which enables you to place the cursor at any given row-column position on the screen. Next is scroll(), which, as you will see later, can be used to build many other functions.

Position the Cursor—*cursor( )*

Positioning the cursor (or cursor addressing) is one of the most fundamental of all screen tools. It is most commonly used to position the cursor at certain row-column coordinates after a prompt has been displayed. For example, suppose you have the following prompt displayed beginning at row 7, column 10, as shown in figure 1.2.

Fig. 1.2. Row-column cursor positioning.

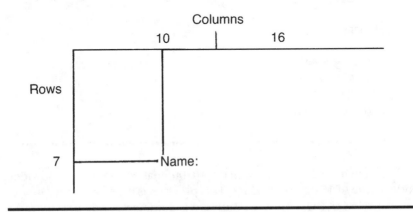

Now suppose you want to place the cursor behind "Name:" so that the user can enter his or her name. This would be done with

```
cursor(7, 16);
```

which places the cursor after "Name:" with one blank space between the colon and the cursor. (The screen looks less cluttered with one space between the cursor and the prompt message.)

The code for cursor positioning is shown in listing 1.7.

Listing 1.7. Position the cursor.

```
/*****


                        cursor()


    This function places the cursor at row-col as given by the
    function arguments. NOTE: For speed reasons, valid row and
    column numbers are NOT checked. getvcols() could be used to
```

check valid columns; rows should not exceed 25. The value 1 is subtracted from row and column so that the upper left corner of the screen is 1,1 rather than 0,0.

```
Argument list:     int row    the row position for the cursor
                   int col    the column position for the
                              cursor


Return value:      void

*****/


#include <dos.h>

void cursor(int row, int col)
{
   union REGS ireg;

   ireg.h.ah = 0x02;                        /* Function number 2 */
   ireg.h.bh = getvpage();                  /* Page ?            */
   ireg.h.dh = row - 1;
   ireg.h.dl = col - 1;

   int86(0x10, &ireg, &ireg);

}
```

As you can see in listing 1.7, interrupt 0x10, function 0x02 is used for cursor positioning. The dh member of the h structure is used to set the row position, and dl is used for the column. Because many programmers prefer to think of the home position on the screen (that is, the upper left corner) as row 1, column 1 rather than row 0, column 0 as the BIOS expects the coordinates to be presented, 1 is subtracted from each function argument. If you prefer to use location 0,0 for the home position, do not subtract 1 from the row-column arguments.

The getvpage() function is covered later in this chapter and does not need to be fully discussed here. For now, it is enough to say that the PC screen enables you to work with more than one video page in your programs. The call to getvpage() simply tells the BIOS which screen page you are using when addressing the cursor. If you do not expect to use video paging, you can remove the call to getvpage() and simply use the default page and set bh equal to 0.

After `ireg` has the proper values loaded, the `int86()` call invokes the video interrupt (0x10), and the cursor is placed at the proper row-column coordinates.

Substituting Book Functions for Vendor Functions

Many of the programs presented in this book call `cursor()` plus other functions discussed earlier in the text. In some cases, compiler vendors have implemented a substitute for these basic screen functions. It is, for example, a simple matter to substitute your vendor's cursor-addressing function for the one presented in listing 1.7 if you want to do so. For example, Borland and Microsoft provide the following cursor-addressing functions:

```
_settextposition(short row, short column)      (Microsoft)
gotoxy(int column, int row);                    (Borland)
```

Both functions serve to position the cursor at the given row-column coordinates. (Note, however, that the arguments are reversed.) If you want to use these functions rather than listing 1.7, you can insert one of the following lines in your program:

```
#define cursor(x,y) gotoxy((y),(x))             /* Borland */
#define cursor(x,y) _settestposition((x),(y))   /* Microsoft */
```

This macro substitution will enable you to use the disks included with this text without needing to change all instances of the `cursor()` function calls. You should notice two things in the `#defines` above. First, the arguments were parenthesized to prevent the side effects that can arise with parametized macros. Second, the order of the parameters for the Borland `gotoxy()` function must be reversed. If you are using some other compiler, the approach shown here will work, but you must supply the appropriate function name.

Scroll the Screen—*scroll( )*

The `scroll()` function enables you to scroll the screen up or down one or more lines. The code for the `scroll()` function appears in listing 1.8.

Listing 1.8. Scroll the screen.

```
/*****

                        scroll()

    This function scrolls the screen via a call to interrupt
0x10. The value of the variable-named function may be either
0x06 for an upward scroll or 0x07 for a downward scroll. The
arguments determine how many columns currently are in use on
the screen.

    Argument list:    int row        the row position for the window
                      int col        the column position for the window
                      int wide       the width of the window
                      int deep       the depth of the window
                      int num        the number of lines to scroll within
                                     the window (all are scrolled if 0)
                      int function   0x07 for up scroll, 0x06 for down

    Return value:     void

*****/

#include <dos.h>

void scroll(int row, int col, int wide, int deep, int num, int function)
{
    union REGS ireg;

    ireg.h.ah = function;
    ireg.h.al = num;
    ireg.h.ch = row - 1;        /* Index from (0, 0) */
    ireg.h.cl = col - 1;
    ireg.h.dh = row + deep;
    ireg.h.dl = col + wide;
    ireg.h.bh = 0;              /* Attribute byte */

    int86(0x10, &ireg, &ireg);
}
```

The first four arguments for the scroll() function define the *window* that will be scrolled. The fifth argument (num) gives the number of lines to be scrolled within that window. The last argument tells the direction in which the lines are to be moved: 6 for up or 7 for down. In the scroll() function, it is assumed that the attribute byte (in bh) is set to 0. (More information on the attribute byte is presented later in this chapter.) Notice that the row-column positions must be adjusted to agree with the home position of (1, 1). Note also that the row-column coordinates are for the upper-left corner of the window to be scrolled.

You might want to experiment with the scroll() function to see how it actually works; it has more possibilities than you might expect. For example, you can use it to scroll a display either forward or backward, perhaps in response to reading an up-arrow or down-arrow key. If the up-arrow key is sensed, you might scroll the window down one line and update the top-most line of the screen. This technique enables you to redisplay output that had been scrolled off the screen. The scroll() function enables you to update the screen quickly, especially when only one line of the screen needs updating. You will see the scroll() function often in this chapter and in subsequent chapters.

Selective Erase Screen— *eraeol( )*, *eral( )*, *erabol( )*, *eraeos( )*, *erabos( )*

This section presents functions that enable you to erase selected parts of the screen. The functions are similar, but each is used in a specific way. Code that erases to the end of a line, for example, might be written in a form similar to the following code:

```
int i;

for (i = col, i < WIDE; i++)
   putchar(' ');
```

in which the cursor is on the line to be erased, col is the column number where erasing should begin, and WIDE defines the screen width. Although this code probably will work, it is less efficient than using the routines provided in the BIOS.

Erase to End of Line—*eraeol( )*

The first of the selective erase commands, eraeol() is used to erase to the end of the line, given a row-column current cursor position. The code is presented in listing 1.9.

Listing 1.9. *Erase to end of line.*

```
/*****
                            eraeol()

    This function erases to the end of the specified line. The
 call to getvcols() determines how many columns currently are
 in use on the screen. Because columns are assumed to begin at
 1 (not 0), the starting column value has 1 subtracted from it.

    Argument list:    int row    the row position for the cursor
                      int col    the column position for the
                                 cursor
    Return value:     void

*****/

#include <dos.h>


#define DOWN      0x07
#define UP        0x06


void eraeol(int row, int col)
{
    scroll(row, col, getvcols() - col, 1, 1, DOWN);
}
```

Notice how the function performs its task by building on the scroll() and getvcols() functions. This procedure is consistent with the design philosophy of creating new functions by reusing functions that already have been debugged and tested. The eraeol() function simply defines a one-line window, using the row and column coordinates given in the function arguments. The scroll() function does all the work. The call to getvcols() determines how many columns are to be erased. The use of these existing functions makes creating the eraeol() function easy.

You could change `eraeol()` to eliminate the need for any function arguments to `eraeol()`, provided the cursor already is at the proper position on the screen to erase to the end of the line. You could use the `find_cursor()` function (discussed later in this chapter) to determine the current row-column position and then call the `scroll()` function. The modified code might look like the following code:

```
void eraeol(void)
{
    int row, col;

    find_cursor(&row, &col);
    scroll(row, col, getvcols() - col, 1, 1, DOWN);
}
```

Notice that this version of `eraeol()` has a `void` argument list. Either form for `eraeol()` would work, but the second version requires that the cursor already be at the proper screen position before `eraeol()` is called. You might want to add both varieties of this function to your set of screen tools.

Erase a Line—*eral( )*

The `eral()` function is used to erase an entire line. The source code for this function appears in listing 1.10.

Listing 1.10. Erase a line.

```
/*****

                              eral()

    This function erases a line on the screen at the specified
  row position.

    Argument list:    int row    the line (row) to be erased

    Return value:    void

*****/

#include <dos.h>
```

```
void eral(int row)
{
    eraeol(row, 1);
}
```

Again, you are building on a function that was written earlier in this chapter. What could be simpler? After all, to erase a line, you need only determine which line must be deleted, and erase to the end of the line, starting in column 1.

Erase to Beginning of Line—*erabol( )*

The erabol() function is used to erase from a given row-column position to the beginning of the line. Note that it is the counterpart of eraeol(). The code is given in listing 1.11.

Listing 1.11. *Erase to beginning of line.*

```
/*****

                        erabol()

    This function erases to the beginning of the line. The
getvcols() call determines the number of columns currently in
use on the screen.

    Argument list:    int row    the row position for the cursor
                      int col    the column position for the
                                 cursor

    Return value:     void

*****/

#define DOWN 0x07

void erabol(int row, int col)
{
    int wide;
```

continues

Listing 1.11. *continued*

```
   wide = getvcols();
   cursor(row, 1);
   if (col > wide)                      /* Is the column value too big */
      col = wide;
   scroll(row, 1, col, 1, 1, DOWN);
}
```

Again, the function builds on getvcols() and scroll() to do most of the work. The call to getvcols() ensures that you do not try to erase more columns than are available, and scroll() erases a one-line window from the column position (col) for the desired row (row).

If you assume that the cursor already is at the desired row-column coordinates, you could use the find_cursor() function to eliminate the need for passing the row-column values to erabol(), in a manner similar to that discussed with eraeol().

Erase to End of Screen—*eraeos( )*

The function eraeos() is used to erase from a given row-column position to the end of the screen. The code is presented in listing 1.12.

Listing 1.12. *Erase to end of screen.*

```
/*****
                             eraeos()

   This function erases to the end of the screen. The call to
   getvcols() determines the number of columns currently in use
   on the screen.

   Argument list:    int row    the row position for the cursor
                     int col    the column position for the
                                cursor
   Return value:     void

*****/
```

```
#include <dos.h>

#define DOWN     0x07

void eraeos(int row, int col)
{
   eraeol(row, col);
   scroll(row, 1, getvcols(), 24 - row, 0, DOWN);
}
```

The call to eraeol() erases the screen from the current row-column position to the end of the line. Then scroll() is used to erase any lines that might appear after the row line passed as a function argument. All the work is done by previously written functions. Notice that you must use the DOWN direction in the scroll() call so that the upper portion of the screen remains unchanged.

Erase to Beginning of Screen— *erabos()*

This function is the opposite of eraeos(): It erases from the current row-column position to the beginning of the screen. The code is presented in listing 1.13.

Listing 1.13. *Erase to beginning of screen.*

```
/*****

                     erabos()

   This function erases to the beginning of the screen. The
   call to getvcols() determines the number of columns currently in
   use on the screen.

   Argument list:    int row    the row position for the cursor
                     int col    the column position for the
                                cursor
   Return value:     void

*****/
```

continues

Listing 1.11. *continued*

```
#define UP        0x06

void erabos(int row, int col)
{

    erabol(row, col);
    scroll(1, 1, getvcols(), row - 1, 0, UP);
}
```

In this case, getvcols(), erabol(), and scroll() are used to accomplish the task at hand. Notice that this time UP is used to leave the lower portion of the screen unchanged.

With the complement of era*() functions presented in this section, you can selectively erase any part of the screen from any given cursor position. Because you use the BIOS interrupt services rather than loops, the functions are fairly fast and generate very little code. (After all, most of the work is done in the BIOS.)

More important, you can create several new functions simply by calling existing functions in a specific way. This concept of building new functions from existing resources (be they in the BIOS or your own functions) makes sense because you have less testing and debugging to do than if everything is built from scratch. You always should design new tools from existing tools whenever possible. It will save you much work.

Clearing the Screen—*cls( )*

If you know how to erase selected portions of the screen, it should be a simple task to erase all of the screen. The cls() function presented in listing 1.14 does just that.

Listing 1.14. *Clear the display screen.*

```
/*****

                              cls()

    This function is used to clear the screen and home (row = 1,
col = 1) the cursor.

    Argument list:      void

    Return value:       void

*****/

#include <dos.h>

void cls(void)
{
    scroll(1, 1, getvcols(), 25, 0, 0x07);
}
```

The cls() function uses scroll() to clear the screen simply by defining a window that is equal to the total screen size. Because all text modes for the screen have 25 rows, the screen's width is the only parameter needed. The screen's width is provided by the call to the getvcols() function. In this case, the window is scrolled down (0x07), but scrolling up (0x06) would have the same effect.

As you saw with the cursor() discussed earlier, you can use a #define statement to substitute any existing clear-screen function that might be provided by your compiler vendor (for example, clrscr()).

Cursor Information— *find_cursor( ), get_cursor( ), set_cursor( )*

You already know how to position the cursor on the screen, but there might be times when you need to know the cursor's current location or need to change the shape of the cursor itself. The functions presented in this section will enable you to do both tasks.

Get Cursor's Row-Column Position— *find_cursor( )*

The purpose of find_cursor() is to determine the current row-column location of the cursor on the screen. Listing 1.15 shows this function's source code.

Listing 1.15. *Find cursor position.*

```
/*****
                          find_cursor()

    This function finds the current row and column position of
    the cursor, and fills in the two pointers with the appropriate
    values. The value of 1 is added to the results to agree with a
    home position of 1,1 rather than 0,0.

    Argument list:    int *row       the row position for the cursor
                      int *col       the column position for the
                                     cursor

    Return value:     void

*****/

#include <dos.h>

void find_cursor(int *row, int *col)
{
    union REGS ireg;

    ireg.h.ah = 0x03;                    /* Function 3 */
    ireg.h.bh = getvpage();              /* Page ?     */
    int86(0x10, &ireg, &ireg);

    *row = (int) ireg.h.dh + 1;
    *col = (int) ireg.h.dl + 1;
}
```

Function 0x03 shows you the cursor's position on the screen. The find_cursor() function requires that two pointers to int be passed as its arguments. A call to getvpage() ensures that you examine the video page currently being used. The dh and dl members of ireg will contain the appropriate row-column values after the video interrupt call is made by way of the int86() function call. The return values then are assigned into row and col. Because row and col are integer variables, find_cursor() must be called as

```
find_cursor(&row, &col);
```

The address-of operator (&) means that the lvalue of the two variables is passed to the function, so you can use indirection to fill in the appropriate values. As mentioned earlier, the find_cursor() function could be used to build new screen functions, such as eraeol(), without function arguments. Such modifications, however, require that the cursor be positioned before calling the function.

Get Cursor Type—*get_cursor( )*

This function helps you determine what type of cursor currently is on the screen. As you know, the cursor is comprised of one or more lines, and each line is the width of a character on the screen. Most PCs use a two-line cursor with the sixth and seventh scan line turned on. The result is an "underline" cursor. Other types are possible, however.

By using get_cursor(), you can determine the type of cursor in use while the program is running (that is, at runtime). The code is presented in listing 1.16.

Listing 1.16. *Get cursor type.*

```
/*****

                    get_cursor()

   This function reads the cursor's starting and ending scan
   lines. Normal values are: start = 6, end = 7. The function
   fills in the two pointers with the appropriate values.

   Argument list:    int *start     the starting scan line for
                                    the cursor
                     int *end       the ending scan line for the
                                    cursor
```

continues

Listing 1.16. continued

```
    Return value:      void

*****/

#include <dos.h>


void get_cursor(int *start, int *end)
{
    union REGS ireg;

    ireg.h.ah = 0x03;                        /* Function 3 */
    ireg.h.bh = getvpage();                  /* Page 0     */
    int86(0x10, &ireg, &ireg);

    *start = (int) ireg.h.ch;
    *end = (int) ireg.h.cl;
}
```

Function 0x03 also is used to determine the cursor type. The two arguments to the function are pointers to int so that the appropriate values can be filled in by the function. The call to getvpage() tells you to examine the cursor on the currently active video page. The int86() call fills in the appropriate values (the ch and cl members of ireg), which then are assigned to start and end. The two arguments tell you the starting and ending scan lines used for the cursor. If your system uses a normal double-underline cursor, the return values will be 6 (start) and 7 (end).

Notice that the arguments to this function are integer pointers. To use this function properly, therefore, you must pass the lvalue of the two variables to the function, as in

```
get_cursor(&ostart, &oend);
```

If your program changes the cursor type as it runs (see set_cursor() in the following call), you can reset the original cursor with the call:

```
set_cursor(ostart, oend);
```

This call restores the original cursor type when the program ends. (The set_cursor() function is discussed in the next section of the chapter.)

Set Cursor Type—*set_cursor( )*

The function set_cursor() enables you to change the type of cursor used in a program. If you use this function, be sure to read the type of cursor before setting it so that the cursor can be returned to its original type when your program finishes. The code appears in listing 1.17.

Listing 1.17. Set cursor type.

```
/*****

                        set_cursor()

    This function changes the size of the cursor. Normal values
would be: start = 6, end = 7. If the value of start is larger
than the value of end, a split cursor results (for example,
start = 8, end = 1).

    Argument list:    int start       the starting scan line for
                                      the cursor
                      int end         the ending scan line for the
                                      cursor

    Return value:     void

*****/

#include <dos.h>

void set_cursor(int start, int end)
{
    union REGS ireg;

    ireg.h.ah = 0x01;
    ireg.h.ch = (char) start;
    ireg.h.cl = (char) end;

    int86(0x10, &ireg, &ireg);

}
```

Suppose you want your program to use a block cursor rather than a double-underline. (This often is done by text editors when you switch from the insert to the overtype mode.) If you call set_cursor() in the following manner:

```
set_cursor(1, 7);
```

a block cursor will result. If the starting line number is greater than the ending line number (for example, start = 8 and end = 1), a split cursor results. Although this might not be very useful, it does create an interesting cursor type.

Video Paging—*getvpage( )*, *setvpage( )*

PCs reserve enough video memory for more than just one screen of information. In fact, they have sufficient memory for up to eight video screens of information (depending on the video mode being used). Obviously, the display device can show only one screen at a time, but that does not mean you cannot take advantage of additional screens.

To give a common example, imagine a series of programs presented in a primary menu. When the user makes a choice, a program is loaded and run and, when the program is finished, the user is returned to the main menu for another selection. You probably have run such programs yourself, and have noticed how quickly the main menu reappeared when the subprogram finished. Actually, the menu never "went away." The programmer might have kept the main menu in one video page and flipped to another one while the subprogram was running. When that program finished, the programmer simply flipped back to the page containing the main menu. By using the getvpage() and setvpage() functions, you can add video paging to your library.

Get the Current Video Page— *getvpage( )*

First, suppose you need to know the video page currently being used for the display. The code presented in listing 1.18 shows how you can find out which video page it is.

Listing 1.18. *Get video page.*

```
/*****
                               getvpage()

     This function gets the active video page.

   Argument list:    void

   Return value:     int         the currently active page

*****/

#include <dos.h>


int getvpage(void)
{
   union REGS ireg;

   ireg.h.ah = 0x0f;                              /* Function 0x0f */

   int86(0x10, &ireg, &ireg);
   return (ireg.h.bh);
}
```

Function 0x0f of interrupt 0x10 enables you to read the video page currently in use. The value is returned from the BIOS in the bh member of the h structure held in ireg. Because there can be as many as eight pages of video memory, the value must fall within the range of 0 to 7.

Other functions presented in this chapter are sensitive to the video page's being used. If you examine the cursor() function in listing 1.7, for example, you will notice that the video page must be passed to the BIOS so that the BIOS will know which page to use for addressing the cursor. As listing 1.7 illustrates, cursor() assumes that the current video page is the one that will use cursor addressing.

Set Video Page—*setvpage( )*

The setvpage() function lets you "flip" from one video page to another. The source code for setvpage() appears in listing 1.19.

Listing 1.19. Set video page.

```
/*****
                           setvpage()

    This function sets the currently active video page. Valid
    page values are influenced by the current screen mode [see
    setvmode()] and the video hardware in use. No checking is
    performed other than ensuring that the page value does not
    exceed 7.

    Argument list:    int page        the page to be activated

    Return value:     void

*****/

#include <dos.h>

#define MAXPAGE    8

void setvpage(int page)
{
   union REGS ireg;

   ireg.h.ah = 0x05;                          /* Function 0x05 */
   ireg.h.al = (page % MAXPAGE);

   int86(0x10, &ireg, &ireg);
}
```

Function 0x05 of interrupt 0x10 is used to change video pages. The page number is passed to setvpage() as an argument. In this case, a modulo operation is performed on page to ensure that the value remains between 0 and 7, to provide some protection in case an improper argument is passed to setvpage(). With the proper arguments loaded, the call to int86() will cause the program to "flip" to the new video page requested.

Test Program for Video Paging

Program 1.1 presents a simple test program that demonstrates how video paging might be used. Even if you have not used video paging before, a little thought will help you produce several ways you might speed up your screen I/O programming.

Program 1.1. *Test of video paging.*

```c
#include <stdio.h>
#include <dos.h>
void show_message_one(void);
void show_page_0(int):
void show_message_two(void);
                    /* Program to test video paging */
void main(void)
{
   int original_page;

   original_page = getvpage();      /* Save the original page */

   show_message_one();
   show_page_0(original_page);
   show_message_two();
   setvpage(original_page);
}

/*****

                    show_message_one()

    This function shows the first message on video page 2. Note
that the user must press Return or Enter for the program to
continue.

   Argument list:    void

   Return value:    void

*****/
```

continues

Program 1.1. *continued*

```
void show_message_one(void)
{
   setvpage(2);
   cls();
   cursor(3, 5);
   printf("This program uses video page 2 to display this message.\n");
   printf("To see what the screen looked like when you started the program,\n");
   printf("press the Return or Enter key. You will have to press Return\n");
   printf("or Enter to return from the original screen, too.");
   printf("\n\n   Press Return to start: ");
   getchar();
}
```

```
/*****
                         show_page_0()
```

This function simply flips to the original video page and displays whatever was on the (DOS) screen when this program first was run. Note that the user must press Enter to continue with the program.

```
   Argument list:    int page       the page number of the original
                                     video page
```

```
   Return value:     void
```

```
*****/
```

```
void show_page_0(int page)
{
   setvpage(page);
   getchar();
}
```

```
/*****
                       show_message_two()
```

This function shows a second message on video page 2.

```
    Argument list:    void

    Return value:     void

*****/

void show_message_two(void)
{
    setvpage(2);
    cursor(10, 5);
    printf("Press the Return or Enter key again to end the program.\n");
    printf("\n\nPress Return or Enter: ");
    getchar();
}
```

The first thing to do in main() is to save the original video page in the variable original_page. This step always is a good idea when doing paging because it returns the user to the video page that was in use when this program started. (After all, the user might run this program as a child process of some other program that was not using the default video page.)

The call to show_message_one() simply tells the user what is going on and to press the Return or Enter key to progress through the program. The call to setvpage(2) means that the text being displayed by way of the call to printf() is being written to video page 2, not page 0. After the user has read the message and pressed the proper key, control returns to main().

The program now calls show_page_0(), using original_page as its argument. When it is in show_page_0(), the call to setvpage() (using the value of the original video page as its argument) enables the user to see the display screen as it appeared at the time this program started execution. When the user presses the Return or Enter key, control again returns to main().

After calling show_message_two() to display the final message, one last call to setvpage()—using the original video page number (original_page)—restores the screen to the proper status, and the program ends.

Adding Color—*c_scroll()*, *cls_c()*, *colorchr()*, *colorstr()*, *border()*

Color adds a new dimension to almost any program. Using color also can add consistency to a program. Error messages, for example, might always appear in red, and help messages and prompts might always appear in another color. The consistent use of color can make a program easier to learn and help hold the user's interest during the learning process.

Color Scroll—*c_scroll()*

The first function to write is a version of scroll() in which a color other than black can be used. The code for scrolling with color is presented in listing 1.20.

Listing 1.20. *Scroll with color.*

```
/*****
                        c_scroll()

    This function scrolls the screen by way of a call to interrupt
0x10. The function is the same as scroll(), except that the color
can be changed.

    Argument list:    int row        the row position for the window
                      int col        the column position for the window
                      int wide       the width of the window
                      int deep       the depth of the window
                      int num        the number of lines to scroll within
                                     the window (all are scrolled if 0)
                      int f          0x06 for up-scroll, 0x07 for down
                      int color      attribute for blanks in window

    Return value:     void

*****/

#include <dos.h>
```

```
void c_scroll(int row, int col, int wide, int deep, int num, int f, int color)
{
   union REGS ireg;

   row--;                                          /* Index from (1, 1)  */
   col--;
   ireg.h.ah = f;
   ireg.h.al = num;
   ireg.h.ch = row;
   ireg.h.cl = col;
   ireg.h.dh = row + deep - 1;
   ireg.h.dl = col + wide;
   ireg.h.bh = color;

   int86(0x10, &ireg, &ireg);
}
```

The code in listing 1.20 is almost the same as the code in listing 1.8 with another argument added, to be used for the color value. When it is used with function 0x06 or 0x07 of interrupt 0x10, only the background color of the scrolled area is affected. Remember, you must change the values of row and col because you are indexing from a home position of (1, 1) rather than (0, 0).

Colors

Some thought must be given to the value passed to c_scroll() for the color argument. Because the background color of the screen is controlled by bits 4 through 6 of the screen's attribute byte, only eight (that is, $8 = 2^3$) background colors are possible, including black. Also notice that, because the background color begins with bit 4, advancing to the next color actually increments the color value by 16 (that is, $16 = 2^4$). Table 1.3 shows the decimal values associated with the background colors:

Table 1.3. *Background color values (decimal).*

Decimal Value	Color
0	Black
16	Blue
32	Green
48	Cyan
64	Red
80	Magenta
96	Brown
112	White

Instead of forcing yourself to memorize these values, try creating a header file (such as color.h) to hold the values as a series of #defines, such as

```
#define BRED    64      /* Background RED */
```

so that the color function could be called with

```
cls_c(BRED);
```

Begin all the background colors with the letter *B*, to distinguish them from possible foreground colors. Or, you might left-shift the color (for example, color = blue << 4) before the call to the function.

Clear Screen with Color—*cls_c( )*

With the help of the next function, you can clear the screen with a background color other than black. Listing 1.21 shows that this function's code is virtually the same as the one used by cls(). Now, however, the background color is being set.

Listing 1.21. *Clear screen with color.*

```
/*****

                        cls_c()


    This function clears the screen using the background color
passed to the function. The colors are the normal background
colors for the attribute byte.
```

```
    Argument list:    int color      the color for the background

    Return value:     void

*****/


void cls_c(int color)
{
    c_scroll(1, 1, getvcols(), 25, 0, 0x07, color);
}
```

The cls_c() function simply is built from the color scroll routine, passing in the desired background color. In all other respects, cls_c() is just a color scroll using the entire screen. Both cls_c() and c_scroll() work on the currently active screen page. You therefore can clear different pages in video memory with different colors.

Color Text—*colorchr( )*, *colorstr( )*

Now that you know how to use color for the entire screen, you should learn how text can be written to the screen in color. Two functions can do this for characters and strings.

Character in Color—*colorchr( )*

Suppose that you want to display a character in color. The function presented in listing 1.22 shows how this can be done.

Listing 1.22. Print a character in color.

```
/*****
                            colorchr()

    This function is used to print a character on the screen in
color and enables foreground-background colors to be set. The
valid colors are the following:


--------- Foreground ------------          -- Background --

0    black        8    gray                 0    black
1    blue         9    light blue           1    blue
2    green       10    light green          2    green
3    cyan        11    light cyan           3    cyan
4    red         12    light red            4    red
5    magenta     13    light magenta        5    magenta
6    brown       14    yellow               6    brown
7    white       15    light white          7    white


    Notice that bit 3 (values above 8) sets the intensity bit. If
bit 7 is set, the data are set to the blink mode.

    Argument list:    int c        the character to be printed
                      int fcolor   the foreground color
                      int bcolor   the background color

    Return value:     void

*****/

#include <dos.h>

void colorchr(int c, int fcolor, int bcolor)
{
    union REGS ireg;

    ireg.h.ah = 0x09;                    /* Function 0x09         */
    ireg.x.cx = 1;                       /* Number of characters  */
    ireg.h.bh = getvpage();              /* Video page            */
    ireg.h.al = (char) c;
    ireg.h.bl = (char) (fcolor | bcolor);
```

```
    int86(0x10, &ireg, &ireg);
}
```

In this case, you can write a character to the screen at the cursor position in fcolor on a bcolor background. You can use the standard color numbers for the background color if you perform a bit shift on the color before calling the colorchr(). For example, if RED is defined as the value 4, you could set the background color by calling

```
    colorchr('A', WHITE, RED << 4);
```

instead of using BRED for the background color. The background values shown in listing 1.22 assume that a bit shift is performed on the color number before calling colorchr().

You can use the symbolic constants for the colors. If the foreground and background colors are defined as follows:

```
    #define RED        4
    #define BWHITE     112
```

then the call

```
    colorchr('A', RED, BWHITE);
```

will display a red letter *A* on a white background. Notice how the foreground and background colors are ORed together to form the attribute byte in listing 1.22. Keep in mind that colorchr() displays the character at the current cursor position. In other words, if you do not keep track of the cursor, multiple characters will be printed on top of each other so that only the last one printed shows on the screen. With this in mind, consider program 1.2.

***Program 1.2.** Color test program.*

```
#include <stdio.h>
#include <dos.h>

#define BWHITE  112
void main()
{
    int i;
```

continues

Program 1.2. continued

```
cls();
for (i = 65; i < 91; i++) {
   cursor(10, i - 63);
   colorchr(i, i%16, BWHITE);
}
}
```

What will the output of this program look like? Think about it, and perhaps try running it to find out.

Printing a String in Color—*colorstr( )*

You can build a color string function using the `colorchr()` function presented in listing 1.22. You must consider some complications, however, to make things work properly. The complications become more apparent if you examine listing 1.23 closely.

Listing 1.23. Display a string in color.

```
/*****


                          colorstr()


     This function is used to print a string in color on the
  screen. The function allows the foreground and background
  colors to be set. No error-checking is performed on the x-y
  coordinates or on the color values.

     Argument list:    char *s       the string to be printed
                       int fcolor    the foreground color
                       int bcolor    the background color

     Return value:     void

*****/

#include <dos.h>
#define TAB    3
#define BELL   7
```

```
void colorstr(char *s, int fcolor, int bcolor)
{
   int col, row, wide;

   wide = getvcols();                          /* Width of display */
   find_cursor(&row, &col);
   while (*s) {
      switch (*s) {
         case '\n':
            s++;
            row++;
            col -- 1;
            break;
         case '\b':
            s++;
            col--;
            break;
         case '\r':
            s++;
            col = 1;
            break;
         case '\t':
            s++;
            col += TAB;
            break;
         case '\f':
            s++;
            break;
         case '\a':
            s++;
            putchar(BELL);
            continue;
         case '\\':
            col++;
            break;
         default:
            col++;
            break;
      }
      cursor(row, col);
      colorchr(*s++, fcolor, bcolor);
      if (col > wide) {
```

continues

Listing 1.23. continued

```
        row++;
        col = 1;
      }
    }
    cursor (row, col);
}
```

As you can see, the escape sequences pose a problem, and only some of these sequences are addressed here. What is required to display a double quotation mark on the screen? Why is there a `continue` statement for the alarm `case`, and why is s incremented in some `cases` and not others? With a little thought, you will figure out the answers to these questions (and better understand what's going on, too).

Direct Memory Access to the Video Display

As you know, you can do direct memory writes to an IBM screen. Simply stated, the fastest way to access the screen is to bypass the BIOS and write directly to the screen. However, some MS-DOS systems (Tandy 2000 and Zenith Z100, for example) do not have the video memory at the "expected" memory address for a true IBM compatible. By doing direct memory writes on such machines, you probably will lock up the system— but you will do it very quickly. By using the resources provided in the BIOS, you sacrifice blazing speed but gain increased portability.

Screen Address

Clearly, you need to know the starting address for video memory if you want to write to it. Although most of the popular C compilers provide support for graphics displays, the concern here is being able to write program output in text form to the video display. You can determine the base address by using the `getvmode()` presented in listing 1.1. The two base addresses of interest are

Video Base Segment Address	Display Types
0xb000	Monochrome Display Adapter for 80x25 text
0xb800	CGA-EGA-VGA for 80x25 text

When you know these base addresses, you can initialize a pointer to point to (and index from) the base address.

The color string function presented in listing 1.23 also can be written using direct video addressing. This variation is shown in listing 1.24.

Listing 1.24. *Color string function using direct video addressing.*

```
/*****


                         colorstr1()

    This function is used to print a string in color on the screen
using direct video access. The function enables the foreground
and background colors to be set. No error-checking is performed on
the x-y coordinates or on the color values. The function assumes
the cursor is positioned before the call.

    Argument list:    char *s        the string to be printed
                      int fcolor     the foreground color
                      int bcolor     the background color

    Return value:     void

*****/

#include <dos.h>

#define TAB    3
#define BELL   7

void colorstr1(char *s, int fcolor, int bcolor)
{
   int col, row, wide;
   unsigned int far *ptr, far *base, attribute;

   wide = getvcols();                        /* Width of display */
   base = ptr = (getvdev() == 2) ? (unsigned int far *) 0xb8000000 :
```

continues

Listing 1.24. continued

```
                                       (unsigned int far *) 0xb0000000;
    attribute = (fcolor + bcolor) << 8;
    find_cursor(&row, &col);
    row--; col--;                    /* Adjust for 0,0       */
    ptr += row * wide + col;         /* Find screen location */
    while (*s) {
        switch (*s) {
            case '\n':
            s++;
            row++;
            ptr = base + row * wide;
            break;
        case '\b':
            s++;
            ptr--;
            break;
        case '\r':
            s++;
            ptr = base + row * wide;
            break;
        case '\t':
            s++;
            ptr += TAB;
            break;
        case '\f':
            s++;
            break;
        case '\a':
            s++;
            putchar(BELL);
            continue;
        case '\\':
            ptr++;
                break;
            default:
            ptr++;
            break;
        }
        *ptr = *s++ + attribute;
    }
}
```

In this version, a call to getvcols() finds the width of the display, and the call to getvdev() determines the start of video memory. The memory address is cast to an unsigned int far pointer and assigned into ptr. For most color text displays, the address is segment 0xb800, offset 0x0000.

The next line

```
attribute = (fcolor + bcolor) << 8;
```

needs some explanation. In video memory, one byte is used for the character to be displayed, and a second byte is used for the attributes of the character (for example, color and blink). These two bytes are treated as a single unit, which is why ptr is a pointer to an unsigned int rather than a char. However, because the 8088 family of CPUs store the data in low-byte, high-byte order, the attribute byte for the character must be shifted eight bits to the left. You then simply add the character to the attribute and display it as a single unsigned int.

The remaining logic is much the same, with only the calculations of the video memory addresses being added to the function. (A full explanation of the memory-addressing appears later in this chapter.) The version shown in listing 1.24 is somewhat faster than the one in listing 1.23 because of direct video memory addressing and fewer function calls in the while loop. In programs with much screen I/O, the speed improvement might be noticeable. You might wish to experiment with both versions.

Change Border Color— *border( )*

As illustrated in listing 1.25, the border() function sets the screen's border color. The border can be changed only when the video mode is set to 4 (see the setvmode() function presented earlier). The border cannot be changed in a text mode.

Listing 1.25. *Change border color.*

```
/*****

                           border()

    This function sets the border to the color specified as the
    argument to this function. This function can be used only when
    mode 4 is active. The symbolic constants are provided in
    color.h.

    Argument list:    int color        the color for the border
                                        with the following values:

              0    black          8    gray
              1    blue           9    light blue
              2    green         10    light green
              3    cyan          11    light cyan
              4    red           12    light red
              5    magenta       13    light magenta
              6    brown         14    yellow
              7    white         15    light white

    Return value:     void

*****/

#include <dos.h>

void border(int color)
{
   union REGS ireg;

   int mode;

   mode = getvmode();
   if ((mode > 3 && mode < 7) || mode > 7)
      return;
   if (getvmode() != 0x04           /* Only set border color in this mode */
      return;
   ireg.h.ah = 0x0b;                /* Function 0x0b                       */
   ireg.h.bh = 0;                   /* Must be 0 to set border             */
   ireg.h.bl = color;
```

```
        int86(0x10, &ireg, &ireg);


}
```

The permissible color values are the same as those of other functions described in this chapter. Notice that you must check to see whether you are in the proper video mode before attempting to change the border color. If the current mode is not equal to 4, execute a simple return statement instead of attempting a BIOS call while the screen is in an improper mode. This precaution ensures that the screen is left unchanged.

Formatted Output to Video Memory—*scrmem( )*

The scrmem() function shown in listing 1.26 is similar to printf(), but scrmem() writes the output directly to video memory instead of using the I/O facilities provided by MS-DOS.

Listing 1.26. *Formatted output to video memory.*

```
/*****
                                scrmem()


   This function is used to format and write an argument
   directly to video memory. The fifth argument is a control
   string (control) that uses the normal printf()-type string with
   conversion characters.The sixth (and subsequent) argument(s)
   must agree with the number and sequence in the control string.

   Argument list:  int row        the row position for output
                   int col        the column position for output
                   int fore       the foreground color
                   int back       the background color
                   char *control  the control string
                   ...            the arguments to print


   Return value:       void
```

continues

Listing 1.26. continued

```
*****/

#define MAXSTR 256

#include <stdlib.h>
#include <stdarg.h>

void scrmem(int row, int col, int fore, int back, char *control, ...)
{
    unsigned char buff[MAXSTR], *ptr;
    unsigned int far *s;                    /* We need large pointer */
    unsigned attr, byte;
    int mode, width;
    va_list parms;

    width = getvcols();                 /* Get columns          */
    mode = getvmode();                  /* Get mode             */
    attr = ((back << 4) + fore) << 8;   /* Set colors           */
                                        /* Which base memory?   */
    s = (mode == 7) ? (unsigned int far *) 0xb0000000L :
                      (unsigned int far *) 0xb8000000L;
    s += row * width + col;
    ptr = buff;
    va_start(parms, control);
    vsprintf(buff, control, parms);

    while (*ptr) {
        *s++ = attr + *ptr++;
    }
    va_end(parms);
}
```

The scrmem() function accepts row-column coordinates (row, col) for setting the location at which output is placed, foreground and background colors (fore, back) for use during display, and a control string used for formatting the output. The final argument is not an argument per se; it is an ellipsis operator that simply tells the compiler that the list contains one or more data items.

The purpose of the vsprintf() call in scrmem() is simply to create one or more pointers based on the conversion characters contained in the control string. va_start() sets up the list of pointers (parms) for use by vsprintf(). (These functions are defined in the ANSI standard library, plus OS/2, UNIX System V, and Xenix.)

Note that a special pointer has been defined in the statement

```
unsigned int far *s;
```

The reserved word far tells the compiler that this particular pointer should be large enough to access memory outside the current data segment. (For MS-DOS machines, this means a four-byte pointer.) The value returned from getvmode() is used to determine the initial value for s. In most instances, the mode value will be 3, which sets s to point to the base of video memory (starting at 0xb8000).

As mentioned earlier in this chapter, a *text screen* is a character byte followed by an attribute byte. As explained earlier, to write both the character and the attribute byte, s must be defined as a pointer to an unsigned int. A char pointer could be used, with a character write to the screen, an increment on s, an attribute write to the screen, another increment on s, and so on. Rather than split the code this way, the variable is defined so that a single increment can be used to move to the next character in video memory.

To determine the screen location, calculate an offset from the base screen address by using

```
s += row * width + col;
```

to get to the row, col screen coordinates. For this to work properly, you need to know the number of columns used on the screen. The call to getvcols() (see listing 1.2) provides the needed information. Note that if you were to define s as a character pointer, you would need to multiply the preceding offset expression by 2. The attribute byte (attr) is built by adding the foreground and background colors together after they have been bit-shifted.

(You might want to change the bit shift on the background color by using #defines for the shifted values. That is, you could define a background color of BRED equal to 4 and let the function shift the value four bits to the left. It is somewhat more efficient, however, simply to define BRED as 64 and remove the bit shifting of the background color from the function. You might want to store these color values in a header file named colors.h.)

A while loop is used to write the formatted output to the video display. Although buff[] could have been used (instead of ptr) to display the information on the screen, that would have required another variable for the index (i, for example, as in buff[i]). Because speed is the primary concern in using video memory, simply initialize ptr to point to buff[] and use the increment operator on ptr rather than an array index.

One final point. scrmem() is extremely versatile; it can handle multiple arguments simultaneously. For instance, you might use it as

```
scrmem(10, 10, 2, 4, "%s %s %x %d", a, b, x, i);
```

Everything will work out properly. The price of this flexibility is that setting up everything within scrmem() takes time. If you simply want to write a single string or character to video memory, it is better to use colorstr() for that purpose. You can use the concepts for establishing a base memory pointer (s) in listing 1.26 and then just write the data to the screen.

Speeding Up *scrmem( )* and Related Video Memory Functions

Another way to improve the performance of scrmem() is to move the determination of the base memory pointer (the ternary in listing 1.26, for example), mode, and width outside the video function and then initialize their values at program start. If s, mode, and width are globals or are passed into the function, the "setup time" for scrmem() can be reduced. An example of how this might be done is presented in program 1.3. This is a complete program, so you can try the identical timing test on your system.

Program 1.3. *Direct writes of a string to video memory using globals.*

```
#include <stdio.h>

unsigned int far *s, far *base;  /* We need a large pointer     */
int mode;
unsigned attr;
void videostr(char *str);

#define GREEN  2

void main(void)
{
   char buff[21];
   int i;
```

```
for (i = 0; i < 20; i++)        /* Fill buff[] with letters   */
    buff[i] = i + 'A';
buff[i] = '\0';                 /* Make it a string           */

mode = getvmode();              /* Get mode for base address  */
attr = GREEN << 8;              /* Stuff attribute byte       */

s = (mode == 7) ? (unsigned int far *) 0xb0000000L :
                  (unsigned int far *) 0xb8000000L;

for (i = 0; i < 100; i++)       /* Do a screenful             */
    videostr(buff);
}

/*****

                        videostr()

    This function is used to write a string directly to video memory.
The function assumes that the memory pointer (s) and attribute byte
have been globally set to proper values.

    Argument list:   char *control       the string to print

    Return value:    void

    CAUTION:   may need to be compiled for large model pointers.

*****/

void videostr(char *str)

{
    while (*str) {
        *s++ = attr + *str++;
    }
}
```

Notice how simple videostr() is. There are two reasons for this
simplicity. First, all the setup variables have been moved outside the
function. They are set once and never assigned again. Contrast the code in
videostr() with that in scrmem(), in which all the setup information is part
of the function. Notice that, if you do another call to videostr(), you should
reinitialize s to point to base before displaying the string. This is because s

has been incremented by previous calls to `videostr()`. You might also have to do some pointer arithmetic (similar to that in listing 1.24) to place the string at the proper screen location.

The second reason for the simplicity is that `videostr()` does only one thing—it writes a string to the video memory. Because `scrmem()` must be able to cope with any and all data types, as well as handle an unknown number of arguments, it is necessarily more complex. This is why designing separate functions for writing specific data types to video memory might be worthwhile.

As an experiment, you should compile and run the program as shown in program 1.3 and note how quickly the screen is filled with data. Having done that, replace the call to `videostr()` in `main()` with

```
printf(buff);
```

and notice the time differences. You also might try calling `scrmem()` after you modify the program a bit; you can see that `videostr()` is more efficient than `scrmem()` at displaying string data.

Conclusion

The functions presented in this chapter represent only some of the many BIOS routines available to you. Others are covered in later chapters.

You might want to experiment with `scrmem()` to get a sense of how direct access to video memory can be used. Try writing a dedicated routine for displaying integers without using any of the `sprintf()` family of functions, and then compare the speed of using `scrmem()` with that needed to display several thousand calls to your routine. Perform the same test using `printf()` to test the relative speed advantages and disadvantages of each alternative.

2

String Processing

This chapter presents several string processing functions that are not found in the ANSI C standard library, but which should be useful additions to your library. The primary objective of the chapter, however, is not so much to describe the functions themselves, but to show you how to develop new and useful additions to your library by building on the functions you already have.

If you are comfortable with pointers and their use in strings, you can skip the next section, which reviews some basic concepts about arrays and pointers.

How to Think About Strings

There is nothing particularly tricky about writing string functions as long as you remember what lvalues and rvalues mean in C. As you recall, a data item's lvalue is where that data item is stored in memory. That is, an lvalue is a memory address. The lvalue enables the compiler to "find" the proper data item when the program is compiled.

An rvalue, on the other hand, is what is stored at that memory address. If you think of a megabyte of memory as a sequence of a million cups, the lvalue is where each cup is stored and the rvalue is what each cup contains. C makes things a bit more interesting by enabling you to have different-sized cups. Figure 2.1 might help tie things together.

Fig. 2.1. *Diagrammatic representation of* lvalue *and* rvalue.

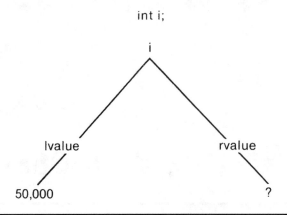

In figure 2.1, it is assumed that you have written a program in which variable i is defined as an integer variable (int i). It also is assumed that the compiler has reserved the memory address starting at 50,000 for variable i. Because the variable is assumed to have auto storage class, the contents of i (that is, its rvalue) are unknown and will be whatever random bits happen to be stored in memory at the time.

So how big is i? The sizeof operator indicates the number of bytes needed to store an integer data type. For most PCs, this is 16 bits, or two bytes. Therefore, the "cup" occupies memory locations 50,000 and 50,001.

If you now write the statement

```
i = 10;
```

figure 2.1 becomes that shown in figure 2.2.

Using the assignment statement, the compiler finds the lvalue of i (memory locations 50,000 and 50,001) and places the integer value 10 at memory locations 50,000 and 50,001.

Character arrays behave in much the same way, but you can do some interesting things with them. Using the same type of example, consider figure 2.3.

In figure 2.3, it is assumed that the compiler placed b[] starting at memory location 600. The memory image would look like figure 2.4.

Fig. 2.2. `lvalue` *and* `rvalue` *after an assignment.*

i = 10;

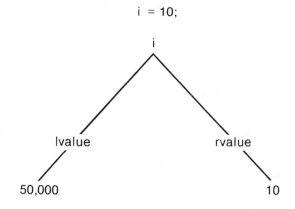

i

lvalue   rvalue

50,000   10

Fig. 2.3. `lvalue` *and* `rvalue` *with an array.*

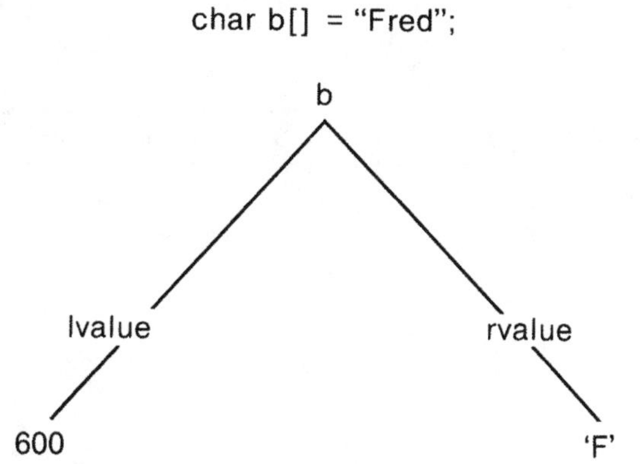

char b[] = "Fred";

b

lvalue   rvalue

600   'F'

    Because the character sequence stored in the b[] array is null termi-
nated, you can treat the character array as a string. So far, all of this is pretty
simple, right?

Fig. 2.4. Memory image of a string.

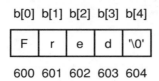

Where the Confusion Usually Begins with String Data

In string handling, the most common problem occurs when an array is passed to a function. It really is not complicated if you remember a few basic rules. First, arrays are different when used as an argument to a function call. For example, if you call a function by using variable i from figure 2.2, the rvalue of i (that is, 10) is passed to the function. To further illustrate, imagine code similar to that shown in code fragment 2.1.

Code Fragment 2.1. Passing an integer value to a function.

```
int main(void)
{
   int i;

   i = 10;
   func(i);
}

int func(int num)
{
    /* Function body for func() */
}
```

The diagrams might look like those shown in figure 2.5.

Fig. 2.5. lvalues *and* rvalues *for code fragment 2.1.*

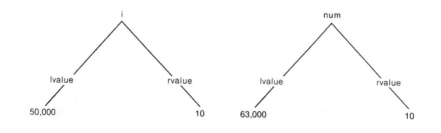

Notice that the variable num in the prototype for func() has an lvalue that is different from i in main(), but that their rvalues are the same. This is what is meant by "call by value" during a function call. The function has a copy of the rvalue of i, but not its lvalue. Because func() does not know the lvalue of i in main(), there is no way func() can find i—it must use the copy of i, which is the rvalue held in num.

Arrays are different, however, and this is where most beginners have problems when dealing with arrays and pointers. Consider code fragment 2.2, which is only somewhat different from code fragment 2.1.

Code Fragment 2.2. *Passing a character array to a function.*

```
int main(void)
{
    char b[] = "Fred";

    func(b);
}

int func(char s[])
{
    /* Function body for func() */
}
```

The memory image might look like that shown in figure 2.6.

Fig. 2.6. lvalues *and* rvalues *for code fragment 2.2.*

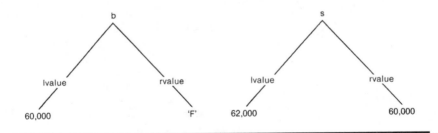

Notice any difference? The first element of b[] in main() is an F (b[0] = 'F'). That is, the rvalue of b in main() is 'F'. Now look at the rvalue for s[] in func(). Its rvalue is 60,000. It seems that the rvalue of s[] is the lvalue of b[] in main(). Precisely! Because arrays are not copied, only their lvalue ends up being passed to the function. As you know, any time an rvalue is a memory address, it can be treated as a pointer. In the example, s actually is a pointer to char, which happens to be the lvalue for the b[] character array defined in main().

Therefore, the only thing to remember when writing a string processing function is that you are working with an lvalue when the character array is passed to your function. This makes things much simpler to understand. For example, what is the difference between the following two function calls?

```
func(&b[2]);
func(b[2]);
```

In the example given in figure 2.6, the first call sends 60,002 to func(), and the second call sends the letter 'e' to the function. If func() does something like

```
*s = 'u';
```

the first call ends up changing "Fred" to "Frud," and the second call writes the letter 'u' to memory address 101 (an 'e' is 101 decimal in the ASCII character set). Because this could be right in the middle of MS-DOS, who knows what might happen? Indeed, the frustrating thing is that nothing might happen...right now.

The lesson is simple: Use the address-of operator (for example, &b[3]), or the array name by itself, when you want to pass an lvalue to a function. If the array name is followed by brackets and an index (for example, b[0]), or it is preceded by the indirection operator (*b), an rvalue is being passed. If you understand the concepts presented in this section, you should be able to understand and write just about any string processing function you need.

Center a String—*centers( )*

One common task of displaying string information is to center the string on the display screen. The string centering function is presented in listing 2.1.

Listing 2.1. *Center a string.*

```
/*****
                              centers()

    This function displays a string so it is centered on the screen.

    Argument list:    int row        the row for centering
                      char *s        pointer to the string to be centered

    Return value:     int            -1 if an error occurred, 0 otherwise

*****/

#include <stdio.h>
#include <string.h>

int centers(int row, char *s)
{
    int wide, len;

    len = strlen(s);
    wide = getvcols();
    if (len > wide)
        return -1;

    cursor(row, (wide - len) >> 1);
    write(fileno(stdout), s, len);
    return 0;
}
```

This function builds on the getvcols() and cursor() functions developed in Chapter 1, "Screen Functions." The call to strlen() determines the length of the string to be centered, and the call to getvcols() indicates the width of the display space. If the string is too long to fit on the screen, a -1 is returned from the function. The programmer then can decide what to do if the string is too long.

If the string will fit on one line, you subtract the length of the string from the number of columns available on the display and divide the result in half to determine the starting column for printing the string. Because the shift right operator (>>) is faster than a divide operation, it is used to determine the starting column.

The program then calls the write() function to display the string on the screen. Because write() expects a file descriptor (used in low-level file I/O) as one of its arguments and stdout is a FILE pointer (used in high-level file I/O), you must convert the FILE pointer to a file descriptor. This conversion from "fp" to "fd" is done by fileno().

The call to write() is used rather than printf() for two reasons. First, write() executes faster than printf(). Second, write() is a very simple function that does not take up much code space. In fact, in a test program, I replaced the call to write() with printf() and checked the code size. It was 9,746 bytes. I then recompiled the same test program using write() without a printf(), and the program size dropped to 2,280 bytes.

Does this mean you always should use write() rather than printf()? Clearly, no. The write() function is small because it does not do much—it lacks the flexibility of printf(). Also keep in mind that after printf() is used anywhere in the program, another call to it does not increase program size beyond the overhead of a function call. Indeed, using write() in the centers() function when the program already uses printf() actually will make the program somewhat larger. You should keep write() in mind, however, whenever code space is tight.

Substring Manipulations— *leftstr( ), rightstr( ), midstr( )*

Some people say that C lacks string processing capabilities. Often they point to COBOL and Basic as examples of languages that have good string processing. Oddly, those people never mention the fact that C has no inherent I/O facilities at all. Indeed, one of C's greatest strengths is that it is not bound by predetermined I/O or string statements. Whatever you need (that isn't already part of the standard library), you can create yourself.

In this section, we will build C equivalents of the LEFT$(), MID$(), and RIGHT$() statements in Basic. Although these functions are useful on their own, they also show how easy it is to duplicate statements found in other languages.

leftstr( )

The LEFT$() statement in Basic has the form

```
LEFT$(A$,N)
```

and is used to create a substring of A$ that consists of the N leftmost characters of A$. For example, if

```
A$ = "SeptemberOctoberNovember"
```

then LEFT$(A$,9) would return "September". Actually, strncpy() is almost a perfect substitute for LEFT$(), with one exception. Before that exception is discussed, look at the source code for LEFT$() as shown in listing 2.2.

Listing 2.2. *Create a left substring.*

```
/*****

                        leftstr()

    This function copies the left-most num characters from the
source string to the destination string. If the length of the
source string is less than num, then NULL is returned. This
function is similar to the LEFT$() statement in Basic.

Argument list:    char *d      the destination string
                  char *s      the source string
                  int num      starting character in the source
                               string

Return value:     char *       pointer to the destination string

*****/
```

continues

Listing 2.2. continued

```c
#include <string.h>

char *leftstr(char *d, char *s, int num)
{
   int len;

   len = strlen(s);
   strncpy(d, s, num);
   if (num < len)
      d[num] = '\0';
   return d;
}
```

Strncpy() is not a perfect replacement because it does not always copy the null termination character. If the length of the source string (s) is greater than the number of characters to copy (num), strncpy() does not append the null termination character. The solution is simple: Just place a null termination character in the numth element of the destination character array when len is greater than num. Voilà. A simple replacement for LEFT$().

Problems with *NULL*

Most compiler vendors define the macro named NULL in the stdio.h header file. The way in which NULL is defined, however, might vary among compiler vendors. Some use

```c
#define NULL 0
```

and others use

```c
#define NULL '\0'
```

There might even be some vendors that don't define NULL at all. If NULL is not defined for your compiler, one of the two preceding forms should work. After that choice is made, however, porting the code to a different compiler might require you to redefine the NULL macro. For example, the Quick C compiler "complains" when NULL is defined as 0, but it is satisfied when NULL is defined as '\0'. Check your vendor's documentation to see which definition is applicable for your compiler.

rightstr( )

Writing an equivalent function to Basic's RIGHT$() statement isn't much more difficult. RIGHT$() has the form

RIGHT$(A$,N)

which says to return the rightmost N characters of A$. Using the string example mentioned earlier, RIGHT$(A$,8) would yield the substring "November". The code for rightstr() appears in listing 2.3.

Listing 2.3. *Create a right substring.*

```
/*****
                              rightstr()


    This function copies the right-most num characters from the
source string to the destination string. If the length of the
source string is less than num, NULL is returned. This function
is similar to the RIGHT$() statement in Basic.


    Argument list:    char *d       the destination string
                      char *s       the source string
                      int num       starting character in the source
                                    string


    Return value:     char *        pointer to the destination string

*****/


#include <stdio.h>

char *rightstr(char *d, char *s, int num)
{
   char *temp;
   int len, offset;

   len = strlen(s);
   if (len < num) {
      return NULL;
   } else {
      temp = d;
```

continues

Listing 2.3. continued

```
    offset = len - num;         /* Starting offset in source string */
    s += offset;
    do {
       *d++ = *s;
    } while (*s++);
  }
  return temp;
}
```

In this function, you want to return a NULL pointer if the string has fewer than num characters. Otherwise, you save the starting address of the destination string (d) in temp and create an offset variable (offset) to the starting character's address in the source string. (You do this outside the do-while loop to avoid an unnecessary subtraction and assignment statement.) The function then copies the last num characters from the source string into the destination string. The function returns a pointer to the destination string.

midstr( )

The last substring function is the equivalent of Basic's MID$() statement:

MID$(A$,N,J)

This says to return J characters from A$, starting with the Nth character. However, the MID$() function also can have the following form:

MID$(A$,N)

which says to return all characters in A$ starting with the Nth character. This makes the midstr() only somewhat more complex than the other functions. The code is presented in listing 2.4.

Listing 2.4. *Create a mid-substring.*

```
/*****
                            midstr()

     This function copies num characters from the source string
  to the destination string, beginning with element start. If
  the length of the source string is less than num, then NULL
  is returned. If num is 0, the function copies all characters
  from the source string beginning with the start character.
  This function is similar to the MID$() statement in Basic.

  Argument list:    char *d    the destination string
                    char *s    the source string
                    int start  starting character in the source
                               string
                    int num    the number of characters to copy

  Return value:     char *     pointer to the destination string

*****/

#include <stdio.h>

char *midstr(char *d, char *s, int start, int num)
{
   char *temp;
   int len, offset;

   len = strlen(s);
   if (len < num + start) {
      return NULL;
   } else {
      if (num == 0) {
         num = len - start + 1;
      }
      temp = d;
      offset = start - 1;  /* Starting offset in source string */
      do {
         *d++ = *(s + offset);
      } while (*s++ && num--);
```

continues

Listing 2.4. continued

```
    }
    *(d - 1) = '\0';
    return temp;
}
```

The function first checks to see whether the length of the string is longer than the starting point in the string plus the number of characters to be copied. If not, a NULL pointer is returned.

Next, if num is 0, you must copy all elements from start to the end of the string. If num is 0, you reset num to equal the remaining number of characters in the string. The variable offset simply calculates the address of the startth character in the string. The loop simply copies the appropriate number of characters into the destination string. The second-to-last statement in the function is necessary to null-terminate the string. You then return the original lvalue of d to the calling function.

If nothing else, this section should show you how easy it is to duplicate any statements you like in other languages.

Display a String as Digits— *strdigit( )*

This function is more useful as a debugging function than as a general-purpose applications function. Sometimes you might need to examine a string's contents in a form other than the straight ASCII representation seen on the string. For example, what character does a newline ('\n') really take in a string? Is it the same for all compilers? What about the character when the Enter key is pressed? The purpose of strdigit() simply is to enable you to display the string as decimal, octal, or hexadecimal digits rather than as ASCII characters.

The source code for strdigit() is presented in listing 2.5.

Listing 2.5. *Display a string as digits.*

```
/*****
                        strdigit()

    This function displays the string passed to the function as
digits in one of three forms: octal, decimal, hexadecimal. If
you want, the ASCII digits can be displayed below the string
with the proper spacing for easy comparison.

    Argument list:    char *s       the string to be displayed
                      int val       the numeric form desired:
                                        1 = octal
                                        2 = decimal
                                        3 = hex
                                    Any other values will be displayed
                                    as characters.
                      int flag      a flag to display ASCII below
                                    digits

                                        0 = no display
                                        1 = display ASCII


    Return value:     void

*****/

#include <stdio.h>

void strdigit(char *s, int val, int flag)
{
    static char *form1[] = {"%3o ", "%3d ", "%3x "};
    char *ptr;

    ptr = s;
    if (val > 0 && val < 4) {              /* Proper range for val?   */
        while (*s) {                       /* If so, show it          */
            printf(form1[val - 1], *s++);
        }
    } else {
        flag = 1;                          /* If not, show ASCII      */
    }
```

continues

Listing 2.5. continued

```
if (flag) {
    s = ptr;
    printf("\n");
    while (*s) {
        printf("%3c ", *s++);
    }
}

}
```

The function has three arguments:

- The string to be displayed.

- A variable to determine which type of digit is to be displayed.

- A flag variable to enable the string to be displayed in ASCII below the digit representation. This last option enables you to inspect the digit and ASCII representations side-by-side.

There are no surprises in the function. Note that in the example the character array named form1[] has been initialized to the three display formats. The array is defined with the static storage class following the old "K&R" style. The ANSI standard now enables you to initialize automatic storage class arrays, so you could remove the static keyword from the data definition.

The purpose of form1[] is to serve as a control string for printf() and to display the string in the format requested by val when the function is called. If val falls outside the range of 1 to 3, the flag variable is set to 1. This causes the function to display the string in standard ASCII format.

Format *double* into Dollar String—*strdollar()*

Sometimes it is convenient to display a dollar amount in a program by using the form $12,345.67 rather than 12345.67. The strdollar() function is used to convert a floating point number into a formatted dollar amount. The code is presented in listing 2.6.

Listing 2.6. *Format double to dollar string.*

```
/*****
                          strdollar()

    This function builds a dollar amount from a double passed to the
function and returns the result into the buffer passed to the
function.

    NOTE: This function:

        1) rounds to the nearest penny
        2) assumes that doubles are capable of 17 significant digits
        3) returns an error message in the string space if the digits
           exceed the sprintf() format string (for example, "%17.2f"
           below)

    These assumptions might require some modifications to the function
    if it does not meet your needs.

    Argument list:     double x        the double to be converted
                       char *s         pointer to a buffer where the
                                       result is to be stored

    Return value:      void

*****/

#include <string.h>
#include <ctype.h>                   /* Need for string functions  */
#include <math.h>                    /* Need for fabs()            */


#define COMMA      1
#define NOCOMMA    0

void strdollar(double x, char *s)
{
    char buff[50];
    int comma, i, len, leadin, neg;

    neg = i = 0;
```

continues

Listing 2.6. *continued*

```
    if (x < 0.0) {                        /* Is it negative?          */
        neg = 1;
    }

    sprintf(buff, "%17.2f", fabs(x));     /* Format into a string     */
    while (isspace(buff[i]))              /* Eat white space          */
        i++;

    len = strlen(&buff[i]) - 3;           /* Ignore pennies .00 for now */

    if (len > 14) {                       /* Too long?  (14 = 17 - 3)  */
        strcpy(s, "**out of range**");
        return;
    }
    if (neg) {
        *s++ = '-';
    }

    comma = (len > 3) ? COMMA : NOCOMMA; /* At least one comma?       */

    *s++ = '$';                           /* Build string             */

    leadin = len % 3;                     /* Digits before first comma */

    while (leadin--) {                    /* Do leading digits        */
        *s++ = buff[i++];
    }

    if (comma && len % 3) {               /* Do first comma if needed  */
        *s++ = ',';
    }

    len -= (len % 3);                     /* Subtract digits written   */

    while (len--) {                       /* Do rest of string        */
        *s++ = buff[i++];
        if (len % 3 == 0 && len) {        /* Another comma?           */
            *s++ = ',';
        }
    }
    *s = '\0';                            /* Make it a string         */
    strcat(s, &buff[i]);                  /* Add the pennies back in  */
}
```

The function is more complex than you might expect. The first task is to see whether x is a negative value and set neg accordingly. Next, you must create a working string from which you can parse the dollar amount in the string to the final dollar format desired. Begin this process by formatting x into a working buffer using sprintf(). As you know, sprintf() writes the formatted output to a string rather than to the display screen. Note how fabs() is used to format the absolute value of x in case x is negative. The result of the call to sprintf() is a string representation of x with two decimal places. (This also will round x to the nearest penny.)

At first glance, it would seem that the while loop should not be necessary to strip away the leading white space. Why not just use a "%-17.2" format string instead? The problem is that you need to know the string's length after the buffer is filled. Either way, the leading or trailing white space must be stripped away to derive the string's "true" length. The call to strlen() gives the string's total length. Subtract 3 from the length so that you can ignore the pennies for the moment.

Next, you must check to see whether the string is greater than 14 digits. This is done to see whether you have exceeded the expected precision for a floating-point number. Some compilers have 17 significant digits; others have fewer. Consult your compiler's documentation (or do a few experiments) to see how many significant digits you have available with a double data type. Change the 17 in the format string and the test on 14 if your compiler is different. If your precision is exceeded, some form of error processing is needed. In listing 2.6, an out-of-range message simply is copied into the string and returned.

The function now begins to create the output string. If the number is negative, the first thing to do is write a minus sign into the output string. Next, if the amount is more than three characters, at least one comma is needed in the output string. Finally, write in the dollar sign ($) and then determine the number of characters to write before the first comma appears in the output string. This is done by using a modulo 3 operation on the string length and assigning the result into leadin.

After copying leadin characters into the output string, write the comma and subtract from the string length (len) the number of characters written thus far. Next, a while loop spins you through the rest of the string, adding commas when necessary. After the while loop ends, a null termination character is written to the string, enabling strcat() to be used to tack on the pennies. The result will be a dollar-formatted string for the double x passed to the function.

Format a String into Fields— *strfld( )*

How many times have you written code to put a string into a specific format, such as a phone number or a Social Security number? Although there is nothing particularly tricky about doing such formatting chores, it would be nice to have a function that could handle them. The purpose of strfld() is to provide a simple means of formatting a string into any desired field arrangement.

This function is flexible because it is data "nonspecific." That is, strfld() performs the formatting according to the format specifications passed to it; the specifics are determined outside the function. Listing 2.7 shows how the function is written.

Listing 2.7. Format string into fields.

```
/*****
                              strfld()

    This function converts a numeric value in "big" into a formatted
    string. The string is formatted according to the delimiter string.
    The f[] and delims[] arrays determine what the final string will
    look like. See the text for further explanation.

    Output is specified in the arguments presented to the function.

    Argument list:  int f[]         an array that tells how the input
                                    fields are organized. That is:

                                       f[0] = total number of input
                                                fields (n)
                                       f[1] = length of field 1
                                         .

                                         .    more field lengths

                                         .
                                       f[n] = ending length of string

                    char delims[]   delimiters to use between fields
                    long big        the number to be formatted
                    char *s         the buffer to receive the string
```

```
          Return value:    void              NOTE: If the string is not the right
                                             length, a null character is returned
                                             in s.


*****/

#include <stdio.h>
#include <string.h>

void strfld(int f[], char delims[], long big, char *s)
{
   char buff[20], *p;
   int count, fields, i, subgroup;

   p = s;
   fields = f[0];                      /* How many fields            */
   sprintf(buff,"%ld", big);           /* Make a string              */
      subgroup = i = 0;
   count = 1;

   while (buff[i]) {                    /* As long as there are digits... */
      if (f[count] == subgroup && delims[count - 1]) {
         *s++ = delims[count - 1];
         count++;
         subgroup = 0;
      }
      *s++ = buff[i];                   /* Fill in digits             */
      i++;
      subgroup++;
   }
   *s = '\0';
   if (strlen(p) != f[fields + 1])   /* Check for correct length     */
      *p = '\0';
}
```

The key to using strfld() is the arguments passed to it. The first argument is an array of integers that details how the field is to be built. An example will best show how this is done.

Suppose that you want to format a string for use as a Social Security ("SS") number in the format

123-45-6789

When formatting an SS number, the first argument to strfld() would be

```
int f[5] = {3, 3, 2, 4, 11};    /* For Social Security # */
```

The first element of the f[] array tells the function how many fields there will be. In an SS number there are three fields, so f[0] equals 3. Because there are three fields to be built, the next three integers in the f[] array indicate the number of characters in each field. The first field of an SS number has three characters, followed by a field of two characters, followed by a final field of four characters. Therefore, the f[] array will contain the following:

```
f[1] = 3    f[2] = 2    f[3] = 4
   123    -     45    -    6789
```

The final value in the f[] array is the resulting string's total length.

The second argument contains the delimiters that will be used to separate the fields. A hyphen usually is used, but others are possible. The delimiters are held in the character array named delims[]. For an SS number, delims[] would hold the string "- -" because only two delimiters are used.

The third argument is a long that holds the number to be formatted. I use this function most often for SS numbers, phone numbers, and nine-digit ZIP codes, although other numbers are possible (ISBN numbers, for example). If you need to convert an input string to a fielded output string, you can modify this function to meet your needs.

The final argument is a pointer to the character array that will hold the final (formatted) string. Obviously, it should be large enough to hold the formatted string and the delimiters.

First, you must format the long value in big into a working buffer and initialize several other working variables. The while loop moves through the working buffer, comparing the field counts in the f[] array with the number of characters being formatted into the field. When the value in f[] equals the count in subgroup, it is time to add in a delimiter. Therefore, with an SS number, f[1] equals 3. When subgroup is incremented to 3, a hyphen should be added to the string. If you examine the statements controlled by the if in the while loop, you will see that this is precisely what happens in the loop.

When the while loop ends, add the null termination character ('\0') to the string, and perform a final check to make sure the overall string length equals the last value in the f[] array. If all goes well, the new formatted string appears in the output string (that is, the fourth argument to the strfld() function). If the string lengths do not match, write a null termination character at the front of the output string and return. This has the effect of returning a null string, which the program can check as a possible error condition.

After the field array (f[]) is built, using strfld() is very convenient.

Dollar Amount to Verbal String—*saydollar( )*

You probably have seen checks on which the dollar amount is written out in words to prevent the check's amount from being altered. The saydollar() function is designed to "verbalize" an amount passed to the function and pass the result back as a string. The code is presented in listing 2.8.

Listing 2.8. *Convert amount into words.*

```
/*****
                              saydollar()

    This function converts a double to its verbal equivalent. It
most likely would be useful for check printing. Note that the
input range for the double should be less than one billion dollars,
although you can extend the limit. Remember, however, that you
will push the double's precision if you go much beyond the limit
set here.

    One final caution: Be sure the character pointer is large
enough to hold the output. You might want to make it at least 150
bytes.

    Argument list:    double x      the amount to convert
                      char *s       the string to hold the result

    Return value:     void

*****/


#include <stdio.h>
#include <string.h>
```

continues

Listing 2.8. *continued*

```c
void saydollar(double x, char *s)
{
    char buff[80], done[200];
    static char *units[] = {"0", "one", "two", "three", "four", "five",
                            "six", "seven", "eight", "nine"},
                *teens[] = {"ten", "eleven", "twelve", "thirteen",
                            "fourteen", "fifteen", "sixteen",
                            "seventeen", "eighteen", "nineteen"},
                *tens[] = {"", "ten", "twenty", "thirty", "forty",
                           "fifty", "sixty", "seventy", "eighty",
                           "ninety"},
                *denoms[] = {"", " hundred ", " thousand ", " million "};

    int len, passes;

    sprintf(buff, "%.2f", x);
    done[0] = '\0';
    passes = len = strlen(buff) - 3;

    while (len > -1) {
        switch (len % 3) {                  /* Divide into groups of 3    */
            case 0:                         /* Millions, thous, hundreds  */
                if (buff[0] == '.') {
                    strcat(done, " dollars and ");
                    len = 3;
                } else {
                    if (len) {
                        if (strlen(done)) {
                            strcat(done, denoms[len / 3 + 1]);
                        }
                        if (buff[0] != '0') {
                            strcat(done, units[(int) (buff[0] - '0')]);
                            strcat(done, denoms[1]);
                        }
                    } else {
                        if (done[strlen(done) - 2] == 'd') {
                            strcat(done, "no");
                        }
                        strcat(done, " cents");
                    }
```

```
            }
            len--;
            break;
        case 1:                         /* Units                     */
            if (buff[0] != '0') {
                strcat(done, units[(int) (buff[0] - '0')]);
            }
            if (buff[0] == '0' && passes == 1) { /* No dollars        */
                strcat(done, "no dollars");
                len--;
                break;
            }
            if (len == 1 && strlen(done) == 1) { /* When just 1 dollar */
                strcat(done, "dollar");
            }
            len--;
            break;
        case 2:                         /* Tens                       */
            if (buff[0] == '1') {       /* Special case for teens amts */
                strcat(done, teens[buff[1] - '0']);
                strcpy(buff, &buff[1]);
                len -= 2;
                break;
            } else {
                strcat(done, tens[buff[0] - '0']);
                if (buff[0] != '0' && buff[1] != '0')
                    strcat(done, "-");
                len--;
            }
            break;
        }                               /* End switch (len)           */
        strcpy(buff, &buff[1]);
    }                                   /* End while (len)            */
    strcpy(s, done);
}
```

The function begins with several definitions for the words that will be used to develop the string output. Although they are defined with the static storage class here, strict ANSI rules now enable variables with the auto storage class to be initialized. If your compiler supports this feature, you can omit the static keyword from the data definitions. Leaving them in, however, will not hurt anything.

First you must format into a working buffer the amount that is passed to the function in argument x. The length of this working string is determined by the call to strlen(), and the length minus three (the decimal point and the pennies) is stored in len and passes.

A while loop is used to process the working string, and a switch is used to determine what is done next within the while loop. Note that a modulo 3 operation is performed on len. This enables you to keep track of whether you will print the word "million" or "thousand" or "hundred" as you advance through the string. If the length (mod 3) is zero but positive, one of the denom[] words must be added to the string. If the modulo length is 1 (for example, case 1), a units[] word must be added. If the modulo length is 2 (for example, case 2), a tens[] word is added. A complication exists because of the way the numbers 10 through 19 are verbalized. A special test is performed for these character sequences and len is double-decremented if one is found.

When len eventually becomes zero, a special test in case 0 replaces the decimal point with the words "dollars and" and proceeds to determine the cents amount. After the cents are determined, the while loop ends, and the working string is copied into the second argument passed to the function.

When you use this function, be sure that the character array passed to the function is big. You will be surprised by how quickly the string space is used up.

Delete a Character from a String—*strdelc( )*

Once I was working with an old database of client information in which the client wanted to change each occurrence of "Mrs." to "Ms." Because of the database's arrangement, the strdelc() function made the job easy. This is the best kind of code—extremely simple and easy to maintain. The code appears in listing 2.9.

Listing 2.9. *Delete character from string.*

```
/*****
                            strdelc()

    This function deletes all occurrences of a character from a
    string.

    Argument list:    char *s      the string to be searched
                      char c       the character to be deleted

    Return value:     void

*****/

#include <string.h>

void strdelc(char *s, char c)
{
    while (*s) {
        if (*s == c) {
            strcpy(s, s + 1);
        } else {
            s++;
        }
    }
}
```

About the only unusual thing in this function is its use of

```
strcpy(s, s + 1);
```

which uses pointer addition to make things work. Because s is a pointer and, hence, holds an lvalue, you simply are copying the base of the string offset by one character into the base of the string. For example, if the string is "target" and you are deleting the letter 'a' from the string, the representation might look like figure 2.7.

Fig. 2.7. Memory image of a string.

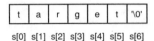

s[0] s[1] s[2] s[3] s[4] s[5] s[6]

When the `if` statement

```
if (*s == c)
```

becomes logical True, the representation becomes

```
if (s[1] == 'a')
```

Therefore, in the `strcpy()` call, the representation becomes

```
strcpy(s[1], s[2]);
```

If you think about this, you end up copying the `'r'` and the rest of the string "on top of" the `'a'` that was there originally. Obviously, there are other ways to do this, but the approach shown in listing 2.9 is simple and easy to understand. It also reinforces the design philosophy of using existing library functions to build new functions whenever possible.

Delete Only *n* Occurrences of a Character—*strdelcn( )*

The `strdelc()` function deletes every occurrence of a specified character from a string. There are times, however, when you want to remove only specific occurrences of the character from the string, rather than every one. This is the purpose of the `strdelcn()` code shown in listing 2.10.

Listing 2.10. Delete n occurrences of a character from a string.

```
/*****

                              strdelcn()

    This function deletes the specified number of occurrences of a
    specified character from a string.
```

```
   Argument list:     char *s       the string to be searched
                      int n         the number of occurrences to delete
                      char c        the character to be deleted


   Return value:      void


*****/


#include <string.h>

void strdelcn(char *s, int n, char c)
{
   while (*s) {
      if (*s == c && n) {
         strcpy(s, s + 1);
         n--;
      } else {
         s++;
      }
   }
}
```

As you would expect, the functions are similar, except that you keep decrementing a counter of the number of occurrences of c that have been removed from the string. The while continues to march through the string as long as there are characters to process and n is positive.

Here is something else to think about: Why don't you increment s when you find a match between s and c? (Hint: You want to remove characters.)

One other variation of these "delete character" functions might be useful. A situation might arise when you want to delete characters from a string, starting at the end of the string rather than the beginning. The standard library function strrchr() can be used to find the last occurrence of a character. A single call to strrchr() does not find multiple occurrences of the letter. Also, strrchr() only returns a pointer to the character; it does not delete it. Overcoming these limitations would be relatively easy by making multiple calls to strrchr() (when needed) and by having your new function delete the characters as it finds them. I will leave this as an exercise for you.

Delete Characters from a String—*strndel( )*

The strndel() function is used to delete n characters from a string, regardless of what those characters are. The code assumes that the pointer passed to the function points to the first character to be deleted. If you need to find a specific pattern string before you know where to begin deleting characters, consult the discussion of strstr() in your standard library documentation.

The code for strndel() appears in listing 2.11.

Listing 2.11. *Delete* n *characters from a string.*

```
/*****
                            strndel()

    This function deletes a specified number of characters from a
    string.

    Argument list:    char *s       the string to be searched
                      int n         the number of characters to be
                                    deleted

    Return value:     int           0 if string unchanged, 1 otherwise

*****/

#include <string.h>

int strndel(char *s, int n)
{
    int len;

    len = strlen(s);
    if (len < n)
        return 0;

    strcpy(s, s + n);
    return 1;
}
```

The function first checks the string's length to make sure it is greater than the number of characters being deleted. The code in listing 2.11 assumes an error exists if the length is less than n, and leaves the string unchanged. If your needs are different, you can modify the length check.

After the length check is passed, the strcpy() function is used to copy the old string with an n offset added back into the original string. As you saw in the discussion of the strdel() function, this has the effect of removing n characters from the original string.

Delete *n* Characters from the End of a String—*strndelend( )*

This function is used to delete a specified number of characters from the end of a string. This function, illustrated in listing 2.12, is useful when an input string must be truncated for some reason (to fit into a fixed field, for example).

Listing 2.12. *Delete* n *characters from the end of a string.*

```
/*****
                      strndelend()

    This function deletes a specified number of characters from the
  end of a string. Note that the function does not change the string if
  you try to delete more characters than actually are in the string.

    Argument list:    char *s      the string to be searched
                      int n        the number of characters to be
                                   deleted

    Return value:     int          0 if string unchanged, 1 otherwise

*****/

#include <string.h>

int strndelend(char *s, int n)
{
   int len;
```

continues

Listing 2.12. continued

```
len = strlen(s);
if (len < n)
   return 0;

s[len - n] = '\0';
return 1;
}
```

The concept used here is similar to that used by other string-delete functions. As soon as the length of the string is known, that length minus n is where the end of the string should be. Therefore, the statement

```
s[len - n] = '\0';
```

simply moves the null termination character to that point in the string. This removes the last n characters from the string.

Remove Trailing White Space from a String—*strbobb( )*

Often, a string is padded with blank spaces on the end to give the string a fixed record length in a disk file. When the string is being processed, however, these extra spaces might need to be removed. The strbobb() function, illustrated in listing 2.13, is designed to strip away the padding white space from the end of a string.

Listing 2.13. *Remove padding from a string.*

```
/*****

                          strbobb()

    This function deletes all white space (as defined by the isspace()
function) from the end of a string.

    Argument list:    char *s      the string to be searched

    Return value:     void

*****/
```

```
void strbobb(char *s)
{
   int len;

   len = strlen(s);
   len--;
   while (isspace(*(s + len) )) {
      len--;
   }
   *(s + len + 1) = '\0';
}
```

Although this function could be written many different ways, the idea here is to examine the contents of the string from the end of the string until the first non-white space character is read. The while loop, in conjunction with isspace(), continues to examine the string and decrement the length of the string until a non-white space character is read.

The statement

```
*(s + len + 1) = '\0';
```

writes the null termination character on top of the last white space character read in the string. Why is 1 added to the offset before the null is written? (Hint: What was the last character read in the while loop?)

Replace *n* Characters in a String—*strreplace( )*

The strreplace() function is used when you need to replace all occurrences of one character with another one. For example, if you store a date as 5/23/89 and you want it to be 5-23-89 instead, you can use strreplace() to make such changes easily. This function is useful in altering many formatting conventions that differ among locales. (Europeans, for example, often use a comma rather than a decimal point in dollar amounts.) The source code for the function appears in listing 2.14.

Listing 2.14. Replace character sequence with another sequence.

```
/*****
                              strrepl()


     This function scans the string passed to the function and
   replaces each occurrence of character "old" with character "new."


   Argument list:    char *s      the string to be searched
                     char new     the replacement character
                     char old     the character to be replaced


   Return value:     void

*****/


#include <string.h>

void strreplace(char *s, char new, char old)
{
   char *ptr;
   int len;

   len = strlen(s);
   while (len) {                         /* While some chars left   */
      ptr = memchr(s, old, len);
      if (ptr) {                         /* Pointer to "old"?       */
         *ptr = new;
         len -= (ptr - s);
         s = ptr + 1;
      } else {                           /* If null, no match       */
         break;
      }
   }
}
```

All the real work is done by the memchr() standard library function. (*Note:* The prototype for the memchr() function might be located in a header other than string.h. Alternative header names to check are memory.h (for Microsoft) and mem.h (for Borland). Although Borland and Microsoft use different "memory" header file names, both also prototype the mem*() family of functions in string.h. Check your compiler's documentation to see which is the appropriate header.) When memchr() is called, as in

```
memchr(s, old, len);
```

it searches `len` bytes in string `s` for the character `old`. If it finds a match, the function returns a pointer to the character in `s` that matches `old`, or a null pointer if no match is found. All the `mem*()` functions are very fast because they do not have much work to do. They are a great way to process strings.

If `memchr()` does find a match, you write the new character into the string where `ptr` points, adjust the `len` and `s` variables for the characters that were read, and continue looking through the string. Eventually all characters are read and the `while` loop terminates.

Again, remember that you should build onto your library, not replace it. As you search for a solution to any task, always look for existing functions, such as `memchr()`, that reduce the coding load.

Insert a Character into a String—*strinsert( )*

The purpose of `strinsert()` is to insert a single character into an existing string. One example might include inserting the necessary punctuation in abbreviations (such as "Mr." rather than "Mr") and contractions ("don't" rather than "dont"). Listing 2.15 presents the code for the `strinsert()` function.

Listing 2.15. *Insert a character into a string.*

```
/*****
                              strinsert()

    This function inserts a character into a string. The function
is passed the address of the point in the string where the
character is to be inserted.

Argument list:    char *s        the point in the string where the
                                 character is to be inserted
                  char insert    the inserted character

Return value:     char *         pointer to the inserted character

*****/
```

continues

Listing 2.15. continued

```c
#include <stdlib.h>

char *strinsert(char *s, char insert)
{
   char *sptr;

   sptr = (char*)calloc(strlen(s)+1, sizeof (char));

   if (sptr == NULL) {                    /* Was there room ?      */
      return NULL;
   }
   strcpy(sptr, s);                       /* Yep. Save old string  */
   *s = insert;                           /* Add new character     */
   strcpy(s + 1, sptr);                   /* Add the old string on */
   free(sptr);                            /* Free the space up     */
   return s;
}
```

There is more to the process of inserting a character than you might think. The previous example's approach to the task involves copying the original string into a new memory allocation (see the call to calloc() in listing 2.15), inserting the new character into the original string, and then copying the copy of the original string back onto the original string with an offset of 1 from the start of the string. If you examine listing 2.15, you will see that that is exactly what was done.

Notice that strcpy() is used with the destination string offset by one byte. The one byte is, of course, the character that has been inserted into the string.

A few words of warning: The function assumes that the lvalue of the place to insert the string is passed to the function. In other words, if you wanted to replace s[5] with the letter 'c', you would call the function

```c
new_ptr = strinsert(&s[5], 'c');
```

and new_ptr would point to the inserted character. You also must be sure to check the return value (for example, new_ptr) for a null pointer. If a null pointer is returned, the character was not inserted into the string. Next, the call to free() must be in the function code. Otherwise, you unnecessarily chew up memory allocations. Finally, this function assumes there is enough space in the character array to hold another character. If not, all bets are off on the data following the array in memory!

Note: The function prototype for calloc() might appear in a header file other than stdlib.h. Check alloc.h, memory.h, and malloc.h if you do not find it prototyped in the stdlib.h header file. (You need the prototype so that your program will know that the calloc() returns a pointer data type.)

Convert Blanks into Tabs— *strentab( )*

When you press the tab key on your keyboard, only one tab character is generated, even though the cursor moves several spaces. When writing strings, however, some editors actually use several blank spaces, rather than the tab character itself, to denote the tab's use within the string. If the string is then stored on disk, more disk space is used than is necessary. The strentab() function shown in listing 2.16 enables you to convert these spaces into a single tab character.

Listing 2.16. *Convert spaces into tabs.*

```
/*****
                            strentab()

    This function converts blank spaces into tabs. Variable num
    determines how many spaces are to be treated as a tab insert.

    Argument list:    char *s        pointer to the string to be
                                     detabbed
                      int num        the number of blanks to insert
                                     for a tab character

    Return value:     char *         pointer to new string
*****/

char *strentab(char *s, int num)
{
    char *sptr, *tptr;
    int flag, count;
```

continues

Listing 2.16. continued

```
    tptr = s;
    while (*s) {                            /* Walk through it       */
        if (*s == ' ') {                    /* Found one...          */
            sptr = s;
            count = num - 1;                /* Enough others for tab */
            flag = 0;
            s++;
            while (count--) {               /* Count spaces for tab  */
                if (*s == ' ') {
                    s++;
                    flag = 1;
                } else {                    /* Not enough for tab    */
                    flag = 0;
                    break;
                }
            }
            if (flag) {                     /* There were enough     */
                *sptr = '\t';               /* Insert the tab        */
                strcpy(sptr + 1, s);        /* Save old string       */
            }
        } else {
            s++;
        }
    }
    return tptr;
}
```

The function has two arguments—the string to be processed, and the number of blank spaces to treat as a tab. The function uses a while loop to examine the string for a space. When one is found, a second while loop checks to see whether enough spaces (num) are present to substitute a tab character into the string. If there are enough spaces, a tab character is inserted at the first space read (sptr), and the remaining part of the string after num spaces is copied back into the string. This substitution process continues until the entire string has been examined.

The function returns a pointer to the beginning of the original string.

Convert Tabs into Spaces—*strdetab( )*

Just as you sometimes need to replace blank spaces with tabs, you sometimes need to convert tabs into spaces. When printing C listings, for example, using three spaces rather than eight for a tab often can mean the difference between folding a source line and not folding it. (I find folded lines difficult to read.) The `strdetab()` function shown in listing 2.17 converts tabs into a specified number of spaces.

Listing 2.17. *Convert tabs into spaces.*

```
/*****
                            strdetab()

    This function converts tabs into spaces. Variable num
determines the number of spaces to be inserted for each tab
read. The function assumes the string is large enough to hold
the output.

    Argument list:    char *s      pointer to the string to be
                                   detabbed
                      int num      the number of blanks to insert
                                   for a tab character

    Return value:     char *       pointer to new string

*****/

#include <alloc.h>            /* Might be malloc.h for some compilers */

char *strdetab(char *s, int num)
{
   char *sptr, *tptr;
   int i;

   tptr = s;
   while (*s) {
      if (*s == '\t') {
          sptr = (char *) calloc(strlen(s), sizeof(char));
          if (sptr == NULL) {                 /* Was there room ?        */
```

continues

Listing 2.17. continued

```
            return NULL;
        }
        strcpy(sptr, s + 1);
        for (i = 0; i < num; i++)          /* Add spaces              */
            *s++ = ' ';

        strcpy(s, sptr);                   /* Save old string         */
        free(sptr);                        /* Free the space up       */
    } else {
        s++;
    }
  }
  return tptr;
}
```

The code in listing 2.17 is similar to the strentab() function, except that the string's length must be increased when a tab character is read. This means that you must allocate space for the old string while you convert the new one. The call to calloc() provides this allocation when needed; the remaining string is copied into this allocation.

Next, you pad the string with num blanks using a for loop. A more efficient way to accomplish the padding would be to replace the following statements

```
for (i = 0; i < num; i++)              /* Add spaces              */
    *s++ = ' ';
```

with

```
memset(s, ' ', num);
s += num;
```

Although the memset() function is part of the ANSI standard library, some compilers might not have the function. If you do have the memset() function in your library, you might want to make the change. Be sure to include the proper header file (stdlib.h, alloc.h, or whatever your compiler requires).

As always, the function assumes there is enough string space in the original character array for the new space characters that will be added into the string.

Count Words in a String— *strcw( )*

The strcw() function produces a word count for the string passed to the function (see listing 2.18). This function has some shortcomings, however. If the string contains a hyphenated word (such as "blue-collar") or a contraction (such as "wasn't"), the word is counted as two words rather than one. You could argue that such constructions should be counted as one word, but I think the function produces a proper count. If you disagree, you can modify the function to suit your needs.

Listing 2.18. *Word count in a string.*

```
/*****
                            strcw()

    This function determines the number of words in a string.

    Argument list:    char *s       pointer to the string to search

    Return value:     int           the number of words found

*****/

#include <stdio.h>
#include <ctype.h>

int strcw(char *s)
{
   int count;

   count = 0;
   while (*s) {                     /* For the entire string...   */
      if (isalpha(*s)) {            /* If a word has started...   */
         while (isalpha(*s)) {      /* ...find its end...         */
            s++;
         }
         count++;                   /* ...and count it            */
      } else {
         while (!isalpha(*s)) {     /* Otherwise, spin though it  */
            if (*s == NULL)         /* unless you find its end    */
```

continues

Listing 2.18. continued

```
                break;
            s++;
        }
    }
}
return count;
}
```

This function relies on `isalpha()` to do most of the work. The `while` loop examines the string one character at a time and checks to see whether the character is an alphabetic character (`'a'-'z'`, or `'A'-'Z'`) and, if it is, enters another `while` loop that keeps checking characters until a non-alpha (end of word) character is read. At that point, the word counter (`count`) is incremented.

If the character read is not alphabetic, a `while` using an `!isalpha()` check continues to spin through the sequence of non-alphabetic characters. This alternating between alpha and non-alpha characters continues until the entire string has been checked. When the process is finished, `count` will equal the word count for the string.

Replace a String Pattern with Another Pattern—*strsub( )*

This function works in a manner similar to the search-and-replace functions of many text editors. The code in listing 2.19 shows that the original and replacement strings do not have to be the same length.

Listing 2.19. String replacement.

```
/*****
                        strsub()

    This function searches a string for a specified pattern and
    replaces it with a new text string. Note that the pattern string
    is replaced with the replacement string, and that the two do not
    have to be the same length. It is assumed, however, that the
    original string is long enough to hold the result.
```

```
    Argument list:      char *s          the string to search
                        char *pat        the pattern to locate
                        char *rep        the replacement string

    Return value:       char *           pointer to the replaced string

*****/

#include <stdio.h>
#include <string.h>
#include <alloc.h>                  /* Might be malloc.h for some compilers */

char *strsub(char *s, char *pat, char *rep)
{
    char *ptr, *tptr;
    int plen, rlen;

    tptr = ptr = s;
    plen = strlen(pat);
    rlen = strlen(rep);

    if ( (ptr = strstr(s, pat)) == NULL) { /* Find a match?              */
        return NULL;
    }
                                            /* Buy some work space       */
    tptr = (char *) calloc(strlen(ptr)+1, sizeof(char));

    if (tptr == NULL)                       /* No memory left            */
        return NULL;

    strcpy(tptr, ptr + plen);               /* If space was left         */

    while (rlen--) {                        /* Copy replacement          */
        *ptr++ = *rep++;
    }

    strcpy(ptr, tptr);                      /* Add old stuff back        */
    free(tptr);

    return ptr - plen;                      /* Return pointer to change  */
}
```

The strstr() function finds the pattern to be replaced. You probably have this ANSI C standard library function, even though you might not use it often. The return value from strstr() is a pointer to the matched pattern if one is found, or a null pointer if no match occurs. If no match is found, the null pointer is returned to the caller.

Assuming a match is found, you call calloc() to reserve enough space to store the string from ptr to the end of the string. If the allocation is made, you copy the string into the allocation pointed to by tptr. Note that you do not copy the pattern used in the search (pat). In other words, if this function is called with

```
strsub("123456789", "234", "xxxx");
```

ptr will point to the '2' in the string, but the call to strcpy() only copies "56789" into the allocation pointed to by tptr.

Next, a while loop copies the replacement pattern into the original string (as pointed to by ptr). When rlen is decremented to zero, the replacement string has been copied into the original string. The call

```
strcpy(ptr, tptr);
```

copies the contents of tptr ("56789") to the location indicated by ptr (it actually points to '6' now). The result is the string

```
"1xxxx56789"
```

Take some time to study how the strsub() function works.

Conclusion

Unique tasks always are popping up where string processing is concerned, and no library can cover all the bases. However, some of the ideas presented in this chapter should help you tackle related string processing problems. If nothing else, this chapter should convince you of the value of knowing the functions that already exist in your standard library. Many are seldom used, but these functions can save you much time now and then, if you know they are there.

You might want to curl up with your library's documentation one night. Doing so could pay big dividends later.

3

Input Functions

A lmost every program, regardless of its language, can be divided into five basic steps. Step one is the setup, or initialization, phase of the program. This first step might be responsible for opening certain data files, doing dynamic allocations, parsing command-line arguments, or completing other similar tasks. The second step involves inputting the data that will be used in the program. Data input might be from the keyboard, disk files, or some other device.

Step three is the processing of data. This step is especially "program dependent"; that is, step three is the most difficult to generalize and, hence, is not likely to produce new functions that can be added to your library of C functions.

The fourth step is the presentation of the program's results. The results can be shown on the screen, written to the printer, or saved to a data file. The fifth step is performing any cleanup task that needs to be done, such as closing data files or freeing pointers.

This chapter discusses several input routines that are not part of the standard C library. The functions in this chapter fall into two broad groups— those that can be used as models for other input functions, and those that are specific to a narrowly defined task and cannot be used in any other way. The first group's functions present ideas that can be used to build new functions.

The second group's functions probably are not good models for new functions, but they still are useful in their own right. For example, this chapter examines several mouse functions used in the menuing functions discussed in Chapter 4, "Menuing Systems."

scanf( ) As an Input Function

When the speed limit was lowered to 55 miles per hour during the energy crisis of the early 1970s, one state erected the new speed-limit signs six inches too low. At considerable expense, the state had to raise every speed-limit sign in the state or risk losing all federal highway funds. When this situation came to light in the press, one person remarked, "They're lucky the federal government didn't do it. The feds would have lowered the road six inches."

I think of scanf() as a federally funded input function. In most situations it is like cutting butter with a chain saw: the tool is much too powerful for the task. The scanf() function also is easily misused even for the most simple tasks, such as inputting strings into a program. The sad thing is that many introductory textbooks use scanf() as the input function of choice. As a result, novice C programmers are not exposed to other input functions, even though better alternatives exist. These programmers continue to use scanf() out of habit, if for no other reason.

A short experiment should convince you that scanf() often is not the best choice for putting data into a program. Write a simple program that does nothing more than get a string from the keyboard. To make it more interesting, use scanf() to input an address such as

123 Main St.

After the program is working correctly, check the .EXE file's size. Then remove the scanf() function and use gets() instead. In my case, the scanf() program was nearly 2.5K larger than the gets() program. In addition, gets() worked on the first try. (I needed several tries to get the scanf() version to work properly.) As a general rule, therefore, I suggest that you avoid scanf() unless you cannot find another alternative.

Basic Input Functions

Programs normally accept keyboard input in one of two forms—buffered or unbuffered. With buffered input, data is written into a buffer using the full keyboard handling facilities. These routines usually are based on interrupt 0x21, function 0x0a of MS-DOS. An example of the C equivalent of buffered input is gets().

Unbuffered keyboard input does not use an input buffer, so the input is processed one character at a time. Unbuffered input routines might call interrupt 0x21, functions 0x06, 0x07, or 0x08. Each function uses a somewhat different method of processing the input. For example, the primary difference between functions 0x07 and 0x08 is that the latter does Ctrl-C and Ctrl-Break checking. The C equivalent of unbuffered input is getch().

Unbuffered Character Input—*getch( )*

Although getch() is not a standard library function, all MS-DOS compilers have this function in one form or another. Listing 3.1 presents an example of how getch() might be written. Because interrupt 0x21 is used for many service routines, compilers supply the intdos() function to do nothing but service interrupt 0x21. Many of the functions discussed in this chapter use the intdos() function.

Listing 3.1. Unbuffered character input.

```
/*****
                            getch()

    This function does unbuffered input from the keyboard and
    performs Ctrl-C and Ctrl-Break checking. If either of these two
    input conditions is sensed, interrupt 0x23 is executed. Note
    that input characters are not echoed.

    Argument list:    void

    Return values:    int       the character entered at the keyboard
*****/

#include <dos.h>

int getch(void)
{
    union REGS ireg;

    ireg.h.ah = 0x08;                          /* Function 8           */
    intdos(&ireg, &ireg);

    return ireg.h.al;
}
```

Not much needs to be said about the getch() function, except that it probably is better to use function 0x08 so that Ctrl-C and Ctrl-Break are active. The Ctrl-C and Ctrl-Break facilities can be useful in debugging sessions when you must terminate the program. If your compiler supports getch(), you might want to write a short test program to make sure your getch() is based on function 0x08. (If it does use function 0x08, the program should end whenever you enter Ctrl-C and Ctrl-Break while the program is calling getch().) If your getch() is not based on function 0x08, you should add the code in listing 3.1 (using a different function name) to your set of library functions.

Checking for Ctrl-C and Ctrl-Break—*brkchk( )*

When you check for Ctrl-C and Ctrl-Break, how can you know whether the checks are active? Fortunately, it is quite simple to find out whether Ctrl-C and Ctrl-Break checks are active, as shown in listing 3.2.

Listing 3.2. *Checking for Ctrl-C and Ctrl-Break.*

```
/*****
                            brkchk()

    This function detects whether the Ctrl-Break or Ctrl-C
    checking flag is set or clear. If the flag is set, a process
    (for example, disk I/O) could be interrupted and cause problems
    later.

    Argument list:    void

    Return value:     int      0 if Ctrl-C-Break is off;
                               1 if it is on

*****/

#include <dos.h>


int brkchk(void)
{
```

```
    union REGS ireg;

    ireg.h.ah = 0x33;                          /* Function 51           */
    ireg.h.al = 0x00;                          /* Just read current status */
    intdos(&ireg, &ireg);

    return ireg.h.dl;
}
```

With `ireg.h.al` set to 0, function 0x33 checks to see whether Ctrl-C and Ctrl-Break checking are active. The return value is 0 if checking is not performed and 1 if the checks are active.

Because there might be times when you do not want the user to be able to use Ctrl-C or Ctrl-Break to terminate a program (for example, before data is flushed to disk), you can disable Ctrl-C and Ctrl-Break. The `set_cntrlbrk()` function shown in listing 3.3 enables you to turn Ctrl-C and Ctrl-Break checking on or off, according to your program's needs.

Listing 3.3. *Setting Ctrl-C and Ctrl-Break.*

```
/*****
                            set_cntrlbrk()

     This function is used to set Ctrl-Break or Ctrl-C checking.
   The state of the flag must be either 0 or 1.

     Argument list:     int flag       0 if no checking wanted;
                                       1 if checking is wanted

     Return value:      int            0 if Ctrl-Break is off;
                                       1 if it is on
*****/

#include <dos.h>


int set_cntrlbrk(int flag)
{
    union REGS ireg;

    ireg.h.ah = 0x33;                              /* Function 51           */
```

continues

Listing 3.3. continued

```
    ireg.h.al = 0x01;                    /* Prepare for setting it    */
    ireg.h.dl = flag;
    intdos(&ireg, &ireg);

    return ireg.h.dl;
}
```

Depending on whether you set flag to 0 (no checking) or 1 (checking), Ctrl-C and Ctrl-Break checking can be turned on or off. As a general rule, if your program uses buffered file I/O or you are otherwise saving information for some form of I/O later in the program, you might want to disable Ctrl-C and Ctrl-Break until those output routines are finished.

Clear Keyboard Buffer—*clrgetch( )*

As you probably know, PCs use a keyboard buffer that can hold keystrokes while the CPU is doing something else. If you type too many characters, an alarm or a bell tone sounds to tell you the buffer is full. After the CPU finishes its task, it can process the keystrokes held in the buffer.

Usually, this "type-ahead" buffer is a convenient feature, but it also can be a problem. Have you ever run a program that used unbuffered input, similar to getch(), and then pressed the Enter key only to find that you answered the first question with the first keystroke and the second question with the Enter key? This can happen when the buffer stores both keystrokes.

You can avoid this problem by clearing the keyboard buffer before each input, using the function presented in listing 3.4.

Listing 3.4. Clear keyboard buffer.

```
/*****
                                    clrgetch()

    This function clears the keyboard type-ahead buffer before
reading a single character from the keyboard. The keyboard input
routine is interrupt 0x21, function 0x08, which waits for a key to
be entered.

    Argument list:      void
```

```
      Return value:      int        the character entered

*****/


#include <dos.h>


int clrgetch(void)
{
   union REGS ireg;

   ireg.h.ah = 0x0c;                       /* Function 12             */
   ireg.h.al = 0x08;                       /* Prepare for function 8  */
   intdos(&ireg, &ireg);

   return ireg.h.al;
}
```

The buffer is cleared (by function 0x0c of interrupt 0x21), and then it waits for a character to be entered. The character entered is then returned from the function.

This function behaves just like the getch() function shown earlier. It probably is a better choice for most applications because it will not accidentally use any keystrokes that might be left over in the buffer. In fact, you might want to replace the getch() function shown in listing 3.1 with the one shown here, in listing 3.4.

Keyboard Character Input, No Waiting—_kbhit( )

Sometimes it is useful to see whether a character has been entered at the keyboard and, if one has not been entered, to go back to processing something else. For example, I wrote a game that presented a series of instructions. When a user pressed the space bar, the value of a counter was used to seed a random-number generator. By using _kbhit() to sense the pressing of the space bar, the program could continue incrementing an internal counter while the user read the instructions. Because people read at different speeds, and because their reaction times are different, I was fairly certain that different seeds would be used for the random-number generator. As a result, the cards used in the game rarely would show the same starting pattern.

Listing 3.5 shows the code for the _kbhit() function. Simply stated, this function polls the keyboard and returns a value of 0x80 (128 decimal) if no key is struck. When a key has been pressed, the function returns the key that was pressed.

Listing 3.5. Unbuffered character input (keyboard polling).

```
/*****
                            _kbhit()

   This function reads a character from the keyboard--if one is
ready--using interrupt 0x21. If a character is not ready, the
function returns zero. If a character is read, it is not echoed to
the screen. If an extended key code is read, the value returned is
the scan code plus 0x100.

Argument list:    void

Return value:     int      0 if no key has been pressed; otherwise,
                           the character pressed


   CAUTION: This version of _kbhit() assumes that the intdos()
function returns the contents of the flag register after the call.
This is not true for the Borland or Microsoft compilers. See
listing 3.5a for an alternative.

*****/

#include <dos.h>

#define ZEROFLAG  0x40

int kbhit(void)
{
    int zflag;
    union REGS ireg;

    ireg.h.ah = 0x06;               /* Function 6                    */
    ireg.h.dl = 0xff;               /* We want to read it, not output */
    zflag = intdos(&ireg, &ireg);

    if ( (zflag & ZEROFLAG) == 0) {  /* A character and 0?            */
```

```
          if (ireg.h.al == 0) {          /* Extended keycode?          */
              ireg.h.ah = 0x06;
              ireg.h.dl = 0xff;
              intdos(&ireg, &ireg);
              return (ireg.h.al + 0x100);
      }
    return ireg.h.al;                     /* An ASCII character          */
      }
      return 0;                           /* No character                */
  }
```

As always, `ireg.h.ah` is set to the function number (0x06) before calling interrupt 0x21. Note that, for the function to perform properly, `ireg.h.dl` must be loaded with 0xff before calling.

Nit-picking

The previously described function is fairly simple, but it still is more complicated than most `_kbhit()` functions. This complexity is due to the manner in which the PC processes the extended key codes (for example, the function or arrow keys). On the first call to interrupt 0x21, function 0x06 returns 0 and the second call returns the scan code for the key pressed. This can cause confusion because two interpretations are possible for a return value of 0 from the interrupt call. That is, a 0 could mean no key or an extended key code.

Many programmers become confused because they make implicit assumptions about the return value (as held in `ireg.h.al`) from function 0x06. Although it appears that `ireg.h.al` is zero when no character is read, the specifications do not say that. What *is* said is that the zero flag is set (for example, 1) when no character is read, and clear when a character is available. Therefore, because the flag register is returned from an `intdos()` call, you assign the return value into `zflag` and use that value to determine whether a character is available. (There is no guarantee that `ireg.h.al` is zero when no character is present.) Because the zero flag is bit 6 of the flag register, `ZEROFLAG` is `#defined` as 0x40. A bitwise `AND` of `zflag` and `ZEROFLAG` will equal 0 if a character is present.

If the test on `zflag` and `ZEROFLAG` is logical True and `ireg.h.al` is not 0, then it is a normal ASCII character. If the `zflag` and `ZEROFLAG` test is logical False, no character is available.

Unfortunately, most compilers do not return the flag register as part of the intdos() function call. Instead, the return value often is the contents of the AX register or perhaps just the carry flag. If your compiler does not return the contents of the flag register, you should use the code in listing 3.5a rather than listing 3.5.

You now have a safe way to read all three possible keystroke types:

1. No keystroke

2. An ASCII character

3. An extended key code

Some of you will "ding" me because I have committed the sin of multiple exit points from the function. It is true, and I will accept the criticism. However, considering the function's small size (the entire function can be viewed at one time) and the rather simple coding used, it seems to be the most direct solution to the problem. Another convenient feature is that it works.

One final note: If the return value from _kbhit() is used for subsequent processing, as in

```
key = _kbhit();
```

key must be either an integer or at least 9 bits long so that the return value can be tested properly. Because some compilers strip the high bit on chars and some extended key codes have values greater than 128, it is not safe to use a char with the return value from _kbhit().

Listing 3.5a presents an alternative for those whose compilers do not return the flag register after an intdos() call.

Listing 3.5a. Alternative _kbhit() function.

```
/*****
                            _kbhit()


    This function reads a character from the keyboard--if one is
ready--using interrupt 0x21. If a character is not ready, the
function returns zero. Characters are not echoed to the screen. An
extended key code is returned as the scan code plus 0x100. ASCII
characters are returned.
```

```
     NOTE: THIS VERSION IS USED INSTEAD OF LISTING 3.5 IF INTDOS()
DOES NOT RETURN FLAG REGISTER.

Argument list:    void

Return value:     int     0              no key pressed
                          1 < c < 128    ASCII character
                          c > 256        extended key code

     CAUTION: Depending on your compiler, you might need to change
the following keyword "asm" to "_asm" or some other keyword. The
following code is for the Borland compiler.

*****/

int kbhit(void)
{
   unsigned c, flag;

   asm mov c, 0
   asm mov flag, 0
 loop1:
   asm mov dl,0ffh
   asm mov ah, 06h
   asm int 21h
   asm jz clear
   asm cmp al, 0
   asm jne good
   asm mov flag, 100h
   asm jmp loop1
 clear:
   asm mov al, 0
 good:
   asm mov c, al

   return (int) (c + flag);
}
```

The code shown in listing 3.5a is written using inline assembler instructions. Most C compilers support inline assembler, and the example here is for the Borland compiler. If you use Microsoft's compiler, simply replace the keyword "asm" in listing 3.5a with "_asm". Other compilers might have other minor deviations from the _asm or asm keyword. Consult your compiler's documentation for details.

One final caution: Many compiler vendors already supply a kbhit() function. The _kbhit() functions presented in listings 3.5 and 3.5a, however, are different because of the way they process extended key codes. If your compiler has an existing kbhit() function, you should be sure to name the functions in listings 3.5 and 3.5a _kbhit() to avoid a name collision.

Keyboard Status—*kbstatus( )*

Suppose that your program uses the arrow keys. As you probably know, when the Num Lock key is on, the return code for the right-arrow key is read as the number 6 rather than as the right-arrow key. In other cases, you might insist that only lowercase letters be returned from the keyboard. If the Caps Lock key is on, you never will see a lowercase letter. It might be useful, therefore, to have a function that can determine whether these (and other) special keys are set properly before continuing the program. Such is the purpose of the kbstatus() function, shown in listing 3.6.

Listing 3.6. Keyboard status.

```
/*****
                        kbstatus()

    This function returns the status of the keyboard. The return
value is an integer whose bit interpretations are explained below.
If the bit is turned on, it means that the key is pressed. Only the
low byte has meaning.

Argument list:    void

Return value:     int       bit: 0    Right Shift key
                                 1    Left Shift key
                                 2    Control key
                                 3    Alt key
                                 4    Scroll Lock key
                                 5    Num Lock key
                                 6    Caps Lock key
                                 7    Insert key

*****/

#include <dos.h>
```

```
int kbstatus(void)
{
    union REGS ireg;

    ireg.h.ah = 0x02;                       /* Function 2, Int 0x16     */
    int86(0x16, &ireg, &ireg);
    return ireg.h.al;                       /* Return status byte       */
}
```

Function 0x02 of interrupt 0x16 is used to check the keyboard's status. The value returned from the function determines whether one of the special keys is active. Each of the lower eight bits of the return value tells the status of one of the keys. These bits can be checked to determine whether some specific action should be taken before continuing the program.

Program 3.1 presents an example of how kbstatus() might be used. The program begins by defining several keyboard-status error messages on which you might want to act while the program is running. For purposes of illustration, assume that you want all the special keys deactivated before running the program.

The error messages are defined in errors[]. In the program, this array of pointers has been defined to char using the static storage class. Although the ANSI standard permits auto storage-class aggregate data items to be initialized, not all compilers support this feature. If your compiler supports initialization of auto aggregates, you can omit the static keyword from the definition of errors[].

The program then calls kbstatus() to check the keyboard's status and assigns the return value into i. If any bit of the return value is set, control enters a while loop and calls kbstatus_off().

Program 3.1. *Check special keyboard status.*

```
#include <stdio.h>
#include <string.h>

#define MAXLINE 128

void kbstatus_off(int row, int col, char *errors[], int status);
void clean_kbemess(int row, int col, char *errors[], int index);
```

continues

Program 3.1. *continued*

```
void main(void)
{
    static char *errors[] = {
      "Release the Right Shift key",
      "Release the Left Shift key",
      "Release the Ctrl key",
      "Release the Alt key",
      "Release the Scroll Lock key",
      "Release the Num Lock key",
      "Release the Caps Lock key",
      "Release the Insert key"
      };
    int i, index;

    clr();
    getch();
    index = i = kbstatus();
    if (i) {
       while (i) {
          kbstatus_off(5, 30, errors, i);
          index = i = kbstatus();
  }
  clean_kbemess(5, 30, errors, index);
    }
}


/*****
                        kbstatus_off()


    This function is used to tell the user that certain keys are
turned on or off. The function places the message at a specified
location on the screen and continues to display it until the user
acts on the message.

    Argument list:    int row       row position for messages
                      int col       column position for messages
                  char *errors[]    array of pointers to error
                                    messages
                    int status      keyboard flags returned
                                    by a call to kbstatus()


    Return value:    void
```

```
*****/

void kbstatus_off(int row, int col, char *errors[], int status)
{
   char buff[MAXLINE];
   int i, mask, test;
   static int flag = -1;

   mask = 1;
   for (i = 0; i < 8; i++) {
      test = status & mask;
      if (test) {
         if (flag != i) {
            cursor(row, col);
            memset(buff, ' ', strlen(errors[flag]));
            write(fileno(stdout), buff, strlen(errors[flag]));
            cursor(row, col);
            write(fileno(stdout), errors[i], strlen(errors[i]));
            flag = i;
      }
      break;
 }
 mask <<= 1;                              /* Test next bit         */
   }
}

/*****

                      clean_kbemess()

    This function is used to clear a keyboard error message
    from the screen if a call to kbstatus_off() produced an error
    message.

    Argument list:    int row        row position for messages
                      int col        column position for messages
                char *errors[]       array of pointers to error
                                     messages
                  int index          the index number of the last
                                     error message displayed

    Return value:     void

*****/
```

continues

Program 3.1. *continued*

```c
void clean_kbemess(int row, int col, char *errors[], int index)
{
   char buff[MAXLINE];

   cursor(row, col);
   memset(buff, ' ', strlen(errors[index]));
   write(fileno(stdout), buff, strlen(errors[index]));

}
```

The purpose of `kbstatus_off()` is to tell the user to disable the special keys that are turned on. The `kbstatus_off()` function performs this task by passing the error message's row-column address and a pointer to the list of error messages that might be displayed. The final argument is the keyboard status word as returned from `kbstatus()`. Notice how the messages in `errors[]` correspond to the type of errors contained in the bit positions of the status word. This data structure permits an easy way to index into the `errors[]` array.

Once into `kbstatus_off()`, you continue to stay in the function until the user has cleared all the bits that were set in the keyboard status word. The way `kbstatus_off()` is written might not suit your needs because it requires all set bits to be cleared before the program can continue; this is why it is not shown here as a stand-alone general library function. The basic concept shown can be used, however, to suit your own programming requirements.

The purpose of `clean_kbemess()` is to clear out any error message that might have been printed as a result of the `kbstatus_off()` function. In both `clean_kbemess()` and `kbstatus_off()`, `write()` is used rather than `printf()` because `write()` is smaller and faster than `printf()`. If you know that `printf()` always will be present in your programs anyway, feel free to modify the function to use `printf()`. This way, you will avoid adding the new function code associated with `write()`, `fileno()`, and `strlen()` at the expense of a somewhat slower function.

Again, the `clean_kbemess()` and `kbstatus_off()` functions shown in program 3.1 are not generalized to the extent that they are ready to be included as library functions. You might want to exclude the cursor-positioning code or modify the function so that only one bit of the status word is tested. Therefore, the code shown in program 3.1 is meant to serve as a model for functions that could be written as library functions based on your specific needs.

Get Integer—*getint( )*

The getint() function is presented here to serve as a model for other functions you might want to write. The integer data type was selected because many people still use scanf() even though better alternatives exist.

Another reason for presenting getint() as a model function is to illustrate an aspect of the ANSI standard that has not received the attention it deserves. One of the ANSI header files—limits.h—contains macro definitions for the ranges of all the fundamental C data types. A partial listing of limits.h is presented in table 3.1.

Table 3.1. *Partial listing of* limits.h.

```
#define SCHAR_MAX    127
#define SCHAR_MIN    -127
#define CHAR_BIT     8
#define CHAR_MAX     SCHAR_MAX
#define CHAR_MIN     0
#define INT_MAX      32767
#define INT_MIN      -32767
#define LONG_MAX     2147483547
#define LONG_MIN     -2147483547
#define SHRT_MAX     32767
#define SHRT_MIN     -32767
#define UCHAR_MAX    255U
#define UINT_MAX     65535U
#define ULONG_MAX    4294967295U
#define USHRT_MAX    65535U
```

The values for the symbolic constants #defined in limits.h will vary from machine to machine. By using the symbolic constants contained in limits.h, however, you remove "magic numbers" that might have to be changed if you move the source code to another environment. Finally, admit it: How many times have you had to look up the range of a signed 16-bit integer because you were not sure of the last digit? The limits.h header file keeps such constants in one handy place.

The basic idea behind getint() is to use as much existing code as you can from the ANSI standard library and related header files to build your input function. The getint() source code appears in listing 3.7.

Listing 3.7. Get integer input.

```
/*****
                          getint()

    This function accepts input from the keyboard to form an integer
    number. When the input is entered, the value is converted to a long
    integer and checked against the symbolic constants as defined in
    the (ANSI) limits.h header file. If the value entered does not fall
    within the limits as defined in the header file, an error condition
    is returned.

    Argument list:     int *ptr      a pointer to the integer that will
                                     hold the integer value on success

    Return value:      int           0 on error, 1 if successful

*****/

#include <stdlib.h>                  /* Need for atol() declaration  */
#include <limits.h>                  /* Need for INT_MAT and INT_MIN */


int getint(int *ptr)
{
   char buff[10];
   long temp;

   gets(buff);
   temp = atol(buff);
   if ( (temp > (long) INT_MAX) ¦¦ (temp < (long) INT_MIN) ) {
     *ptr = 0;
     return 0;
   } else {
     *ptr = (int) temp;
     return 1;
   }
}
```

The key to the function is the use of a data-conversion routine that is *larger* than the data type desired. In the example, because you want to get an integer value from the keyboard, you first treat the input as though it were a long data type. The statements

```
gets(buff);
temp = atol(buff);
```

build on gets() to collect the input from the keyboard. Why not? The gets() function already exists, it has some editing features, and it does not use much code space. The call to atol() converts the contents of buff[] to a long integer. You #include stdlib.h so that the prototype for atol() is included in the program.

In actual programming situations, most C programmers probably would write the two previous statements as

```
temp = atol(gets(buff));
```

The condensed version offers no real advantage, however, and makes the code more difficult to read.

The if statement

```
if ( (temp > (long) INT_MAX) ¦¦ (temp < (long) INT_MIN) )
```

uses the symbolic constants INT_MAX and INT_MIN to check the range of the long integer named temp. If the checks are passed, it is safe to use indirection and assign the integer value into ptr.

Because 0 is a valid integer value, you cannot use the integer to indicate an error condition. The method used in listing 3.7 is to set the integer to zero *and* return an integer value of 0 if an error occurs. Otherwise, the return value is set to 1. Therefore, this function assumes that you check the return value from getint() to determine whether the return value is a valid integer data type.

The code in listing 3.7 can be changed slightly for the other data types presented in the limits.h header file. The double floating point numbers pose more of a problem for testing, especially if your compiler does not support the long double data type. One way to address the problem is to use strtod() from the standard C library and then test the value against something slightly smaller than the floating point limits found in the float.h header file. A better solution would be to parse the input string for the exponent part of the number (who's going to input a number with 307 digits?) and see whether the exponent exceeds the limits defined in float.h.

A Potential Problem

The code presented in listing 3.7 still suffers from one real potential danger—the chance that you easily could overflow the 10-character input buffer buff[]. The easiest solution is to make buff[] larger than you could possibly expect (for example, 256 characters). Although this solution would solve the problem for most situations, it is not very elegant. The alternative is to set the buffer size to a few characters larger than the data item could possibly be (MAXINTLEN) and use a for loop to input no more than MAXINTLEN characters. For a signed integer, for example, the maximum character space needed would be for a number such as −32767.

Counting a space for the null character, the buffer never should exceed 7 characters. MAXINTLEN, therefore, would be set to 7. A simple test between MAXINTLEN and the for's loop counter variable could activate code for the error condition. Therefore, you might have something like the example shown in code fragment 3.1.

***Code Fragment 3.1.** Modifying getint().*

```c
#define MAXINTLEN    7

.

.

int getint(int *ptr)
{
    char buff[MAXINTLEN], c;
    int i;

    for (i = 0; i < MAXINTLEN - 1; i++) {
      c = getch();

        /* Code to allow for backspace, arrow keys, */
        /* and/or other editing features            */

      buff[i] = c;
    }
    buff[i] = '\0';

    .
```

The cost of this alternative approach is added complexity. You also would have to use something like the getch() function for keyboard input. This means losing the editing features of gets() and then having to add those features to the getint() function. Code fragment 3.1 gives a starting point for such changes.

Code Abstraction
As a Design Tool

Code fragment 3.1 illustrates something else as well. Look closely at the middle of the code fragment, and you will notice that the comments serve as a reminder that additional code is needed to accomplish the editing task. Comments are a form of code abstraction, and they let you concentrate on the task at hand (while things are fresh in your mind) and postpone other details until another time. This is no different than using pseudocode to lay out the program's general design.

If you use comments as code abstractions in a situation like the one in code fragment 3.1, a code abstraction often is a candidate for a new library function. Think about it. If you use listing 3.7 as a general model for getting char, unsigned ints, longs, and others, they all will need some editing capability. The same editing function could be used for all the different data types. The new function could be as simple as just allowing for a backspace, or as complex as allowing for full cursor control with inserts, deletes, and arrow keys for line editing. (The geditstr() function discussed in Chapter 9, "Odds and Ends," could be used directly or as a model for writing such a function.)

Get String with a Maximum
Character Limit—*getsm( )*

In the long run, simple often is best. For general data-input functions, all you really need is a gets() function with a maximum input length. The getsm() function does just that. It is presented in listing 3.8.

Listing 3.8. *Get maximum character string.*

```
/*****
                            getsm()

    This function behaves in a manner similar to gets(), except that
it allows for a maximum number of input characters. The carriage
return is not part of the character count.

    Argument list:    char *buff        the character array to hold the
                                        input
                      int max           maximum characters allowed

    Return value:     char *            pointer to start of string

*****/

#include <stdio.h>

#define ENTER  '\r'                      /* Might also be '\n'           */

char *getsm(char *buff, int max)
{
   char *ptr;
   int c, fd, i;

   ptr = buff;
   fd = fileno(stdout);                  /* So we can use write()        */
   for (i = 0; i < max; ) {
      c = getch();
      if (c == ENTER) {                  /* End of input?                */
         break;
      }
      if (c == '\b' && i > 0) {          /* Backspace but not first char */
         write(fd, "\b \b", 3);
         i--;
         buff--;
         continue;
      }
      if (c == '\b') {                   /* Backspace and is first char  */
         write(fd, "\a", 1);
      } else {                           /* Looks OK now                 */
         *buff++ = (char) c;
         write(fd, &c, 1);
         i++;
```

```
    }
  }
  *buff = '\0';             /* Make it a string        */
  if (i > max)              /* It was too long         */
    return '\0';
  else
    return ptr;
}
```

There is nothing fancy about this function. One argument is simply a pointer to the character array that will hold the input; the other argument is the maximum allowed string length. Again, the write() function is used to display output on the screen, although other functions could be used (such as printf() and putchar()). You should use printf() if you are certain it will be included in the final program.

The actual input is done by the getch() function, shown earlier in this chapter. The character returned by getch() is checked to see whether the user pressed the Enter key. Note that some compilers might use the carriage return ('\r') to indicate the Enter character, and others might use the newline character ('\n'). You might have to experiment to find out which character your compiler uses.

Next, the function checks to see whether a backspace character was typed at the keyboard. If so, you should check to see whether there is a character to be erased or whether the backspace was issued when no characters were present. If there is a character, the backspace-space-backspace sequence erases the character and repositions the cursor in the proper place. If no character is present, an alarm is sounded.

If all the checks are passed, the character is written into the pointer and the program waits for the next character. If max characters are entered, the loop terminates. You then add the null and return a pointer to the beginning of the string. If too many characters are entered, a null pointer is returned.

Now that the getsm() function is written, you can change the general model (see code fragment 3.1) to the one shown in code fragment 3.2.

If you compare code fragments 3.1 and 3.2, you easily can see how the function is simplified by creating a generalized function. Indeed, all the get*() functions could use getsm().

With a little practice, the idea of coding by abstraction will help you identify likely candidates for new functions to add to your library of tools.

Code Fragment 3.2. Modifying getint().

```
#define MAXINTLEN    7

.

.

int getint(int *ptr)
{
    char buff[MAXINTLEN], c;
    int i;

    getsm (buff, MAXINTLEN-1);
    .
```

Get a Choice from the Keyboard—*getchoice( )*

A program's user often must enter one of two choices into the program. The function shown in listing 3.9 is designed for situations in which the user must select one of two options. Because some choices are selected more often than others, the getchoice() function allows for a default choice that will be selected automatically should the user elect simply to press the Enter key.

Listing 3.9. Get one of two options from the keyboard.

```
/*****
                        getchoice()

    This function offers the user an either-or choice. The prompt
    presents the options, with the default choice indicated first. For
    example, if the prompt is "Enter Yes or No (Y, N): ", a Yes answer
    is the default choice because it is first in the list. The second
    argument to the function then becomes the nondefault option.

    The program displays the prompt and asks for a single-keystroke
    (unbuffered) input from the user.
```

```
Argument list:    char *prompt      the prompt string for input as
                                    a single keystroke
                  char *choice      the list of nondefault responses
                                    that will indicate that the
                                    default is not wanted

Return value:     int               0 if the default is not selected,
                                    1 if the default is selected

*****/

#include <stdio.h>
#include <mem.h>          /*Might be memory.h for some compilers */

int getchoice(char *prompt, char *choice)
{
   int c;

   write(fileno(stdout), prompt, strlen(prompt));
   c = getch();
   putchar(c);
   if (memchr(choice, c, strlen(choice) ) ) {
      c = 0;
   } else {
      c = 1;
   }
   return c;
}
```

The arguments to the function present a prompt and a nondefault choice list. For example, if you called the function with

```
choice = getchoice("Erase the File, No or Yes (N, Y): ", "Yy");
```

"No" is assumed to be the default response because it appears first in the list of options. Also, because the nondefault choice might be more dangerous (go ahead and erase all of my accounting data for the year!), the user must enter a 'Y' or a 'y' response to activate it.

After displaying the prompt, the program asks the user to indicate a choice by entering a letter. The call to memchr() then searches the nondefault option list (choice) to see whether any match occurs between a character in choice and the character in c. This approach means that you will act on the nondefault choice only if you find a match between choice and c. Otherwise, the default option is selected.

Get an MS-DOS File Name—
getfilename( )

You probably have written at least one program that needed to get a
file name from the user. That is the easy part. The hard part is making sure
that the user enters a valid file name. Listing 3.10 illustrates a function
designed to parse a specified file name and determine whether it meets the
rules for a valid MS-DOS file name.

Listing 3.10. Check for valid MS-DOS file name.

```
/*****
                                getfilename()

    This function determines whether the string passed to it is a
    valid MS-DOS file name.

    Argument list:    char *s      the string to be tested

    Return value:     int          0 if not valid, 1 if okay

*****/

#include <ctype.h>
#include <mem.h>                      /*Might be memory.h for some compilers*/

#define MAXFILELEN    12
#define PRIMARY       8
#define SECONDARY     3

int getfilename(char *s)
{
    char *ptr, *tptr;
    int i, len;

    ptr = s;
    len = strlen(s);
    if (len > MAXFILELEN || len == 0)
        return 0;

    tptr = memchr(s, '.', len);
    if (tptr) {                           /* There is an extension        */
```

```
        i = tptr - ptr;
        if (i > PRIMARY) {              /* Does primary name exceed 8?   */
          return 0;
        }                              /* Does secondary name exceed 3? */
         if (len - (i + 1) > SECONDARY) {
          return 0;
        }
    }

    while (*s) {
        if (!isprint(*s) ) {           /* Any ctrl or graphics chars?   */
          return 0;
        }
        switch (*s) {
          case ' ':                    /* Check for illegal characters  */
          case '^':
          case '+':
          case '=':
          case '/':
          case '[':
          case ']':
          case '\"':
          case ':':
          case ';':
          case ',':
          case '?':
          case '*':
          case '\\':
          case '<':
          case '>':
          case '¦':
              return 0;
          default:
              s++;
        }
    }
    return 1;
}
```

Actually, MS-DOS is rather forgiving when it comes to file names. The function first inspects the file name's length, which should be greater than zero but not more than MAXFILELEN characters. Next, the program scans the file name to see whether a period is present. If there is a period, the primary name length and extension length are checked to make sure they are within limits.

Finally, a `while` loop is used to scan the file name for any illegal characters. The `isprint()` macro makes sure that only printable, legal characters are used. The `switch` statement checks for characters that are not legal in a file name. If any of these checks fails, a zero is returned. If all the checks are passed, the function returns 1 to indicate that a valid file name has been entered.

Although it usually is not a problem, you should remember that this function does not check for certain string constants that might be an illegal file name (such as "prn"), or files that you probably do not want to change (command.com). If this makes you uncomfortable, you can use `strcmp()` to scan a list of "reserved" file names that should not be used.

Get String from Right to Left—*getstrleft()*

Quite honestly, this is just a "gee-whiz" function you can use to liven up the keyboard entry process. If you are tired of entering data into a program and watching the characters march across the screen from left to right, this function makes them march from right to left. The code appears in listing 3.11.

To understand what the function does, consider a program prompt to input my name into a field whose maximum length is 10 characters. The screen might look like this:

```
Enter your first name: _ _ _ _ _ _ _ _ _ _
```

After I type the first letter, the screen looks like this:

```
Enter your first name: _ _ _ _ _ _ _ _ _J
```

After the second letter:

```
Enter your first name: _ _ _ _ _ _ _ _Ja
```

and so on. When I type the last character and press the Enter key, the field is left-justified and looks like this:

```
Enter your first name: Jack_ _ _ _ _ _ _ _
```

The function has no more utility than `gets()`, but it does offer the user a change of pace.

Listing 3.11. *Get keyboard input from right to left.*

```
/*****
                            getstrleft()

     This function uses cursor control to accept string input, but
it displays the characters to the left as they are entered rather
than to the right. When the input string is completed, the string
is displayed, left-justified, in the input field width.

     Argument list:    int row       starting row position for input
                       int col       starting column position for input
                       char buff[]   where the input is placed
                       int max       the maximum field length of string
                       char plot     the character to be used for
                                     displaying field length


     Return value:     void

*****/

#include <stdio.h>

#define ENTER   '\r'              /* NOTE: Some might use a newline  */
#define DEL     0x53             /* Special Function key Del        */
#define BACK    '\b'
#define BELL    7

void getstrleft(int row, int col, char buff[], int max, char plot)
{
   int fd, i;

   cursor(row, col);
   for (i = 0; i < max; i++)
     putchar(plot);

   fd = fileno(stdout);          /* Find fd for stdout              */
   col += max;
   i = 0;
   for (i = 0; i < max; ) {
     buff[i] = getch();
     if (buff[i] == ENTER) {     /* If end of input, make a string  */
```

continues

Listing 3.11. continued

```
            buff[i] = '\0';
            break;
    }
    if (buff[i] == 0) {              /* If special DEL function key    */
        buff[i] = getch();
        if (buff[i] == DEL) {
            buff[i] = BACK;          /* Make it a backspace           */
        }
    }
    switch (buff[i]) {
        case BACK:                   /* Do backspace                  */
            if (i < 1) {             /* Make sure something is left   */
                putchar(BELL);
            } else {
                cursor(row, col - i);
                putchar(plot);       /* Rewrite prompt line character */
                i--;
                if (i) {             /* Don't bother if nothing there */
                    write(fd, buff, i);
                }
            }
            break;
        default:                     /* Write the character moving left */
            cursor(row, col - (i + 1));
            i++;
            write(fd, buff, i);
            break;
    }
}
cursor(row, col - max);              /* Rewrite string left justified */
write(fd, buff, i);
for ( ; i < max; i++)
    putchar(plot);
}
```

The function requires the row-column coordinates for the input prompt, a pointer to the area where the input is to be placed, a maximum number of characters allowed for the input, and a plot character to use for printing the input field on the screen.

The code is rather simple, and its only idiosyncrasy appears when you address the simultaneous handling of both the Backspace and the Delete keys. The Backspace key is no problem, but the Del key is a little different because it is treated as part of the PC's extended character set. If the first call to getch() returns a zero, a second call to getch() is needed to see whether

the key was part of the extended character set. If it was the Del key, simply write a backspace into the buffer and let the code in the switch statement process the Del key as though it were a backspace.

After each character is entered, cursor control is used to update the screen so that the characters appear to move from right to left. The final string in the field is left-justified by the final call to cursor() and write(), near the end of the function.

Get "Fielded" Input from Keyboard—*getfld( )*

The getfld() function is used whenever you want to retrieve information in a specific format. Common examples are dates (MM/DD/YY), phone numbers (1-800-123-4567), or Social Security numbers (123-45-6789). This function enables you to control the number of fields, the number of characters in each field, and the separator used between fields. The code appears in listing 3.12.

Listing 3.12. *Fielded keyboard input.*

```
/*****

                        getfld()

   This function gets input from the keyboard as a formatted
string. The function uses getch() to input the characters
entered. Because getch() is not buffered, no carriage-return
(Enter key) needs to be pressed. Also note that because getch()
does not echo the input to the screen, getch() is followed by a
putchar() for the character entered. Some compilers provide
the function getche(), which does echo the character entered
and could be used instead of the getch()-putchar() pair.

   Output is specified in the arguments presented to the function.
```

continues

Listing 3.12. *continued*

```
Argument list:    int row       row position for cursor
                  int col       column position for cursor
                  int f[]       an array that tells how the input
                                fields are organized. That is:

                                  f[0] = total number of input
                                           fields (n)
                                  f[1] = length of field 1
                                       .
                                       . more field lengths
                                       .
                                  f[n] = total input length

            char delims[]       delimiters to use between fields
            char *s             string to receive the input

    Return value:     void

*****/

#include <stdio.h>

#define EVER    ;;

void getfld(int row, int col, int f[], char delims[], char *s)
{
   int count, i, fields, sub;

   fields = f[0];                              /* How many fields        */
   cursor(row, col);
   sub = i = 0;
   count = 1;
   for (EVER) {
      if (i == f[fields + 1]) {
         break;
      }
      if (f[count] == sub && delims[count - 1]) {
         *s++ = delims[count - 1];
         putchar(delims[count++ - 1]);
         sub = 0;
         i++;
      }
```

```
    *s = getch();
    putchar(*s++);
    i++;
    sub++;
  }
  *s = '\0';
}
```

An example helps explain what the function does. Suppose that the `fields[]` argument is defined as follows:

```
static int fields[5] = {3, 3, 2, 4, 11};
```

The array's first element (`fields[0]`) is the number of fields that will be used during input—three in this example. The next three elements state that the first field will have three characters, the next field will have two characters, and the final field will have four characters. The statement

```
strcpy(delims,"--");
```

is a cheap way to initialize the delimiter field with the characters to be used as delimiters on input. Using what you know thus far, the input field should produce a string that looks like

xxx-xx-xxxx

when the function is finished—perhaps a Social Security number. The `fields[]` array's last value is the length of the final input string—11 in the example.

The code is fairly simple. The hardest part is remembering when a separator character must be inserted into the string. The variable sub keeps a count of the number of characters entered into the field, and when its value matches the count in `fields[]`, the next delimiter is inserted into the string.

The function is flexible enough to handle most types of input that need to be entered in a fielded format. You must, of course, be sure that the output buffer is large enough to hold the total field, including the delimiters.

Read Video Memory— *read_scr( )*

You probably have a program (perhaps your own text editor) that enables you to move the cursor to a word and, with the press of a key, get information about that word displayed on the screen. What actually takes place is a simple reading of the word from the section of memory where the screen image is stored. Reading video memory, therefore, can be a form of data input to a program.

The `read_scr()` function presented in listing 3.13 enables you to retrieve a word as a string from video memory. With a little modification, it also can retrieve a line or n characters from the screen.

Listing 3.13. Input from video memory.

```
/*****
                            read_scr()

   This function reads video memory and attempts to form a string
using the word currently under the cursor. The program first scans
left to find the start of the word and then scans right to find
the end of the word. Scanning ends (in either direction) when the
character read returns !isalpha(). If the cursor is not sitting on
an alpha character (if it is sitting on a blank space, for example),
a null string is returned.

   This function should be used only in the text mode--not graphics.


Argument list:    int row      row cursor position
                  int col      column cursor position
                  char *buff   pointer to char to hold the string

Return value:     void


   CAUTION: Because this function uses direct reads of video memory,
it might not work on some not-so-compatible compatibles. Also, the
function can be used only when compiled with a memory model using
four-byte pointers (a large-model or a mixed-model compiler).
*****/

void read_scr(int row, int col, char *buff)
{
   char c, far *ptr;
   unsigned int mode, wide;

   mode = getvmode();                    /* Get video mode            */
   if (mode > 7 || (mode > 3 && mode < 7)) {
```

```
        *buff = '\0';                  /* Can't be in graphics mode      */
        return;
    }

    wide = getvcols();                 /* Get column width               */

                                       /* This is why the large pointers */

    ptr = (mode == 7) ? (char far *) 0xb0000000 :
                        (char far *) 0xb8000000;

    ptr  += ((row - 1) * wide + col - 1) * 2;

    if (!isalpha(*ptr)) {              /* Are we in a word?              */
        *buff = '\0';                  /* Nope                           */
        return;
    }

    for (;;) {                         /* Scan left to start of word     */
        c = *ptr;
        if (isalpha(c))                /* Quit when no letter read       */
            ptr -= 2;
        else
            break;
    }

    for (;; buff++) {                  /* Build string via screen        */
        ptr += 2;
        c = *ptr;
        if (!isalpha(c)) {             /* Quit when not a letter         */
            break;
        } else {
            *buff = c;
        }
    }
    *buff = '\0';
}
```

The call to getvmode(), a function discussed in Chapter 1, "Screen Functions," is necessary for two reasons. First, if the screen is in a graphics mode, the function will not work properly. Second, the mode value is used to determine where the base of video memory begins (0xb0000000 or 0xb8000000). Because the base address of video memory is not in the same segment as the program code and data, this function can be used only with large (four-byte) pointers. (Borland C and Microsoft C support a mixed model that enables you to define a "far" pointer. Other compilers require a memory model with four-byte pointers.) If you try to compile the program with small (two-byte) pointers, you probably will lock up the system.

Next, the program calls getvcol() to find out how many columns are available for display. This information enables you to index from the base address of video memory to the proper screen location defined by row and col. Notice that the calculated index is multiplied by two because each character on the screen actually uses two bytes of memory: one for the character and a second for the character's attribute (for example, color). This also explains why the video memory pointer (ptr) is changed by two each time the screen is scanned left or right.

After ptr is properly indexed using row and col, examine the character stored at that address. If the character is not alphabetic, buff is set to null and you return to the caller. If a character is read, begin scanning to the left to find the beginning of the word. A non-alphabetic character terminates the scan.

The for loop then scans to the right, beginning with the first character in the word, filling in buff as it goes. Again, a non-alphabetic character ends the scan. The program then adds a null to the end of the word, and control returns to the caller.

One possible modification warrants consideration. If you assume that the cursor is sitting on the word prior to calling read_scr(), you could do away with the row and column arguments and place a call to find_cursor() (as discussed in Chapter 1, "Screen Functions") near the beginning of the function. This change removes two arguments from the function, but is somewhat restrictive in that the cursor must be on the word before the call. As the function is written in listing 3.13, the cursor can be anywhere on the screen before the call and the word still can be retrieved, if its screen coordinates are known.

Mouse Functions

More and more commercial software uses a mouse as an input device. This section presents a dozen functions used to support a mouse. You will use some of these functions in Chapter 4, "Menuing Systems," during the discussion of different menuing systems. Chapter 10, "Text Windows," and Chapter 11, "Putting It All Together," also discuss extensive use of the mouse functions.

Mouse Virtual Screen

Before learning the mouse functions, you should understand how the mouse interacts with the screen. As you learned in Chapter 1, "Screen Functions," different screen modes can be used with a PC. In the text mode, the screen is defined as 80 columns by 25 lines. In the graphics mode, the resolution can be as much as 640 by 480 pixels. Because of the different resolutions, the mouse uses what is called a *virtual screen* composed of a matrix of 640 horizontal points by 200 vertical points. Each possible screen mode is mapped into this 640x200-coordinate space, with position (0,0) being the screen's upper-left corner.

The actual screen mode determines how the mouse can access the virtual screen. For example, if your program has set the screen mode to 640x200 graphics, there is a one-to-one correspondence between the virtual and the actual screen. That is, a one-unit move on the actual screen corresponds to a one-unit move on the virtual screen. If you use the 80x25 text mode, however, there is an eight-to-one correspondence between the virtual and the actual screens. Therefore, a one-unit move in the actual screen looks like an eight-unit move to the virtual screen.

Suppose that you have set the screen mode to 40x25. In this case, a one-column movement in the actual screen corresponds to a 16-unit move in the virtual screen. It is up to you to maintain the translation of screen values to the virtual screen.

Several of the mouse functions discussed in this chapter have arguments that use the row-and-column position of the mouse. These row-column values always are in terms of the virtual screen. This means that if the screen is set to 80x25 text mode, mouse coordinates always will be reported in multiples of eight because of the eight-to-one correspondence between the virtual and the actual screens. To determine the actual screen position, you must divide the virtual screen coordinates by eight.

You will find mouse programming much easier if you remember that the mouse always thinks in terms of the virtual screen.

Get Mouse Status—*mouse_status( )*

If you want to use a mouse, it seems logical to start by checking to see whether one is present in the system. All the mouse functions make use of interrupt 0x33. Because this interrupt is a bit unusual, most compilers do not supply a predefined interrupt 0x33 function as they do for interrupt

0x21. Therefore, you must use the general interrupt function int86(), which requires you to pass the interrupt number as one of its arguments. The function that checks the mouse status is presented in listing 3.14.

Listing 3.14. Check mouse status.

```
/*****
                              mouse_status()

    This function determines whether the mouse driver is installed
and how many buttons the mouse has. The ax is loaded with the
function number (0x00), and interrupt 0x33 is called.

    Argument list:    int buttons     pointer to the number of mouse
                                      buttons available

    Return value:     int             nonzero if the mouse is installed;
                                      0 if not. Note that after the call
                                      to int86(), the bx holds the number
                                      of mouse buttons.

*****/

#include <dos.h>

int mouse_status(int *buttons)
{
   union REGS ireg;

   ireg.x.ax = 0x00;                /* Function 0x00--mouse status    */
   int86(0x33, &ireg, &ireg);       /* bx is number of mouse buttons */
   *buttons = ireg.x.bx;
   return ireg.x.ax;
}
```

Function 0x00 is used to determine whether a mouse is present in the system. After returning from the int86() function call, two pieces of information are available. First, if ireg.x.ax is nonzero, a mouse is installed. Second, if ireg.x.ax is nonzero, ireg.x.bx will hold the number of mouse buttons available. This is summarized as follows:

.x.ax = status (1 = mouse installed, 0 = no mouse installed)

ireg.x.bx = number of mouse buttons

Although the most common mouse has only two buttons, some have three. The buttons' uses are described later in this chapter.

Because you might want to use the information about the number of mouse buttons later in a program, a pointer to a "button counter" is filled with the contents of ireg.x.bx.

Turn Mouse Cursor On—
mouse_cursor_on( )

If mouse_status() determines the presence of a mouse, then one of the first things you might want to do is turn on the mouse cursor. Listing 3.15 illustrates the code for this function.

Listing 3.15. *Turn mouse cursor on.*

```
/*****
                            mouse_cursor_on()

    This function enables you to turn the mouse cursor on. The
    function maintains an internal counter that determines whether the
    cursor is on; if the counter is 0, the cursor is on. By calling this
    function and function 0x02, you can turn the mouse cursor on and off.

    Argument list:     void

    Return value:      void

*****/

#include <dos.h>

void mouse_cursor_on(void)
{
   union REGS ireg;

   ireg.x.ax = 0x01;                        /* Toggle cursor on        */
   int86(0x33, &ireg, &ireg);

}
```

The function's default setting is for the mouse cursor to be turned off. When the mouse cursor is turned on, it defaults to a block-style cursor. Function 0x01 of interrupt 0x33 is used to turn the mouse cursor on.

Turn Mouse Cursor Off— *mouse_cursor_off( )*

You probably will not want the mouse cursor on all the time. (Later chapters, especially Chapters 10 and 11, give examples of why this is true.) If the cursor is turned on, you can turn it off by using the code shown in listing 3.16.

Listing 3.16. *Turn mouse cursor off.*

```
/*****
                         mouse_cursor_off()

    This function enables you to turn the mouse cursor off. The
    function decrements the internal cursor counter. You should alternate
    calls to mouse_cursor_on() and mouse_cursor_off() for things to work
    properly.

    Argument list:    void

    Return value:     void

*****/

#include <dos.h>

void mouse_cursor_off(void)
{
    union REGS ireg;

    ireg.x.ax = 0x02;                        /* Toggle cursor off        */
    int86(0x33, &ireg, &ireg);
}
```

Function 0x02 of interrupt 0x33 is used to turn the mouse cursor off. Keep in mind that even if the cursor is turned off, the mouse is still active.

That is, functions 0x01 and 0x02 do not turn the *mouse* itself on or off; they determine only whether the cursor is visible.

Read the Mouse—*read_mouse( )*

As an input device, there really is not much a mouse can tell its user. To be more precise, about all you can find out from a mouse is where the mouse is located on the screen and whether a mouse button has been pressed. The read_mouse() function can give you both pieces of information. The function is presented in listing 3.17.

Listing 3.17. *Read mouse.*

```
/*****
                        read_mouse()

    This function enables you to read the mouse's position and status.
On return from the interrupt, the following information is available:

        ireg.x.bx  =  button status, where bits 0 and 1 are for the
                      left and right buttons. If the button is pressed,
                      the bit is 1. If there is a middle button, it
                      uses bit 2.

        ireg.x.cx  =  horizontal cursor position
        ireg.x.dx  =  vertical cursor position

    Therefore, the return values in ireg provide the necessary
information.


    Argument list:   int *row      pointer to the row position of
                                   mouse cursor
                     int *col      pointer to the column position of
                                   mouse cursor
                     int *button   pointer to return the button status

    Return value:    void

*****/
```

continues

Listing 3.17. *continued*

```c
#include <dos.h>


void read_mouse(int *row, int *col, int *button)
{
   union REGS ireg;

   ireg.x.ax = 0x03;                    /* Read mouse position and status */
   int86(0x33, &ireg, &ireg);
   *button = ireg.x.bx;
   *col = ireg.x.cx;
   *row = ireg.x.dx;

}
```

The argument is passed three integer pointers— one each for the row-and-column position and one for the buttons' status. On return from function 0x03, ireg.x.cx and ireg.x.dx contain the current column-and-row position of the mouse.

It is important to note that with the read_mouse() function, the mouse's row-column positions are updated continuously. *The status of the buttons does not affect the tracking of the mouse's movement.* Therefore, read_mouse() can be used whenever you need to know where the mouse is but do not care about the buttons' status.

The buttons' status is returned in ireg.x.bx. Bit 0 of the return value references the left button, bit 1 is for the right button, and bit 2 is for the middle button (if one is present). You might find it useful to define these bit positions as symbolic constants for use in your programs:

```c
#define LBUTTON      0x01
#define RBUTTON      0x02
#define MBUTTON      0x04
```

Because the buttons' status often is used in switch and in other control statements, the symbolic constants make it easier to understand code than if the bit positions were used.

Get Mouse Press—*mouse_ press( )*

The `mouse_press()` function is used when you want to know the mouse's current position on the screen. In other cases, however, you might want to know where the mouse was the last time a certain mouse button was pressed. The function given in listing 3.18 determines the mouse's status under such circumstances.

Listing 3.18. *Get mouse press.*

```
/*****
                            mouse_press()

    This function enables you to check which mouse button was pressed
    and the mouse's row-column position when the press occurred. The
    button passed in is the one that is checked.

    Argument list:    int row      the new row position
                      int col      the new column position
                      int button   button to check

    Return value:     int          the button status

*****/

#include <dos.h>


int mouse_press(int *row, int *col, int button)
{
   union REGS ireg;

   ireg.x.ax = 0x05;              /* Function to get mouse data      */
   ireg.x.bx = button;            /* Update only on this button press */
   int86(0x33, &ireg, &ireg);
   *col = ireg.x.cx;
   *row = ireg.x.dx;
   return (ireg.x.ax);            /* Return button status            */
}
```

The `mouse_press()` function is different from `mouse_read()` in one very important way: *The row-column values are changed only when the button associated with the third argument to the function (button) has been pressed.* That is, the row and column values do not change unless the button stored in button has been pressed. For example, suppose that you call mouse_press(), with the third argument being MBUTTON. Suppose also that you press the middle button when the mouse is at row 50 and column 100. The row-column values returned from the call are 50 for row and 100 for column. If you slide the mouse to some other row-column coordinates, the row-column values do not change unless the middle button is pressed again.

The mouse_press() function gives you a way to read the row-column coordinates on the condition that a certain button has been pressed.

Get Mouse Release—*mouse_release( )*

Using the mouse_release() function, you can check the row and column coordinates when a certain mouse button is released. The code is presented in listing 3.19.

Listing 3.19. *Get mouse release.*

```
/*****
                    mouse_release()

    This function enables you to see whether the mouse button has been
    released. The row and column values are those that existed when the
    button was released.

    Although it is not included in this function, ireg.x.bx holds the
    number of releases for the button after the interrupt. This counter
    is set to zero after the call.

    Argument list:     int row      the new row position
                       int col      the new column position
                       int button   the button to check

    Return value:      int          the button status: 1 if the button is
                                     pressed, 0 if not

*****/

#include <dos.h>
```

```
int mouse_release(int *row, int *col, int button)
{
   union REGS ireg;

   ireg.x.ax = 0x06;                      /* Function to get mouse data */
   ireg.x.bx = button;                    /* The button to inspect      */
   int86(0x33, &ireg, &ireg);
   *col = ireg.x.cx;
   *row = ireg.x.dx;
   return (ireg.x.ax);                    /* Return button status       */
}
```

The function behaves much the same as mouse_press(), but *the updating of row and col occurs only when the button is released* rather than when it is pressed. Therefore, if the user moves the mouse while button is pressed, row and col will hold the mouse's row-column position when the button finally is released. This information would be useful if the user were "dragging" something (an icon of some sort, for example) across the screen.

If you want to keep track of the number of button presses, you can pass another pointer to the function and fill the pointer with the value contained in ireg.x.bx. The counter falls within the range of a signed integer (0 to 32767) and is set back to zero after the call.

Set Mouse Vertical Range— *mouse_vrange( )*

In some applications you will want to restrict the range that the mouse can use. If you were writing a one-line menu bar, for example, you would want to limit the mouse's vertical travel range to the line used for the menu. Listing 3.20 presents the code to set the vertical limits for the mouse.

Listing 3.20. *Set vertical range for mouse.*

```
/*****

                         mouse_vrange_()

   This function enables you to set the mouse max-min values for the
   row coordinates. The range permitted falls within 0, 200.
```

continues

Listing 3.20. *continued*

```
    Argument list:      int min        the min row position
                        int max        the max row position

    Return value:       void

*****/

#include <dos.h>


void mouse_vrange(int min, int max)
{
   union REGS ireg;

   ireg.x.ax = 0x08;                    /* Function to set vertical range */
   ireg.x.cx = min;
   ireg.x.dx = max;
   int86(0x33, &ireg, &ireg);
}
```

The two arguments for `mouse_vrange()` are the minimum and maximum row positions that the mouse can use. Function 0x08 is used to set the vertical limits. Again, keep in mind that the minimum and maximum values are for the virtual screen. For example, if the call

```
mouse_vrange(0, 7);
```

is made when the screen is in the text mode, only the first line of the screen can be used by the mouse. Note, however, that the call

```
mouse_vrange(0, 8);
```

would enable the first two lines of the text screen to be used by the mouse. The vertical limits are inclusive, therefore, in that the 0–7 range restricts the mouse to the first row for the virtual screen, and the 0–8 range includes the first and second rows when in text mode. This might seem odd until you remember that the extreme upper left corner of the virtual screen is location (0, 0). Therefore, the first eight rows of the virtual screen use the values 0–7 and correspond to row one of the actual text screen. It also follows that a vertical position with the value 8 in the virtual screen must fall in the second row of the text screen.

Set Mouse Horizontal Range— *mouse_hrange( )*

The mouse's horizontal range can be set in much the same way as the vertical range. The code is presented in listing 3.21.

Listing 3.21. *Set horizontal range for mouse.*

```
/*****

                            mouse_hrange_()


    This function enables you to set the mouse max-min values for the
column coordinates. The range permitted must fall within 0-640.

    Argument list:    int min      the min column position
                      int max      the max column position

    Return value:     void

*****/


#include <dos.h>


void mouse_hrange(int min, int max)
{
   union REGS ireg;

   ireg.x.ax = 0x07;                /* Function to set horizontal range */
   ireg.x.cx = min;
   ireg.x.dx = max;
   int86(0x33, &ireg, &ireg);
}
```

Again, the minimum and maximum values passed to the function are in terms of the virtual screen. This means that any values based on the actual screen in the text mode must be multiplied by eight for use in this function. For example, restricting the movement to the first 40 columns in the text mode means that the value of max passed to the function would have to be 320. This is because of the eight-to-one correspondence ratio between the actual and virtual screens.

Set Mouse Position—*set_mouse( )*

You can set the mouse to a specific row-column position by using the
set_mouse() function. The code for set_mouse() appears in listing 3.22.

***Listing 3.22.** Set mouse position.*

```
/*****
                              set_mouse()

    This function enables you to set the mouse position. The new
values must fall within the row-column ranges that have been set.
When in the text mode, values are rounded to the nearest values
permitted.

    Argument list:     int row      the new row position
                       int col      the new column position

    Return value:      void

*****/

#include <dos.h>

void set_mouse(int row, int col)
{
    union REGS ireg;

    ireg.x.ax = 0x04;                  /* Function to set mouse position */
    ireg.x.cx = col;
    ireg.x.dx = row;
    int86(0x33, &ireg, &ireg);
}
```

The row and col values are in terms of the virtual screen and must be
within the horizontal and vertical ranges that might have been set. This
function is useful when you want the mouse to appear at some specific
location (such as a default menu selection) when the program starts.

Set Text Mouse Cursor— *mouse_cursor_t( )*

The `mouse_cursor_t()` function enables you to define the type of mouse cursor used. This function should be used only when the screen is in the text mode. This function permits the use of two types of cursors—a hardware-defined cursor or a software-defined cursor. It will be easier to explain how these cursors can be set after illustrating the code for the `mouse_cursor_t()` function in listing 3.23.

Listing 3.23. *Set text mouse cursor.*

```
/*****
                        mouse_cursor_t()

   This function enables you to redefine the mouse cursor when in the
text mode. Note that this function works only when in the text (not
graphics) video mode, hence the 't' at the end of the function name.

   NOTE: If a hardware cursor is selected, the screen and mask
arguments are interpreted to be the beginning and ending scan lines
for the cursor.

Argument list:    int type      the type of cursor:

                                 0 = software will define the
                                     cursor
                                 1 = hardware will define it


                  int screen    defines the cursor screen
                  int mask      defines the cursor mask

   Return value:    void

*****/

#include <dos.h>

void mouse_cursor_t(int type, int screen, int mask)
{
   union REGS ireg;
```

continues

Listing 3.23. *continued*

```
    struct SREGS s;                    /* CAUTION: MUST BE "SREG" FOR ECO-C88 */

    segread(&s);                       /* Read segment reg        */
    s.es = s.ds;                       /* Load es with dseg       */
    ireg.x.ax = 0x0a;                  /* Set text cursor         */
    ireg.x.bx = type;                  /* Type of cursor          */
    ireg.x.cx = (unsigned) screen;     /* Screen mask             */
    ireg.x.dx = (unsigned) mask;       /* Cursor mask             */
    int86x(0x33, &ireg, &ireg, &s);    /* Set all registers       */
}
```

A hardware-defined cursor is the one usually seen at the MS-DOS prompt. If you want to use the hardware cursor, the first argument (type) of the mouse_cursor_t() function is set to 1. The hardware cursor is limited to a block-type cursor, and only the block's width can be set. This width is defined by the second and third arguments of the function. The ranges for the arguments are 0–7 for a CGA display adapter and 0–11 for a Monochrome Display Adapter. The variable named screen is used as the starting line for the cursor, and mask is the ending line. Therefore, if you are using a CGA, the call

```
mouse_cursor_t(1, 0, 7);
```

will define a full block cursor. On the other hand, the call

```
mouse_cursor_t(1, 6, 7);
```

will produce the more familiar underline cursor.

With a software-defined cursor, the possibilities are more varied. To select a software cursor, the first argument to mouse_cursor_t() must be 0. The second and third arguments then are interpreted as masks that are to be applied to the data on the screen. The masks are 16-bit values with the interpretations shown in figure 3.1.

The remaining (low) eight bits are the character representation on the screen. Both the screen and the cursor masks have the same interpretations shown in figure 3.1.

With the two masks defined, the mouse_cursor_t() function first logically ANDs the screen mask with the character data on the screen. (Remember that each character on the screen represents two bytes in memory—one each for the character and its attribute.) The result of this AND operation then is logically ORed with the cursor mask to determine the mouse text cursor.

Fig. 3.1. Screen and cursor masks.

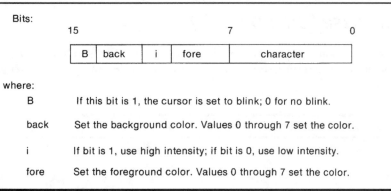

Bits:

where:

B	If this bit is 1, the cursor is set to blink; 0 for no blink.
back	Set the background color. Values 0 through 7 set the color.
i	If bit is 1, use high intensity; if bit is 0, use low intensity.
fore	Set the foreground color. Values 0 through 7 set the color.

A common example would be to set the screen mask to 0x77ff and the cursor mask to 0x7700. This is shown in figure 3.2.

Fig. 3.2. Sample screen and cursor masks.

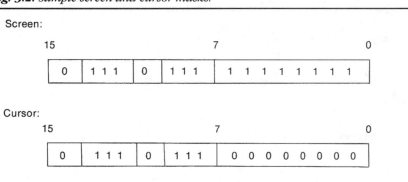

The screen and cursor masks shown in figure 3.2 result in a mouse cursor that inverts the foreground and background colors for the mouse cursor. Because the mouse cursor screen and mask values shown in figure 3.2 are used so often, you might want to create #defines for them for use in your program:

```
#define MCSCREEN    0x77ff    /* Mouse Cursor SCREEN */
#define MCMASK      0x7700    /* Mouse Cursor MASK   */
```

Set Graphics Mouse Cursor— *mouse_cursor_g( )*

If you are using the screen in the graphics mode, you have even greater flexibility in defining the mouse cursor. A sample function is presented in listing 3.24.

Listing 3.24. *Set graphics mouse cursor.*

```
/*****
                          mouse_cursor_g()

    This function enables you to redefine the mouse cursor. The
    code shown here defines an arrow to use as the mouse cursor. Note
    that this function works only when in the graphics (not text)
    video mode, hence the 'g' at the end of the function name.

    If you write out the binary bit positions for the mask[] array,
    you can see how the cursor is defined.

    Argument list:    void

    Return value:     void

*****/

#include <dos.h>


void mouse_cursor_g(void)
{
    static unsigned int mask[] = {
        0x3ff, 0x1ff, 0x0fff, 0x7ff, 0x3ff, 0x1ff, 0xff, 0x7f,
        0x3f, 0x1f, 0x1ff, 0x10ff, 0x30ff, 0xf87f, 0xf87f, 0xfc3f,
        0x00, 0x4000, 0x6000, 0x7000, 0x7800, 0x7c00, 0x7e00, 0x7f00,
        0x7f80, 0x78c0, 0x7c00, 0x4600, 0x0600, 0x0300, 0x300, 0x0180};
    union REGS ireg;
    struct SREGS s;              /* CAUTION: MUST BE "SREG" FOR ECO-C88 */

    segread(&s);                          /* Read segment reg         */
    s.es = s.ds;                          /* Load es with dseg        */
    ireg.x.ax = 0x09;                     /* Set graphics cursor      */
    ireg.x.bx = 0x01;                     /* Column hot spot          */
```

```
    ireg.x.cx = 0x01;                   /* Row hot spot              */
    ireg.x.dx = (unsigned) mask;        /* Pointer to mask           */
    int86x(0x33, &ireg, &ireg, &s);     /* Set all registers         */
}
```

The mouse_cursor_g() function shown in listing 3.24 is defined for an arrow cursor. The first 16 values in the mask[] array are similar in interpretation to the screen mask in the mouse_cursor_t() function; the values are used for the screen mask. The remaining 16 values define the cursor mask. These two masks must be in contiguous memory, so they simply are made one array of values.

The call to segread() is necessary so that the function can find the data that define the graphics cursor. The segment address is copied into ES before the call, and ireg.x.dx points to the mask.

Remember that you must call mouse_cursor_on() before you can see the arrow cursor, and that the function works only in the graphics mode.

Count Mouse Movement—
mouse_counters( )

Using the mouse_counters() function, you can maintain a count of the mouse's movement. Vertical or horizontal movement is kept in a unit of measurement called a "mickey." (I wonder why?) Each mickey corresponds to a 1/100-inch movement of the mouse. Because a signed int is used to maintain the counters, the range is limited to –32768 to 32767. The code for the mouse_counters() appears in listing 3.25.

Listing 3.25. *Count mouse movement.*

```
/*****
                        mouse_counters()

    This function enables you to read the mouse row-col counters.
Each unit represents about .01 inch and has the range of a signed
int (about plus/minus 32000).

    Note that the values returned represent the changes in the
counts since the last call.
```

continues

Listing 3.25. *continued*

```
   Argument list:     int *row      pointer to the row count
                      int *col      pointer to the column count

   Return value:      void

*****/

#include <dos.h>


void mouse_counters(int *row, int *col)
{
   union REGS ireg;

   ireg.x.ax = 0x0b;                   /* Function to read motion counts */
   int86(0x33, &ireg, &ireg);
   *col = ireg.x.cx;
   *row = ireg.x.dx;
}
```

Two pointers to signed integers are passed to the function. Function 0x0b of interrupt 0x33 is used to fill in the pointers with the appropriate counts. A positive value for col indicates a mouse movement to the right. Because the upper left corner of the virtual screen is address (0, 0), a positive count for row indicates a downward movement for the mouse.

Coping with Compiler Differences

Writing "generic code" for a half-dozen different compilers is not easy. Writing perfectly portable code for all compilers is impossible. Part of this difficulty arises because this book must rely on non-ANSI standard library functions. The difference between SREG (for example, as defined by Ecosoft) and SREGS (for example, defined by Borland and Microsoft) in the dos.h header file is just one example of the many nuances that must be addressed. How those differences might be dealt with is the subject of this section.

I have tried to point out the instances in which you can expect differences to occur. In most cases, I have placed a comment in the function code to alert you to these differences. You probably already have selected a compiler, and you probably will continue to use only that compiler. If this is the case, I suggest that you simply change the function code to meet your needs and be done with it. I urge you, however, to leave the warning comment in the source code in case you switch compilers later.

Perhaps you expect to switch from the compiler you are using now to a different one in the future. This often happens when you switch jobs. If you want to use some of your previously written code at your new job, you must be aware of the code that will need to be changed. In these situations, several solutions are available.

First, consider the SREG-SREGS problem. In listing 3.24 the line

```
struct SREGS s;    /* CAUTION: MUST BE "SREGS" FOR Eco-C88 */
```

tells you that SREGS must be changed if you want to use the Ecosoft compiler. If you are using Ecosoft C, your source code line should be changed to read:

```
struct SREG s;     /* CAUTION: MUST BE "SREGS" FOR Microsoft */
```

Notice what has been done. The code for the Ecosoft compiler was corrected, but the comment also was changed. Thus, you know what needs to be done if you switch to the Microsoft compiler. Changing the function's source code is very simple now—at least for the Ecosoft and Microsoft compilers.

Another alternative is to let the preprocessor do the work. For example:

```
#ifdef ECOC88
    struct SREG s;     /* Use with the Ecosoft compiler */
#else
    struct SREGS s;    /* Use with most other compilers */
#endif
```

If you have a preprocessor directive

```
#define ECOC88 1
```

before the #ifdef, the preprocessor toggles the SREG definition into the code. If ECOC88 is not defined, the SREGS definition is used. This approach makes the differences between the two compilers very clear.

On the downside, the preprocessor approach adds clutter to the code and makes it somewhat more difficult to read. Also, the #ifdef (and related) preprocessor directives must be added to all the functions in the library. Although this is not hard to do, it is inconvenient.

A third alternative is to place as many of the compiler differences as possible in a single place. For example, suppose you create a header file named compiler.h. Perhaps the first two lines of the header file read as follows:

```
#define SREGS      SREG      /* SREG Eco-C88; SREGS Microsoft */
#define asm        _asm      /* asm  Borland; _asm Microsoft  */
```

If the compiler.h header file is read first, the preprocessor can make the changes throughout the program for you. That is, SREGS is changed to SREG (for example, listing 3.23), and asm is changed to _asm (listing 3.5a). The advantage is that most of the compiler differences are isolated in a single file. This makes it easier to cope with such differences because you need to edit only a single source file.

The bad news is that you cannot use the preprocessor to handle all the compiler differences. For example, Borland calls its memory allocation header file alloc.h, and Microsoft calls its file malloc.h. Because the preprocessor does not make macro substitutions within double quotes or angle brackets ("<" or ">"), this approach won't work for header files. This isn't as bad as it sounds, however, because many compiler vendors duplicate nonstandard function prototypes in stdlib.h. A little trial-and-error will uncover the needed information found in nonstandard header files.

Of the three options presented, I think the third option is the best. It isolates the compiler differences in one place, adds less clutter to the source code, and makes any future editing much easier. Use whatever alternative you think best suits your own needs.

For the remainder of this book, however, assume that the third option is used. I will continue to point out potential problem areas, but assume that these are handled in something similar to a compiler.h header file. This assumption will help you avoid many #ifdefs and related preprocessor directives and will make the code easier to read.

The next chapter discusses menuing systems and builds on several of the functions presented in this chapter. You should take the time necessary to understand the material presented here before you read Chapter 4, "Menuing Systems."

4

Menuing Systems

Introducing Menus

When I was a graduate student, a menu was something you ordered lunch from; it had nothing to do with computer programs. In those days, you handed your program through a small window in the wall to an anonymous face, and, 24 hours later, the program emerged from the bowels of the earth along with a printout of its errors. The down side of this process was the long turnaround time for debugging a program. The up side was that, because of the terrible turnaround time, you spent more time thinking about and designing your program in the first place.

The first "menu" I saw was the log-on request issued by an old Teletype machine. It was amazing to be able to change things "on the fly" while sitting at your terminal. Times have changed. Today's user is accustomed to fancy slidebar menus in full color. Other systems are icon-based and use a mouse as their primary input device.

Two Types of Menus: Slidebar and Box

This chapter takes a middle ground and presents two basic types of menus. The first is the slidebar menuing system that is common to many programs today, especially spreadsheet programs. The slidebar menu is

161

characterized by a top menu line that offers the basic menu choices. Under the menu line (or near the bottom of the display screen), a second line provides a short description of the currently active (highlighted) menu option. As you move from one menu item to the next on the top line, the description is updated on the second line. Because of the way the slide-bar menu operates, its orientation is horizontal. This type of menu can be used with either a mouse or the arrow keys.

The second type of menu is the window, or box, menu. This menu is vertically oriented, and the user manipulates the arrow keys or a mouse to move up and down through the list of menu items. The window menu can be as small or as large as you like. If a small window is used with a long list of items, the list is "scrolled" through the window.

This menuing system is not a true windowing environment, at least not in the sense often associated with the word *windows*. A true window can be "popped" onto the screen and used in whatever way the programmer wants. The window is then closed, leaving the original screen intact. Such "pop-up" windows complicate the programmer's work because they involve direct memory reads and writes to the screen, and they require storage management to save and restore the original screen. Although the techniques shown in this chapter for reading from the screen are much the same as writing to the screen, such a windowing system is not used in this chapter. (Several functions to help you write pop-up-type menus are presented at the end of this chapter. A full discussion of pop-up windows is included in Chapter 10, "Text Windows.")

Slidebar Menuing System

Before designing a menu system, you first must define what the menu system should do. Figure 4.1 shows how a sample slidebar menu will look on the screen.

Fig. 4.1. A slidebar menu.

```
+------------------------------------------+
| Screen      Printer      Disk file       |    Line 1
| Output will be displayed on the screen   |    Line 2
+------------------------------------------+
```

In figure 4.1, it is assumed that on line 1 of the list, the first option (the Screen option) is highlighted. The second line provides a brief description of the highlighted option on line 1. In this case, the Screen option causes the output of the program to be displayed on the screen. Note that line 2 in figure 4.1 also could be placed near the bottom of the screen. Commercial software packages use both variations.

Menu Selection

The user can select an option from a slidebar menu in several ways. First, each menu option has one capital letter associated with it. In figure 4.1, the letters S, P, and D will select from the Screen, Printer, or Disk file output options. The user can select a menu option simply by typing the appropriate capital letter.

When a single letter (often called a "hot key") is used to make a menu selection, it always is the capitalized letter that appears in the menu option. Obviously, this means that you must write your menu option strings with only one capital letter per menu option. This also implies that no two options on the menu line can use the same capital letter as the hot key. In the code presented later in the chapter, the user is not required to enter a capital letter; either an uppercase or a lowercase letter for the hot key will work.

The user also can manipulate the arrow keys on the keyboard to highlight the desired menu option. When the correct option is highlighted, the user makes the selection by pressing the Enter key.

As a variation on the second selection method, the user can highlight the desired option by using the mouse to slide across the menu. When the appropriate option is highlighted, it is selected by pressing a button on the mouse, usually the left one. Pressing the left mouse button is the same as pressing the Enter key, and most users are familiar with this convention.

Now you know some of the design elements that must be considered. Your program and its data structures must cope with the five following design considerations:

1. A (very) short first-line menu option

2. A (brief) second-line description of the first-line option

3. A unique single-character letter associated with each option (that is, a hot key)

4. A means of highlighting each option

5. Mouse support for menu selection

The design criteria suggest other factors as well. If you want to be able to highlight an option, you must be able to "unhighlight" it, too. This means you will need to know the length of each option in the list. And you will need some way of erasing the descriptions on the second line; there is little reason to assume that all descriptions will be the same length.

The system should be as flexible as possible. For example, although most programs place slidebar menus on the top two lines of the screen, perhaps your menu should be designed so that it can be used anyplace two consecutive lines are available on the screen.

It also would be convenient if the menu could handle more than one screen mode. I recently saw a golf handicap program that was written in the 40x25 text mode. Although I do not like that mode of text very much, the choice made good sense after I gave it a little thought. A lot of golfers do not need glasses to play golf but do need them to read. Because golf scores are posted immediately after playing, the larger character size made it easier to read the menu prompts on the screen. This resulted in fewer posting errors.

The Menu Data Structure

The menu's nature immediately suggests that a structure should be used for the menu's list of options. A sample structure is presented in listing 4.1.

Listing 4.1. Menu option data structure.

```
typedef struct {
   char *prompt;            /* First line menu prompt     */
   int  plen;               /* Its length                 */
   char *desc;              /* Second line menu prompt     */
   int  dlen;               /* Its length                 */
   char letter;             /* Single-letter choice option */
   } MENU;
```

The sample uses a `typedef` to declare a data structure named `MENU`. The structure's first member, `prompt`, is a character pointer to the menu prompt that appears on the first line of the menu. Immediately following is the `plen` member of the structure. This integer holds the length of `prompt`. The third member of the MENU structure, desc, is a character pointer to the second-line description of the first-line menu item (prompt). The fourth member is an integer to hold the length of the desc string. The last member of the structure is the single-letter character (letter) recognized for selecting a menu option (that is, it's the hot key). Using the example discussed earlier, letter might be S, P, or D.

Because menus offer multiple options, a program menu probably will consist of an array of MENU structures, each of which represents a single menu option.

Initializing a Menu Structure

Now you need a simple way to fill in the MENU structure. A direct solution is to create a macro that provides the correct initialization of the MENU structure. The macro definition is presented in listing 4.2.

Listing 4.2. OPTION macro definition.

```
#define  OPTION(a, b, c)   {a, sizeof(a) - 1, b, sizeof(b) - 1, c},
#define  OPTIONEND         {0}
```

The macro named OPTION has three arguments. However, the macro expansion is such that it fills in all members of the MENU structure. An example will help explain how this works. Consider the following code fragment:

```
OPTION("Screen", "Send output to screen", 's')
        (a)              (b)              (c)
```

The word "Screen" becomes the 'a' argument to the OPTION macro, and 'a' is used in the first two parts of the macro expansion. The first simply passes the argument through; it is a pointer to char. The macro expansion's second element takes the sizeof() argument 'a' and subtracts 1 from it. Because you are taking the size of a string constant that includes the null termination character, you must subtract 1 from the result to get the equivalent string length. This second term, therefore, is exactly what the structure member plen needs to do its job. The same reasoning applies to argument 'b' and its expansion in the macro. The last argument simply is the single letter associated with selection of this menu option (s).

Note that the macro uses the sizeof operator to calculate the length of the two strings. I chose not to use strlen() even though you must adjust the size of the strings for the null termination character. The reason for using sizeof is that it is a compile-time evaluation, whereas strlen() must be evaluated at runtime. If the program is run on a slow machine and many menu options are used, strlen() causes some performance slowdown, whereas sizeof does not.

There is one more thing to remember about listing 4.2. Notice that the OPTION macro expansion has a trailing comma, but OPTIONEND does not. This is because there is no comma operator after the last item in an initialized list. Therefore, a MENU data structure's last item is a null field as represented by OPTIONEND. This makes it easy to detect the end of a list of menu options.

Now you can define a sample using your menu structure.

```
MENU menu0[] = {
    OPTION("Screen", "Send output to screen", 's')
    OPTION("Disk-File", "Output written to disk file", 'd')
    OPTION("Printer", "Output listed on the printer", 'p')
    OPTIONEND
    };
```

This example defines an array of data structures of type MENU named menu0[]. If you use the macro definitions shown in listing 4.2, and fill them in with the information presented in the menu0[] example, you will see how the structure is initialized to the proper values.

Your next task is to open, or present, the menu on the screen. The function menu_start(), presented in listing 4.3, shows how this is done.

Note that the function begins with an #include statement for a header file named menu.h. This header file is presented in listing 4.9. It contains a number of macro and global data definitions not found in the menu_start() source code.

Listing 4.3. *The menu_start() function.*

```
/*****

                            menu_start()


    This function displays the menu options on the screen, using a
two-line menuing system. The first argument is a typedef for a menu
structure. The two lines first are cleared to the background color,
and then the menu options are displayed.


    This function assumes that the cursor is sitting at the desired
row-column coordinates BEFORE the function is called.
```

NOTE: This function uses the colorstr(), c_scroll(), and
find_cursor() functions discussed in Chapter 2, "String Processing."

```
Argument list:     MENU s[]     an array of MENU structures
                   int fore     the foreground color to use
                   int back     the background color to use

Return value:      void
```

```c
*****/

#include "menu.h"
#include <stdlib.h>
#include <string.h>

#define MARGIN  "  "

void menu_start(MENU s[], int fore, int back)
{
   int buttons, i, r, c, wide;

   wide = getvcols() - 1;
   find_cursor(&prow, &pcol);                  /* Find out where to put it */
   c_scroll(prow, pcol, wide, 2, 0, 6, back << 4);
   last = 0;

   nptr = (int *) calloc(wide, sizeof(int));   /* Store col positions  */
   cptr = (char *) calloc(wide, sizeof(char)); /* Store letter options */

   for (menulen = i = 0; s[i].prompt; i++) {
      find_cursor(&r, &c);
      nptr[i] = c;                             /* Fill in columns       */
      cptr[i] = s[i].letter;                   /* Single-letter choices */
      colorstr(s[i].prompt, fore, back << 4);
      colorstr(MARGIN, fore, back << 4);
      menulen += s[i].plen;                    /* Find total menu length */
   }
   menucount = i;                              /* Items in this menu     */
                                               /* Length of menu line    */
   menulen += (strlen(MARGIN) * (menucount - 1) );

   mouse_here = mouse_status(&buttons);        /* See if there is a mouse */
   cursor(prow, pcol);
```

continues

Listing 4.3. continued

```
    colorstr(s[last].prompt, back, fore << 4);
    cursor(prow + DLINE, pcol);
    colorstr(s[last].desc, fore, back << 4);
}
```

The menu_start() function is responsible for initializing several global variables for use by subsequent functions. (These globals are defined in the menu.h header file, which is presented in listing 4.9.) The arguments to the function establish which MENU array is used, as well as the foreground and background colors.

The call to getvcol() returns the width of the current display device (normally 80 columns, but possibly 40). You must subtract 1 from the return value because you can reference only columns 0 through 79 (or 0 through 39). The call to find_cur() determines the menu's row-column address on the screen.

Note: The slidebar menuing system assumes that the cursor is at the desired screen location before this function is called. In the example, the calling sequence must be as follows:

```
    .
    cursor(1, 1);
    menu_start(menu0, BLUE, CYAN);
    .
```

This sequence assures you that the row and column positions (prow and pcol) are initialized properly. (It is assumed that you have defined BLUE and CYAN as 1 and 3 earlier in the program. Obviously, you can use whatever colors you like, as long as the foreground and background colors equate to the values 0 through 7. You can use the higher-numbered values 8 through 15 for the foreground color, but those values will turn on the blink attribute when the field is inversed. The blink is a bit much for most users.)

The call to c_scroll() is used to clear the two menu lines to the background color. (You can review the c_scroll() function in Chapter 1, "Screen Functions.") Notice how the background color is bit-shifted before the call. This lets you call the function using the normal background color numbers (0 through 7) without calculating their values.

As you can see in listing 4.3, the background color is bit-shifted four bits to the left before the call to c_scroll() (and other functions). Doing the bit-shifting in the function enables you to use the "normal" color numbers associated with background text colors. (See listing 1.22 in Chapter 1,

"Screen Functions.") This means you can call `c_scroll()` with the value 7 (white) as the background color. The code in the function then bit-shifts this value four bits to yield the value 112 for the actual function call to `c_scroll()`.

As an alternative, you could use a macro definition for the white background color

```
#define BWHITE 112
```

and remove the bit-shifting code from the `menu_start()` function. Because bit-shifting is so fast, it is unlikely that a user would notice any difference in performance. Such a change would save a few bytes of code space, however. From the learning point of view, I left the bit shifts in the code so you can better understand what the code is doing. If you want, you can `#define` the background colors for their shifted values and remove the shift operations from the code. The new `#defines` for the shifted background colors should be placed in the menu.h header file, which is presented in listing 4.9.

If you elect to make this change, be sure to change all subsequent functions that do bit-shifting on the background color. If you neglect to make the necessary changes, some functions will generate some pretty weird color combinations.

The global variable `last` represents the last menu option selected. Because the menu is just being started, `last` is initialized to zero, which is the first option in the menu list ("`Screen`").

Next, there are two calls to the storage-allocation function `calloc()`. The first allocation, `nptr`, is filled in later with the starting column position of each menu item as it appears in the list. The second allocation, `cptr`, is filled in later with the single-letter responses associated with each menu option (for example, `S`, `P`, and `D`). These values are filled in by way of the `for` loop that follows the allocations.

Each option is printed on the first line of the slidebar menu, and the menu's total length is calculated in the loop. When you exit from the loop, `menulen` is increased by the length of the `MARGIN` constant for all but the last item in the list.

Next, you call `mouse_status()` to see whether a mouse is present in the system. The global variable `mouse_here` will be set to nonzero if a mouse is available.

The final series of calls to `cursor()` and `colorstr()` is used to highlight the first option in the list and display its description (line 2 in the menu). Note that in the sample menu the foreground and background colors have been alternated to achieve an inverse color effect. This approach works fine unless you choose a foreground color greater than 7. (Values 8 through 15 will turn on the blink attribute, remember?)

If you want to place the menu description line at a location other than the second line on the screen, simply change the value of DLINE (Description LINE) in the menu.h header file. If you wanted the description line to appear on line 23, you would change DLINE to the value 22. The value is one less than the actual row position because DLINE is added to the existing row of the menu line (as stored in the global variable prow).

When menu_start() finishes executing, the slidebar menu will be on the screen, and the first option will be highlighted with inverse attributes. Its associated description line will appear on the second line below the menu line (unless you changed the value of DLINE).

Making a Menu Selection

Now the user can make a menu choice. The function that gets the user's menu choice is menu_choice(), shown in listing 4.4.

Listing 4.4. *The* menu_choice() *function.*

```
/*****
                            menu_choice()

     This function handles the menu display options on the screen
and returns the choice selected by the user. The user may use the
mouse, arrow keys, or capitalized letters to select a menu option.

     NOTE: This function uses the colorstr() and c_scroll() functions
discussed in Chapter 2, "String Processing."

Argument list:    MENU s[]      an array of MENU structures
                  int fore      the foreground color to use
                  int back      the background color to use
                  int button    the button number to signal that a
                                choice was made

Return value:     void

*****/

#include "menu.h"
```

```c
int menu_choice(MENU m[], int fore, int back, int button)
{
    int delta, temp;
    unsigned int select;


    while (TRUE) {
        temp = last;
        select = read_key(button);
        delta = last;
        switch (select) {
            case ENTER:                     /* They selected with CRLF   */
                last = temp;
                menu_off(m, fore, back);    /* Restore to not active     */
                last = delta;
                menu_on(m, fore, back);
                break;
            case RARROW:                    /* Used the right arrow      */
                menu_off(m, fore, back);    /* Restore to not active     */
                if (last + 1 >= menucount)  /* Wrap menu around          */
                    last = 0;
                else                        /* Move one to the right     */
                    last++;
                menu_on(m, fore, back);
                break;
            case LARROW:                    /* Used the left arrow       */
                menu_off(m, fore, back);
                if (last - 1 < 0)
                    last = menucount - 1;
                else                        /* Move one to the right     */
                    last--;
                menu_on(m, fore, back);
                break;
            default:                        /* Don't know what it was    */
                break;
        }
        if (select == ENTER)
            break;
    }
    return last;
}
```

The arguments to menu_choice() are the array of MENU structures, the foreground and background colors, and the mouse button that will be used to indicate a choice (if a mouse is present). In most commercial programs, the left mouse button is equivalent to the Enter key.

In menu_choice(), an infinite while loop is entered and read_key() is called to get a keystroke from the user. (For now, don't worry about the read_key() function's details; concentrate instead on menu_choice().) The last variable is a global variable used to keep track of the last menu selection made, and the working variables temp and delta keep track of the current and previous menu choices. This enables you to "unhighlight" the old menu option and highlight the new one as the user moves through the menu options.

Menu Wrapping

The value returned from read_key() accommodates only three possible states:

- ENTER. The Enter key (or the mouse equivalent) was pressed.

- RARROW, or right arrow. The current option is unhighlighted, and the next one to the right is highlighted.

- LARROW, or left arrow. The option to the left is highlighted, after the current option is unhighlighted. The program should check to see whether there is an option to the left or right of the currently active option. If the rightmost option is active, another right arrow keystroke will cause the first option in the menu list to become active. That is, the menu is designed to "wrap around" when the user tries to move past either the extreme-right or the extreme-left option.

Support Functions

Three support functions are used by menu_choice(). The first two support functions are used to turn the menu options on (highlight) and off (unhighlight). These two functions are called menu_on() and menu_off(). A third function, active(), supports both menu_on() and menu_off().

menu_on( )

The first support function, menu_on(), is shown in listing 4.5.

Listing 4.5. *The menu_on() function.*

```
/*****

                          menu_on()

    This function highlights the menu option just selected and
displays it in reverse video.

    Argument list:    MENU s[]      an array of MENU structures
                      int fore      the foreground color to use
                      int back      the background color to use

    Return value:     void

*****/

#include "menu.h"

void menu_on(MENU m[], int fore, int back)
{
    active(m[last].prompt, prow, nptr[last], back, fore);
    active(m[last].desc, prow + DLINE, pcol, fore, back);
}
```

The MENU structure array and the foreground and background colors
are passed to the function. The primary row (prow) is used for the row
position, and nptr[] is used to set the column. The call to active() sets the
cursor and displays the prompt, starting at the column position held in
nptr[]. The second call to active() simply prints the detailed description
of the currently active menu option. In other words, menu_on() sets the
visual attributes on the screen for the currently active menu option.

menu_off( )

The menu_off() function is illustrated in listing 4.6.

Listing 4.6. *The* menu_off() *function.*

```
/*****
                            menu_off()

    This function turns the menu option that currently is in reverse
video back to the normal display colors.

    NOTE: This function uses the c_scroll() function discussed in
Chapter 2, "String Processing."

    Argument list:    MENU s[]      an array of MENU structures
                      int fore      the foreground color to use
                      int back      the background color to use

    Return value:     void

*****/

#include "menu.h"


void menu_off(MENU m[], int fore, int back)
{
    active(m[last].prompt, prow, nptr[last], fore, back);
    c_scroll(prow + DLINE, pcol, m[last].dlen, 1, 1, 6, back << 4);
}
```

The menu_off() function does the opposite of menu_on(): it unhigh-lights a menu option. Notice that c_scroll() is used to set the background color of the description line (prow + DLINE).

Now you can see why it is important to keep track of old and new menu options. You must first unhighlight the old option by using the previous value of last as an index into the MENU structure array, and then use the new value of last to highlight the newly selected menu option.

active()

Listing 4.7 describes the active() function.

Listing 4.7. The `active()` *function.*

```
/*****
                           active()

    This function is used to highlight the menu option on the first
menu line.

    Argument list:    char *m       the string to be printed
                      int row       row for the string
                      int col       column for the string
                      int fore      the foreground color to use
                      int back      the background color to use

    Return value:     void

*****/

void active(char *m, int row, int col, int fore, int back)
{
   cursor(row, col);
   colorstr(m, fore, back << 4);
}
```

The `active()` function sets the cursor to the row-column coordinates passed to it and calls `colorstr()` to display the string passed to it. If you look again at the `menu_on()` function in listing 4.5, you will notice that the first call to `active()` reverses the order of the foreground and background colors. This is how you can use the same function to highlight (and unhighlight) a menu option.

Reading the Keyboard— *read_key()*

The real workhorse of the menu system is the `read_key()` function, which performs two basic tasks. First, it determines whether the mouse or an arrow key was used to move among menu options. Next, it determines whether the user selected a menu option by typing a corresponding letter (such as S, P, or D), or by pressing the (active) mouse button. The code for `read_key()` is presented in listing 4.8.

Listing 4.8. *The* read_key() *function.*

```
/*****

                            read_key()

    This function gets a keystroke from the keyboard and decodes it
for return to the calling function.

    NOTE: This function uses the _kbhit() function discussed in
Chapter 3, "Input Functions."

    Argument list:    int button        the mouse button that signifies
                                         a choice has been made

    Return value:    unsigned int       the keystroke code

*****/

#include "menu.h"
#include <stdlib.h>                /* Needed for the memchr() function */

unsigned int read_key(int button)
{
   char press, *tptr;
   int dhm, vmove, hmove, temp;

   hide_cursor();

   dhm = 0;
   while (TRUE) {
      if (mouse_here) {                  /* If there is a mouse       */
         press = mouse_press(&temp, &temp, button);
         if (press == button) {
            return ENTER;
         }
         mouse_counters(&vmove, &hmove); /* Get relative movement     */
         dhm += hmove;
         if (dhm > delta) {              /* Enough to move it right    */
            return RARROW;
         }
         if (dhm < -delta) {             /* How about left?           */
            return LARROW;
         }
```

```
    }
    temp = _kbhit();                    /* Poll the keyboard     */
    if (temp == 0) {                    /* No key                */
        continue;
    }
    if (temp == ENTER)                  /* Pressed Enter key?     */
        return ENTER;

    if (temp < ASCII_LIMIT) {           /* Single character?     */
        tptr = memchr(cptr, tolower(temp), menucount);
        if (tptr) {
            last = tptr - cptr;         /* Found a match          */
            return ENTER;
        }
    }
    return temp - EXTEND_OFF;           /* Extended keycode?      */
  }
  return 0;                             /* Should never be here   */
}


/*****
                        hide_cursor()

    This function simply parks the cursor so it does not show on the
    screen.

    Argument list:     void

    Return value:      void

*****/

void hide_cursor(void)
{
    cursor(26,1);
}
```

The only argument to read_key() is the button that represents the equivalent of pressing the Enter key. The purpose of the hide_cursor() function is to simply "park" the cursor so that you cannot see it while the menuing system is in use.

If *hide_cursor( )* Does Not Work Properly

If you are using the cursor-addressing function provided by the compiler vendor (rather than the one shown in listing 1.5), the hide_cursor() function might not work properly. You might have this problem if you have adjusted your cursor routine so that the upper left corner of the screen is position 1,1 (row, col) rather than 0,0. This positioning might cause all cursor functions to work differently than the code examples in this book expect.

A second reason why hide_cursor() might not work properly is that some vendors appear to do modulo operations on the row-column coordinates before executing the cursor-addressing interrupt call. That is, if the vendor does something such as

```
row %= 25;
```

before calling the cursor-addressing interrupt, it is impossible to place the cursor at row 26.

These problems might force you to use the cursor-addressing function presented in listing 1.5 or to modify all source codes to account for the addressing differences. We will assume that you chose to use listing 1.5 for the cursor() function.

As soon as you are inside the function, and after the cursor is parked out of sight, you enter an infinite while loop. The first if test checks to see whether a mouse is available. If it is, call the mouse_press() function discussed in Chapter 3, "Input Functions." The return value from mouse_press() indicates whether a mouse button was pressed. If press is equal to button, the user has made a menu choice, and you return a value equal to ENTER.

Mouse Sensitivity

If no choice was made, you can call mouse_counters() to see whether the mouse has been moved since the last call. A running total of the mouse's movement is held in dhm (delta horizontal movement). If the total in dhm is greater than delta, return a RARROW code. If the total in dhm is less than negative delta, return a LARROW code. delta is a symbolic constant for the amount of mouse movement necessary to interpret the movement as a "real" mouse change. Because mouse_counters() can detect movements as small as .001 inch, the mouse would move things on the screen so quickly that the user would have a hard time making the proper selection. Therefore, delta is a mouse-sensitivity constant that can increase the amount of mouse travel necessary to change menu selections. The higher the value of delta, the less sensitive the mouse is to movement.

You might want to make delta a true variable and have the user set the value as part of a setup program. This value could be stored in a disk file and read into the program during initialization. Although this probably is overkill for most applications, it would not be difficult to do. In most circumstances, a value of 50 is fast enough to change among menu items quickly, but not so fast that the user "overshoots" the desired menu option.

If the mouse was not used, you can call _kbhit() to see whether a key on the keyboard was pressed. The _kbhit() function does not wait for a keystroke if one was not made. (Remember that the _kbhit() function supplied in this book probably is different from any kbhit() that might be supplied with your compiler.) If a key was pressed, temp holds the keystroke. You check temp to see whether the keystroke was the Enter key. If it was, that value is returned to menu_choice(). If not, you fall into the next if statement.

If you reread the discussion of _kbhit() in Chapter 3, "Input Functions," you will find that the possible return values are

```
temp == 0          no character
temp <  128        ASCII character
temp >  0x100      extended key code
```

Therefore, if _kbhit() returns a value of 0, you execute the continue statement in listing 4.8 and continue polling the input devices. If the value is greater than 0x100, the user must have pressed one of the extended keys (an arrow key, for example).

If the return value from _kbhit() is less than 0x100 and not 0, the key must be an ASCII character. You now must test the character to see whether it matches one of the letters in the list of single-letter menu options; use memchr() to perform the test. You can do this by scanning the letters pointed to by cptr (which was filled in by menu_start()). The tolower() macro is used so that the user can type either uppercase or lowercase letters when making the menu selection. If memchr() finds a match, set last using pointer subtraction, and return ENTER. The switch statement in menu_choice() performs the proper processing of the possible return values. If no match is found, the entire process is repeated until a menu selection is made.

An Example Showing How to Use the Slidebar Menu

Now you have seen all the functions needed to use a slidebar menu. This section shows you how the pieces fit together to form a complete menuing system. First, however, you should look at a list of the menu.h header file, which contains all the macros, global variables, and other information needed to use both menuing systems discussed in this chapter. Although the file's entire contents are presented in listing 4.9, some items are not used by the slidebar menuing system. These items are discussed in later chapters.

Listing 4.9. The menu.h header file.

```
/*****
                              menu.h


                   Ref. 1.0    3/14/89
                   Ref. 1.1    7/05/89
                   Ref. 1.2    5/15/90
                   Ref. 1.3    6/13/91


      This header file contains the necessary overhead information
   for the slidebar, box menuing system, and other functions.

*****/

#include <stdio.h>
#include <stdlib.h>
#include <string.h>
#include <ctype.h>
#include <dos.h>
#include <alloc.h>            /* Might be malloc.h for some compilers */
#include <mem.h>              /* Might be memory.h for some compilers */


         /******* Data Structures and Definitions ***********/

                                   /* Slidebar menu structure    */
typedef struct {
   char *prompt;                   /* First line menu prompt      */
   int  plen;                      /* Its length                  */
```

```c
    char *desc;                     /* Second line menu prompt     */
    int  dlen;                      /* Its length                  */
    char letter;                    /* Single-letter choice option */
    } MENU;


                                    /* Structures in Chapters 10-11 */
typedef struct {
    char fname[13];                 /* The file name               */
    char use;                       /* File use flag               */
    } FILEDIR;

struct WINDOW {
    char title[30];
    int num_win;
    unsigned int far *base;         /* Base memory for window      */

    int x,         /* Upper left x                                */
        y,         /* Upper left y                                */
        wide,      /* Lower right x                               */
        deep,      /* Lower right y                               */
        border,    /* 0 = no border, 1 = single line, 2 = double line */
        wbcolor,   /* Window background color                     */
        wfcolor,   /* Window foreground color                     */
        bbcolor,   /* Border background color                     */
        bfcolor,   /* Border foreground color                     */
        mcolor,    /* Foreground message print color (back = wbcolor) */
        vscrollbar, /* Vertical scroll bar; 0 = No, 1 = Yes       */
        hscrollbar, /* Horizontal scroll bar; 0 = No, 1 = Yes     */
        hotspot,   /* 0 if no close button, 1 for close button    */
        shadow;    /* Does window have a shadow; 0 = No, 1 = Yes  */
};


struct DIALOG {
    char *messages,    /* Input prompt messages                   */
         *buttons;     /* Button messages                         */

    unsigned int far *base; /* Base memory for dialog box         */

    int *locations,    /* Start of button locations; x then y     */
        *buttonlen;    /* Length of each button string            */

    int bfcolor,       /* Background input field color            */
```

continues

Listing 4.9. continued

```
        bmcolor,         /* Background message color              */
        buttonnum,       /* Number of buttons in dialog box       */
        dbcolor,         /* Dialog background color               */
        deep,            /* Dialog depth                          */
        dfcolor,         /* Dialog foreground color               */
        ffcolor,         /* Foreground input field color          */
        fmcolor,         /* Foreground message color              */
        shadow,          /* Does dialog have a shadow; 0 = No, 1 = Yes */
        wide,            /* Dialog width                          */
        x,               /* Upper left x                          */
        y;               /* Upper left y                          */

};


#ifdef EXTERN
    extern
#endif
    FILEDIR *fptr;              /* Pointer to FILEDIR structure      */


#ifdef EXTERN
    extern
#endif
        char *cptr,             /* Vector of single char choices     */
        old_source[128],        /* Starting directory                */
        file_source[128],       /* Input file path name              */
        file_dest[128];         /* Output file path name             */


#ifdef EXTERN
    extern
#endif
        int delta,              /* Make delta available              */
        increment,              /* Relative movement of marker       */
        last,                   /* The last menu choice made         */
        menucount,              /* The number of items in the menu   */
        menulen,                /* The length of all menu choices    */
        mouse_here,             /* Is there a mouse present          */
        *nptr,                  /* Pointer to menu column positions  */
        pcol,                   /* Primary column                    */
        prow;                   /* Primary row                       */
```

```
#ifdef EXTERN                        /* Start of video memory         */
   extern
#endif
   unsigned int far *start_video_memory, hot_key_color;



                    /******* Macros **********/

#ifndef TRUE
   #define TRUE  1
#endif


#define HOME    71                   /* Extended key codes for keypad */
#define UARROW  72
#define PAGEUP  73
#define LARROW  75
#define RARROW  77
#define END     79
#define DARROW  80
#define PAGEDN  81


#define OBRACKET   91                /* Open bracket                  */
#define CBRACKET   93                /* Close bracket                 */


#define LBUTTON  1                   /* Define mouse buttons          */
#define RBUTTON  2
#define MBUTTON  4


#define SIDEWAYS 0                   /* Direction of mouse travel     */
#define UPDOWN   1
#define ANYWAY   2


#define SINGLEBAR 1                  /* For box drawing               */
#define DOUBLEBAR 2

#define UL  218                      /* Graphics characters for       */
#define UR  191                      /* single-line box               */
#define LL  192
#define LR  217
#define VB  179
#define HB  196
```

continues

Listing 4.9. continued

```
#define DUL  201                    /* Double-line box              */
#define DUR  187
#define DLL  200
#define DLR  188
#define DVB  186
#define DHB  205


                        /* Graphics characters                      */

#define RARROWH        16           /* Right arrowhead              */
#define LARROWH        17           /* Left arrowhead               */
#define UDARROW        18           /* Up-down arrow symbol         */
#define UARROWSYM      24           /* Up arrow symbol              */
#define DARROWSYM      25           /* Down arrow symbol            */
#define UARROWH        30           /* Up arrowhead symbol          */
#define DARROWH        31           /* Down arrowhead symbol        */
#define LITEBOX        176          /* Light hatch area             */
#define MEDIUMBOX      177          /* Horizontal background field  */
#define HSCROLLFIELD   177          /* Horizontal background field  */
#define HEAVYBOX       176          /* Heavy hatch area             */
#define BLANK          219          /* Solid hatch area             */
#define VSCROLLBAR     219          /* Vertical scroll bar          */
#define HALFBLOCK      220          /* Half block                   */
#define HALFSQUARE     223          /* Half square                  */
#define CHECK          251          /* Check                        */
#define HOTSPOT        254          /* Square                       */
#define HSCROLLBAR     254          /* Horizontal scroll bar        */

#define SPACE          32


#define ENTER          '\r'    /* This might be '\n' on some compilers */
#define ESCAPE         27
#define BACKSPACE      8
#define DELETE         127
#define TAB            9
#define BELL           7            /* Terminal alarm               */

                             /* Macros for two-line menu bar        */

#define ifbars(x, y)    (c = (bars == 1) ? (x) : (y) )
```

```
#define OPTION(a, b, c)   {a, sizeof(a) - 1, b, sizeof(b) - 1, c},
#define OPTIONEND         {0}

#define MARGIN       " "          /* Spacing between menu items       */

#define MAXWIDE      80           /* Maximum screen width-depth       */
#define MAXDEEP      24

#define delta        50           /* Mickeys/menu change              */

#define ASCII_LIMIT 128
#define EXTEND_OFF  0x100

#define MAXLINE      256
#define MAXITEM      50
#define EVER         ;;
#define UP           72
#define DOWN         80
#define WIDTH        80
#define ROW          5

#define MENUCOL      1
#define DLINE        1           /* Description line placement        */

#if DLINE > 2                    /* Used in Chapter 11                */
   #define MENUROW   1
#else
   #define MENUROW   2
#endif

                  /* Color definitions                               */

#define FBLACK       0           /* Foreground colors                */
#define FBLUE        1
#define FGREEN       2
#define FCYAN        3
#define FRED         4
#define FMAGENTA     5
#define FBROWN       6
#define FWHITE       7
#define FGRAY        8
#define FLBLUE       9
```

continues

Listing 4.9. continued

```
#define FLGREEN      10
#define FLCYAN       11
#define FLRED        12
#define FLMAGENTA    13
#define FYELLOW      14
#define FLWHITE      15


#ifdef NOSHIFT                      /* The shift operators have been    */
                                    /* removed from all functions, so   */
                                    /* no bit-shifting is necessary.    */

    #define BBLACK    0             /* Background colors (values shifted) */
    #define BBLUE     16
    #define BGREEN    32
    #define BCYAN     48
    #define BRED      64
    #define BMAGENTA  80
    #define BBROWN    96
    #define BWHITE    112

#else                               /* Source has not been modified     */

    #define BBLACK    0             /* Background colors (no shift)     */
    #define BBLUE     1
    #define BGREEN    2
    #define BCYAN     3
    #define BRED      4
    #define BMAGENTA  5
    #define BBROWN    6
    #define BWHITE    7

#endif

                                    /* Function prototypes              */

unsigned int read_key(int button),
    get_mouse_or_key(int button, int direction, int *row, int *col),
    read_key_all(int *row, int *col),
    read_key_d(int button, int dir);                /*SEE LIST0414.C */

int box_menu_start(MENU s[], int fore, int bk, int frame, int bar, int wdeep),
    box_select(MENU m[], int fore, int bk, int button, int limit, int marker),
```

```
    box_menu_start(MENU s[], int fore, int bk, int frame, int bars,
     int wdeep),
    create_w(int y, int x, int wide, int deep, struct WINDOW *m),
    get_string(int row, int col, char *m, char *buff, int field_width,
              struct DIALOG mine, int len),
    menu_choice(MENU m[], int fore, int back, int button);

void active(char *m, int row, int col, int fore, int back),
    cbox(int row, int col, int wide, int deep, int color, int bars),
    close_box(void),
    close_window(struct WINDOW m),
    draw_box(struct WINDOW m),
    hide_cursor(void),
    highlight(MENU m[], int row, int fore, int back),
    indicator(int fore, int marker, int limit),
    init_window(struct WINDOW *w),
    menu_end(void),
    menu_off(MENU m[], int fore, int back),
    menu_on(MENU m[], int fore, int back),
    menu_start(MENU s[], int fore, int back),
    mouse_cursor_on(void),
    mouse_counter(int *r, int *c),
    mouse_cursor_off(void),
    prepare(void),
    read_mouse(int *row, int *col, int *button),
    redraw_window(MENU m[], int first, int fore, int limit),
    restore(MENU m[], int row, int fore, int back),
    save_screen(int row, int col, int wide, int deep, char *s),
    show_window(struct WINDOW m),
    wprintf(int row, int col, struct WINDOW hwnd, char *c, ...),

    write_screen(int row, int col, int wide, int deep, char *s);
```

The menu.h listing presents much information that has not yet been covered in this book. Many of the entries in menu.h are discussed in Chapters 10 and 11. For now, I will limit the discussion to only those items that are of immediate interest.

Data Definitions and Declarations Using Multiple Files

One technique presented in listing 4.9 needs to be explained. Consider the following lines from menu.h:

```
#ifdef EXTERN
    extern
#endif
        char *cptr;           /* Vector of single char choices */
```

This technique is used to toggle the keyword extern into or out of a program module. For example, suppose that you have two source files named file1.c and file2.c that are used in a program. Also suppose that both files use the menuing system, but that the main() function is in file1.c. Clearly, cptr should be *defined* in file1.c but *declared* in file2.c.

To refresh your memory, when a data item is defined, storage is allocated for the item. When you declare a data item, you simply are telling the compiler that the item already is defined elsewhere, but that you want to use it in this module. In the example, cptr is defined in file1.c, but parts of the program in file2.c need access to it. Therefore, you should place the preprocessor directives

```
#define EXTERN 1
#include "menu.h"
```

near the top of file2.c. Because EXTERN is #defined in file2.c, the translation of the preprocessor directives associated with cptr in file2.c becomes

```
extern char *cptr;
```

That is, you have declared cptr in file2.c so that it can be used in file2.c.

On the other hand, in file1.c you would simply have the line

```
#include "menu.h"
```

(that is, no #define for the EXTERN macro). This causes the preprocessor to translate the same lines as

```
char *cptr;
```

Therefore, you have *defined* cptr in file1.c but only *declared* it in file2.c. This is exactly what you must do if you want to use the menuing system across multiple program files. The rule is simple:

Add the preprocessor directive

```
#define EXTERN 1
```

just before the #include "menu.h" directive in all program files, *excluding* the one that contains main().

This will result in only one definition of any specified data item but will enable access to the data item across multiple files.

Now, examine a short example of how you might use the slidebar menuing system. The code is presented in program 4.1.

***Program 4.1.** Example using slidebar menu.*

```
#include <stdio.h>
#include <stdlib.h>
#include <alloc.h>               /* Might be malloc.h for some compilers */
#include <mem.h>   /* Might be memory.h or string.h for some compilers */
#include <dos.h>

#include "menu.h"                /* Header file with menu macros        */


MENU menu0[] = {
   OPTION("Screen", "Send output to screen", 's')
   OPTION("Disk-file", "Output written to disk file", 'd')
   OPTION("Printer", "Output listed on the printer", 'p')
   OPTIONEND
   };


void main()
{
   int back, choice, fore, mode;

   cls();
   mode = getvmode();
   if (mode == 1 || mode == 3) {                 /* Color... */
      fore = 1;               /* Blue */
      back = 3;               /* Cyan */
   } else {                                      /* or B&W   */
      fore = 0;               /* Black */
      back = 7;               /* White */
   }
```

continues

Program 4.1. *continued*

```
    cursor(1, 1);
    menu_start(menu0, fore, back);
    choice = menu_choice(menu0, fore, back, LBUTTON);
    menu_end();
    printf("\nchoice = %d", choice);
}
```

Next, take a look at the definition of the MENU structure array:

```
MENU menu0[] = {
    OPTION("Screen", "Send output to screen", 's')
    OPTION("Disk-file", "Output written to disk file", 'd')
    OPTION("Printer", "Output listed on the printer", 'p')
    OPTIONEND
    };
```

The OPTION macro, defined in menu.h, was discussed earlier in this chapter, in the section entitled "Initializing a Menu Structure." The first parameter in the OPTION macro is the string constant that will appear on the first line of the slidebar. The second parameter is the string constant that will appear on the second line of the menu. The final argument is the single-letter keystroke used to indicate the selection of the menu option. Again, this letter corresponds to the only uppercase letter in the first parameter. The OPTIONEND macro simply is a null macro that defines the end of the menu list.

Although the example shows the menu options defined within the program itself, there is no reason why these could not be read from a disk file and read into a dynamically allocated space at runtime. Program 4.1 illustrates the easiest method, but the final method will be dictated by your needs.

Inside main(), you clear the screen and make the call to getvmode() to determine whether the screen is monochrome or color. If color is present, set the foreground color to blue on a cyan background. (Monochrome displays do not leave much choice.)

Next, call cursor() to establish the two menu lines' screen location. This is important because menu_start() reads the current cursor position into the two global variables prow and pcol. All subsequent cursor addressing is referenced from these initial coordinates.

After the menu is opened by way of the call to menu_start(), the call to menu_choice() gets the menu selection from the user. The return value will be the selected option. The option list begins at 0. After the choice is made, the call to menu_end() is made to free up the memory allocations made by menu_start(). The code for menu_end() is shown in listing 4.10.

Listing 4.10. The menu_end() *function.*

```
/*****
                            menu_end()

    This function simply frees the allocations used by the menuing
    system.

    Argument list:    void

    Return value:     void

*****/

#include "menu.h"

void menu_end(void)
{
   free(nptr);
   free(cptr);
}
```

As you can see, menu_end() releases the storage associated with the starting column address for each menu item (nptr), as well as the storage used by the single-letter keystrokes used for menu selection (cptr). After menu_end() is called, the program simply displays the menu choice. In an actual programming situation, choice probably would be used in a switch to cause some subsequent action in the program. If you run the sample program, you will notice that the selected menu option remains highlighted after the selection is made.

Box Menuing System

The slidebar menuing system can handle most menuing tasks, but there might be times when you want to present more options than a slidebar menu can hold easily. In most commercial programs, for example, a box menu helps the user choose from what could be a long list of disk files. A box menuing system creates a small "window box," within which the user can scroll through the menu list.

The box menuing system is not a true "window" menuing system in which a window opens, does its task, and then disappears, leaving the screen as it was just before the window opened. Such systems require you to save the screen (or at least the portion that must hold the window) before the window is opened. The screen (or that portion of it that held the window) then must be rewritten when the window is removed. The last section of this chapter, "Box Embellishments," presents three functions to help you implement such windows if you want to use them. (A more complete discussion of such windowing functions is presented in Chapter 10, "Text Windows.")

The box menuing system presented in this section assumes that you can use the screen as you like, without having to restore it when you are done. If you need to preserve the original screen, you can use setvpage() to write the box menu to a different page of video memory, get the user's menu choice, and then set the video page back to the original page after you are finished with the menu. This easily implemented technique is used in some commercial programs.

With all the caveats out of the way, you now can consider the new functions you will need to implement a box menu system.

First you must be able to draw a box on the screen where your list of menu options can be displayed. It would be convenient if the function could handle color and single- and double-bar boxes. Perhaps another function should give some indication (a menu marker) of your position on the menu relative to the list's total length. That is, if the list is longer than the box is deep, a visual indicator will tell the user that the list can be scrolled.

You will need to modify read_key() so that it can process up-and-down movement. The user also should be able to use the Page Up, Page Down, Home, and End keys for rapid movement through a long menu. To allow for paging up and down, you will need a function that can redraw the window. As in the slidebar system, functions are needed that can highlight and unhighlight a menu selection. Compared to the slidebar counterpart, however, the box menu system uses a rather complex function to move the menu through the box.

Activate a Box Menu— *box_menu_start( )*

You still can use your MENU data structure in a box menu, even though you might not need all the structure's features (for example, the description line could be a null string). If you would rather use another structure, simply change the references from MENU m[] to the array of pointers to char that holds the menu list. In either case, you should pass the array containing the list to the menuing system as one of the arguments.

The foreground, background, and box frame colors all should be passed to the function. Because you want the ability to use single- or double-bar boxes, you should pass that information as well. Finally, the box's depth must be determined. Because the box must be wide enough to hold the largest data item, you will have to determine that parameter "on the fly."

Listing 4.11 presents the function that will open a menu box.

Listing 4.11. *The* box_menu_start() *function.*

```
/*****
                            box_menu_start()

     This function performs the code necessary to display the
 menu box and the menu list. The first choice is automatically
 highlighted. The variable "bars" determine whether single or double
 lines are used for the menu box. The background color is used only
 for highlighting the active menu option.

     Argument list:      struct MENU m[]       the array of structures that
                                               contains the menu choices
                         int fore              the foreground color used
                         int back              the background color
                         int frame             the box color
                         int bars              flag: 1 = single bars,
                                                     2 = double bars
                         int wdeep             depth of window

     Return value:       void

*****/

#include "menu.h"

int box_menu_start(MENU s[], int fore, int back, int frame,
                            int bars, int wdeep)
{
    int buttons, i, limit, wide;
```

continues

Listing 4.11. continued

```c
    last = menulen = 0;
    find_cursor(&prow, &pcol);
    mouse_here = mouse_status(&buttons);
    nptr = '\0';
    for (i = 0; s[i].prompt; i++) {
        if (s[i].plen > menulen)            /* Max menu width        */
            menulen = s[i].plen;
    }
    menucount = i;
    cptr = (char *) calloc(menucount, sizeof(char)); /* Letter options */
    for (i = 0; i < menucount; i++) {
        cptr[i] = s[i].letter;              /* Single-letter choices   */
    }
    wide = menulen + 3;
    if (wdeep > MAXDEEP)
        wdeep = MAXDEEP;
    limit = (wdeep >= menucount) ? menucount : wdeep;
    increment = (int) ( (double) menucount / (double) limit + .5);
    cbox(prow, pcol, wide, limit + 1, frame, bars);

    prow++;                                 /* Work inside the box     */
    pcol += 2;
    for (i = 0; i < limit; i++) {
        cursor(prow + i, pcol);
        colorstr(s[i].prompt, fore, 0);
    }
    highlight(s, prow, fore, back);         /* Highlight choice        */
    return limit;
}
```

The `box_menu_start()` function assumes that the cursor is at the desired row and column coordinates before the menu is opened. The call to `find_cursor()` then fills in the global variables `prow` and `pcol` in the same manner as the slidebar menu. A check also is done to see whether a mouse is present; `mouse_here` then is set accordingly. The `for` loop is used to find the widest item in the menu list. The maximum width is assigned into `menulen`. When the `for` loop terminates, the variable `i` equals the number of items in the menu list, and it is used to set the value for `menucount`.

Next, a call to `calloc()` allocates enough space to hold all the single-letter menu options. The second `for` loop is used to fill in the single-letter options. The variable wide is set to menulen plus 3, to account for the outside of the box when it is drawn. The variable named limit sets the maximum number of menu items that can be displayed at one time.

Later, by using the increment variable, you can determine the number of rows that must be advanced in the menu, to show a corresponding one-row advance in the menu position marker. Now, however, you are ready to call cbox() to draw the menu box outline. (The code for cbox() will be described later.)

Now that the box is drawn, you need to reference everything from within the box. Therefore, you advance prow by one row and pcol by two columns. The two columns leave a small black border around the menu list, which you can change if you like.

The final for loop fills in the box with the maximum (limit) number of menu items that can be displayed in the box. The call to highlight() simply uses the foreground and background colors to highlight the first item in the list of menu options.

Draw a Box with Color—*cbox( )*

The cbox() (color box) function, which draws the menu box, is presented in listing 4.12.

***Listing 4.12.** The cbox() function.*

```
/*****
                            cbox()

    This function is used to draw a character graphics box on the
screen with color. The box can use single or double lines. The
macro ifbars() determines which one is selected, based on the last
argument.

    Argument list:    int row        starting row for box
                      int col        starting column for box
                      int wide       width of box
                      int deep       depth of box
                      int color      color of frame lines
                      int bars       1 = single bar, 2 = double bars
```

continues

Listing 4.12. *continued*

```
    Return value:      void

*****/

#include "menu.h"

#define ifbars(x, y)    (c = (bars == 1) ? (x) : (y) )

void cbox(int row, int col, int wide, int deep, int color, int bars)
{
   char c;
   int i;

   cursor(row, col);
   ifbars(UL, DUL);                        /* Do upper left corner    */
   colorchr(c, color, 0);
   ifbars(HB, DHB);
   for (i = 1; i < wide; i++) {            /* Do top and bottom       */
      cursor(row, col + i);
      colorchr(c, color, 0);
      cursor(row + deep, col + i);
      colorchr(c, color, 0);
   }
   cursor(row, col + wide);
   ifbars(UR, DUR);                        /* Do upper right corner   */
   colorchr(c, color, 0);
   cursor(row + deep, col);
   ifbars(LL, DLL);                        /* Do lower left corner    */
   colorchr(c, color, 0);
   cursor(row + deep, col + wide);
   ifbars(LR, DLR);                        /* Do lower right corner   */
   colorchr(c, color, 0);
   ifbars(VB, DVB);
   for (i = 1; i < deep; i++) {            /* Do left right side      */
      cursor(row + i, col);
      colorchr(c, color, 0);
      cursor(row + i, col + wide);
      colorchr(c, color, 0);
   }
}
```

The arguments to cbox() determine the row-column coordinates for the box, its width and depth, the box frame's color, and whether single or double bars will be used to draw the box. The macro

```
#define ifbars(x, y)    (c = (bars == 1) ? (x) : (y) )
```

is used to decide which graphics character will be used for drawing the box at various positions on the screen. For example, the call

```
ifbars(HB, DHB);
```

expands to

```
c = (bars == 1) ? (HB) : (DHB);
```

Therefore, if the value for bars is passed in as a 1, a single horizontal bar (HB) is used to draw the box. If bars equals 2, double horizontal bars (DHB) are used. If you study the code, you will see that the ifbars() macro must be invoked for each corner of the box and for drawing the top and bottom lines. The colorstr() function uses the color argument when drawing the box.

The only other new function in box_menu_start() is highlight(), shown in listing 4.13.

***Listing 4.13.** The highlight() function.*

```
/*****

                        highlight()

    This function is used to print a string in the menu box in its
    highlighted state.

    Argument list:    struct MENU m[]      the array of structures that
                                           contains the menu choices
                      int first            screen position
                      int fore             the foreground color used
                      int back             the background color used

    Return value:     void

*****/


#include "menu.h"
```

continues

Listing 4.13. continued

```
void highlight(MENU m[], int row, int fore, int back)
{
   char buff[MAXWIDE], t[MAXWIDE];

   memset(buff, ' ', MAXWIDE);                 /* Set the buffer to blanks  */
   strcpy(t, m[last].prompt);
   strncat(t, buff, menulen - m[last].plen);/* Pad string with blanks  */

   cursor(row, pcol);
   colorstr(t, fore, back << 4);
}
```

This function simply takes the currently active menu option as determined by the global variable last, pads the option with blanks (if necessary) so that it will fill the menu box's width, and then prints the option in color, using the foreground and background colors. Briefly stated, the highlight() function is used simply to show which menu option is currently active.

Get the Selection from the User— *box_select( )*

The return value box_menu_start() (limit) equals the number of menu choices that can appear in the box at one time. The call to box_select() passes the foreground-background colors, the MENU structure array, the active mouse select button, and the marker flag as arguments. The source code for box_select() appears in listing 4.14.

Listing 4.14. The box_select() function.

```
/*****

                    box_select()

   This function is used to select an item from the menu box.

   Argument list:    struct MENU m[]    the array of structures that
                                        contains the menu choices
                     int fore           the foreground color used
```

	int back	the background color
	int button	the button for selection
		(usually the left button)
	int limit	the maximum number of items
		for the box
	int marker	character for fuel gauge
Return value:	int	the choice made, or -1 if
		no choice

```
*****/


#include "menu.h"



int box_select(MENU m[], int fore, int back, int button, int limit, int marker)
{
    int active, bottom, delta, temp, top;
    int select;

    top = temp = last;
    bottom = limit - 1;
    active = prow;
    while (TRUE) {
        if (marker) {
            indicator(fore, marker, limit);
        }
        temp = last;
        select = read_key_d(button, UPDOWN);
        delta = last;
        switch (select) {
            case DARROW:                        /* Used the down arrow   */
                if (last + 1 > menucount - 1) { /* At end of menu        */
                    if (limit == menucount)      /* If one big window     */
                        restore(m, active, fore, 0);
                    top = last = 0;
                    bottom = limit - 1;
                    active = prow;
                    if (limit < menucount)
                        redraw_window(m, last, fore, limit);
                    highlight(m, active, fore, back);
                    break;
                }
```

continues

Listing 4.14. continued

```
        if (last + 1 > bottom) {        /* At bottom of menu    */
            restore(m, active, fore, 0); /* Restore to not active */
            scroll(prow, pcol - 1, menulen, limit - 2, 1, 6);
            last++;
            highlight(m, active, fore, back);
            top++;
            bottom++;
            break;
        }
        restore(m, active, fore, 0);     /* All other options    */
        last++;
        active++;
        highlight(m, active, fore, back);
        break;
    case UARROW:                         /* Used the left arrow  */
        if ( (last - 1) < 0) {           /* At top of list       */
            if (limit == menucount)
                restore(m, active, fore, 0);
            last = bottom = menucount - 1; /* Reset to bottom     */
            top = bottom - limit + 1;
            active = (limit - 1) + prow;
            if (limit < menucount)
                redraw_window(m, top, fore, limit);
            highlight(m, active, fore, back);
            break;
        }
        if ( (active - 1) < prow) {      /* Top screen, not list */
            restore(m, active, fore, 0); /* Restore to not active */
            scroll(prow, pcol - 1, menulen, limit - 2, 1, 7);
            last--;
            highlight(m, active, fore, back);
            top--;
            bottom--;
            break;
        }
        restore(m, active, fore, 0);
        active--;
        last--;
        highlight(m, active, fore, back);
        break;
    case PAGEUP:
        top -= limit;
        if (top < 0) {
```

```
        if (limit == menucount)
            restore(m, active, fore, 0);
        top = 0;
        bottom = top + limit - 1;
        last = top;
        active = top + prow;
        if (limit < menucount)
            redraw_window(m, top, fore, limit);
        highlight(m, active, fore, back);
        break;
    }
    if (limit == menucount)
        restore(m, active, fore, 0);
    last -= limit;
    bottom -= limit;
    if (limit < menucount)
        redraw_window(m, top, fore, limit);
    highlight(m, active, fore, back);  /* Highlight choice  */
    break;
case PAGEDN:
    bottom += limit;
    if (bottom > menucount - 1) {
        if (limit == menucount)
            restore(m, active, fore, 0);
        last = bottom = menucount - 1;
        top = bottom - limit + 1;
        active = (limit - 1) + prow;
        if (limit < menucount)
            redraw_window(m, top, fore, limit);
        highlight(m, active, fore, back);
        break;
    }
    if (limit == menucount)
        restore(m, active, fore, 0);
    top += limit;
    last += limit;
    if (limit < menucount)
        redraw_window(m, top, fore, limit);
    highlight(m, active, fore, back);  /* Highlight choice  */
    break;
case HOME:
    if (limit == menucount)
        restore(m, active, fore, 0);
```

continues

Listing 4.14. continued

```
            top = last = 0;
            bottom = limit - 1;
            active = prow;
            if (limit < menucount)
                redraw_window(m, last, fore, limit);
            highlight(m, active, fore, back);
            break;
        case END:
            if (limit == menucount)
                restore(m, active, fore, 0);
            last = bottom = menucount - 1;
            top = bottom - limit + 1;
            active = (limit - 1) + prow;
            if (limit < menucount)
                redraw_window(m, top, fore, limit);
            highlight(m, active, fore, back);
            break;
        case ESCAPE:
            restore(m, active, fore, 0);
            last = -1;
            break;
        case ENTER:                          /* User selected with CRLF */
            last = temp;
            restore(m, active, fore, 0);   /* Restore to not active   */
            last = delta;
            highlight(m, active, fore, back);
            break;

        default:                             /* Don't know what it was  */
            break;
        }
    if (select == ENTER ¦¦ select == ESCAPE)
        break;
    }
    return last;
}
```

As you can see, the function is rather large. Its size is necessary, however, because it enables the user to do many things in the menu. All the cursor keys (Home, End, Page Up, Page Down, and the arrow keys) can be used to scroll the list of options. Actually, the code just keeps track of which menu item currently is being highlighted, and that item's location on the screen.

Because the code is quite repetitive, you need to consider how only one of the `switch` cases works: for example, the down-arrow key (`DARROW`). Three possible situations must be addressed:

1. When the cursor is at the bottom of the screen

2. When the cursor is at the bottom of the list

3. When the cursor is somewhere between 1 and 2

The first `if` statement in `case DARROW` checks for situation 2. Will advancing one item farther down the list exceed the number of items in the list? The second `if` statement checks to see whether the box is large enough to hold all the items in the list. (If this is the case, there is no reason to redraw the screen.) If the entire menu is on the screen, the call to `restore()` simply turns off the currently highlighted menu option.

If the list is larger than the box, the `if` check will be logical `FALSE`, and a number of assignments will take place. (Table 4.1 gives a list of the most important variables used in `box_select()`.) At this point in the first `if` statement, you know that you are at the bottom of the menu list. When the user wants to continue going down the list even though he already is at the bottom, it is assumed he wants to "wrap around" and return to the top. Therefore, assignments are made to reset the menu so that the list's beginning is shown.

Table 4.1. *Key variables used in* `box_select()`.

Variable Name	Description
`top`	The index number of the topmost item appearing in the menu box
`bottom`	The index number of the bottommost item appearing in the menu box
`active`	The currently highlighted menu option
`delta`	A temporary holding place for the index number between inputs; also used to highlight the final choice made by the user
`select`	The value returned from `read_key()`

continues

Table 4.1. *continued*

Variable Name	Description
marker	If nonzero, the "fuel gauge" marker to show the relative position in the menu list
limit	The maximum number of menu items that can appear in the menu box

The statement

```
if (limit < menucount)
```

checks to see whether the box is smaller than the number of items in the menu. You must redraw the box if it is smaller than the list. This is done by the call to redraw_window(). Finally, call highlight() to "turn on" the currently active menu option. In this case, it would be the first item on the list. You now can show the beginning of the menu list with its first item highlighted.

When you reach the statement

```
if (last + 1 > bottom)
```

you must be at the bottom of the box, but not at the end of the menu. Therefore, you first must unhighlight the option at the bottom of the screen to "deactivate" it. This is done by the call to restore(). Next, scroll the contents of the menu box by one line, which is done by the call to scroll(). Increment last so that it is the currently active menu item, and then call highlight() to highlight the new option. Finally, increment top and bottom to keep those two indexes in sync. The break statement sends control out of the switch so that you can read the next keystroke.

The third option is processed by the remainder of the code associated with the DARROW case. In this case, a down-arrow key was pressed, but you are not at the bottom of either the menu box or the list. For example, if the menu's first option is currently active and the user presses the down-arrow key, the highlighting simply should advance to the second item in the menu. This process is carried out by turning off the currently active option by the call to restore(), incrementing last and active, and highlighting the new option by a call to highlight().

All the cursor key movements behave similarly, but the direction or the extent of the movement is changed. Several support functions, however, should be discussed. The first is the read_key_d() function. Because this function must do more than the read_key() function in listing 4.8, an enhanced function named `read_key_d()` (that is, read a key or direction) is needed. This new function is shown in listing 4.15. Notice the new second argument that tells you in which direction you want to move the menu selection.

The new `read_key_d()` function also has a check for MBUTTON, which enables the use of the middle button on any three-button mouse. Even though MBUTTON causes a PAGEDN code to be returned in all cases, you can decode this into any specific action you like.

Listing 4.15. *The read_key_d() function.*

```
/*****
                            read_key_d()

    This function gets a keystroke from the keyboard and decodes it
for return to the calling function. Only one direction is readable
on a specified call, as determined by the second argument.

    NOTE: This function uses the getch() function discussed in
Chapter 3, "Input Functions."

    Argument list:    int button      the button to check for press
                      int direction   the travel direction desired
                                       0 = sideways, 1 = up-down

    Return value:     unsigned int    the keystroke code

*****/

#include <mem.h>                  /* May be memory.h for some compilers */
#include <ctype.h>

#include "menu.h"


unsigned int read_key_d(int button, int direction)
{
    char press, *tptr;
    int dhm, dvm, vmove, hmove,temp;

    hide_cursor();
```

continues

Listing 4.15. continued

```
dvm = dhm = 0;
while (TRUE) {
    if (mouse_here) {                    /* If there is a mouse      */
        press = mouse_press(&temp, &temp, button);
        if (press == button) {
            return ENTER;                /* User made a choice       */
        }
        if (press == RBUTTON) {
            return ESCAPE;               /* Return without choice    */
        }
        if (press == MBUTTON) {          /* Third button???          */
            return PAGEDN;
        }
        mouse_counters(&vmove, &hmove);  /* Get relative movement    */

        dhm += hmove;                    /* Get horizontal movement  */
        dvm += vmove;                    /* Get vertical movement    */

        switch (direction) {
            case SIDEWAYS:               /* How about right?         */
                if (dhm > delta) {
                    return RARROW;
                }                        /* How about left?          */
                if (dhm < -delta) {
                    return LARROW;
                }
            case UPDOWN:                 /* How about down?          */
                if (dvm > delta) {
                    return DARROW;
                }                        /* How about up?            */
                if (dvm < -delta) {
                    return UARROW;
                }
            default:
                break;
        }
    }
    temp = _kbhit();                     /* Poll the keyboard        */
    if (temp == 0) {                     /* No key press             */
        continue;
    }
```

```
    if (temp == ENTER) {              /* Pressed Enter key?      */
        return ENTER;
    }
    if (temp == ESCAPE) {             /* Escape key?             */
        return ESCAPE;
    }
    if (temp < ASCII_LIMIT) {         /* Single character?       */
        tptr = memchr(cptr, tolower(temp), menucount);
        if (tptr) {
            last = tptr - cptr;       /* Found a match           */
            return ENTER;
        }
    }
    return temp - EXTEND_OFF;         /* Extended keycode?       */
    }
}
```

Another thing to notice is that the call to mouse_counters() keeps track of both vertical (dvm) and horizontal (dhm) movements. The switch statement and the direction value determine which value to return to the calling program. If no mouse press or movement is read, _kbhit() is called in the same way as in the previous version of read_key(). This variation of the function is a little smarter than the version presented earlier, because the user can press the Escape key to abort the menu-selection process. The remainder of the read_key() function is the same as the version shown in listing 4.8.

Again, notice that you use the special _kbhit() rather than any kbhit() that might be supplied with your compiler. This is necessary because of the special way that the _kbhit() decodes the function keys.

Other Support Functions for Box Menus

Although most of the difficult parts of the box menu system have been covered, there still are a few support functions that need to be discussed.

Unhighlight a Menu Option—*restore( )*

Several smaller functions are called by the box menuing system. The first discussed is restore(), seen in listing 4.16.

Listing 4.16. *The* restore() *function.*

```
/*****
                            restore()

    This function is used to print a string in the menu box in its
    unhighlighted state.

    Argument list:     struct MENU m[]      the array of structures that
                                            contains the menu choices
                       int row              the row to unhighlight
                       int fore             the foreground color used
                       int back             the background color used

    Return value:      void

*****/

#include "menu.h"

void restore(MENU m[], int row, int fore, int back)
{
    char buff[MAXWIDE];

    memset(buff, ' ', MAXWIDE);
    buff[menulen + 1] = '\0';
    cursor(row, pcol);
    printf("%s", buff);
    cursor(row, pcol);
    colorstr(m[last].prompt, fore, back << 4);
}
```

The restore() function's job is to turn off the currently highlighted menu option. To do this, you must erase the option from the menu and then restore it to its unhighlighted state. There are several ways to do this, but the one used here is rather simple yet efficient. The call to memset() has the effect of initializing buff[] to MAXWIDE blank spaces. (MAXWIDE is defined in menu.h.) Because buff[] is to be used as a string, you use menulen to write a null termination character at the appropriate spot in buff[]. After the string is constructed, position the cursor and print out the string. You should use printf() rather than the shorter puts() function because puts() always writes a new line after the string. This could scroll the screen in some situations.

After the string of blanks has erased the highlighted option, call colorstr() to display the same string in its unhighlighted state.

Redraw the Contents of the Box Window—*redraw_window( )*

Eventually, you will need to erase and redraw everything in the box. It is tempting to call this function redraw_box(), but that is not what the function actually does. Rather, it cleans and redraws the window within the box. That is, only the menu options presented within the box are redrawn. The code is shown in listing 4.17.

Listing 4.17. *The* redraw_window() *function.*

```
/*****

                        redraw_window()

    This function redraws the list of menu options when certain
    keystrokes require it (for example, Page Up).

    Argument list:    MENU m[]       the array of menu entries
                      int first      the top menu item in the window
                      int fore       the foreground color
                      int limit      the number of lines in the window

    Return value:     void

*****/

#include "menu.h"
```

continues

Listing 4.17. continued

```
void redraw_window(MENU m[], int first, int fore, int limit)
{
    int i;
    scroll(prow, pcol - 1, menulen, limit - 2, 0, 6);
    for (i = 0; i < limit; i++) {
        cursor(prow + i, pcol);
        colorstr(m[first + i].prompt, fore, 0);
    }
}
```

The function first scrolls the entire window inside the box. This has the effect of erasing everything within the box. A for loop then prints out the new menu options, using first as the index for displaying the proper options. Because the last argument to colorstr() is 0, the function always displays the new options on a black background.

Relative Menu Position Indicator—
indicator( )

If you call box_select() with something other than 0 as the last argument, you are requesting that a position indicator also be shown as part of the menu display. The actual value passed can be whatever symbol you want to use. However, a left-pointing triangle (a decimal value of 17) looks nice. When the menu first is called, the marker will appear on the immediate right of the menu box, aligned with the first menu option.

The indicator's usefulness is most apparent when the list of options is much longer than the box's depth. For example, if the menu includes 18 items and limit equals 6, you must press the down-arrow key three times before the indicator moves down one line. That is, the indicator's position is scaled to the size of the menu list relative to the box size. The indicator, therefore, gives you an idea of your relative position when the menu is longer than the box.

The code for indicator() is presented in listing 4.18.

Listing 4.18. *The* `indicator()` *function.*

```
/*****
                            indicator()

    This function keeps track of the scroll indicator's location on
    the screen. It gives an approximation of where the user is in the
    menu.

    Argument list:    int fore       foreground color
                      int marker     the symbol used
                      int limit      the number of lines in the window

    Return value:     void

*****/

#include "menu.h"

void indicator(int fore, int marker, int limit)
{
    static int offset = 0;

    cursor(prow + offset, pcol + menulen + 2);    /* Erase old marker   */
    colorchr(' ', fore, 0);

    offset = last / increment;                    /* Find position      */
    if (offset > limit - 1)                       /* Keep within bounds */
        offset = limit - 1;
    cursor(prow + offset, pcol + menulen + 2);    /* Show it            */
    colorchr(marker, fore, 0);
}
```

The indicator's old position must be erased before its new position is drawn. The first calls to `cursor()` and `colorstr()` erase the old indicator. The new position is calculated using the value for `increment`, as determined in `box_menu_start()` and `last`. Because `last` represents your last menu position, `offset` is the indicator's new position. Then `offset` is used to position the cursor and call `colorstr()` to display the indicator at its new location.

Close the Box—*close_box( )*

The final function, `close_box()`, simply clears off the window and frees the allocation that was used for `cptr`. The code appears in listing 4.19.

Listing 4.19. *The* `close_box()` *function.*

```
/*****
                            close_box()

    This function is used to remove the menu box from the screen.
The offsets are necessary because of the way the arguments in
box_menu_start() have been altered.

    Argument list:     void

    Return value:      void

*****/

#include "menu.h"

void close_box(void)
{
    scroll(prow - 1, pcol - 2, menulen + 3, menucount + 1, 0, 6);
    free(cptr);
}
```

The function calls `scroll()` to erase the box menu from the screen and `free()` to release the storage associated with `cptr`. You should note that this does not restore the screen. (See the discussion of the `box_select` function earlier in this chapter.)

One final note: The return value from `box_select()` is the index number into the MENU structure array. That is, if the user selects the first option on the list, the return value from `box_select()` is 0. Also keep in mind that a number of the support functions (such as `read_key()` and `read_key_d()`) in the menuing system are useful as stand-alone functions.

Box Embellishments

You might want to experiment with a box menu system that overlays the screen, presents the box menu, and then restores the screen to its original state after the menu selection has been made. This subject is discussed in detail in Chapter 10, "Text Windows." Chapter 11, "Putting It All Together," shows a complete application using this type of windowing system (plus many other functions presented in this book). The rest of this section presents a simplified view that lets you experiment with such a windowing system until you read about the details in Chapter 10.

You can implement a windowing system in several ways. The easiest is simply to switch the video page number when the box menu is presented and then switch it back when the selection is made. This is not a true windowing system, but when it is properly coded it gives the appearance of being one.

The second (and preferred) method requires saving the contents of the screen before activating the box menu, and restoring it when the selection is made. A simple demonstration of a windowing system can be shown with as few as three functions. The first of these demonstration functions, prepare(), is presented in listing 4.20.

Listing 4.20 The prepare() *function.*

```
/*****
                        prepare()

    This function is called before using either save_screen() or
    write_screen(). It sets the base address from which the screen is
    referenced and determines how many columns are in use.

    The variable start and maxwide are assumed to be global variables
    capable of holding a 4-byte pointer (for example, a far pointer).

    Argument list:    void

    Return value:     void

*****/

extern char far *start;
extern int maxwide;
```

continues

Listing 4.20. *continued*

```
void prepare(void)
{
    int mode;

    mode = getvmode();
    maxwide = getvcols();

    start = (mode == 7) ? (char far *) 0xb00000001 : (char far *) 0xb80000001;
}
```

The purpose of prepare() is to determine the width of the video display (it could be 40 columns) and to set the base memory address of the display. Because you will be using only the text mode, the base address will be either 0xb0000000 (monochrome) or 0xb8000000 (color). The function assumes that the variables maxwide and start are globals. (You could add them to the menu.h header file.) The next function to consider is save_screen(), shown in listing 4.21.

Listing 4.21. *The save_screen() function.*

```
/*****
                        save_screen()

    This function is used to save the contents of a text screen,
starting at row-col for deep rows. Each row has wide characters in
it. The contents are copied into the buffer pointed to by s.

    Argument list:    int row      starting row position
                      int col      starting column position
                      int wide     the width of each row to save
                      int deep     the number of rows to save
                      char *s      a buffer to hold the data

    Return value:     void

*****/

extern char far *start;
extern int maxwide;
```

```
void save_screen(int row, int col, int wide, int deep, char *s)
{
   char far *base;
   int col_offset, i, j, pass, row_offset;

   prepare();
   base = start;

   row--;                                  /* Screen based on 0,0     */
   col--;
   row_offset = maxwide * sizeof(int);   /* For a row increment     */
   col_offset = col * sizeof(int);       /* A column offset         */
   pass = wide * 2;                       /* One element width       */

   base += (row * row_offset + col_offset);
   for (i = 0; i < deep; i++) {
     for (j = 0; j < pass; j++, s++) {
        *s =  *(base + (i * row_offset) + j);
     }
   }
}
```

The purpose of save_screen() is to store the contents of the screen that will be overlaid by the box menu. The function assumes that a buffer has been allocated with sufficient size to store the screen information. Consider the following example:

```
 char *s;

s = (char *) calloc(rows * width, 2);
if (s == '\0') {
   printf("No memory\n");
   exit(0);
}
```

In the example, it is assumed that the box menu will be rows deep and width wide. However, because each character on the screen will have a character and an attribute byte, each character on the screen actually requires two bytes of storage. The storage allocated for s becomes the last argument in save_screen().

The variable named row_offset determines how much to increment the screen address each time you want to store another row. The pass variable tells you how many bytes to store, and col_offset tells you where on the screen to begin storing the data.

When save_screen() returns to the caller, s will contain the contents of the screen (with the attribute byte) for the area of the screen that eventually will hold the box menu.

If you assume that you have presented the box menu and the user has made a selection, you need to restore the screen to its original status by writing the contents of s back to the screen. The function to do this is shown in listing 4.22.

Listing 4.22. *The* write_screen() *function.*

```
/*****
                              write_screen()

     This function is used to write the contents of s to a screen
  position, starting at row-col for deep rows. Each row has wide
  characters in it. The contents are copied from the buffer to the
  screen.

     Argument list:    int row       starting row position
                       int col       starting column position
                       int wide      the width of each row to write
                       int deep      the number of rows to write
                       char *s       the buffer that holds the data

     Return value:     void

*****/

extern char far *start;
extern int maxwide;

void write_screen(int row, int col, int wide, int deep, char *s)
{
   char far *base;
   int col_offset, i, j, pass, row_offset;

   base = (char far *) start;

   row--;
   col--;
   row_offset = maxwide * sizeof(int);    /* For a row increment   */
   col_offset = col * sizeof(int);        /* A column offset       */
   pass = wide * sizeof(int);             /* One element width     */
```

```
    base += (row * row_offset + col_offset);
    for (i = 0; i < deep; i++) {
        for (j = 0; j < pass; j++, s++) {
            *(base + (i * row_offset) + j) = *s;
        }
    }
}
```

The code presented in listing 4.22 is virtually the opposite of save_screen(). The contents of s simply are written back to the screen as set by base. Because the box menu is overwritten with the previous contents of the screen, the box menu takes on a "pop-up menu" appearance.

If you experiment with the previous three functions, you will gain an understanding of how a windowing system works. Chapter 10, "Text Windows," expands on the basic concepts presented in this chapter to build a more complex menu system. The new menuing system draws on both the slidebar and box menus, but it uses a windowing system to restore whatever is on the screen when a menu list is presented. Chapter 10 also tells how to construct message boxes (for example, program alerts or on-line help messages) and dialog (input) boxes. For now, however, listings 4.20 through 4.22 lay the groundwork for Chapter 10.

Conclusion

The slidebar and box menuing systems give two different ways of presenting menu selections to the user. The slidebar menu is most useful when the number of options is rather small but a description of each menu option is desired. Additionally, a slidebar menu can be left on the screen as the program runs, with the output presented in lines 3 through 24.

The primary advantage of the box menu is that the number of items in the menu is not limited to the width of a single line or the depth of the screen. Because the contents of a box menu can be scrolled within the box, any reasonable number of menu options can be processed easily.

The two menuing system alternatives presented here should satisfy most of your menuing requirements. (If not, read Chapter 10, "Text Windows," before you give up!)

If you want to experiment with a system that can flip quickly through multiple menus, refer to Chapter 1, "Screen Functions," and restudy the getvpage() and setvpage() functions. Chapter 2, "String Processing," describes the cursor() function, which enables you to use any video page you want. Using these functions, you can write different menus on different pages of video memory and flip through them as needed.

Searching, Sorting, and Parsing

I n the previous chapters, you learned how to create new functions to accomplish specific tasks. This chapter, however, is a bit different. Because the tasks of searching, sorting, and parsing are common to many programming situations, the standard C library already contains the functions you need to perform these operations. So rather than reinventing the wheel, this chapter focuses on the use of standard C library resources to solve the problems of searching, sorting, and parsing (which will be called *SSP* from now on).

In almost any SSP task, the primary complication arises from the different data types that must be handled. If one program sorts a list of integer data types, for example, another program sorts character arrays. If one task searches for a person's name, the next task searches for a phone number or wage rate. If programmers always used the same data type, life would be easier. Life and programs, however, do not work that way.

All searching and sorting routines involve a common task. That is, they must compare two data items before advancing to the next step. The code to perform the comparison, however, must be written specifically for the data type to be compared. In some languages, the programmer is doomed to writing a sort routine for each data type.

Fortunately, C has a wonderful way of coping with such difficulties— the pointer to function. Using the pointer to function, you can write a generalized sort routine that is data *un*specific. The approach is simply

219

"divide and conquer," and it involves separating the general tasks from the specific ones. In a sorting problem, for example, the data comparison requires a data-specific solution; the rest of the sort algorithm does not care what data type is used. Therefore, many SSP functions actually have two parts: the generalized, data-unspecific part, and a part that deals with a specific data type. As a general rule, the standard C library provides the first part. You must provide the second.

So how do you make these two parts communicate with each other? The most common solution is to pass the standard library function (part 1) a pointer to the function that you write (part 2) to solve the data-specific elements of the problem. The beauty of this approach is that you do not need to worry about how the sort algorithm works; you instead can concentrate on the parts that need your attention.

This chapter, therefore, has two purposes. First, it shows you how to use the SSP (part 1) functions in the standard C library. Second, it shows you how to write support functions that make the SSP functions work properly.

Searching

Many programming tasks are based on the need to find a single data item in a large group of items. In some cases, the group already is ordered, and a binary search is possible. In other cases, when the data items are in random order, either another algorithm must be used, or the data must be sorted before the search. This section presents existing standard C library routines for searching through a group of data.

Binary Search—*bsearch( )*

A local radio show has a daily game in which a listener tries to guess a secret, preselected number between 1 and 1,000. After each guess, the announcer says "higher" or "lower," depending on where the target number is relative to the listener's guess. If the listener guesses the number before the allotted time runs out, he wins that number of dollars.

Most listeners use a binary search algorithm to play the game, although I doubt that most of them have any idea what the definition of a "binary search algorithm" is. The principle of the binary search algorithm is simple: Start at the list's midpoint and see whether the desired value is above or below that point. If the midpoint is too low, discard the lower half and set the new midpoint halfway between the old midpoint—plus one—and the end point. In the radio game example, the first guess would be 500. If the announcer says, "Too low," the next guess is 750 (that is, approximately (501 + 1000) / 2). If that number still is too low, the next guess is 875 ((751 + 1000) / 2). If 875 is too high, the next guess is 812 ((751 + 874) / 2). Eventually, the listener closes in on the proper number.

For a binary search to work properly, you first must know how many items are in the list to be searched. Without this information, there is no way to set the midpoint. Next, the list of data items must be in sorted order. If both of these conditions are met, you can use a binary search on the data, regardless of the type of data being searched.

Your only task in using bsearch() is to set up the function call properly and develop the compare function. Two examples will show you how to do this. The first, shown in listing 5.1, is a simple search of a list of integer values. The second example illustrates a search of a list of strings, which forces you to work with more complex attribute lists.

Listing 5.1. *Binary search on an integer list.*

```
/*
                    Integer binary search example
*/

#include <stdio.h>
#include <stdlib.h>                  /* Normally the prototype is here */

#define MAXNUM 100

int list[MAXNUM];

void main(void)
{
   char buff[20];
   int i, compare(int *s1, int *s2), *ptr, val;

   for (val = i = 0; i < MAXNUM; i++, val += 5)
      list[i] = val;

   for (;;) {
      printf("\nEnter value to find (-1 = End): ");
      val = atoi(gets(buff));
      if (val == -1) {
```

continues

Listing 5.1. *continued*

```
        break;
    }
    ptr = (int *) bsearch(&val, list, MAXNUM, sizeof(int),
                (int(*)(const void *, const void *))compare);
    if (ptr != NULL) {
        printf("\nFound %d in the list", *ptr);
    } else {
        printf("\n%d not in list", val);
    }
    }
}


/*****

                        compare()

    This function compares two integers for use with the bsearch()
    function.

    Argument list:    int *s1      pointer to first argument (target)
                      int *s2      pointer to second argument (from
                                   list)

    Return value:     int          0 if a match; otherwise, the net of
                                   s1 - s2.
*****/

int compare(int *s1, int *s2)
{
    return (*s1 - *s2);
}
```

This example defines an array of integers named list[], which are stuffed with 100 (MAXNUM) values using a for loop. To make the example a little more interesting, the values are multiples of five; therefore, you can enter a value that is not on the list but still is within the list's range limits. After list[] is initialized, the user enters a value (val) to be used in the search.

The call statement

```
ptr = (int *) bsearch(&val, list, MAXNUM, sizeof(int),
                (int(*)(const void *, const void *))compare);
```

initiates the binary search. The first argument is the value that must be found in the list. Because bsearch() expects the first argument to be a pointer, the "address of" operator (&) must appear in the argument. The second argument is the base address of the list to be searched. The third argument tells bsearch() how many items are in the list, and the fourth argument is the size of each item in the list.

The final argument is the name of the function that is responsible for comparing two items in the list. Whenever you use a function name without trailing parentheses, the expression resolves to a pointer. The pointer contains the address of the function's location in memory. In other words, compare becomes a pointer whose rvalue is the memory address of compare's location. You also must declare what compare is before calling bsearch(). This is why the statement

```
int i, compare(int *s1, int *s2), *ptr, val;
```

contains the declaration of compare(). Because the compiler knows that compare() is a function by the time it reaches the call to bsearch(), it will convert the compare argument to the proper pointer to function.

Some compilers (for example, Borland) are particular about how the pointer to the compare function appears in the bsearch() call. Specifically, the pointer must be cast to match the function prototype that appears in the stdlib.h header file. In our case, the cast is

```
( int(*) (const void *, const void *) ) compare
```

which says that compare is a pointer to an integer function (the int (*) part of the cast) that has two arguments (the two const void * type specifiers). Note that the cast matches the function prototype with respect to the function arguments, not the arguments themselves. That is, even though you know you are using integer pointers in the compare() function, some compilers might insist that you treat them as const void pointers in the bsearch() function call.

The compare() function itself is very simple. Just remember that bsearch() always passes the comparison routine two pointers, not the actual values themselves. You also should note that the return value from the compare() function must be zero if a match is found, a negative value if the target value is less than the current item being compared on the list, or a positive value if the target value is greater than the current item on the list. In fact, you would write the compare() function as shown in listing 5.2.

Listing 5.2. *Alternative* compare() *function.*

```
int compare(int *s1, int *s2)
{
    if (*s1 == *s2)            /* Match             */
        return 0;
    if (*s1 < *s2)            /* s1 smaller than s2 */
        return -1;
    else
        return 1;              /* s1 larger than s2  */
}
```

If a match occurs, compare() must return zero. In all other cases, only the result's sign is important; the magnitude of the return value is not important. Although listing 5.2 is wordier than the compare() function in listing 5.1, either will work. Also, the version shown in listing 5.1 might have problems if something other than the normal ASCII character set is used.

One word of caution: Although the comparison routine's first argument normally is the value being searched for, using the first argument as the search key is not actually required by the specifications on bsearch(). Therefore, if your compare() routine does not work properly, insert a printf() near the top of the compare() function to see whether the arguments are reversed.

A Second *bsearch()* Example

Because this example changes things slightly, you must write a compare() function that uses arguments with a different attribute list. In this case, you are searching the function names in list[]. The code is presented in listing 5.3.

Listing 5.3. bsearch() *using an array of pointers to* char.

```
#include <stdio.h>
#include <string.h>

char *list[] = {
    "abs", "bsearch", "fclose", "fgetc", "fileno", "fputs",
    "gets", "putchar", "strcat", "strchr", "strtok", "toupper"
    };
```

```
#define SIZE (sizeof(list) / sizeof(list[0]))

void main(void)
{
   char buff[20], **ptr;
   int compare(char *s1, char **s2);

   buff[0] = '\0';
   for (;;) {
      printf("\nEnter word to find: ");
      gets(buff);
      if (buff[0] == '#') {
         break;
      }
      ptr = (char **) bsearch(buff, list, SIZE, sizeof(list[0]),
                  (int(*)(const void *, const void *))compare);
      if (ptr != (char **) NULL) {
         printf("\nFound %s in the list", *ptr);
      } else {
         printf("\n%s not in list", buff);
      }
   }
}

/*****

                           compare()
```

This function compares two strings for use with the bsearch()
function. Note that the function arguments are defined with
different attribute lists.

```
Argument list:     int *s1       pointer to target string
                   int **s2      pointer to list member

Return value:      int           0 if a match; otherwise, the net of
                                 s1 - s2.
*****/


int compare(char *s1, char **s2)
{
   return (strcmp(s1, *s2));
}
```

In this case, the list is an array of pointers to char, so the comparison function must be written differently. In buff[], the user enters a name to be used in the search. The attribute list for buff is pointer to char. The list to be searched, however, is an array of pointers to char. The compare() function, therefore, must account for the different attribute lists.

By the way, an extensible yet portable way to determine an array's size is shown in the line

```
#define SIZE (sizeof(list) / sizeof(list[0]))
```

This method works with any array size. Furthermore, the array's size automatically is adjusted when items are added to or taken from the list.

In listing 5.3, the compare() function's first argument is pointer to char (the attribute list for buff). The second argument is pointer to pointer to char (the attribute list for list[]). Because pointer to pointer to char is syntactically the same as an array of pointers to char, the function arguments are set up correctly.

The compare() function simply returns the result of a call to strcmp(). This works because strcmp() just happens to return (negative, zero, or positive) values in a manner that bsearch() requires. Also notice that the cast in listing 5.3 for the compare() function is the same as that in listing 5.1.

Finally, novice programmers often forget that, because strcmp() expects pointers to be passed to it, they must back up one level of indirection when calling strcmp(). This is why s2 shows two levels of indirection in the function prototype for compare(), but only one level when used in the call to strcmp(). Think about it.

The bsearch() function is simple to use, but it also is flexible because it can be used with a variety of data types. When you write the compare function, however, be sure that the attribute lists are the same for the two variables being compared. With that caveat, you should have no difficulty using bsearch() in many searching tasks.

Searching for Characters—*memchr()*

Sometimes you need to find a single character in a character array. The ANSI standard C library's memchr() function efficiently accomplishes the task. The prototype for memchr() is

```
char *memchr(const void *s1, int letter, size_t num)
```

in which

s1   is the string to be searched

letter   is the character to be found

num   is the maximum number of characters to search

Listing 5.4 presents a sample program using memchr().

Listing 5.4. *Character searching with* memchr().

```
/*
                        memchr() example
*/

#include <stdio.h>
#include <string.h>          /* Prototype might be in mem.h or memory.h */

void main(void)
{
   char c, s1[500], *ptr;

   printf("\nEnter a sentence: ");
   gets(s1);
   printf("\nNow enter the character to find:");
   c = getch();
   ptr = memchr(s1, c, strlen(s1));
   if (ptr == NULL) {
     printf("\nCould not find %c in the string.", c);
     } else {
         printf("\nMatch at s1[%d] in the string.", ptr - s1);
     }
}
```

The string to be searched is held in s1[], and the character to locate is c. If the ptr returned from memchr() is non-null, a match was found, so the appropriate message is displayed. A null pointer means that no match was found.

The string.h header file should contain the memchr() prototype. Some compilers (like UNIX System V), however, place the prototype in memory.h, and others might place it in a header file of their own choice (such as mem.h). Check your documentation to see which one is applicable for your compiler.

While `memchr()` is being discussed, you should note that the family of "mem" functions (`memccpy()`, `memchr()`, `memcmp()`, `memcpy()`, and `memset()`) are more efficient than their "str" counterparts. Still, you might see published code similar to the following code:

```
int i;
double x[MAXNUM];

.
.

for (i = 0; i < MAXNUM; i++)
   x[i] = 0.0;
.
.
```

The loop does nothing more than set all elements of the `x[]` array to zero. The same task is accomplished more efficiently with the statement:

```
memset(x, 0, sizeof(double) * MAXNUM);
```

The first argument simply is the `lvalue` of the data item to set to zero. The second argument is the initialized value for each byte in the array. The third argument is the number of bytes to initialize. Because `x[]` is a `double` data type, `sizeof(double)` calculates the proper number of bytes per element. Multiplying by `MAXNUM` gives the total number of bytes to initialize.

In timing tests on double-dimensioned floating-point arrays, the `memset()` version was more than twice as fast as the loop version. If your program needs to initialize large arrays multiple times, using `memset()` might produce a noticeable speed improvement.

Generally, the "mem" functions are somewhat more efficient than their "str" cousins. You might want to experiment with your compiler and compare the two alternatives. Because the "menu" functions are defined in the ANSI standard library and in UNIX System V, they should be rather portable across environments.

Searching for Strings—*strstr( )*

One rather common programming task involves finding a certain character pattern within a larger number of characters. An example is the search function used in most word processors. The user types in the word or words to be found, and the program searches through a file until the match is (or is not) located. You can think of this process as searching for strings within strings.

Every ANSI-compatible compiler provides a function called strstr() that searches a string for a specified pattern. Although pre-ANSI compilers (modeled after the UNIX System V library) did not supply the strstr() function, almost all compilers now include it.

The function declaration for strstr() is

```
char *strstr(const char *s1, const char *s2);
```

in which

s1 is a pointer to the string to be searched

s2 is a pointer to the pattern string to be searched for

Simply stated, you want to look through s1 for any occurrences of s2. A test program for strstr() is given in listing 5.5.

Listing 5.5. *Example of* strstr().

```
/*
                              strstr() example
*/

#include <stdio.h>
#include <string.h>

void main(void)
{
   char s1[500], s2[100], *ptr;

   printf("\nEnter a sentence or two: ");
   gets(s1);
   printf("\nNow enter the pattern to search:");
   gets(s2);
   ptr = strstr(s1, s2);
   if (ptr == NULL) {
      printf("\nCould not find %s in the string.", s2);
   } else {
      printf("\nMatch at %d characters into the string.", ptr - s1);
   }
}
```

The string to be searched is entered into the character array s1[]. The pattern string to search for is held in character array s2[]. The call to strstr() simply uses these two strings to see whether s2[] exists as a subset of s1[]. If a match is found, ptr returns a pointer to the match. Otherwise, a null pointer is returned. The if test on ptr prints out the appropriate message.

If you expect to find multiple occurrences of the pattern string, you can place strstr() in a loop and base the search on the pointer. Code fragment 5.1 shows how this modification might look.

Code Fragment 5.1. *Using* strstr() *for multiple matches.*

```
ptr = s1;
while (ptr != NULL) {
   ptr = strstr(ptr, s2);
   if (ptr == NULL) {
      printf("\nCould not find %s in the string.", s2);
      break;
   } else {
      printf("\nMatch at %d characters into the string.", ptr - s1);
   }
   ptr += strlen(s2);
}
```

In this case, ptr simply is initialized to point to s1[] and is used as the argument to strstr(). Note that ptr is incremented on each pass through the loop.

Using a Sentinel to Speed Up String Searches

Although the searching method presented works fine, it is not very efficient compared to some alternatives. One alternative involves the use of a *sentinel*—a data item that is added to the end of a list to speed up the search process. A sentinel can be used to improve search speed on any list that must be searched in linear fashion (that is, from beginning to end). Unlike a binary search, a linear search does not require the list to be in sorted order. An example will help explain what a sentinel is and how it is used.

Suppose you have a list of 1,000 random numbers stored on disk and you want to see whether a specific value is in the list. Let's assume the value you want to find is 7,777. You probably will use calloc() to reserve enough storage for the 1,000 numbers read from the disk. After that is done, you might have a piece of code that looks something like the following:

```
target = 7777;
for (i = 0; i < 1000; i++)
   if (val[i] == target)
      break;
}
/* The rest of the program */
```

Although it might look as though the loop contains only one statement, actually it contains three. The most obvious is the if statement. The second is the test to see whether you are at the end of the list (i < 1000). The last statement is the increment on i. Now you'll see how a sentinel can be used to speed things up a bit.

When you do the memory allocation to store the 1,000 values, increase the allocation by 1. That is, instead of allocating storage for 1,000 values, allocate storage for 1,001. Now place the target value at the end of the list. This becomes the sentinel value. You now know with certainty that you will find the target value. The issue is whether the match was in the list or on the sentinel value. The modified code might look like this:

```
target = 7777;
while (TRUE) {
   if (val[i] == target)
      break;
   i++;
}
if (i > MAXNUM)
   printf("No match -- found sentinel");
else
   printf("Match at element %d", i);
/* The rest of the program */
```

So what do you gain by using the sentinel? Notice that you no longer have to check for the end of the list—you have eliminated one of the three statements from the loop. Instead, you check i after the loop finishes to see whether you found a true match or the sentinel that was added to the end of the list. Although this simple example wouldn't save much time, using a sentinel can save considerable time when the number of loop iterations is large.

Listing 5.5a shows how the sentinel might be used instead of strstr(), used in listing 5.5.

Listing 5.5a. *Using a sentinel instead of* strstr().

```
/*
                        Sentinel example
*/

#include <stdio.h>
#include <string.h>

#ifndef TRUE
    #define TRUE 1
#endif

void main(void)
{
    char s1[500], s2[100], *ptr, *target;
    int len1, len2;

    printf("\nEnter a sentence or two: ");
    gets(s1);
    len1 = strlen(s1);
    target = s1;
    printf("\nNow enter the pattern to search:");
    gets(s2);
    len2 = strlen(s2);
    strcat(s1, s2);
    while (TRUE) {
        ptr = memchr(target, *s2, len1);
        if (ptr) {
            if (memcmp(target, s2, len2) == 0)
                break;
        }
        target++;
    }
    if (ptr - s1 < len1) {
        printf("\nMatch at %d characters into the string.", ptr - s1);
    } else {
        printf("\nCould not find %s in the string.", s2);
    }
}
```

In this example, the sentinel is the pattern to locate in the string (s2). The call to strcat() places the sentinel at the end of the string. You use memchr() to find a match on the first character of the string being searched because it is somewhat more efficient than strchr(). If the first character in the pattern matches a character in the string being searched, ptr will be non-NULL. You then call memcmp() to see whether there is a match on the entire pattern. If ptr is NULL after the call to memchr(), you increment the pointer to the string and keep looking.

Eventually, you will find a match either in the string or on the sentinel. The last if statement checks to see which was found. Again, the time savings in this trivial example won't be much, but you can expect to save as much as 20 percent in processing time when a sentinel is used. If you want to check this out, try creating a 30K text file and placing a specific pattern near the end of the file. Then modify listings 5.5 and 5.5a to search the file. I think you will find that it is worth the effort to incorporate a sentinel in some of your programming tasks.

Sorting

Like searching, the sorting of data is fundamental to many programming tasks. Indeed, sorting often is a preliminary step to many other tasks (such as using the bsearch() function, mentioned earlier in this chapter). Entire volumes have been written about various sorting algorithms; a short discussion cannot do full justice to sorting. Instead, this section quickly shows you how to make use of the qsort() function provided by the ANSI (and UNIX System V) standard C library.

Generalized Sort Function—*qsort( )*

The arguments to the qsort() function are much the same as those used in the bsearch() function discussed earlier in this chapter. The declaration for qsort() is

```
void qsort(void *base, size_t num, size_t size,
           int (*comp)(const void *arg1, const void *arg2));
```

in which

*base	is a pointer to the start of the list to be sorted
num	is the number of elements in the list
size	is the size of each element in the list
comp	is a pointer to the compare function

As you can see from the prototype, the compare function's code must be supplied. To understand the use of qsort(), look at a reworked version of the bsearch() example (see listing 5.3). The revised example is shown in listing 5.6.

Listing 5.6. *The* qsort() *example.*

```c
#include <stdio.h>
#include <stdlib.h>
#include <string.h>

char *list[] = {
    "strcat", "bsearch", "putchar", "fclose", "strchr", "gets",
    "fileno", "strtok", "toupper", "abs", "fgetc", "fputs"
    };

#define SIZE (sizeof(list) / sizeof(list[0]))

void main(void)
{
   int compare(char **s1, char **s2), i;

   qsort(list, SIZE, sizeof(list[0]),
        (int(*)(const void *, const void *)) compare);
   for (i = 0; i < (int) SIZE; i++) {
      printf("\n%s", list[i]);
   }
}


/*****

                            compare()

    This function compares two pointers to char for use with qsort().

    Argument list:    int **s1      pointer to first comparison argument
                      int **s2      pointer to second comparison argument

    Return value:     int           0 if a match; otherwise, the net of
                                    s1 - s2.
*****/
```

```
int compare(char **s1, char **s2)
{
    return (strcmp(*s1, *s2));
}
```

The contents of list[] have been scrambled so that they are not in sorted order. All main() does is call qsort() and then print out the sorted list. The compare() function is the same as the one seen in listing 5.3, except that the attribute lists for both arguments are now the same (pointer to pointer to char, or an array of pointers to char). The strcmp() function simply returns a value based on the comparison of the two strings. (If you want to see what is going on, insert a printf() at the top of the compare() function to print the contents of s1 and s2.)

Again, some compilers complain if the cast for the last argument to qsort() is not stated explicitly.

To underline the importance of using the correct attribute list in the compare() function, consider code fragment 5.2.

Code Fragment 5.2. *An alternative* compare() *using the same attribute list.*

```
int compare(char *s1[], char *s2[])
{
    return (strcmp(s1[0], s2[0]));
}
```

Keeping the Attributes Matched

Even though the function has a somewhat different syntax, the function arguments' attribute list is the same for the compare() function in listing 5.6 and code fragment 5.2. In both cases, the attribute list is an array of pointers to char. The primary concern when writing the compare() function, therefore, is keeping the attribute list for the arguments correct. If you remember that qsort() passes pointers to the compare() function, you should not have any problems.

Parsing

Parsing is somewhat different from searching. In parsing, you primarily are concerned with breaking a large data item into smaller parts so that a specific action can take place. A common example is parsing a program's command line into separate arguments and then using those arguments in the program. This section presents two standard C library functions that can be used for parsing.

Parse a String—*strtok( )*

The `strtok()` function is an ANSI standard C library function that can be used to parse a string into substrings. The prototype for `strtok()` is

```
char *strtok(char *s1, const char *s2);
```

in which

s1   is the string to be parsed

s2   is the delimiters, or separators, for tokens

The purpose of `strtok()` is to break a large string (s1) into tokens whenever a delimiter is read. A simple example will show how `strtok()` works. Suppose that s1 looks like the following:

```
s1 = "Jones,Sam#123 Main Street:Indianapolis,IN,46220"
```

and that the separator string contains

```
s2 = ",#:";
```

When `strtok()` first is called using s1 and s2, the function scans s1 from the first character *not* in s2 to the first character in s2, and it writes a null into s1 at that point. It then returns a pointer to the first character in that token. If `strtok()` is called a second time with a NULL pointer as the first argument (replacing s1), the parse continues, with the character immediately following the separator character found on the first call to `strtok()`. This continues until s1 is exhausted.

Using the example just given, the delimiters are a comma (,), the pound sign (or sharp, #), and a colon (:). Therefore, the tokens returned from `strtok()` would be

```
Jones
Sam
123 Main Street
```

```
Indianapolis
IN
46220
```

The code in listing 5.7 contains a simple shell program that can be used to experiment with strtok(). It will help make clear exactly what strtok() does.

Listing 5.7. *Program using strtok().*

```
/*
                          strtok() example
*/

#include <stdio.h>
#include <stdlib.h>
#include <string.h>

void main(void)
{
   char buff[200], delim[50], *ptr;

   printf("Enter up to 175 characters to examine (s1): ");
   gets(buff);
   printf("Enter a string for the delimiter (s2): ");
   gets(delim);
   ptr = strtok(buff, delim);
   for (;;) {
      if (ptr == NULL) {
         break;
      }
      printf("\nptr = %s", ptr);
      ptr = strtok( (char *) 0, delim);      /* Note the null pointer */
   }
}
```

With some experimenting, you will find that strtok() can be used for all kinds of parsing tasks, from extracting information from data files to tokenizing C source files as part of the compilation process. This function is a good solution to many parsing problems.

Parse Command-Line Arguments— *getopt( )*

Like `strtok()`, the `getopt()` function is a parsing function, but it is designed to handle different tasks. The `getopt()` function parses a program's command line into one or more arguments for use by the program. The `getopt()` function is not part of the ANSI standard C library, but it is included in the UNIX System V standard C library.

You first should examine the `getopt()` function declaration and the supporting data definitions that make the function work properly. The function prototype is

```
int getopt(int argc, char *argv[], char *optstring);
```

in which

`argc`	is the argument count
`*argv[]`	is the argument vector
`*optstring`	is a pointer to a string of valid arguments

In addition, `getopt()` relies on the following support variables:

```
extern char *optarg;
extern int optind, opterr;
```

in which

`*optarg`	is a pointer to a command-line argument if one is required by a command-line option.
`optind`	is the option index. It is initialized to 1 and is used for indexing into `argv[]`.
`opterr`	is the option error flag. If the flag is set to 1, the function prints a question mark (?) on `stderr` along with a predefined error message if an argument is read that is not found in `optstring`. If set to 0, the error message is not printed.

Although the UNIX standard library documentation does not explicitly say so, each command-line argument is assumed to be preceded by a dash (-) character. If a colon follows a character in `optstring`, that character can be followed by an argument. Finally, if a double dash (--) is read, command-line parsing stops. This feature enables you to pass additional command-line arguments that might not be parsed by `getopt()`.

A sample command line illustrates how all this fits together. Suppose that optstring is defined as

```
static char *optstring = "dDl:L:vV";
```

and the command line is

```
program -d -ltest.obj -V -- X
```

When getopt() parses the command line, it recognizes -d, -l, and -V as valid command-line options because they all are included in optstring. Note that uppercase and lowercase are different to getopt(). If you want your program to recognize either upper- or lowercase letters for the same option, you must include both upper- and lowercase letters.

Notice that the letters l and L are followed by a colon in optstring. The colon indicates that this letter can be followed by an argument string. In the example, the argument associated with the -l option is test.obj. When such an argument is detected, getopt() sets optarg to point to the argument. In this example, optarg will point to test.obj, which can be treated as a string. You also can have a space between command-line options with arguments, as in

```
program -d -l test.obj -V -- X
```

Note the blank space between -l and test.obj. The space has no impact on the parsing of the command line; either form yields the same results.

When the double dash is read, getopt() stops parsing the command line and returns EOF (usually -1). This means that the last argument on the command line (X) is never read by getopt(). Because optind is incremented each time another command-line argument is processed, however, a check against optind and argc reveals any "unparsed" command-line arguments. Another section of the program might use argument X, using the normal argc-argv processing.

The double dash is not required to terminate parsing by getopt(). The function also returns EOF when no command-line arguments are left. The double dash is used to terminate getopt() only before all command-line arguments are parsed.

Although the ANSI standard C library does not provide a getopt(), it still can be an extremely useful function. Listing 5.8 illustrates the use of getopt() and presents the function's source code.

Listing 5.8. *Example using* getopt().

```c
/*
                            getopt() example
*/

#include <stdio.h>
#include <stdlib.h>
#include <string.h>

extern char *optarg;
extern int optind, opterr;

void main(int argc, char *argv[])
{
    int i;
    static char *optstring = "EeCcVvL:l:";

    optind = 0;
    opterr = 1;                              /* You want error messages    */

    while ((i = getopt(argc, argv, optstring)) != EOF) {
        switch (i) {
            case 'C':
            case 'c':
                printf("\nCase c detected");
                break;
            case 'E':
            case 'e':
                printf("\nCase e detected");
                break;
            case 'V':
            case 'v':
                printf("\nCase v detected");
                break;
            case 'L':
            case 'l':
                printf("\nCase l detected with arg %s", optarg);
                break;
            default:
                printf("\nUnknown command-line option");
                break;
        }
    }
}
```

```
/* getopt() can be compiled and placed in your library */

/*****
                            getopt()

    This function performs command-line parsing. The function uses the
    following external variables:

            char *optarg      a pointer that is initialized to NULL on
                              entry to the function; if a command-line
                              option has an argument, optarg points to
                              the argument

            char *index       a pointer to the next character in the
                              command line

            int optind        an index into the argument vector

            int opterr        a flag that, if set to 0, turns off the
                              display of a predefined error message
                              on stderr; if nonzero, the message is
                              displayed when an error occurs

    In addition, the function uses the following variables in its
    argument list.

    Argument list:   int argc          the argument count from the
                                       command line

                     char *argv[]      the command-line vector
                     char *optstring   a list of valid command-line
                                       options

    Return value:    int               the command-line option or EOF
                                       on error or when parsing is
                                       finished
*****/

#include <stdio.h>
#include <stdlib.h>
#include <string.h>
```

continues

Listing 5.8. *continued*

```c
char *optarg;
static char *index = NULL;
int optind, opterr;

static void get_next_index(void)
{
    ++optind;
    index = NULL;
}

int getopt(int argc, char *argv[], char *optstring)
{
    int fd, i;
    char *ptr = NULL;

    optarg = NULL;
    if (!optind) {                      /* If not set to 1, set it to 1  */
        index = (char *) NULL;
        optind++;
    }
    fd = fileno(stderr);
    while (argv[optind]) {              /* Used for the write() function */
        if (!index) {                   /* If no index string yet        */
            index = argv[optind];
            if (!index || *index != '-') {  /* If still no index and      */
                index = NULL;               /* no dash, we're done        */
                return (EOF);
            }
            if (*(++index) == '-') {    /* Double dash?                  */
                get_next_index();       /* Don't parse any more          */
                return EOF;
            }
            if (!*(index)) {            /* Ready for next iteration       */
                get_next_index();
            }
            continue;
        }
        i = (int) *index++;             /* Look at next character         */
        if (i != ':') {                 /* No command-line argument       */
            ptr = strchr(optstring, i); /* Is i in list of options?       */
            if (ptr && *(ptr + 1) == ':') { /* Yes plus an argument       */
```

```
            if (*index) {              /* If non-NULL index...     */
                optarg = index;         /* set optarg to point to it  */
            } else {                   /* Else get the next argv     */
                optarg = argv[++optind];
            }
            get_next_index();
            if (!optarg) {             /* Colon but no argument    */
                i = EOF;
                if (opterr) {
                    write(fd, argv[0], strlen(argv[0]));
                    write(fd, ": option requires an argument ", 30);
                    write(fd, &i, sizeof(char));
                    write(fd, "\r\n", 2);
                }
            }
            return (i);                /* Must be an error         */
        }
    }
    if (!(*index)) {                  /* If a null character      */
        get_next_index();
    }
    if (ptr) {                        /* Return the command option */
        return (i);
    } else {                          /* Not in the list          */
        if (opterr) {
            write(fd, argv[0], strlen(argv[0]));
            write(fd, ": illegal option ", 17);
            write(fd, &i, sizeof(char));
            write(fd, "\r\n", 2);
        }
        return ('?');
    }
}
return EOF;                           /* None left                */
}
```

The definition

```
static char *optstring = "EeCcVvL:l:";
```

tells getopt() which characters represent valid command-line options. In the example, upper- and lowercase letters e, c, v, and l are valid options. In addition, the l option can be followed by a command-line argument, such as a file name. The `while` and `switch` statements control the parsing of the command line. The `getopt()` function does all the work, freeing you to concentrate on the command options' role in the program.

If this program were called `getopt()`, loading the program using the command line

```
getopt -v -l source.c -- -e
```

would display

```
Case v detected
Case l detected with arg source.c
```

Even though the `-e` is a valid option, it would not be read because it is preceded by a double dash (`--`). When the entire command line is read, `getopt()` returns EOF and sends control out of the `while` loop, and the program ends.

Conclusion

This chapter discusses only some of the functions provided in the ANSI and UNIX System V standard C libraries. Many of today's C compilers have additional functions for sorting, searching, and parsing, as well as other nonstandard functions that can be used to build new functions for extending those presented here. If you have not already done so, you should spend a day or two just reading about everything in your C library. You might be surprised at what you find.

CHAPTER 6

Time and Dates

This chapter presents several functions that concern times and dates. ANSI has recognized the importance of these two features and has enhanced its standard library to account for programming considerations that must be made because of geography. The format used for stating dates, for example, varies according to locale. Although Americans prefer to record dates in a month/day/year format (MM/DD/YY), Europeans use a day/month/year format (DD/MM/YY), and the Japanese follow a year/month/day format (YY/MM/DD). Time formats are less variable, but programmers still must cope with the 12-hour clock versus the 24-hour clock.

This chapter does not attempt to duplicate the time and date functions found in the ANSI standard C library. Rather, it presents several functions that might be available in some form with your compiler. There are three reasons for presenting these functions here. First, the functions might not be available with your compiler. Second, the functions presented here are considerably more flexible than those shipped with some compilers. Finally, because this text supplies the functions' source code, you can modify them to suit your needs; they might provide a framework on which you can build.

245

Get System Time— *maketime( )*

Most PCs have a system clock that can be read by way of interrupt routines. The maketime() function simply shows you how to gain access to the system time. The code is presented in listing 6.1.

Listing 6.1. *Get system time.*

```
/*****
                              maketime()

    This function formats the system time into the string passed to
    the function, using interrupt 0x21. The function allows for a 12-
    or a 24-hour clock. If a 12-hour clock is used, the input string
    must allow for three more characters to hold the time.

    Argument list:    char *buff      pointer to a character array for
                                      the time
                      int sep         the character to be used to space
                                      the time fields
                      int mode        0 if a 12-hour clock is wanted,
                                      nonzero for a 24-hour clock.

    Return value:     void

*****/

#include <dos.h>

void maketime(char *buff, int sep, int mode)
{
   char time[3];
   union REGS ireg;

   ireg.h.ah = 0x2c;
   intdos(&ireg, &ireg);

   time[0] = '\0';
   if (mode == 0) {
```

```
    if (ireg.h.ch > 12) {
        ireg.h.ch -= 12;
        strcpy(time, " PM");
    } else {
        strcpy(time, " AM");
    }
}
sprintf(buff, "%02d%c%02d%c%02d %s", ireg.h.ch, sep, ireg.h.cl,
            sep, ireg.h.dh, time);

}
```

The function uses interrupt 0x21, function 0x2c to retrieve the system time. As you can see by the arguments passed to the function, this function differs from others like it in several ways.

First, you can use any separator character you like. Most people prefer the HH:MM:SS format, and others like HH MM SS (using a blank space as a separator) or HH-MM-SS. Whatever your preference, you are not limited to a fixed separator character.

Second, the mode argument lets you select a 12-hour or 24-hour format. If the 12-hour format is chosen, the program automatically appends the appropriate "a.m." or "p.m." designator.

Finally, the output is returned in the buffer passed to the function (buff) as a string instead of filling in pointers to the hours, minutes, and seconds. You can, of course, change the function to fill in such variables if you need them. In many situations, however, the time is needed only to time-stamp a piece of information or to be displayed periodically on the screen, so the string should be a useful alternative. (If you need actual time variables, most compilers provide a gettime() function that can be used when a time counter is needed.)

The format for the returned string is such that, if the time is 2:30 in the morning, the output becomes

`02:30:00 AM`

assuming that a colon is the separator character (sep). Note that blank spaces are filled in with zeros, yielding a fixed field width. (This fixed field width can be useful in some database applications.) This "zero-filling" feature is caused by the "%02d" conversion character in the call to sprintf(). If you use "%2d" the field is padded with blank spaces when necessary. If you use "%d" no filling is done, and the return string does not have a fixed field length. Use the format that best suits your needs.

Set System Time—*timeset( )*

The maketime() function assumes that the system clock is correct. Sometimes you will need to set the time yourself. Although MS-DOS provides a program to do this, you might need to set the time while the program is running. The timeset() function presented in listing 6.2 shows how this is done.

Listing 6.2. *Set system time.*

```
/*****
                            timeset()

    This function sets the system time using interrupt 0x21. The
time uses the 24-hour clock.

    Argument list:    int hour      the hour
                      int min       the minute

    Return value:     int           0 if successful, 0xff if not

*****/

#include <dos.h>

int timeset(int hour, int min)
{
    union REGS ireg;

    ireg.h.ah = 0x2d;
    ireg.h.ch = hour;
    ireg.h.cl = min;
    ireg.h.dh = ireg.h.dl = 1;              /* Set seconds and 1/100th   */
    intdos(&ireg, &ireg);
    return (ireg.h.al);
}
```

Function 0x2d of interrupt 0x21 is used to set the system clock. You can set the seconds and even hundredths of a second, but this is unnecessary for most applications. In timeset(), simply set the seconds and hundredths of a second to one and call the interrupt. If your applications need more refinement, simply rewrite the function to pass in the seconds and hundredths of a second.

The return value should be checked because the time might not have been properly set by the function call. (Anyone with a dead CMOS battery knows what I mean.)

Get System Date— *makedate( )*

The makedate() function is comparable to maketime() in that it provides similar format control. The source code is presented in listing 6.3.

Listing 6.3. *Get system date.*

```
/*****
                            makedate()

    This function formats the system date into the string passed to
    the function using interrupt 0x21.

    Argument list:    char *buff    pointer to a character array for
                                    the date
                      int sep       the character to be used to space
                                    the fields
                      int zpad      0 =  no leading zeros
                                    1 =  leading zeros to be printed
                                    ? =  free-form

    Return value:     void

*****/

#include <dos.h>

void makedate(char *buff, int sep, int zpad)
{
    char form[20];
    union REGS ireg;
    ireg.h.ah = 0x2a;
    intdos(&ireg, &ireg);
```

continues

Listing 6.3. *continued*

```
    switch (zpad) {
        case 0:
            strcpy(form, "%02d%c%02d%c%02d");        /* Zero padding  */
            break;
        case 1:
            strcpy(form, "%2d%c%2d%c%2d");            /* Blank space   */
            break;
        default:
            strcpy(form, "%d%c%d%c%d");               /* Free form     */
            break;
    }
    sprintf(buff, form, ireg.h.dh, sep, ireg.h.dl, sep, ireg.x.cx -
        1900);
}
```

Listing 6.3 presents an alternative way of choosing between several output formats. Here, zpad determines which of the three output formats is used to fill in the pointer to the character array pointed to by buff. For example, if the date is May 3, 1991, and you choose a hyphen as the separator character, the various output formats look like this:

```
    05-03-91      /* zpad = 0                */
     5- 3-91      /* zpad = 1                */
     5-3-91       /* zpad = any other value */
```

The switch statement just creates a format string (form[]) that is used in sprintf(). You can change form[] to meet many formatting needs.

Set System Date—*dateset( )*

This function enables you to set the system date in a manner similar to that used in timeset() (see listing 6.2). The source code for dateset() is shown in listing 6.4.

Listing 6.4. *Set system date.*

```
/*****
                            dateset()

    This function sets the system date by using interrupt 0x21. The
date must fall between 1980 and 2099.

    Argument list:    int day      the day
                      int month    the month
                      int year     the year

    Return value:     int          0 if successful, 0xff if not

*****/

#include <dos.h>

int dateset(int day, int month, int year)
{
   union REGS ireg;

   ireg.h.ah = 0x2b;
   ireg.h.dl = day;
   ireg.h.dh = month;
   ireg.x.cx = year;
   intdos(&ireg, &ireg);
   return (ireg.h.al);
}
```

The system date is restricted to dates between 1980 and 2099. (The range's upper end is not a serious restriction for most of us.) Again, the return value should be checked to ensure that the date was set properly.

Pack Time—*packtime()*

One disadvantage of using the system time as a string is that it can take more storage than it might otherwise use. By converting the hours, minutes, and seconds into a different data structure, you can squeeze— or pack—the data into two bytes. Indeed, MS-DOS uses only two bytes for storing the time stamp on disk files.

The MS-DOS format is shown in figure 6.1. As you can see, five bits are allocated for the seconds, six bits for the minutes, and five bits for the hours.

Fig. 6.1. *Packed time format.*

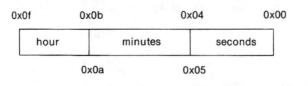

It might seem confusing that 60 seconds can be represented with only five bits. Because 2^5 is 32, there might seem to be a shortage of storage for seconds. MS-DOS solves this problem by storing the seconds as two-second increments, reducing the count stored in the seconds field to 30. The system clock, therefore, has resolution to only two seconds when displaying the clock.

Listing 6.5 presents a packtime() that uses the same scheme for storing the time in one 16-bit quantity.

Listing 6.5. *Pack system time.*

```
/*****

                           packtime()

    This function collapses the time into an unsigned integer using
    the DOS disk format with bits: 0x00 - 0x04 = sec, 0x05 - 0x0a =
    minutes, and 0x0b - 0x0f = hour. Seconds are in two-second
    increments (0 - 29).

    Argument list:    int sec        seconds
                      int min        minutes
                      int hour       hour

    Return value:     unsigned int   the packed time

*****/

unsigned int packtime(int sec, int min, int hour)
{
    unsigned int result;
```

```
    sec >>= 1;                      /* Divide seconds in half        */
    result = sec;
    min <<= 0x05;
    hour <<= 0x0b;
    result += min;
    result += hour;
    return result;
}
```

The function receives the time as three arguments and then simply does some bit-shifting and stores the result in an unsigned int, which then is returned from the call. Be sure to declare that packtime() returns an unsigned int, or you might not get the proper results. You now can store the system time in the least possible space and still have fairly good time resolution.

Unpack Time—*unpacktime( )*

Now you need a function that can unpack the system time from the unsigned int that was created by packtime(). This is the unpacktime() function's purpose. The code for unpacktime() is presented in listing 6.6.

Listing 6.6. *Unpack system time.*

```
/*****

                            unpacktime()

    This function collapses the time into an unsigned integer using
    the DOS disk format with bits: 0x00 - 0x04 = sec, 0x05 - 0x0a =
    minutes, and 0x0b - 0x0f = hour. Seconds are in two-second
    increments (0 - 29).

    Argument list:    int *sec      the day
                      int *min      the month
                      int *hour     the hour
                      int num       the packed number

    Return value:     void

*****/
```

continues

Listing 6.6. *continued*

```
void unpacktime(int *sec, int *min, int *hour, int num)
{
    *sec = (num & 0x1f) * 2;
    *min = (num & 0x7e0) >> 0x05;
    *hour = (num & 0xf800) >> 0x0b;
}
```

The arguments passed to the function are pointers that are used to fill in the appropriate time variables. Each variable is masked with the appropriate bit pattern and then is shifted as needed. The seconds must be multiplied by two because they are stored as two-second increments.

Pack a Date—*packdate( )*

If you can pack time, you also can pack dates. The date field is similar to the MS-DOS time format as shown in figure 6.2.

Fig. 6.2. *Packed date format.*

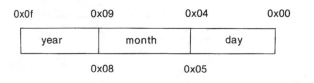

The month and year fields trade a few bits relative to the time format, so the number of years can be extended. All dates assume a base year of 1980. Listing 6.7 presents the code to pack a date.

Listing 6.7. *Pack a date.*

```
/*****

                          packdate()

    This function collapses the date into an unsigned integer, using
    the DOS disk format: 0x00 - 0x04 = day, 0x05 - 0x08 = month, 0x09 -
    0x0f = year. The year is formed relative to 1980.
```

```
        Argument list:    int day       the day
                          int month     the month
                          int year      the year

        Return value:     unsigned int

*****/

unsigned int packdate(int day, int month, int year)
{
   unsigned result = 0;

   result = day;
   month <<= 0x05;
   if (year < 100)                        /* No century given?       */
      year -= 80;
   else
      if (year >= 1980)
         year -= 1980;
   year <<= 0x09;
   result += month;
   result += year;
   return result;
}
```

The function's primary job is to bit-shift the date fields so that they fit the MS-DOS date format. The program will accept a date even if the year is passed in without the century (for example, "91" rather than "1991"). The result is returned as an unsigned integer, so be sure to declare the function before you use it.

Unpack a Date— *unpackdate( )*

A function also is needed to unpack the date. Considering its similarity to the `unpacktime()` function, the source code presented in listing 6.8 should be fairly clear.

Listing 6.8. *Unpack a date.*

```
/*****
                        unpackdate()

    This function unpacks the date from an unsigned integer, using
    the DOS disk format with bits: 0x00 - 0x04 = day, 0x05 - 0x08 =
    month, 0x09 - 0x0f = year. The year is formed relative to 1980.

    Argument list:    int *day       the day
                      int *month     the month
                      int *year      the year
                      int num        the packed number

    Return value:     void

*****/

void unpackdate(int *day, int *month, int *year, unsigned int num)
{
    *day = num & 0x1f;
    *month = (num & 0x1e0) >> 0x05;
    *year = (num & 0xfe00) >> 0x09;
    *year += 1980;                          /* Add offset back in     */
}
```

So that they can be filled in by way of indirection, pointers for the date fields are passed to the function. The variable num is the packed date. Each date field is retrieved using a bit mask on the packed date; the field then is assigned to the appropriate variable. Again, the year is relative to 1980.

Julian Dates—*julian( )*

The Gregorian calendar (which divides the year into 12 months, and each month into a certain number of days) replaced the Julian calendar in 1582. Still, Julian dates are useful in many date and time calculations. Simply stated, the Julian calendar numbers each day of the year according to its ordinal value, from 1 to 365 (or, in a leap year, from 1 to 366). Therefore, February 1 has a Julian date of 32. Listing 6.9 illustrates the code for determining a Julian date.

Listing 6.9. *Julian dates.*

```
/*****
                            julian()

    This function determines the Julian date for the date specified.
    The count includes the day specified.

    Argument list:    int month      the month
                      int day        the day
                      int year       the year

    Return value:     int            the days from Jan 1 to the date

*****/

int julian(int day, int month, int year)
{
    static int runsum[] = {0, 31, 59, 90, 120, 151, 181, 212,
                           243, 273, 304, 334, 365};
    int total;

    total = runsum[month - 1] + day;
    if (month > 2) {
       total += leapyear(year);
    }
    return (total);
}
```

The static array runsum[] is initialized to a running total of the number of days in each month. Because 1 is used as the first month, the array's first element is set to 0. This simplifies the use of the day, month, and year function arguments to determine the Julian date. All you do is index into the runsum[] array.

As you might expect, however, leap years can cause problems. But the problems are easily solved. The leapyear() function (which is presented next) returns 1 if the year is a leap year, 0 otherwise. When the return value from leapyear() is added to the total, the correct Julian date is calculated.

Is It a Leap Year?—*leapyear( )*

A well-known algorithm is used to see whether a year is a leap year: If the year can be evenly divided by 4, but not by 100, it is a leap year. However, years that are evenly divisible by 400 also are leap years. Listing 6.10 presents the algorithm's C code.

Listing 6.10. Leap year calculation.

```
/*****
                              leapyear()

    This function determines whether a certain year is a leap year.

    Argument list:    int year       the year

    Return value:     int            1 if it is a leap year, 0 if not

*****/

int leapyear(int year)
{
   if (year % 4 == 0 && year % 100 != 0 || year % 400 == 0)
      return 1;
   else
      return 0;
}
```

The single if statement does all the work. By making the return value 1 for a leap year and 0 otherwise, you simply can add the return value from leapyear() to any Julian date after February 28.

Day of the Week— *datename( )*

Sometimes you must know not only the date, but the day of the week as well. The next algorithm, based on Zeller's Congruence, uses the date to determine the day of the week. Listing 6.11 presents the code.

Listing 6.11. *Determining the day of the week.*

```
/*****
                            datename()

     This function returns the day of the week for a date. It is
  based on Zeller's Congruence.

     Argument list:    int month      the month
                       int day        the day
                       int year       the year


     Return value:     char *         a pointer to the day of the week

*****/

char *datename(int day, int month, int year)
{
   static char *days[] = {"Sun.", "Mon.", "Tues", "Wed.",
                          "Thur", "Fri.", "Sat.", "Sun."};

   int index;

   if (year < 100)                        /* If century is missing      */
      year += 1900;

   if (month > 2) {                       /* Everything is from February */
      month -= 2;
   } else {
      month += 10;
      year--;
   }

   index = ((13 * month - 1) / 5) + day + (year % 100) + ( (year % 100) / 4)
          + ((year / 100) / 4) - 2 * (year / 100) + 77;
   index = index - 7 * (index / 7);

   return days[index];
}
```

The function's return value is a character pointer to the day of the week.

Difference Between Two Dates—*datecmp( )*

Julian dates are used in financial calculations based on time (interest rate calculations, for example). These calculations often require the number of days between two dates, such as the number of days between a loan's issue and due dates. The datecmp() function in listing 6.12 is designed to return the number of days between two dates.

Listing 6.12. *Number of days between two dates.*

```
/*****

                              datecmp()

     This function returns the number of days elapsed between two
   dates.

   Argument list:    int d1      the day for year 1
                     int m1      the month for year 1
                     int y1      the year for year 1
                     int d2      the day for year 2
                     int m2      the month for year 2
                     int y2      the year for year 2

   Return value:     unsigned int  the number of days from date1
                                   to date2

*****/

unsigned int datecmp(int d1, int m1, int y1, int d2, int m2, int y2)
{
   int i, max, min, t1, t2, years = 0;

   t1 = julian(d1, m1, y1);
   t2 = julian(d2, m2, y2);

   if (y1 != y2) {                          /* Must go across years    */
      if (y1 > y2) {
         max = y1;
         min = y2;
         t2 = julian(31, 12, y2) - t2;   /* Days to end of year      */
```

```
      } else {
         max = y2;
         min = y1;
         t1 = julian(31, 12, y2) - t1;
      }
      for (i = max; i > min + 1; i--) {   /* For all years        */
         years += 365 + leapyear(i);
      }
   } else {
     t1 = julian(d1, m1, y1);
     t2 = julian(d2, m2, y2);
     return (abs(t1 - t2));
   }
   return (t1 + t2 + years);
}
```

The datecmp() function builds on the julian() and leapyear() functions developed earlier in this chapter. The function first finds the Julian dates for the two calendar dates that are passed to datecmp() as function arguments. Next, it must be determined whether the two dates are of the same year and, if not, which of the two dates is the earlier. If the year is the same for both dates, simply return the absolute difference between them.

(The function's return value might seem strange at first, but it is correct. Most people think that there are 365 days between January 1 and December 31 of a non-leap year. Actually, the correct answer is 364 days. The answer is 365 only when the dates are the same.)

If the years are different, you need to know which date is "older." To determine the number of days to the year's end, you must subtract the older date's Julian value from the number of days in the year. Do just the opposite with the "younger" date; calculate from the year's beginning to the date specified. This is the Julian date. Therefore, for the older date the calculation is from the date to the end of the year, but it is simply the Julian date for the younger date. The for loop calculates the number of days for the years between the two dates, accounting for leap years. The return value is an unsigned int, so be sure to declare datecmp() before you use it.

Is the Date Valid?— *valid_date( )*

Now that you can use dates in several ways, you need a function that judges a date's validity. You can do this by using the code presented in listing 6.13.

Listing 6.13. Check for valid date.

```
/*****
                          valid_date()

      This function determines whether a date is valid.

        Argument list:    int month      the month
                          int day        the day
                          int year       the year

        Return value:     int            1 if valid, 0 if not

*****/

int valid_date(int day, int month, int year)
{
   static int days[] = {0, 31, 28, 31, 30, 31, 30,
                           31, 31, 30, 31, 30, 31};

   if (month > 12 ¦¦ month < 1 ¦¦ day > 31 ¦¦ day < 1)
      return 0;

   if (day > days[month]) {
      if (month == 2 && day == 29) {    /* Special check for leap year */
         if (leapyear(year)) {
            return 1;
         }
      }
      return 0;
   }
   return 1;
}
```

Again, `leapyear()` is used to see whether February 29 is a valid date. Because the `days[]` array holds the monthly day totals, the leap year check is the adjustment needed to check for a valid date entry outside the `days[]` array. The function returns 1 if the date is valid and 0 if it is not.

Format Dates for Geographic Area—*natldate( )*

In the United States, dates normally are formatted in order of month, day, and year (MM/DD/YY). In Europe, however, the preferred format is DD/MM/YY, whereas the Japanese use YY/MM/DD. Such varying formats can be confusing, particularly with certain dates. A European bill requesting payment by 10/04/91 sets the deadline at April 10, not October 4. The `natldate()` function (see listing 6.14) enables you to format a date in any of the three formats.

Listing 6.14. *Formatting dates for different localities.*

```
/*****
                                    ` `
                             natldate()


    This function returns the date in different formats.

    Argument list:    char *buff      to hold the resulting date string
                      int day         the day
                      int month       the month
                      int year        the year
                      int sep         the character used to separate
                                      dates
                      int where       which format to use:
                                          0 = US        mm/dd/yy
                                          1 = Europe    dd/mm/yy
                                          2 = Japan     yy/mm/dd


    Return value:     void

*****/
```

continues

Listing 6.14. continued

```
void natldate(char *buff, int day, int month, int year, int sep, int where)
{
    char form[20];

    while (year > 100)
        year -= 100;
    strcpy(form, "%02d%c%02d%c%02d");        /* Zero padding  */

    switch (where) {
        case 0:                              /* US           */
            sprintf(buff, form, month, sep, day, sep, year);
            break;
        case 1:                              /* Europe       */
            sprintf(buff, form, day, sep, month, sep, year);
            break;
        case 2:                              /* Japan        */
            sprintf(buff, form, year, sep, month, sep, day);
            break;
        default:                             /* Default is US */
            sprintf(buff, form, month, sep, day, sep, year);
            break;
    }
}
```

The format assumes that only two digits are used for the year. The function arguments pass in the date, the separation character, and a flag variable (where) that indicates the correct format. The form[] array is such that single-digit dates are zero-filled. That is, April 5, 1991, becomes 04/05/91, using the North American format. If you want to use blanks or free form for the fields, change the form[] array accordingly.

On return from the function, buff[] will hold a formatted date. You must make sure that buff[] is large enough to hold the output.

Break Date String into Values—*datevals( )*

Many of these functions require that the date values be integer data types. On the other hand, some of the functions assume that the dates are held in character arrays as string variables. The datevals() function sepa-rates a date string into integer variables for the day, month, and year, as shown in listing 6.15. The function assumes that a date is contained in the string before the function is called. (You easily can request the date string from the user by calling the strfld() function, which was presented in Chapter 2, "String Processing.")

Listing 6.15. *Decompose a date string into integer values.*

```
/*****
                            datevals()

    This function breaks a date string into integer variables.
The input string may use any nondigit separator (such as a
slash, as in MM/DD/YY) and may be in any of the formats given
for w below.

    Argument list:    char *s      buffer to hold result
                      int *d       the day
                      int *m       the month
                      int *y       the year
                      int w        the format, where:
                                   0 = MM/DD/YY
                                   1 = DD/MM/YY
                                   2 = YY/MM/DD

    Return value:     void

*****/

void datevals(char *s, int *d, int *m, int *y, int w)
{
   char *ptr, temp[5];
   int i, vals[3];

   ptr = s;
   i = 0;
   for (;;) {
      if (isdigit(*s)) {                  /* Loop for separator    */
         s++;
         if (*s != '\0') {
            continue;
```

continues

Listing 6.15. continued

```
      }
    }
    strncpy(temp, ptr, s - ptr);        /* Form a digit string    */
    temp[s - ptr] = '\0';
    vals[i++] = atoi(temp);             /* Make it a number       */
    if (*s == '\0') {                   /* If done, end it...     */
      break;
    }
    s++;                                /* otherwise keep parsing */
    ptr = s;
  }
  switch (w) {
    case 0:                 /* Do MM/DD/YY */
      *m = vals[0];
      *d = vals[1];
      *y = vals[2];
      break;
    case 1:                 /* Do DD/MM/YY */
      *m = vals[1];
      *d = vals[0];
      *y = vals[2];
      break;
    case 2:                 /* Do YY/MM/DD */
      *m = vals[1];
      *d = vals[2];
      *y = vals[0];
      break;
    default:                /* Error       */
      *d = *m = *y = 0;
      break;
  }
}
```

The date string is passed to datevals() in s. Three integer pointers for the day (d), month (m), and year (y) also are passed to the function. The last argument (w) tells which of the three possible formats is used in the date string.

An infinite for loop is used to parse the date into three integer variables. The if statement and the call to isdigit() cause the s pointer to increment until a separator character is read. At that point, you strncpy()

the digit portion read from the string into `temp[]`, add a null termination character so that you can use it as a string, and call `atoi()` to convert the substring into a number. The number then is stored in the `vals[]` array. Continue this process until the null character of s is read.

Using w, the `switch` statement assigns the values into the proper variables for the day, month, and year. If w is not within proper limits, all date values are returned as zero to indicate an error condition. Of course, you can call `valid_date()` after the date values have been filled in by `datevals()`, to make sure that the proper date was constructed.

Easter—*easter( )*

This is one of those functions that is not very useful until you need it. The function shown in listing 6.16 calculates the date on which Easter falls on a certain year.

Listing 6.16. *Find the date for Easter.*

```
/*****
                              easter()

    This function returns the date for Easter. If the return value
is greater than 31 (the number of days in March), the return value
minus 31 is the date in April. Otherwise, the return value is the
March date.

    Argument list:    int year      the year desired (such as 1991)

    Return value:     int           the date for Easter (see note
                                     above)

*****/

int easter(int year)
{
    int cen, leap, days, temp1, temp2;

    cen = year % 19;
    leap = year % 4;
```

continues

Listing 6.16. continued

```
    days = year % 7;
    temp1 = (19 * cen + 24) % 30;
    temp2 = (2 * leap + 4 * days + 6 * temp1 + 5) % 7;
    return (22 + temp1 + temp2);
}
```

The function returns an integer value that must be interpreted. If the value is greater than 31, subtract 31 to get the date for Easter in April. If the value is less than or equal to 31, the value is the date for Easter in March. If you prefer, you can modify the function to return a string that constructs a full date string (like MM-DD-YY).

Pack System Date and Time— *packsdate( ), packstime( )*

Chapter 7, "Disk and Directory Control Functions," discusses the importance of maintaining access to the system date and time in their packed format. Listings 6.17 and 6.18 show functions that convert the system date and time to a DOS-packed number.

Listing 6.17. System date as a packed number.

```
/*****

                        packsdate()

    This function takes the system date and converts it to a packed
    DOS value for the date.

    Argument list:    void

    Return value:     unsigned int     the date as a DOS-packed number

*****/

#include <dos.h>
```

```
unsigned int packsdate(void)
{
   union REGS ireg;

   ireg.h.ah = 0x2a;
   intdos(&ireg, &ireg);
   return packdate(ireg.h.dl, ireg.h.dh, ireg.x.cx);
}
```

The function simply uses function 0x2a of interrupt 0x21 to fill in the registers with the appropriate date values. These values then are passed to packdate() to form the system date as a packed number.

Listing 6.18. *System time as a packed number.*

```
/*****
                          packstime()

    This function takes the system time and converts it to a packed
DOS value for the time.

    Argument list:    void

    Return value:     unsigned int       the time as a DOS-packed number

*****/

#include <dos.h>

unsigned int packstime(void)
{
   union REGS ireg;

   ireg.h.ah = 0x2c;
   intdos(&ireg, &ireg);
   return packtime(ireg.h.dh, ireg.h.cl, ireg.h.ch);
}
```

This function works in the same manner as packsdate(), but packstime() is called to form the appropriate system time as a packed number. Because both functions return an unsigned int data type, their declarations must appear before the functions are called in a program. You should create a new header file containing the function prototypes presented in this chapter, or add them to an existing header file (such as time.h).

Conclusion

The functions presented in this chapter should meet most of your time and date needs that are not covered by the ANSI standard C library. You should examine your compiler's documentation, however, for the time functions included as part of the ANSI standard C library. In particular, see whether your compiler supports asctime(), setlocale(), and strftime(). These functions can be useful in some programming situations.

Disk and Directory Control Functions

The ANSI standard C library includes most of the file functions you are likely to need. The pre-ANSI (K&R) standard library distributed with most C compilers actually had more file I/O functions, however, because ANSI has dropped its library's low-level file I/O functions (such as `read()` and `write()`). Yet all of the C compilers with which I am familiar still distribute the low-level file I/O functions. With such a robust collection of file functions, what possibly needs to be covered in this chapter?

This chapter's purpose is to provide several useful functions that are not found in the standard ANSI C library. In some cases the text draws from nonstandard library functions to build new functions. These nonstandard functions provide a means of extracting the host operating system's unique disk file information (MS-DOS, in this case). Fortunately, even though these nonstandard functions might go by different names in different compilers, most of them still exist in the libraries distributed with the various MS-DOS C compilers, and they can be quite useful.

Working with File Directories

Most MS-DOS C compilers provide functions for searching file directories. These functions are built around functions 0x11 (search for first match) and 0x12 (search for next match) of interrupt 0x21. Different compilers often give different names to the library functions built from interrupt calls, however, and this creates a problem. The Borland compiler, for example, names the functions findfirst() and findnext(), Microsoft uses _dos_findfirst() and _dos_findnext(), and the Eco-C88 compiler names them opendir() and readdir(). As you might expect, the functions' uses also are somewhat different, even though their goals are the same.

Listing 7.1 shows how the findfirst() and findnext() functions are typically used.

Listing 7.1. Example of findfirst() and findnext().

```
#include <stdio.h>                          /* Borland version */
#include <dir.h>

#ifndef NULL
   #define NULL    '\0'
#endif

#define ERROREND -1

void main(void)
{
   char buff[50];
   int done;
   struct ffblk p;

   printf("Enter file mask: ");
   gets(buff);
   done = findfirst(buff, &p, 0);
   if (done == ERROREND) {
      printf("\nCould not search directory");
      exit(1);
   }
   while (done != ERROREND) {
      printf("\n%-14s%9ld", p.ff_name, p.ff_fsize);
      done = findnext(&p);
   }
}
```

The Borland compiler defines the structure ffblk in the dir.h header file as follows:

```
struct ffblk {
   char ff_reserved[21];
   char ff_attrib;
   int ff_ftime;
   int ff_fdate;
   long ff_fsize;
   char ff_name[13];
};
```

The equivalent structure for the Microsoft compiler is defined in dos.h as follows:

```
struct find_t {
   char reserved[21];
   char attrib;
   unsigned wr_time;
   unsigned wr_date;
   long size;
   char name[13];
};
```

As you can see, the function of the structure members is almost identical, and the purpose of each member is the same. Rather than duplicate the discussion, I use the Borland structure definition in the text that follows. If you are using the Microsoft compiler, simply make the appropriate substitutions (for example, find_t instead of ffblk, and _dos_findfirst() instead of findfirst()). Also note that the structure is defined in the dos.h header file for the Microsoft compiler.

The call to findfirst() establishes overhead information used by MS-DOS (for example, File Control Block and Disk Transfer Area information) when searching disk directories. If a match is found on the file mask (for example, test.c), the ffblk structure is filled in with the appropriate information, which then can be used in the program. If no entry can be found, a –1 is returned from the function. If a match is found, the return value is 0.

If the file mask contains wild-card characters (such as * or ?), the call to findnext() first finds the next directory entry that matches the file mask and then refills the ffblk structure. The findnext() function assumes that a previous call to findfirst() was made so that things can work properly.

Listing 7.2 illustrates the same program using the _dos_findfirst() and _dos_findnext() functions for the Microsoft compiler.

Listing 7.2. *Example of* _dos_findfirst() *and* _dos_findnext().

```c
#include <stdio.h>                    /* Microsoft version */
#include <dos.h>
#include <dir.h>

#ifndef NULL
   #define NULL        '\0'
#endif

#define ERROREND    -1

void main(void)
{
   char buff[50];
   int done;
   struct find_t p;

   printf("Enter file mask: ");
   gets(buff);
   done = _dos_findfirst(buff, _A_NORMAL, &p);
   if (done) {
      printf("\nCould not search directory");
      exit(1);
   }
   while (!done) {
      printf("\n%-14s%9ld", p.name, p.size);
      done = _dos_findnext(&p);
   }
}
```

Actually, the program is nearly the same for both the Borland and the Microsoft compilers. The Microsoft compiler has similar arguments for _dos_findfirst(), but their order is different. And Microsoft has a series of #defines for the various file attributes that can be used with the call to _dos_findfirst(). The macro _A_NORMAL is used to locate files with normal DOS attributes. The dos.h header file contains a list of the file attributes that can be used. Other than the name of the structure and its members, the program is almost identical to the Borland version presented in listing 7.1.

Listings 7.1 and 7.2 show that the key functions perform the same task even though there are minor variations in each. The following text provides similar information about disk files, but in smaller chunks.

Get File Size—*getfsize( )*

The first example draws from the code presented in listings 7.1 and 7.2, and creates a new function that simply returns a disk file's size. Listing 7.3 shows the code for the Borland compiler; listing 7.4 shows the same function for Microsoft C.

Listing 7.3. *Get file size (Borland).*

```
/*****
                              getfsize()

      This function returns a disk file's size. If wild cards are
   used (such as * or ?), the function returns the size of each file
   that matches the file mask.

      Argument list:    char *buff      pointer to the file mask. If
                                        multiple searches are made,
                                        all calls after the first call
                                        must pass a null pointer.
                        long *size      pointer to the long that will
                                        hold the file size

        Return value:   int             0 if all goes well, -1 if error
                                        or if all files have been found

*****/

#include <dir.h>

#define ERROREND    -1


int getfsize(char *buff, long *size)
{
   int done;
   static struct ffblk p;

   if (buff != NULL) {
      done = findfirst(buff, &p, 0);
      if (done == ERROREND) {
         return ERROREND;
```

continues

Listing 7.3. continued

```
    }
  } else {
    done = findnext(&p);
  }
  if (done != ERROREND) {
    *size = p.ff_fsize;
  } else {
    return ERROREND;
  }
  return 0;
}
```

The program is designed for use with single or multiple calls. That is, if you search a directory for a file named test.c, there can be only one match in any specified directory. If you search using *.c, there can be multiple calls to the function. In this situation, the second and subsequent calls to getfsize() must be made with the first argument as a null pointer, as in

```
getfsize( (char *) 0, size);
```

The call with the null pointer is made to avoid calling findfirst() again. Otherwise, you will end up in an infinite loop by reading the first file match repeatedly. By using static variables for p, you can keep track of your location in the directory search between calls.

If a 0 is returned, the code assumes that it is safe to make additional calls to the function. If ERROREND (−1) is returned, either an error occurred or there are no more files that match the mask.

Listing 7.4 presents a version of this function for the Microsoft C compiler.

Listing 7.4. Get file size (Microsoft C).

```
/*****
                        getfsize()

   This function returns a disk file's size. The file to search is
   held in buff. If buff is null, it is assumed that the file name was
   passed to the function on a previous call.

   Argument list:    char *buff      the file name
                     long *size      pointer to variable to hold the
                                     file size
```

```
    Return value:     int            -1 if no match or an error occurs;
                                     any other value is OK
*****/

#include <dos.h>

#define ERROREND -1

int getfsize(char *buff, long *size)
{
   int done;
   static struct find_t p;

   if (buff != NULL) {
      done = _dos_findfirst(buff, 0, &p);
      if (done) {
         return ERROREND;
      }
   } else {
      done = _dos_findnext(&p);
   }
   if (done == 0) {
      *size = p.size;
   } else {
      return ERROREND;
   }
   return 0;
}
```

The getfsize() functions presented in listings 7.3 and 7.4 behave similarly, but you should be aware of several differences. First, the structure and member names are different for the p structure, and different header files are required. Second, as was mentioned earlier, the argument order for _dos_findfirst() is different for each compiler. Finally, _dos_findnext() does not necessarily return ERROREND after an unsuccessful call. Because it returns 0 on successful calls, however, I simply altered the check on done in listings 7.3 and 7.4.

One final word of caution: Be sure to make the second and subsequent calls to getfsize() with a null pointer. Otherwise, the function will not perform correctly.

Get File Date or Time—
getfdate_time( )

Now that you can use the structure that contains the disk file information, you can write one double-duty function. The code for Turbo C is shown in listing 7.5. (Listing 7.5 represents only a slight modification to listing 7.3; therefore, it is not necessary to present duplicate code for the Microsoft compiler. Just keep in mind the difference in the return value for _dos_findnext(), as mentioned earlier.)

Listing 7.5. *Get file date or time.*

```
/*****

                         getfdate_time()

     This function returns the date or time associated with a disk
     file. The function can be used with wild cards (*, ?) if buff is
     passed as a null pointer on the second and subsequent calls.


     Argument list:    char *buff       pointer to the file mask. If
                                        multiple searches are made,
                                        all calls after the first call
                                        must pass a null pointer.

                       char *out        pointer to the string that will
                                        hold the date or time

                       int which        0 for the date, 1 for the time

     Return value:     int              0 if all goes well, -1 if error
                                        or if all files have been found

*****/

#include <stdio.h>
#include <dir.h>

#define ERROREND -1

int getfdate_time(char *buff, char *out, int which)
{
    int done, d, m, y;
```

```
    unsigned int temp;
    static struct ffblk p;

    if (buff != NULL) {
       done = findfirst(buff, &p, 0);
       if (done == ERROREND) {
          return ERROREND;
       }
    } else {
       done = findnext(&p);
    }
    if (done != ERROREND) {
       if (which) {                          /* Time */
        temp = p.ff_ftime;
        unpacktime(&d, &m, &y, temp);
        sprintf(out, "%02d:%02d:%02d", y, m, d);
       } else {                              /* Date */
        temp = p.ff_fdate;
        unpackdate(&d, &m, &y, temp);
        sprintf(out, "%02d/%02d/%02d", m, d, y);
       }
    } else {
       return ERROREND;
    }
    return 0;
}
```

In the getfdate_time() function, two pointers are passed to the function. The first pointer, buff, holds the file mask during the first call to getfdate_time(). If multiple searches are made, buff must be replaced with a null pointer on the second and subsequent calls. The second character pointer is filled in with the file's date or time. The third argument, which, determines whether out is filled in with the date or the time.

As with all arrays in C, the function does not (indeed, cannot) check to ensure that out is large enough to hold the output. Therefore, it is your responsibility to ensure that out is large enough to hold the output produced by the function.

Fortunately, the file date and time use the same storage format as the MS-DOS date and time bytes discussed in Chapter 6, "Time and Dates." Therefore, you can use unpackdate() and unpacktime() (as described in Chapter 6) to fill in the date or the time. If you want to get fancy, you can draw from other Chapter 6 functions to format the time or the date in a variety of ways.

Get Current Working Directory— *getcurdir( )*

Sometimes you want your program to go to another directory. Before you make the switch, however, it is helpful to know the directory in which you are currently working. This way, you can return to the current working directory when your program is finished. To do this, you must save the current working directory's path name. Listing 7.6 shows how this is done.

Listing 7.6. Get current working directory (Borland C).

```
/*****
                            getcurdir()

    This function gets the current working directory's path name.

    Argument list:    char *s      pointer to buffer to hold path name

    Return value:     int          0 if no error, nonzero on error

*****/

#include <dos.h>

int getcurdir(char *s)
{
   union REGS ireg, oreg;
   struct SREGS sreg;

   ireg.h.ah = 0x47;
   ireg.x.si = (unsigned) s;
   sreg.ds = _DS;
   ireg.h.dl = 0;                        /* Default drive        */
   if (intdosx(&ireg, &oreg, &sreg)) {   /* An error?            */
      return oreg.x.ax;
   }
   return 0;
}
```

The program passes getcurdir() a buffer that should be large enough to hold a fully expanded directory path name. Although most DOS manuals suggest a 64-byte buffer, there is no reason to skimp on its size. I make the buffer one byte longer than the DOS input buffer (129 bytes).

Because function 0x47 of interrupt 0x21 needs the buffer's segment and offset addresses, use the Borland C _DS pseudoregister to set DS and place the rvalue of s into SI. DL is set to 0 if you want to use the default disk drive code (the case for most uses of this function). If you want to use other drive codes, they proceed sequentially with drive A equal to 1, drive B equal to 2, and so on.

If an error occurs, the carry flag is set (oreg.x.cflag) and oreg.x.ax contains the error code. If no error occurs, the buffer is filled in with the current working directory's path name. You can treat the buffer's contents as a string.

Listing 7.7 presents the same function, but uses the Microsoft C syntax.

Listing 7.7. *Get current working directory (Microsoft C).*

```
/*****
                            getcurdir()

        This function gets the current working directory's path name.

    Argument list:    char *s        pointer to buffer to hold path name

    Return value:     int            0 if no error, nonzero on error

*****/

#include <dos.h>

int getcurdir(char *s)
{
    union REGS ireg, oreg;
    struct SREGS sreg;

    segread(&sreg);
    ireg.h.ah = 0x47;
    ireg.x.si = (unsigned) s;
    sreg.ds = sreg.ss;
    ireg.h.dl = 0;
    intdosx(&ireg, &oreg, &sreg);      /* An error?              */
```

continues

Listing 7.7. *continued*

```
if (oreg.x.cflag) {
    return oreg.x.ax;
}
return 0;
}
```

The only important difference is that Microsoft C does not use pseudovariables for the registers. Use the segread() function provided with the Microsoft library to fill in the segment address.

After control is returned from the call to getcurdir(), you can use chdir() to change the current working directory. When you finish working in the new directory, you can call chdir() a second time, using the path name stored in s as the argument to chdir(), to restore control to the original working directory.

Default Disk Drive—*getcurdrive( )*, *change_drive( )*

The getcurdir() function enables you to determine the current default directory being used. It does not, however, enable you to change disk drives or determine the default drive directly. (You could determine the drive by parsing the current working directory.) The getcurdrive() and change_drive() functions enable you to find out which drive currently is the default drive and to change disk drives if necessary.

Listing 7.8 shows the code for getcurdrive(), which enables you to determine the default working disk drive directly.

Listing 7.8. *Get current default disk drive.*

```
/*****

                        getcurdrive()

    This function is used to get the currently active drive. The
    function returns the drive designator as an int (i.e. A = 0,
    B = 1, and so on). If your code needs the drive letter, simply add
    "A" to the return value.

    Argument list:     void
```

```
    Return value:      int        the drive number where drive 0 is
                                   drive "A," 1 is drive "B," and so on

*****/

#include <dos.h>

int getcurdrive(void)
{
   union REGS ireg;

   ireg.h.ah = 0x19;
   intdos(&ireg, &ireg);
   return ireg.h.al;
}
```

The function uses function 0x19 to retrieve the default disk drive. Although the return value is an integer, you easily can change it to an alphabetic correspondence by adding "A" to the return value. For example, study the call

```
drive = getcurdrive() + 'A';
printf("\nThe current drive is %c", drive);
```

If the current default disk drive is drive C, the message displayed is: "The current drive is C." If you know that you always will want the representation as an ASCII letter rather than a drive number, you can modify the return statement in Listing 7.8 to

```
return ireg.h.al + 'A';
```

You then can treat the return value as a character representing the disk drive directly. Use the method that best suits your needs.

Changing the Default Disk Drive— *change_drive()*

The chdir() library function provided with most MS-DOS compilers is not capable of changing between disk drives. Rather, it is designed to change directories on the default disk drive. That is, if you are on drive C and want to change to drive D, you cannot use chdir() to change drives. The code presented in listing 7.9 enables you to change disk drives.

Listing* 7.9. *Change current default disk drive.

```
/*****
                          change_drive()

     This function is used to change the default drive used with
  the copy aspects of the program. This function is used when
  you need to change from drive to drive, not just between
  subdirectories (use chdir() for that).

  Argument list:    int drive       the drive to change to. It is
                                    assumed that the drive is a
                                    letter ("A", "B", "C", and so on).

  Return value:     int             last valid drive on the system
                                    (A = 1, B = 2, and so on)
*****/

#include <dos.h>

int change_drive(int drive)
{
   union REGS ireg;

   ireg.h.ah = 0x0e;
   ireg.h.dl = toupper(drive) - 'A';
   intdos(&ireg, &ireg);
   return ireg.h.al;
}
```

The function presented in listing 7.9 uses interrupt 0x21, function 0x0e to change the default disk drive. The argument to the function is a character representing the drive you want to change to (for example, "D"). Because the DL register must be loaded with a drive number (rather than a character), you subtract "A" from the function argument before the interrupt call. The call to toupper() enables you to use lower- or uppercase letters for the function argument.

Note that the return value from the function is somewhat strange—it is one-based rather than zero-based. For example, if the return value is 4, drive D is the last valid drive on the system. If the return value is zero-based, a return value of 4 means that drive E is the last valid drive (that is, 0 through 4 inclusively, or five drives). Other than that quirk, the function is straightforward.

Get Disk Storage Capacity— *get_disk_size( )*

Function 0x36 of interrupt 0x21 provides a simple method for determining a disk drive's storage capacity. Listing 7.10 shows the code that accomplishes this.

Listing 7.10. *Disk capacity.*

```
/*****

                              get_disk_size()

   This function determines the amount of storage space on the
   specified disk drive.

   Argument list:    char drive      the drive prefix (such as "A")

   Return value:     long            the drive's total space, in bytes

*****/

#include <dos.h>

long get_disk_size(char drive)
{
   union REGS ireg, oreg;

   ireg.h.ah = 0x36;
   ireg.h.dl = toupper(drive) - 'A' + 1;
   intdos(&ireg, &oreg);
   return (long) ( (long) oreg.x.dx * (long) oreg.x.ax * (long) oreg.x.cx);
}
```

The get_disk_size() function's only argument is the name of the drive to be measured. This is passed as a character (for example, "C"), which is assigned into ireg.h.dl. DOS views the drives numerically, so you convert the drive's associated character to an appropriate DOS number. As shown in the discussion of getcurdir() earlier in this chapter, drive A corresponds to a 1, drive B to a 2, and so on. Therefore, the statement

```
ireg.h.dl = toupper(drive) - 'A' + 1;
```

sets up everything properly for the interrupt call.

On return, the union members have the following interpretation:

oreg.x.ax   the number of sectors per cluster

oreg.x.bx   the number of free sectors

oreg.x.cx   the number of bytes per sector

oreg.x.dx   the number of clusters per drive

Therefore, the statement

```
return (long) ( (long) oreg.x.dx * (long) oreg.x.ax * (long) oreg.x.cx);
```

multiplies the number of clusters per drive by the number of sectors per cluster by the number of bytes per sector to calculate the drive's storage space. The casts are used to make sure that intermediate results do not overflow the (default) integer limits of the oreg members.

Get Amount of Free Disk Storage—
get_disk_free( )

If you followed the calculation of disk drive storage capacity in listing 7.10, you probably noticed that the amount of free storage space left can be calculated by using similar code. The code is presented in listing 7.11.

***Listing 7.11.** Get free drive storage.*

```
/*****
                          get_disk_free()

    This function determines the amount of free space on the
    specified disk drive.

    Argument list:    char drive      the drive prefix (such as "A")

    Return value:     long            the drive's free space, in bytes

*****/
```

```
#include <dos.h>

long get_disk_free(char drive)
{
   union REGS ireg, oreg;

   ireg.h.ah = 0x36;
   ireg.h.dl = toupper(drive) - 'A' + 1;
   intdos(&ireg, &oreg);
   return (long) ( (long) oreg.x.ax * (long) oreg.x.bx * (long) oreg.x.cx);
}
```

The get_disk_free() function works in the same manner as get_disk_size(), but you use the number of free clusters available on the drive rather than the total number of clusters. That is, in this function, you use oreg.x.bx rather than oreg.x.dx.

When you use get_disk_size() and get_disk_free(), remember to declare that each function returns a long data type. Otherwise, the return values probably will not be correct.

Does the File Exist?—*fexist( )*

An unnerving aspect of some file I/O commands in C is that opening a file can truncate it to zero length. This is a euphemistic way of saying that you just lost everything in the file. True, it should not happen if you pay attention to details, but it is likely that most C programmers have lost at least a file or two this way.

This kind of mistake often occurs when you ask the user to enter a file name from the keyboard and then attempt to open the file for writing. If the user happens to pick a name that matches a file that already exists, the contents of the file might be lost.

Listing 7.12 presents a simple function that tells you when a specified file already exists. If the file already exists and you do not want to lose its contents, you can ask the user to enter another file name.

Listing 7.12. Does the file exist?

```
/*****
                              fexist()

     This function determines whether a specified disk file exists in
     the current working directory.

     Argument list:    char *buff      pointer to the file name

     Return value:     int             0 if it does not exist, 1 if
                                        it does

*****/

#include <stdio.h>

int fexist(char *buff)
{
   int flag;
   FILE *fp;

   if ((fp = fopen(buff, "r")) == NULL) {
      flag = 0;
   } else {
      flag = 1;
      fclose(fp);
   }
   return flag;
}
```

The function simply attempts to open the file for reading. In terms of protecting a file from truncation, opening a file for reading does not truncate it or alter its contents. If a file can be opened for reading, therefore, it obviously already exists. If the file cannot be opened, you probably can create a new file, using the file name passed to the function.

The function is limited in that there is no way to distinguish whether a file cannot be opened because it does not exist, or because of a failure (for example, in the hardware).

puts( ) Without the Newline—*nputs( )*

The puts() function's major advantage is that it is relatively small and displays a string very quickly when compared with a call to printf(). One disadvantage, however, is that it appends a newline character to the end of the string. In some situations, such as direct cursor addressing, the newline can cause annoying scrolling problems. The code is very simple, as seen in listing 7.13.

Listing 7.13. *Put string without newline.*

```
/*****
                                nputs()

    This function displays a string on stdout without adding a
    newline at the end of the string. (It is puts() without the
    newline.)

    Argument list:    char *buff      the string to be printed

    Return value:     void

*****/

#include <stdio.h>

void nputs(char *buff)
{
    write(fileno(stdout), buff, strlen(buff));
}
```

The first argument to write() is a file descriptor, which is supplied by the call to fileno(), using stdout as the argument to fileno(). (All fileno() does is return the file descriptor [that is, the handle] that is part of the FILE structure.) The second argument is the string, and the third argument is the number of characters to write. The function then simply writes the string pointed to by buff on stdout. No newline is appended to the output.

The primary advantage of nputs() is that it generates smaller code than does an equivalent program that uses printf(). A test program using printf() compiled to 8,752 bytes using the Borland compiler (7,857 bytes for Microsoft C). When printf() was replaced with nputs(), the code size dropped to 6,505 bytes (5,951 bytes for Microsoft C). If, however, your program already uses printf(), the smaller code size advantage is lost.

When this book first was written, the speed improvement for most compilers was approximately 10 to 20 percent. The time improvement with the latest compilers reduced the time savings to about six percent for Microsoft C and less than one percent for the Borland compiler. Obviously, today's compilers are generating better code than three years ago. You must decide for yourself whether the speed and size improvements warrant using nputs(). You might find more advantages in using printf().

Get File Attribute—*getfatrib( )*

The getfatrib() function finds the attribute of a specified disk file. Listing 7.14 presents the code for getfatrib().

Listing 7.14. Get disk file attribute.

```
/*****
                        getfatrib()

    This function returns the attribute of a disk data file.

    Argument list:    char *fname      the name of the file

    Return value:     int               0 = normal disk file
                                         1 = read-only file
                                         2 = hidden file
                                         4 = system file
                                         8 = volume label
                                        16 = subdirectory
                                        32 = archive

*****/

#include <errno.h>
#include <dos.h>

int getfatrib(char *fname)
{
    union REGS ireg;

    ireg.h.ah = 0x43;
    ireg.h.al = 0;
    ireg.x.dx = (unsigned) fname;
```

```
    intdos(&ireg, &ireg);
    if (ireg.x.cflag) {                /* An error              */
        errno = ireg.x.ax;             /* Global error variable */
        return -1;
    } else {
        return ireg.x.ax;              /* Attribute of file     */
    }
}
```

If you are using something other than the Borland or the Microsoft compiler, you might need to modify the code somewhat. For example, the Eco-C88 compiler returns the flag register from the intdos() call. Therefore, you must logically AND the return value with 0x01 to retrieve the carry flag and check for an error condition. With the Borland and Microsoft compilers, on the other hand, you can test the flag register (that is, the ireg.x.cflag structure member) to test for an error condition. In addition, the Borland compiler has a global variable (_doserrno) defined in the dos.h header file that is set to the specific error code when an error condition is sensed.

You easily can write the converse of this function to set the file attribute. Even though chmod() is not part of the ANSI C standard library, it is defined as part of the UNIX System V library. As a result, almost all compilers provide a chmod() function.

One final note: The code presented in listing 7.14 assumes that you are using a small model. This assumption means that you do not have to worry about which data segment holds the file name. If you want to use getfatrib() in a large model (multiple data segments), you must add the statements

```
struct SREGS sreg;
union  REGS ireg;

sreg.ds = FP_SEG(frame)
ireg.dx = FP_OFF(frame)
```

to the Borland C and Microsoft code in listing 7.14. If you are using some other compiler (for example, Eco-C88), you might need to change the lines to:

```
struct SREG sreg;

segread(&sreg);
```

These modifications will cause the compiler to look in the proper memory segment for the file name.

Delete a File—*kill_file()*

The `kill_file()` function in listing 7.15 deletes a file using interrupt 0x21, function 0x41.

Listing 7.15. *Delete a file (Borland C).*

```
/*****
                              kill_file()

    This function deletes the specified disk file, and sets the
    global system variable (named errno) to the error condition.

    Argument list:    char *fname      the name of the file to delete

    Return value:     int              0 if OK, -1 on error

*****/

#include <dos.h>
#include <errno.h>
extern int errno;           /* Remove this line for Microsoft compilers */


int kill_file(char *fname)
{
    union REGS ireg, oreg;

    ireg.h.ah = 0x41;
    ireg.x.dx = (unsigned) fname;
    intdos(&ireg, &oreg);
    if (oreg.x.cflag) {                    /* An error?              */
        errno = oreg.x.ax;
        return -1;
    }
    return 0;
}
```

The code holds no surprises, but a global system variable named `errno` holds the error code if an error occurs while the file is being deleted.

Using *errno*

The errno variable is defined in the errno.h header file and is used in many functions to hold an integer value that can be used to index into a predefined list of error messages. Actually, three system variables can be used when working with error messages. They are:

errno	The error number
sys_nerr	The number of error messages defined for the system
sys_errlist[];	An array of pointers to the error messages

Program 7.1 presents a program that uses these variables to print the complete list of possible error messages defined for the compiler you are using.

Program 7.1. *Test program for* errno.

```c
#include <stdio.h>

void main(void)
{
    extern char *sys_errlist[];
    extern int errno, sys_nerr;

    for (errno = 0; errno < sys_nerr; errno++) {
        printf("\nerrno = %d, sys_errlist[%d] = %s",
                        errno, errno, sys_errlist[errno]);
    }
}
```

The actual number of error messages printed varies among compilers, but most have at least a dozen predefined error messages. In program 7.1, sys_nerr is used to control the number of iterations made in the loop. You just need to find out how many error messages exist for your compiler. To do this, simply print the value of sys_nerr. If you run the program, however, you will find that although some compilers have rather large values for sys_nerr, many of the error codes return null messages. Still, the program gives you an idea of the predefined messages available for use in your own programs.

Get DOS Version Number— *getversion( )*

You probably are familiar with the DOS environment block. The environment block commonly is used to set the PATH variable to a directory path and use the PATH variable for running a single program from multiple directories. Indeed, most compilers create their own environment variables to determine where to find the library, header, and compiler files. For example, both Borland and Microsoft C use an environment variable named include to determine the path for finding the #include header files.

Conveniently enough, you can access environment variables with the getenv() function while the program is running. However, you should remember that the getenv() function must find an exact match on the desired environment variable. If you have created an environment variable named TEMP, calling getenv() using "temp" as its argument will not work: getenv() is case-sensitive.

When you call getenv() with the environment variable (in capital letters), a pointer that points to the environment variable is returned if there is a match, and a null pointer is returned if there is not a match. For example, if you define an environment variable (usually as part of AUTOEXEC.BAT) as

TEMP=C:\COMPILE\WORK

and call getenv() using

ptr = getenv("TEMP");

then ptr will point to "C:\COMPILE\WORK". You can use this pointer as a path name for working files or for whatever else you need. Remember, however, that only versions 2.x and later allow directory path names. Therefore, you need a function that tells you the runtime version of DOS being used. The getversion() function presented in listing 7.16 enables you to get the DOS version for the system.

Listing 7.16. Get DOS version number.

```
/*****
                              getversion()

   This function retrieves the DOS version number from the system.
```

```
Argument list:      char *s        a pointer that is filled in with
                                   the DOS version number

Return value:       int            the primary version number

*****/

#include <dos.h>

int getversion(char *s)
{
   union REGS ireg;

   ireg.h.ah = 0x30;
   intdos(&ireg, &ireg);
   sprintf(s, "%d.%d", ireg.h.al, ireg.h.ah);
   return ireg.h.al;
}
```

Function 0x30 of interrupt 0x21 enables you to get the DOS version number, which is divided into the major and minor version numbers. For example, if you are running DOS V3.1, *3* is the major version number and *1* is the minor version number. Function 0x30 returns the major version number in AL register and the minor version number in AH. On return from the intdos(), the version number is formatted into a string, and the major version number is returned from the call to getversion(). You can use the return value to determine whether path names can be used in your program (if the major version number is greater than 1), or you can use the full version number in string form, if necessary.

Get Verify Flag—*getvflag( )*

The DOS verify flag's status determines whether a read-after-write is performed when data are written to disk. Data transfers to disk are faster if the verify flag is off. Because of the increased speed, most programs do not set the verify flag. However, if you want to ensure a data file's integrity, you can set the verify flag on. Listing 7.17 shows how to determine the verify flag's status.

Listing 7.17. Get status of verify flag.

```
/*****
                              getvflag()

    This function returns the verify flag.

    Argument list:    void

    Return value:     int       0 if verify flag is off, 1 if on

*****/

#include <dos.h>

int getvflag(void)
{
    union REGS ireg;

    ireg.h.ah = 0x54;
    intdos(&ireg, &ireg);
    return ireg.h.al;
}
```

Function 0x54 of interrupt 0x21 returns the verify flag's status. If the return value is zero, no data verification takes place.

Set the Verify Flag Status—*setvflag( )*

You can set the verify flag using the DOS commands VERIFY ON and VERIFY OFF. The code in listing 7.18 does the equivalent of the DOS VERIFY command.

Listing 7.18. Set the verify flag.

```
/*****
                              setvflag()

    This function turns the verify flag on or off.

    Argument list:    int flag       a value of 1 turns verify on; 0
                                     turns it off
```

```
    Return value:      void

*****/

#include <dos.h>


void setvflag(int flag)
{
   union REGS ireg;

   ireg.h.ah = 0x2e;
   ireg.h.al = flag;
   ireg.h.dl = 0;
   intdos(&ireg, &ireg);
}
```

To be sure that a disk transfer is verified, you simply call with flag set to 1. You might want your program to read the verify flag's status before setting it so that you can return the flag to its original status after the program terminates.

Get File Date and Time—*gfiledate( )*, *gfiletime( )*

Earlier in this chapter you learned how to use getfdate_time() to get the date and time for a file. The getfdate_time() function enables you to use wild cards in the file name so that multiple files can be used. The function can use wild cards because the findfirst() (or _dos_findfirst) and findnext() (or _dos_findnext()) functions are used to perform directory searches.

Now you can develop similar functions, but this time the date and time stamps are relative to only one file. Furthermore, the file must be opened when the function is called. The advantage is that the functions presented here are smaller and execute somewhat more quickly. (Complementary functions that enable you to set the time and the date are presented in the next section.)

The two functions are almost identical, as shown in listings 7.19 and 7.20.

Listing 7.19. *Get date stamp for a disk file.*

```
/*****
                            gfiledate()

     This function gets the date stamp for the specified disk file.

   Argument list:     FILE *fp         pointer to the open file

   Return value:      int              the date as a DOS packed number

*****/

#include <stdio.h>

#include <dos.h>

int gfiledate(FILE *fp)
{
   union REGS ireg;

   ireg.h.ah = 0x57;
   ireg.h.al = 0;
   ireg.x.bx = fileno(fp);
   intdos(&ireg, &ireg);
   return ireg.x.dx;
}
```

Listing 7.20. *Get time stamp for a disk file.*

```
/*****
                            gfiletime()

     This function gets the time stamp for the specified disk file.

   Argument list:     FILE *fp         pointer to the open file

   Return value:      int              the time as a DOS packed number

*****/

#include <stdio.h>
```

```
#include <dos.h>


int gfiletime(FILE *fp)
{
   union REGS ireg;

   ireg.h.ah = 0x57;
   ireg.h.al = 0;
   ireg.x.bx = fileno(fp);
   intdos(&ireg, &ireg);
   return ireg.x.cx;
}
```

Both functions use interrupt 0x21, function 0x57; the only difference is in the return value. The date function returns the date as a packed number in `ireg.x.dx`, and the time function returns the time as a packed number in `ireg.x.cx`. Because the return values are DOS-packed numbers for the time and date, you can use `unpacktime()` and `unpackdate()` from Chapter 6, "Time and Dates," to break the packed data into a usable format.

Also note that `ireg.x.bx` expects a file *descriptor* rather than a FILE pointer. As you saw earlier in this chapter, the `fileno()` function's purpose is to convert a FILE pointer into its associated file descriptor. Use the FILE pointer rather than a file-descriptor approach for the function because the ANSI standard C library does not support low-level file I/O.

Even though low-level file I/O is not supported by ANSI, all the compiler vendors supply a `fileno()` as part of their standard library. You shouldn't worry about using `fileno()` in any of your code. Because `fileno()` is defined under the UNIX System V specification, it is portable across most environments.

Set File Date and Time—*sfiledate( )*, *sfiletime( )*

The `sfiledate()` and `sfiletime()` functions set the date and time stamp for an open disk file. These two functions provide a way to "touch" a file without using the archive bit (which is not available on all versions of DOS). You can use the date and time stamp, for example, to decide whether a file has been updated recently, and then take appropriate action in your program based on that information. You can write your own "backup" program that reads a file's time and date stamps, and then you can decide whether the file needs to be copied.

Again, the functions are virtually identical, as shown in listings 7.21 and 7.22.

***Listing 7.21.** Set file date stamp.*

```
/*****
                            sfiledate()

    This function sets the date stamp for the specified disk file.

    Argument list:    FILE *fp      pointer to the open file
                      unsigned d    the date as a packed number

    Return value:     int           the date as a DOS-packed number

*****/

#include <stdio.h>

#include <dos.h>

void sfiledate(FILE *fp, unsigned d)
{
   union REGS ireg;

   ireg.h.ah = 0x57;
   ireg.h.al = 1;
   ireg.x.bx = fileno(fp);
   ireg.x.dx = d;
   intdos(&ireg, &ireg);
}
```

***Listing 7.22.** Set file time stamp.*

```
/*****
                            sfiletime()

    This function sets the time stamp for the specified disk file.
```

```
    Argument list:     FILE *fp      pointer to the open file
                       unsigned d    the time as a packed number

    Return value:      int           the time as a DOS-packed number

*****/

#include <stdio.h>

#include <dos.h>

void sfiletime(FILE *fp, unsigned d)
{
   union REGS ireg;

   ireg.h.ah = 0x57;
   ireg.h.al = 1;
   ireg.x.bx = fileno(fp);
   ireg.x.cx = d;
   intdos(&ireg, &ireg);
}
```

Both functions are passed as an integer that contains either the date or the time as a packed number. You can get the packed number in one of several ways. One method involves passing the time or the date to the packtime() or packdate() functions discussed in Chapter 6, "Time and Dates." Or, you simply can pack the time and date with your own code. If you choose to use the system's date and time values, you should use the packsdate() and packstime() functions from Chapter 6.

Conclusion

Most C compilers offer a variety of file I/O functions that are specific to the host operating system. A multiuser environment, such as UNIX, offers many functions that do not exist in MS-DOS. Even under MS-DOS, many functions are not provided as part of the standard C library. It would be worthwhile to review the I/O functions provided with your compiler and see what additional resources are available.

Finally, many add-on libraries are available to tackle more specific programming tasks, such as database libraries with a variety of retrieval methods. If you are working on a large database project, you might consider such packages because they can save you months of development time.

CHAPTER 8

Working with Numbers

This chapter discusses functions that manipulate numeric data, and it generally covers the areas of statistics, matrices, and financial calculations. By the way, if you are a serious programmer and do not have a copy of *Collected Algorithms from ACM*, published by the Association for Computing Machinery, you should consider buying one. Some of the functions presented here are derived from this source.

Statistics

Most people use statistics all the time without realizing it. Perhaps more important, many spreadsheet users should use statistics but do not. I am amazed by the number of businesses that use spreadsheets to do their financial planning but do not support their planning with statistics. Many small businesses, for example, use a spreadsheet to forecast income and expenses for the next fiscal year. They may have no idea, however, how reliable their forecast is. They play the "what if" game with great expertise but do not realize that they also are playing "what if you are wrong."

Statistics are useful when you change a condition of uncertainty to one of risk. Under conditions of uncertainty, you have two or more outcomes but cannot place any estimate of probability on them. Under conditions of risk, you have the same outcomes, and you can estimate the probability of each event's likelihood. This is done with the aid of statistics.

303

Because statistics is such a broad and important subject, it cannot be covered adequately in this text. You owe it to yourself, however, to become familiar with this field of study, even if you are not involved in business. (Two very readable texts are *Identifying and Solving Statistical Problems with Microstat-II* by Peter Rob, Wadsworth Publishing Company; and *Statistics*, 2nd Ed., by Moshe Ben-Horim and Haim Levy, Random House Books. Both books cover all the statistical functions presented in this section.)

Standard Deviation—*sd( )*

The most basic statistical measures are the mean and the standard deviation of a data set. Concentrating on just the mean, however, often can lead to erroneous conclusions about the data. For example, a number of years ago I worked as a consultant for a major insurance company. Twice a year, the employees evaluated their division's manager, using a questionnaire with questions ranked on a scale from 1 to 5. One year, even though all the division managers had received ratings around the central value of 3, one division nevertheless was having severe productivity problems. A quick check of the questionnaires showed that the division was split almost in two: Half of the employees had given their manager rankings of 1, and the other half had given rankings of 5. That division's standard deviation was almost twice that of the other divisions.

Had the company looked at the standard deviation in the first place, it would have known that the division had been "politicized" into two counter-productive factions. A management change was made, and productivity levels soon returned to normal. Examination of both the mean and its standard deviation always sheds more light on a data set than just the mean alone.

Listing 8.1 presents a function that calculates the mean and the standard deviation. Either the population or the sample standard deviation is calculated.

Listing 8.1. Mean and standard deviation.

```
/*****

                              sd()


    This function calculates the standard deviation of the n values
pointed to by x. It also fills in the value of the mean.
```

```
Argument list:     double *x        pointer to the array of doubles
                   double *mean     pointer to the mean
                   int n            the number of doubles
                   int which        0 = sample standard deviation
                                    1 = population standard deviation

Return value:      double           the standard deviation for the
                                    values

*****/

#include <math.h>

double sd(double *x, double *mean, int n, int which)
{
   int i;
   double sum, ss;

   sum = ss = 0.0;
   for (i = 0; i < n; i++, x++) {
      sum += *x;
      ss += (*x * *x);
   }
   *mean = sum = sum / (double) n;
   if (which == 1) {                         /* Population        */
      return sqrt( (ss - n * (sum * sum)) / ( (double) n) );
   } else {                                  /* Sample            */
      return sqrt( (ss - n * (sum * sum)) / ( (double) n - 1.0) );
   }
}
```

The function's arguments are a pointer to the data set, a pointer to the mean (which is to be filled in by the function), the number of data items in the set, and a flag variable that determines whether the sample or the population standard deviation is calculated. In most cases, the sample standard deviation is the proper measure, which is why the sample is calculated in all cases in which the flag's value is not 1. The standard deviation gives you some measure of a data set's variability.

The standard deviation's square is the variance of the data set. Therefore, if a statistical routine calls for the variance and the standard deviation, you can get the variance by simply squaring the return value from sd().

The Median—*median( )*

Usually a data set's values are close to a central value, but sometimes a set has a few "wild" values that can distort the interpretation of the mean for the data set. For example, suppose a salary survey has the following values:

15,000 12,000 16,000 18,000 75,000

Although the mean salary is $27,200, most of the salaries center closer to a value of $15,000. Indeed, if you discard the $75,000 salary, the mean drops to $15,250. In other words, the "wild" value of $75,000 distorts the picture of the true distribution of salaries. In cases such as these, the median often presents a better picture of the central value of the data set.

In calculating the median, the data set is sorted and the "middle" value becomes the median. If the number of elements in the set is odd, the middle value is the median. If the number of elements in the set is even, the median is the average of the two central values in the data set. Using this approach, any "wild" values have less impact on the median than they would on the mean.

The code for calculating the median is presented in listing 8.2.

Listing 8.2. *Find the median of a data set.*

```
/*****
                            median()

    This function computes the median of a set of data.

    Argument list:    char *n      pointer to the data set
                      int size     the number of elements in the set
                      int width    the size of one element in the set

    Return value:     double       the median of the set

*****/

#include <stdio.h>
#include <stdlib.h>

static int i_compare(int *, int *),
       c_compare(char *, char *),
       d_compare(double *, double *);
```

```c
double median(char *n, int size, int width)
{
    int index, *iptr;
    double *dptr, medi;

    index = size >> 1;                      /* Find a middle value     */
    switch (width) {
      case sizeof(char):
        qsort(n, size, width,
            (int (*)(const void *, const void *)) c_compare);
        if (size & 0x01) {
        medi = (double) n[index];
        } else {
            medi = (double) ( (n[index] + n[index - 1]) / 2.0);
        }
      break;

      case sizeof(int):
        iptr = (int *) n;
        qsort(iptr, size, width,
            (int (*) (const void *, const void *)) i_compare);
        if (size & 0x01) {
            medi = (double) iptr[index];
        } else {
            medi = (double) ( (iptr[index] + iptr[index - 1]) / 2.0);
        }
        break;

      case sizeof(double):
                dptr = (double *) n;
        qsort(dptr, size, width,
            (int (*) (const void *, const void *)) d_compare);
        if (size & 0x01) {
            medi = (double) dptr[index];
        } else {
            medi = (double) ( (dptr[index] + dptr[index - 1]) / 2.0);
        }
        break;
    }
    return medi;
}

/*****
c_compare()
```

continues

Listing 8.2. continued

```
i_compare()
d_compare()
```

These functions are support routines for the median() function.
Each performs a comparison on the data item being tested (char,
int, or double). The functions are made static so that they will
not collide with other functions with the same name. They are not in
scope outside this module.

| Argument list: | XXXX *s1 | pointer to 1st type XXXX data element |
| | XXXX *s2 | pointer to 2nd type XXXX data element |

Return value:	int	> 0 if *s1 > *s2
		0 if *s1 == *s2
		< 0 if *s1 < *s2

```
*****/

static int c_compare(char *s1, char *s2)
{
    return (int) (*s1 - *s2);
}


static int i_compare(int *s1, int *s2)
{
    return (*s1 - *s2);
}


static int d_compare(double *s1, double *s2)
{
    if (*s1 > *s2)
        return 1;
    else
        if (*s1 < *s2)
            return -1;
        else
            return 0;
}
```

The median() has three arguments. The first is a pointer to the data set, the second is the number of elements in the data set, and the third is the width of each element in the data set. Inside median(), you first find the index of the central element. You do this by bit-shifting the number of elements to the right by one position. (This is the same as dividing by 2.) Next, a switch statement is used to select the proper code sequence, depending on the type of data for which you are trying to find the median. The function provides for character, integer, and floating-point data. If you need other data types, simply use listing 8.2 as a model to add the new data type.

Because you pass the base address of the array to median() as a pointer to char, you must cast that address to a pointer of the appropriate data type before calling qsort(). The pointer then is used in all subsequent processing.

The function then calls qsort() to sort the data into ascending order. (If you want to preserve the data's original order, copy the array before calling this function. A call to calloc() and memcpy() could be used.) As you saw in Chapter 5, "Searching, Sorting, and Parsing," qsort() requires a pointer to a comparison function. I wrote three comparison functions (c_compare(), i_compare(), and d_compare()) to handle the three data types. If you add new data types, you must provide an appropriate comparison function. Note that I have defined the comparison function with the static storage class so that the names of the comparison functions will be invisible (out of scope) outside the median() module.

After the data have been sorted, you check to see whether the number of items in the data set is even or odd. (The low bit will be on if the set is odd.) Based on the check, you perform the necessary calculation to find the median. Note that the return value is a double in all cases. This is necessary because even integer data can have a fractional value if the number of cases is even.

Some compilers enable you to use the name of the comparison function without the casts shown in listing 8.2. Other compilers (for example, Borland), however, are rather particular, and insist that the explicit cast be performed. The code in listing 8.2 works with all compilers that support prototyping. If your compiler does not support prototyping, try using just the name of the comparison function.

The Normal Distribution—*normal( )*

If the number of data items in a data set is rather large (for example, more than 50), the data's distribution tends to follow something called a normal distribution, often referred to as the "bell curve." Many things follow a normal distribution, from people's height and weight to cotton yields in the South. A Russian mathematician named Chebyshev demonstrated that at least $1 - 1/k^2$ percent of the data must lie within k standard deviations of the mean. His work shows, for example, that 95 percent of a data set falls within plus or minus 1.96 standard deviations about the mean. Therefore, if a car's mean gas mileage is 20 miles per gallon, with a standard deviation of two miles per gallon, then 95 percent of the car's gas mileage readings will fall between 16.08 ($= 20 - 1.96 * 2$) and 23.92 ($= 20 + 1.96 * 2$) miles per gallon.

The normal distribution can be thought of as a hypothetical distribution with a mean of 0.0 and a standard deviation of 1.0. Therefore, if you write a function that passes in a value for the standard deviation, you should be able to get back a probability measure for the area under the curve. This function is presented in listing 8.3.

Listing 8.3. *Probability of the normal deviate.*

```
/*****
                            normal()

    This function returns the probability associated with the
normal deviate from the maximum ordinate of the normal distribution.
(For example, if x = 1.96, the return value from normal() is
.9750021048. The algorithm is from Collected Algorithms from
CACM, #209, Vol. 1, by Ibbetson and Brothers.)

    Argument list:    double x     the normal deviate (sigma)

    Return value:     double       the probability associated with x
                                   for the normal distribution.

*****/

#include <math.h>

double normal(double x)
{
    double w, y, z;

    if (x == 0.0)
        z = 0.0;
```

```
  else {
     y = fabs(x) / 2.0;
     if (y >= 3.0) {
        z = 1.0;
     } else {
        if (y < 1.0) {
           w = y * y;
           z = (((((((0.000124818987 * w
           -.001075204047) * w + .005198775019) * w
           -.019198292004) * w + .059054035642) * w
           -.151968751364) * w + .319152932694) * w
           -.531923007300) * w + .797884560593) * y * 2.0;
        } else {
           y = y - 2.0;
           z = ((((((((((((-.000045255659 * y
           +.000152529290) * y - .000019538132) * y
           -.000676904986) * y + .001390604284) * y
           -.000794620820) * y - .002034254874) * y
           +.006549791214) * y - .010557625006) * y
           +.011630447319) * y - .009279453341) * y
           +.005353579108) * y - .002141268741) * y
           +.000535310849) * y + .999936657524;
        }
     }
  }
  if (x > 0.0)
     return (z + 1.0) / 2.0;
  else
     return (1 - z) / 2.0;
}
```

The function has just one argument, which is the standard deviation. (The normal distribution's standard deviation often is called the *normal deviate*.) The function returns the cumulative probability up to the normal deviate. Therefore, if you call this function with the value 1.96, the return value will be .975002. If you call the function with the value –1.96, the return value will be 0.024998. Those familiar with statistics can see that this makes it easy to calculate results for a one- or two-tailed probability test.

Be sure to include math.h, or the appropriate header file, for the fabs() function.

Student's t Distribution—*tvalue()*

Sometimes you cannot get enough observations from a data set to meet the normal distribution's requirements. There are no laws carved in stone about the precise number, but most statisticians agree that approximately 30 cases is the minimum for assuming a normal distribution for a data set—although 50 might be a safer number.

If you were in charge of doing crash tests for Lamborghini Motors, you might want to find a less expensive way to sample the distribution. When you think that the distribution is normal, but the number of cases is less than 30, you should use the Student's t distribution. Because the distribution is sensitive to the number of cases used in the sample, however, the function requires an additional argument relative to the normal() function. The code for the Student's t distribution is shown in listing 8.4.

Listing 8.4. *Student's t distribution.*

```
/*****
                            tvalue()

    This function computes the area under the curve for the Student's
    t distribution. The area reflects the probability for the given t.

    Argument list:    double t       the given t value for use
                      double df      the degrees of freedom

    Return value:     double area    the area under the curve

*****/

#include <math.h>

double dint(double x);


#ifndef M_PI
   #define   M_PI        3.14159265358979323846    /* pi */
#endif

double tvalue(double t, double df)
{
    double cn, i, r, sn;
    double area, atg, cum, term;
```

```
t = fabs(t);
r = t / sqrt(df);

atg = atan(r);

if (df != 1.0) {
   sn = sin(atg);
}
if (df >= 3.0) {
   cn = cos(atg);
}
if (df == 1.0)
   area = 2.0 * atg / M_PI;
if (df == 2.0)
   area = sn;
if (df == 3.0)
   area = 2.0 * (atg + cn * sn) / M_PI;
if (df <= 3.0 || dint(df / 2.0) == df / 2.0) {
   if (df == 2.0 || dint(df / 2.0) != df / 2.0)
      return area;
   term = cum = 1.0;
   for (i = 2.0; i <= df - 2.0; i += 2.0) {
      term = term * cn * cn * (double) ((i - 1.0)/ i);
      cum += term;
   }
   area = sn * cum;
   return area;
}
term = cum = 1.0;
for (i = 3.0; i <= df - 2.0; i += 2.0) {
   term = term * cn * cn * ((i - 1.0) / i);
   cum += term;
}
area = 2.0 * (atg + cn * sn * cum) / M_PI;
return area;
}

/*****

                         dint()
```

This function returns the integral part of a floating point number. It truncates the double at the decimal point. Because it does not round the number, it is not the same as floor().

continues

Listing 8.4. continued

```
   Argument list:     double x      the value to be truncated

   Return value:      double        the truncated double

*****/

#include <stdlib.h>

double dint(double x)
{
   char buff[25], *ptr;

   ptr = (char *) memchr(buff, '.', sprintf(buff, "%24F", x));
   if (ptr) {
      *ptr = '\0';
      return atof(buff);
   }
   return 0.0;
}
```

The first argument is the t value itself. The second argument is the degrees of freedom in the sample. The degrees of freedom is the number of cases (*n*) available, minus the number of estimated parameters. Because the mean is almost always used as one of the parameters, the degrees of freedom is never more than $n - 1$. It is likely that one of your header files defines the constant pi to machine accuracy for your system. You might need to change the M_PI constant to match that for your machine.

The dint() function is designed to truncate a floating point number at the decimal point. Because it is not part of the ANSI library and because a similar function might not be provided with your compiler, the source code is presented as part of listing 8.4. The function simply formats the double passed to the function into a buffer for conversion by sprintf(). By placing the sprintf() call inside memchr(), you avoid the use of a local variable to store the length of the string held in buff[]. (You can do this because sprintf() returns the number of bytes placed in the buffer.) If memchr() finds a decimal point, you replace the decimal point with a null termination character. The final call to atof() converts the string back to a (truncated) double. This value then is used in tvalue() to calculate the probability value.

Note that you could use strtod() instead of atof() in dint(). The strtod() function provides a means of checking for conversion errors—a feature not found in `atof()`. However, `strtod()` requires an additional character pointer in the call. Check your compiler's documentation to see whether `strtod()` better suits your needs.

The exact values calculated by `tvalue()` varies somewhat among compilers, sometimes to as little as the fourth decimal point. It appears that the Borland and Microsoft compilers carry out the transcendental math functions only to the precision associated with a `float` data type (that is, 32 bits). The Eco-C88 compiler, on the other hand, uses the full 64 bits for the math functions. In most cases, this difference should pose no problems.

All statistics books publish probability tables for the t value, in which each degree of freedom has its own probability distribution. The `tvalue()` function presented here provides fairly good accuracy relative to the published tables, it requires less storage than a table, and it can calculate values not in the table.

Chi-Square Distribution— *chi_square( )*

Sometimes you must study samples taken randomly from a population and make inferences about the data. The chi-square distribution often is used to examine the variance of a certain sample, or to determine whether a variable follows some other distribution (such as the normal distribution). Whether the chi-square distribution is used in tests for data independence or to determine accuracy of fit, it is a valuable tool for studying the variance of a variable.

As before, because the chi-square distribution is an approximation of the normal distribution, two arguments must be passed: the chi-square value and the degrees of freedom. The `chi_square()` function is presented in listing 8.5.

Listing 8.5. Chi-square distribution.

```
/*****
                        chi_square()

    This function computes the area under the curve for the chi-
square distribution. The algorithm is a modified version from ACM's
Collected Algorithms, #299 by I.D. Hill and M.C. Pike. (Also see:
Hastings, Approximations for Digital Computers, p. 195.)
```

continues

Listing 8.5. *continued*

```
       Argument list:      double x        the specified chi-square value
                           double df       the degrees of freedom

       Return value:       double area     the area under the curve

*****/

#include <math.h>
#include <errno.h>


double chi_square(double x, double df)
{
    int f, bigx, even;
    double a, c, chiprob, e, y, z, s, normal();
    extern int errno;         /* Remove this line for Microsoft compilers */

    errno = 0;
    exp(-.5 * x);
    if (errno)
        bigx = 1;
    else
        bigx = 0;

    f = (int) df;
    if (x < 0.0 || f < 1.0)
        return -1.0;

    a = .5 * x; even = (f % 2);
    even = !even;
    if (even || f > 2 && ! bigx)
        y = exp(-a);
    if (even)
        s = y;
    else
        s = 2.0 * normal(-sqrt(x));

    if (f > 2) {
        x = .5 * (df - 1.0);
        if (even)
            z = 1.0;
```

```
        else
           z = .5;
        if (bigx) {
          e = (even) ? 0.0 : .572364942925;
          c = log(a);
          for ( ; z <= x; z += 1.0) {
             e = log(z) + e;
             s = exp(c * z - a - e) + s;
          }
          chiprob = s;
        } else {
          e = (even) ? 1.0 : .564189583548 / sqrt(a);
          c = 0.0;
          for ( ; z <= x; z += 1.0) {
             e = e * a / z;
             c += e;
          }
        }
        chiprob = c * y + s;
    } else
        chiprob = s;
    return chiprob;
}
```

There is nothing tricky in the code, but it does use the external variable errno to trap any exponentiation problems that occur. Therefore, errno.h must be included in the code. Furthermore, the normal() function, discussed earlier in this chapter, also is called as part of the function.

F Distribution—*fdist( )*

The F distribution is a natural extension of the chi-square distribution because it simply is a ratio of two chi-square variables. The F distribution usually concerns relationships between two or more variables, such as Analysis of Variance (ANOVA).

Because the F distribution works with two chi-square variables, the argument list needs two measures of the degrees of freedom. The F distribution's code is shown in listing 8.6.

Listing 8.6. F distribution.

```
/*****
                              fdist()

    This function calculates the F probability, given the F value
and the degrees of freedom for the numerator and the denominator.
(The sample algorithm is from ACM #322 by Egon Dorrer.)

    Argument list:    double x    the F value
                      int m       degrees of freedom for the numerator
                      int n       degrees of freedom for the denominator

    Return value:     double      the probability for the F distribution

*****/

#include <math.h>

#ifndef M_1_PI
    #define   M_1_PI      0.31830988618379067153    /* 1 / pi          */
#endif

#define BIGNUM 180                          /* Limit on exponent for pow */

double fdist(double x, unsigned m, unsigned n)
{
    unsigned int a, b, i, j;
    double w, y, z, zk, d, p, temp;


    if (x <= 0.0)                           /* F is too low            */
       return 0.0;

    if (x >= 1000.0 && n >= 2u) {           /* Check for huge values   */
       return 0.0;
    }

    a = 2 - (m & 1); b = 2 - (n & 1);

    w = x *  m / n; z = 1.0 / (1.0 + w);

    if (a == 1) {
       if (b == 1) {
```

```
            p = sqrt(w); y = M_1_PI;
            d = y * z / p; p = 2.0 * y * atan(p);
        } else {
            p = sqrt(w * z); d = .5 * p * z / w;
        }
    } else {
        if (b == 1) {
            p = sqrt(z); d = .5 * z * p; p = 1.0 - p;
        } else {
            d = z * z; p = w * z;
        }
    }
    y = 2.0 * w / z;
    if (a == 1) {
        for (j = b + 2; j <= n; j += 2) {
            d =  (1 + ( (double) a) / ((double) (j - 2))  ) * d * z;
            p = p + d * y / ( (double) (j - 1) );
        }
    } else {
        temp = (double)(n - 1) / 2;
        if (temp > BIGNUM) {
            return 0.0;
        }
        zk = pow(z, temp);
        d = d * zk * n / b;
        p = p * zk + w * z * (zk - 1.0) / (z - 1.0);
    }
    y = w * z; z = 2.0 / z; b = n - 2;
    for (i = a + 2; i <= m; i += 2) {
        j = i + b; d = y * d * ( (double) j) /( (double) (i - 2) );
        p = p - z * d / (double) j;
    }
    return p;
}
```

The macro M_1_PI is the reciprocal of pi, and it might be defined in your math.h header file. BIGNUM represents an exponential limit to the exp() function. The number shown here should work for most MS-DOS compilers using IEEE floating point, but it might have to be changed in other environments. The return value is the cumulative probability for the arguments given.

Simple Regression—*regression( )*

Simple regression is a statistical procedure used to estimate a linear equation between two variables, using the general form

```
y = b0 + b1(x)
```

in which

```
y  = the dependent variable
x  = the independent variable
b0 = the constant term
b1 = the slope coefficient
```

Suppose that you operate a pizza store. You think that the price you charge affects the number of pizzas you sell, but you don't know the exact relationship between the two. You might use regression analysis to estimate the regression equation

```
pizza sales = b0 + b1(pizza price)
```

This equation assumes that you have collected data for sales and prices over a certain period. The implicit assumption about the regression equation is that pizza sales are a linear function of pizza price. Having collected the data, you can use the regression() function to perform the regression, shown in listing 8.7.

***Listing 8.7.** Simple regression.*

```
/*****
                        regression()

   This function performs a simple regression between variables
x and y. The function also fills in support statistics using the
following structure:

struct regres {
   double b0,              Constant term
          b1,              Slope coefficient
          se,              Standard error of estimate
          sy,              Standard of regression
          sdb1,            Std error of b1
          tval,            t value for b1
          r;               Coef of determination
   };
```

```
      Argument list:    double *x              pointer to independent
                                               variable

                        double *y              pointer to dependent
                                               variable

                        int n                  number of cases
                        struct regres *result  support statistics


      Return value:     void

*****/

#include <math.h>

struct regres {
      double b0, b1, se, sy, sdb1, tval, r;
      };

void regression(double *x, double *y, int n, struct regres *result)
{
   int i;
   double dev, se, sumxy, xbar, ybar, sumx2, sumy2, temp;

   sumxy = xbar = ybar = sumx2 = 0.0;
   for (i = 0; i < n; i++) {
      xbar += x[i];
      ybar += y[i];
      sumxy += (x[i] * y[i]);
      sumx2 += (x[i] * x[i]);
      sumy2 += (y[i] * y[i]);
   }
   xbar /= (double) n;
   ybar /= (double) n;
   result->b1 = (sumxy - ( (double) n * xbar * ybar)) /
              (sumx2 - ( (double) n * xbar * xbar));
   result->b0 = ybar - result->b1 * xbar;
   result->sy = sqrt( (sumy2 - ( (double) n * ybar * ybar)) /
              (double) (n - 1) );
   result->se = sqrt( (sumy2 - result->b0 * ybar * (double) n -
              result->b1 * sumxy) / (double) (n - 2) );
   if (result->sdb1 == 1.0) {
      dev = 0.0;
      for (i = 0; i < n; i++) {
```

continues

Listing 8.7. continued

```
        temp = (x[i] - xbar);
        dev += (temp * temp);
    }
    result->sdb1 = sqrt((result->se * result->se) / dev);
  }
  result->r = 1.0 - (result->se * result->se) /
            (result->sy * result->sy) * ( (double) (n - 2) / (n - 1));
  result->tval = result->b1 / result->sdb1;
}
```

The regression() function's first two arguments are the independent (x) and dependent (y) variables. The third argument is the number of observations existing for each of the dependent-independent variables. (The data must exist in pairs.) The final argument is a structure that holds the support statistics for the regression. Therefore, the call

```
regression(price, sales, 20, &answer);
```

is an example of how to call the regression function. Note that the call means that there are 20 observations for price[] and sales[].

The support statistics are very important because they indicate the validity of the regression results. You can think of the estimate's standard error (result.se) as the amount of variation explained by the regression, and the regression's standard error is the total variation (result.sy). The difference between the total and explained variation is called the unexplained variation. An adjusted ratio of the explained to the total variation is called the coefficient of determination (result.r). This coefficient indicates the amount of variability in the data that can be explained with the regression equation.

The coefficient's standard error (result.sdb1) is important because it can be divided into the estimated slope coefficient (result.b1) to get a t value. Therefore, if you want to know the probability that the slope coefficient is not zero, simply call the tvalue() function with result.tval and $n-2$ degrees of freedom.

Most regression experiments have a target *confidence level* of .95. That is, the support statistics for the regression should indicate that estimated values using the regression will be "correct" 95 out of 100 times. This means you can take the estimated regression equation, plug in the appropriate value for the independent variable (pizza price), estimate the dependent variable (pizza sales), and be confident that the estimated sales figure will be correct 95 percent of the time.

The question is, What is the "correct" value for the dependent variable? The estimated result of the regression is a number, but it is like a middle value for a range of possible values. For example, suppose that you have 20 degrees of freedom and that the estimated regression coefficient (b1) is 100 and the standard error is 10. At the .95 confidence level, the t value would have to be 2.086. If this is true, you know with 95 percent confidence that the true slope coefficient will fall within the range

```
b1 - t value *  s.e     to      b1 + t value *  s.e
100 - 2.086  *  10      to     100 + 2.086  *  10
100 - 20.86             to     100 + 20.86
       79.14            to            120.86
```

Notice how important the support statistics are. They give you a quantitative way to judge the confidence you can place in the estimated dependent variable. Using the preceding information, if the intercept term (b0) was 500 and the pizza price was $10, you could be 95 percent certain that your sales would fall within the range of 1,291 and 1,709 units. Remember that the regression equation estimates sales of 1,500 units, but the 95 percent confidence interval implies that the 1,500 units is more like a central tendency value within a range of 1,291–1,709 units.

If the t value from the regression is not statistically significant at the .95 confidence level, the range increases in value, making the estimate less reliable. Don't be lured into believing that the number your spreadsheet gives you is *the* sales figure, however. Without the regression supports statistics, the estimated number could be nothing more than garbage.

If you are not familiar with regression analysis, you should read a good introductory statistics book. If you work with spreadsheet analysis, regression analysis can be a valuable ally.

Reducing Storage Requirements for Symmetrical Matrices

There are many situations in which a data matrix, or table, must be processed. In some cases you can be reasonably certain that the matrix is symmetrical. That is, the value of element a[i][j] in the matrix, for example, is the same as that of element a[j][i]. In statistics, the correlation matrix commonly is a symmetrical matrix, as is the mileage table found in a road atlas.

Consider the matrix displayed in figure 8.1.

Fig. 8.1. *A symmetrical matrix.*

```
 0  10  25  18
10   0  33  20
25  33   0  15
18  20  15   0
```

The line of zeroes from a[0][0] to a[3][3] is called the *main diagonal* of the matrix. Notice how the diagonal "bisects" the matrix into two equal parts. Also notice that elements a[0][1] and a[1][0] are equal, as are all other elements in which the subscripts are reversed (for example, a[0][3] and a[3][0]). When a matrix exhibits this property, it is called a *symmetrical matrix*.

If the matrix is symmetrical, you should be able to reduce its storage requirements simply by storing everything either above or below (and including) the main diagonal.

Check Matrix for Symmetry— *check_symmetry( )*

The first task is to determine whether a certain matrix is symmetrical. If it is symmetrical, you can try reducing its size. The check_symmetry() function examines a matrix for symmetry. The function is presented in listing 8.8.

Listing 8.8. *Symmetrical matrix check.*

```
/*****

                    check_symmetry()

  This function checks to see whether the matrix is symmetric.
```

```
        Argument list:      char *a      pointer to the matrix to be checked
                            int size     size of the matrix
                            int type     the data type in the matrix

        Return value:       int          0 if not symmetric, 1 if it is

*****/

int check_symmetry(char *a, int size, int type)
{
    int i, j, *iptr;
    double *dptr;

    switch (type) {
        case sizeof(char):
            for (i = 1; i < size; i++) {
                for (j = 0; j < i; j++) {
                    if ( *(a + i * size + j) !=  *(a + j * size + i)) {
                        return 0;
                    }
                }
            }
            break;
        case sizeof(int):
            iptr = (int *) a;
            for (i = 1; i < size; i++) {
                for (j = 0; j < i; j++) {
                    if ( *(iptr + i * size + j) !=  *(iptr + j * size + i)) {
                        return 0;
                    }
                }
            }
            break;
        case sizeof(double):
            dptr = (double *) a;
            for (i = 1; i < size; i++) {
                for (j = 0; j < i; j++) {
                    if ( *(dptr + i * size + j) !=  *(dptr + j * size + i)) {
                        return 0;
                    }
                }
            }
            break;
```

continues

Listing 8.8. continued

```
    default:
        return 0;


    }
    return 1;
}
```

Listing 8.8 assumes that the matrix is either a char, an int, or a double data type. If you need to check a matrix containing another data type, use listing 8.8 as a model and add the new data type. The first argument is a pointer to the matrix. Because you do not know the type of data at runtime, simply define the matrix pointer as a pointer to char. Within each case statement, a cast is used, if needed, to change the scalar of the pointer to the appropriate data type.

The second function argument (size) simply tells the matrix's size. Because you are interested in only symmetrical matrices, the matrix is assumed to be square. The third argument (type) tells the function what type of data the matrix contains. Based on this argument, a switch statement determines which data type is processed by the function.

The function's work is performed by two nested for loops. The function is efficient because it does not double-check the matrix. For example, early in the loop when i = 1 and j = 2, you check a[1][2] against element a[2][1]. A less efficient algorithm also would check a[2][1] against a[1][2] when j = 1 and i = 2. This algorithm avoids such double checks. Notice also that the check_symmetry() function does not bother checking the main diagonal (a[1][1], a[2][2], and so on), because this amounts to checking a value against itself. The best way to understand how the algorithm works is to perform the calculations by hand, using the matrix in figure 8.1 as an example.

If the matrix is symmetrical, the value of 1 is returned; otherwise, the return value is 0. If the matrix is not symmetrical, you cannot use the space-reduction techniques discussed in the following section.

Considerations for Symmetrical Matrices

If `check_symmetry()` returns 1, then almost half of the matrix is redundant. (The redundancy is not exactly half because all the matrix's main diagonal elements still must be maintained.) For example, given the matrix

```
static int a[][4] = {
    {110,  45,  97,   35},
    { 45, 200,  33,   11},
    { 97,  33,  10,   29},
    { 35,  11,  29,  300}
    };
```

you can see that element a[0][3] is the same as a[3][0]. If you change all the redundant values in the a[][] to 0, you can rewrite the matrix as

```
static int b[][4] = {
    {110,   0,   0,    0},
    { 45, 200,   0,    0},
    { 97,  33,  10,    0},
    { 35,  11,  29,  300}
    };
```

In the b[][] matrix, only the nonzero values must be preserved. You need a way to rewrite the matrix and discard its redundant values.

Without going through the mathematical proof, the following relationships exist for a symmetrical matrix:

Rule 1: When i is greater than or equal to j, the proper element to read is

$$\frac{i * (i + 1)}{2} + j$$

Rule 2: When i is less than j, the proper element is

$$\frac{j * (j + 1)}{2} + i$$

You can read any value in the a[][] matrix using the b[][] if you use the indexing relationship suggested by the two preceding rules.

After you have convinced yourself that the relationship indeed holds true, you also might convince yourself that the b[][] matrix can be stored as a vector. That is, given the a[][] matrix, you can use a vector c[] using the indexing rules if c[] contains the values

```
int c[] = {110, 45, 200, 97, 33, 10, 35, 11, 29, 300};
```

As a further example, consider element a[i][j] when i = 0 and j = 3, or the value 35 in the a[][] matrix. Using Rule 2 from before, with i = 0 and j = 3:

$$\frac{j * (j + 1)}{2} + i$$

which is

$$\frac{3 * (3 + 1)}{2} + 0$$

and reduces to

```
12 / 2 = 6;
```

When you use the value 6 as the subscript into the c[] vector, c[6] is, in fact, equal to 35 and equals a[0][3] or a[3][0] in the original matrix.

Open a Symmetrical Matrix— *open_matrix( )*

Listing 8.9 illustrates the use of the open_matrix() function with a symmetrical matrix.

Listing 8.9. *Open a symmetrical matrix.*

```
/*****
                            open_matrix()

   This function attempts to allocate enough storage to hold the
reduced-size matrix.

   Argument list:    int msize      the size of the matrix (one side)
                     int dsize      size of the data type in the matrix
```

```
    Return value:     char *          pointer to allocation if available;
                                      a null pointer otherwise


*****/


#include <alloc.h>                          /* Might also be malloc.h   */

char *open_matrix(int msize, int dsize)
{
   int small;

   small = ( (msize * msize) + msize) / 2;
   return (calloc(small, dsize));
}
```

Two arguments are passed to the function. The first argument indicates the matrix's size; the second argument gives the size of the data type stored in the matrix. If the matrix is 10x10 in size and contains double data types, for example, the call should be

```
    char *open_matrix(int, int);          /* Declare it */
    double *dptr;


    .
    .
    .

    dptr = (double *) open_matrix(10, sizeof(double));
    if (dptr == NULL) {
       printf("Out of memory");
       exit(1);
    }
```

The open_matrix() function simply calculates the vector's storage requirements and then attempts to get an allocation for the vector. A non-null pointer is returned if the allocation is successful.

Fill in the Symmetrical Vector—
fill_vector( )

You use the pointer returned from open_matrix() to hold the vector equivalent of the symmetrical matrix. Listing 8.10 shows the code for the fill_vector() function, which fills in the vector.

Listing 8.10. *Fill in vector values from symmetrical matrix.*

```
/*****
                              fill_vector()

        This function fills in the storage for the reduced-size
    matrix.

        Argument list:     char *a       pointer to original matrix
                           char *b       pointer to vector
                           int dsize     which type of data to be used
                           int msize     size of one side of matrix

        Return value:      int           1 if vector filled, 0 if not

*****/


int fill_vector(char *a, char *b, int dsize, int msize)
{
    char *crptr, *csptr;
    int i, j, *rptr, *sptr, term;
    double *drptr, *dsptr;

    switch (dsize) {
        case sizeof(char):                    /* For char data types       */
            crptr = b;
            csptr = a;
            for (i = 0; i < msize; i++) {
                term = i * msize;
                for (j = 0; j <= i; j++) {
                    *crptr++ = *(csptr + term + j);
                }
            }
            break;

        case sizeof(int):                     /* For integer data types    */
            rptr = (int *) b;
            sptr = (int *) a;
            for (i = 0; i < msize; i++) {
                term = i * msize;
                for (j = 0; j <= i; j++) {
                    *rptr++ = *(sptr + term + j);
```

```
            }
        }
        break;
    case sizeof(double):                /* For double data types    */
        drptr = (double *) b;
        dsptr = (double *) a;
        for (i = 0; i < msize; i++) {
            term = i * msize;
          for (j = 0; j <= i; j++) {
              *drptr++ = *(dsptr + term + j);
          }
        }
        break;
    default:
        return 0;
    }
    return 1;
}
```

The function serves as a model that can be modified if you work with matrices that contain date types other than char, int, or double. The arguments are a pointer to the original matrix, the pointer returned from open_matrix(), the size of the data type stored in the matrix, and the size of the matrix.

The statement fragment

```
*(dsptr + i * msize + j);
```

is used to calculate the offset from the matrix's base address. This can be improved by moving the calculation of i * msize outside the inner (j) loop. This is done with the term variable shown in listing 8.10.

The nested for loops read the matrix and assign the values into the appropriate locations in the vector. When the function ends, b points to the storage that will contain the vector equivalent of the symmetrical matrix.

You can make the fill_vector() function more flexible. For example, you can modify the function to work directly from disk data files.

Read Values from the Vector— *read_mat( )*

The next function enables you to access values in the vector in much the same way you would if the entire symmetrical matrix were in memory. The read_mat() function is presented in listing 8.11.

Listing 8.11. Read vector values.

```
/*****

                            read_mat()

     This function reads one value from the vector.

        Argument list:    char *vec      pointer to vector to be read
                          int i          the row element to be read
                          int j          the column element to be read
                          int dsize      the data type in the matrix

        Return value:     char *         pointer to data value read or null
                                         if not valid

*****/


char *read_mat(char *vec, int i, int j, int dsize)
{
    int *iptr;
    double *dptr;

    switch (dsize) {
        case sizeof(char):
            if (i >= j)
                return &vec[ ( (i * (i + 1)) >> 1) + j];
            else
                return &vec[ ( (j * (j + 1)) >> 1) + i];
        case sizeof(int):
            iptr = (int *) vec;
            if (i >= j)
                return (char *) &iptr[ ( (i * (i + 1)) >> 1) + j];
            else
                return (char *) &iptr[ ( (j * (j + 1)) >> 1) + i];
```

```
       case sizeof(double):
          dptr = (double *) vec;
          if (i >= j) {
             return (char *)&dptr[ ( (i * (i + 1)) >> 1) + j];
          } else {
             return (char *)&dptr[ ( (j * (j + 1)) >> 1) + i];
          }
       default:
          return (char *) 0;
    }
}
```

Again, the read_mat() function can be used as a model if you want to add new data types to those presented here. The first argument is declared as a pointer to char, even though it might be another type of data. A cast is used on non-char data types to access the data in the vector.

The second and third arguments are the i-j indexes that would be used to access the value from a normal matrix (as in a[i][j]). The final argument tells which type of data will be read.

The return value is a pointer to the value read. Therefore, you probably will declare read_mat() to return a pointer to char, as in the statement

```
char *read_mat(char *, int, int, int);
```

and cast the result if the matrix holds data of a type other than char. If the matrix contains integer data types, for example, you might call read_mat() as follows:

```
val = *(int *) read_mat( (char *) ptr, i, j, sizeof(int) );
```

The char pointer cast is necessary if the read_mat() prototype is to agree with the function call. You can use a void pointer cast for ptr, if you like. This is allowed by ANSI but might not be supported by non-ANSI compilers. Use indirection (the asterisk before the cast) to make the assignment into val.

Change a Value in a Matrix— *put_mat()*

Now that you can initialize and read a matrix stored as a vector, you might need another function to change an existing value in the matrix. Such changes are made with the put_mat() function, presented in listing 8.12.

Listing 8.12. _Change a value in the matrix._

```
/*****
                              put_mat()

    This function reads one value from the vector.

    Argument list:      void *vec    pointer to vector to be read
                        int i        the row element to be read
                        int j        the column element to be read
                        int dsize    the data type in the matrix
                        void *val    the value to write in

    Return value:       void

*****/


void put_mat(void *vec, int i, int j, int dsize, void *val)
{
    char *cptr;
    int *iptr;
    double *dptr;

    switch (dsize) {
      case sizeof(char):
        cptr = (char *) vec;
        if (i >= j)
            cptr[ ( (i * (i + 1)) >> 1) + j] = *(char *) val;
        else
            cptr[ ( (j * (j + 1)) >> 1) + i] = *(char *) val;
      case sizeof(int):
        iptr = (int *) vec;
        if (i >= j)
            iptr[ ( (i * (i + 1)) >> 1) + j] = *(int *) val;
        else
            iptr[ ( (j * (j + 1)) >> 1) + i] = *(int *) val;
      case sizeof(double):
        dptr = (double *) vec;
        if (i >= j) {
            dptr[ ( (i * (i + 1)) >> 1) + j] = *(double *) val;
        } else {
            dptr[ ( (j * (j + 1)) >> 1) + i] = *(double *) val;
```

```
            }
        break;
    default:
        break;
    }
}
```

The arguments are the same as in read_mat(), with a fifth argument added for the value to be entered into the vector. The fifth argument is declared as a pointer to void, but you can use a pointer to char if your compiler does not support a void pointer.

The rest of the code is much the same as read_mat(), but you are writing a value into the vector instead of reading it. The value is cast to the proper data type to avoid a type mismatch error.

Close the Vector—*close_mat( )*

Because a dynamic memory allocation has been done for the vector, that storage must be freed when you are finished with it. The close_mat() function, shown in listing 8.13, does this for you.

Listing 8.13. Free vector storage.

```
/*****
                            close_matrix()

    This function frees the storage associated with the reduced-size
    matrix.

    Argument list:    char *ptr      pointer to the open matrix

    Return value:     void

*****/

void close_matrix(char *ptr)
{
    free(ptr);
}
```

You can, of course, do this as inline code, but the function call is logically consistent with the other functions discussed. That is, you now have a set of functions that open, fill, read, and close the matrix.

Using the Symmetrical Matrix Functions

You can access any element in the matrix by using the read_mat() function. This section demonstrates the ways in which you might modify existing code to use the symmetrical matrix functions. Listing 8.14 shows the normal code used to add two matrices together.

Listing 8.14. *Add two matrices.*

```
/*****
                              matadd()

    This function returns a matrix that is the sum of two matrices.
The function assumes that the number of rows in m1 is equal to the
number of columns in m2. Otherwise, all bets are off.

Argument list:    double *m1      pointer to the matrix 1
                  double *m2      pointer to the matrix 2
                  double *result  pointer to the resulting matrix
                  int m           the rows in the m1
                  int n           the columns in the m2

Return value:     void

*****/


void matadd(double *m1, double *m2, double *result, int m, int n)
{
   int i, j, term;

   if (n != m) {
      *result = 0.0;
      return;
```

```
    }
    for (i = 0; i < m; i++) {
        term = i * m;
        for (j = 0; j < n; j++) {
            *(result + term + j) = *(m1 + term + j) + *(m2 + term + j);
        }
    }
}
```

The arguments are two input matrices (m1 and m2), the matrix for the sum of the two matrices (result), the number of rows in m1, and the number of columns in m2. Matrix addition requires that the rows (columns) in one matrix be equal to the columns (rows) in the other matrix. If this is not true, the function fills in 0.0 for the first element in the result matrix and then returns.

If everything proceeds properly, a nested for is used to add the two matrices together, using the normal pointer indexing scheme for double-dimensioned arrays.

Listing 8.15 shows the same function, but assumes that the first input matrix is symmetrical.

Listing 8.15. *Add two matrices together (assume that the first matrix is a vector).*

```
/*****

                        matadd()

    This function returns a matrix that is the sum of two matrices.
The function assumes that the number of rows in m1 is equal to the
number of columns in m2. Otherwise, all bets are off.

Argument list:      double *m1      pointer to the matrix 1
                    double *m2      pointer to the matrix 2
                    double *result  pointer to the resulting matrix
                    int m           the rows in the m1
                    int n           the columns in the m2

Return value:       void

*****/
```

continues

Listing 8.15. continued

```
void matadd(double *m1, double *m2, double *result, int m, int n)
{
   int i, j, term;
   char *read_mat(double *, int, int, int);

   if (n != m) {
      *result = 0.0;
      return;
   }
   for (i = 0; i < m; i++) {
      term = i * m;
      for (j = 0; j < n; j++) {
         *(result + term + j) = *(double *) read_mat(m1, i, j, sizeof(double))
                              + *(m2 + term + j);
      }
   }
}
```

The matadd() function (in listing 8.15) assumes that the first matrix actually is a symmetrical matrix that has been stored as a vector. The only difference between the two functions is the addition of the declaration for read_mat(), and its use in accessing the proper element in the symmetrical (vector) matrix m1.

In many situations you probably will use either symmetrical or nonsymmetrical matrices and will not have to "mix" the two, as shown in listing 8.15. Even if you do have to mix them, however, writing the code is not much different than using standard matrices.

Using a vector has a substantial advantage. For example, a correlation matrix with 100 variables normally uses 80K just for the matrix. Because a correlation matrix is symmetrical, the same matrix could be stored in a vector using only 40.4K. Sometimes, the savings can mean the difference between processing the data and issuing an "out of memory" error.

Financial Calculations

Most financial calculations involve the flow of income over time, compound interest, and present value calculations. In a very real sense, compound interest is the inverse of present value analysis. For example, if you place $95.24 in the bank at 5 percent interest, the value at the end of one year would be $100.00. Conversely, if someone offers to sell you a bond guaranteed to pay you $100.00 a year from now, and the prevailing interest rate is 5 percent, then you should pay no more than $95.24 for the bond.

Compound Interest Multiplier— *compound( )*

Listing 8.16 presents the compound() function, which returns a multiplier value. This value can be used for figuring compound interest.

Listing 8.16. *Compound interest.*

```
/*****
                            compound()

    This function returns a multiplier that can be used to figure
compound interest.

    Argument list:    double year      the number of years to compound
                      double irate     the interest rate

    Return value:     double           the value of 1 compounded for
                                       year at irate percent
*****/

#include <math.h>

double compound(double year, double irate)
{
    return (pow(1.0 + irate, year));
}
```

If you call compound() with the year set to 10 and the interest rate set to 0.05 (5 percent), the return value will be approximately 1.55297. Therefore, if you placed $1,000 in an IRA paying 5 percent interest, the balance after 10 years would be

```
value = 1000.0 * compound(10.0, .05);
value = 1552.97;
```

Although you can write the function to figure the final amount as part of the function code, there is little reason to do so; it just adds another argument to the function. Also, other financial calculations use the compound interest calculations.

Present Value Discount Factor— *present_value( )*

A relatively new financial instrument is the "zero coupon" bond. (The concept is not new; only the name is.) The bonds promise to pay the face amount *n* years from now. Normally, there is no coupon rate on these bonds, which is why they are called zero coupon bonds. Instead, market forces set their sales price.

An example helps show how these bonds are priced. Suppose that a company issues 10-year bonds in $1,000 units, and the prevailing rate of interest is 11.5 percent. If you purchase a bond on the day it is issued, you should pay no more than $336.71. That is, if you place $336.71 in the bank at ll.5 percent interest, the balance will be $1,000 at the end of 10 years. The code for present_value() is shown in listing 8.17.

Listing 8.17. Present value factor.

```
/*****
                        present_value()

    This function returns a multiplier that can be used to figure
    the present value of a future income stream.

    Argument list:    double year      the number of years to compound
                      double irate     the interest rate

    Return value:     double           the discounted value of 1 for
                                       year at irate percent
*****/

#include <math.h>

double present_value(double year, double i)
{
    return (1.0 / (pow(1.0 + i, year)));
}
```

Using the numbers in the example, calling the function with an interest rate of 11.5 and years equal to 10 returns a discount factor of 0.336706. To calculate the value of a $1,000 bond, your code might look like this

```
value = 1000.0 * present_value(10.0, .115);
```

yielding 336.71 for value.

The present_value() function returns a discount rate whose reciprocal is equal to the number returned from compound(), if the same arguments are used. Therefore,

```
compound(10.0, .115) = 1.0 / present_value(10.0, .115);
        2.96995       =       1.0 / .336706
        2.96995       =       2.96995
```

By omitting the dollar amount from the calculations in both functions, you can use this relationship to build other functions.

Payments to Reach a Financial Goal— *future_amt( )*

When you calculate compound interest and present value equations, you might need to determine how much money should be regularly set aside to attain a financial goal. For example, if you will need $20,000 to send a child to school 10 years from now, how much should you pay monthly into a 6 percent savings account to attain that sum? The future_amt() function (see listing 8.18) shows how to calculate the required amount.

Listing 8.18. *Payments to reach a financial goal.*

```
/*****

                    future_amt()

    This function determines the amount a payment must be to
accumulate a specified amount of money in the future.

    Argument list:     double p      the amount desired
                       double n      the number of yearly payments
                       double i      the annual interest rate
                       double y      the number of years payments are
                                     made
```

continues

Listing 8.18. continued

```
   Return value:     double       the monthly payment


*****/


#include <math.h>


double future_amt(double p, double n, double i, double y)
{
   return p * ((i / n) / (pow(1.0 + i / n, n * y) - 1.0));
}
```

The number of payments (n) is the number of payments *per year*. If monthly payments are made, the value of n is 12. The return value is the amount that must be paid each (n) period. In the example, if you need $20,000 at the end of 10 years at 6 percent interest, the monthly payment would be $122.04.

Compound Interest (Annual)— *compoundy( )*

Some assets compound interest annually. Listing 8.19 shows the compoundy() function for such calculations.

Listing 8.19. Compound interest (yearly).

```
/*****

                              compoundy()


   This function returns a multiplier that can be used to figure
   annual compound interest.

   Argument list:    double year      the number of years to compound
                     double irate     the interest rate

   Return value:     double           the value of 1 compounded for
                                      year at irate percent
*****/


#include <math.h>
```

```
double compoundy(double year, double irate)
{
    return (pow(1.0 + irate, year));
}
```

Your calculations are limited here because the compounding is done only yearly. The next function generalizes this to compounding for any annual compounding period. The function's returned value is a multiplier that must be multiplied by the principal amount to determine the principal and interest total. Therefore, if $1,000.00 is deposited for two years at 6 percent interest, the balance would be $1,123.60 at the end of two years. This means that compoundy() returns a value of 1.1236.

Compound Interest (X Periods per Year)—*compoundx( )*

The compoundx() function also calculates compound interest, but allows for compounding any number of times during the year (such as daily compounding, monthly compounding, and so on). The compoundx() function is presented in listing 8.20.

Listing 8.20. Compound interest (x periods per year).

```
/*****
                        compoundx()

    This function returns a multiplier that can be used to figure
compound interest for any number of annual compounding periods.

    Argument list:    double year      the number of years to compound
                      double irate     the interest rate
                      double factor    the number of times per year
                                       that compounding is done

    Return value:     double           the value of 1 compounded factor
                                       times per year at irate percent
                                       for year years

*****/
```

continues

/Listing 8.20. continued

```
#include <math.h>

double compoundx(double year, double irate, double factor)
{
    return (pow(1.0 + (irate / factor), factor * year));
}
```

Again, the return value is a multiplier that must be applied to the principal amount to determine the principal and interest balance. For example, $1,000.00 for two years at 6 percent interest with monthly compounding has an ending balance of $1,127.16; daily interest produces a balance of $1,127.49. Therefore, in these two examples, the returned multipliers are 1.12716 and 1.12749.

It is interesting to note that banks used to advertise that interest was compounded daily on savings accounts. If they raised their compounding rate to hourly instead of daily, the balance of the savings account in this example would increase by one penny.

Loan Payment—*payment( )*

No discussion of financial calculations would be complete without the old loan-payment routine. The payment() function in listing 8.21 calculates the monthly payment needed to retire a specified loan in a specified amount of time.

Listing 8.21. Monthly loan payment.

```
/*****
                            payment()

    This function determines the monthly payment for a loan.

    Argument list:    double p     the amount borrowed
                      double m     the number of monthly payments
                      double i     the annual interest rate
```

```
    Return value:      double         the monthly payment

*****/

#include <math.h>

double payment(double p, double m, double i)
{
   double mi;

   mi = i / 12.0;                          /* Monthly interest rate    */

   return (mi * p * ( (pow(1.0 + mi, m)) / (pow(1.0 + mi, m) - 1.0)));
}
```

Because the loan's principal amount is passed in as an argument, the return value is the monthly payment (not a multiplier). Therefore, a loan of $14,600.00 at 13.5 percent for 60 months would require a monthly payment of about $335.94.

Conclusion

This chapter presented a variety of statistical, math, and financial functions. The accuracy of the probability distributions exceeds those published in most statistics texts. When you use the functions presented in this chapter, be sure to use function prototyping. Most of the functions do not return an int data type.

9

Odds and Ends

Don't let this chapter's title fool you. This chapter is called "Odds and Ends" simply because the functions found here would not fit conveniently into any of the previous chapters. This chapter also breaks with tradition by presenting several complete programs that should be useful in your programming projects. Therefore, although this chapter's name is a bit strange, I think you will find the programs presented in it quite useful.

This chapter introduces you to functions of diverse nature. With one function, for example, you can use (and restore) the 43-line mode on an EGA or a VGA display device. Another function enables you to edit an input line in a manner similar to many text editors. Another function shows how to use splines for graphics work. All the functions are useful tools.

Get and/or Edit a String— *geditstr( )*

By using the `geditstr()` function, you can either edit an existing character string or input a string and then edit it. This function enables much more editing than does the standard C library's `gets()` function. Furthermore, adding new editing features to `geditstr()` or redefining the function's existing features is simple.

Table 9.1 presents the symbolic constants that define the editing features of `geditstr()`.

***Table 9.1.** Defined editing features (`keys.h`).*

```
#define NEWLINE    '\r'    /* End input             */
#define BACKSPACE  '\b'    /* Backspace char        */
#define BELL       7       /* ASCII bell code       */
#define ESCAPE     27      /* Abort edit            */


#define FKEY       0       /* Special function keys */
#define HOME       71      /* Start of input        */
#define UARROW     72
#define PGUP       73
#define RARROW     77      /* Letter right          */
#define PGDN       81
#define DARROW     80
#define END        79      /* End of input          */
#define LARROW     75      /* Letter left           */
#define DELETE     83      /* Delete at cursor      */
#define INSERT     82      /* Open space for char   */


                          /* Control keys           */
#define CTRL_A     1       /* Word left             */
#define CTRL_D     4       /* Letter right          */
#define CTRL_F     6       /* Word right            */
#define CTRL_G     7       /* Delete at cursor      */
#define CTRL_S     19      /* Letter left           */
#define CTRL_T     20      /* Delete word right     */
```

The first set of definitions (NEWLINE through ESCAPE) simply defines standard keystrokes for the ASCII character set. The NEWLINE macro actually is a carriage return, not the line-feed character. When you do "raw" keyboard I/O with the getch() function, the carriage return usually is the return code when the Enter key is pressed. Your compiler, however, might return the newline character (\n). If the function does not terminate when the Enter key is pressed, try switching from the carriage-return character to the newline character.

The next set of definitions (FKEY through INSERT) includes the special function keys found on the numeric keypad. All the cursor-control functions are presented, even though the geditstr() function does not use them all. If you want to use the macros in table 9.1 in other programs, you can find the macros in the keys.h header file on the disk included with this book.

The last macros are standard features you use when you edit text. Most of the popular C compilers use editing key sequences similar to those found in WordStar. Many programmers know that among these sequences, for example, pressing Ctrl-T deletes the word to the right of the cursor. Because many programmers are used to these key sequences, they are retained here for use in the geditstr() function.

Of course, if you prefer different key sequences, you easily can change the macros shown in table 9.1. In fact, you can replace them with a corresponding set of variables and let the user define a customized set of editing key sequences for storage in the variables. A program can save the user's key sequences in a file for subsequent use in a program.

The geditstr() code is presented in listing 9.1.

Listing 9.1. *Edit a string.*

```
/*****

                            geditstr()

    This function enables input and editing of string data. If the
input strings are empty, the function receives the data in the
normal manner. If the first character of s is non-null, it is
assumed that a valid string has been passed for editing. When the
Enter key is pressed (that is, c == NEWLINE), the new string data
is copied into s. If Escape is pressed, the edit is aborted and no
change is made to the contents of s.

    Argument list:    int row      the row address for the cursor
                      int col      the column address for the cursor
                      char *s      the input string

    Argument list:    int          NEWLINE if data accepted,
                                   ESCAPE if edit aborted

*****/


#include <string.h>
#include <mem.h>                         /* This might be memory.h    */
#include "keys.h"

#define MAXSLEN    256
```

continues

Listing 9.1. continued

```c
#ifndef TRUE
   #define TRUE   1
#endif

#define MAXSLEN    256

int geditstr(int row, int col, char *s)
{
   char buff[MAXSLEN], *ptr;
   int bindex, c, c1, len, temp;

   c1 = col;
   bindex = 0;
   memset(buff, 0, MAXSLEN);              /* Clear buffer           */
   if (*s) {
      cursor(row, col);
      strcpy(buff, s);
      puts(buff);
   }
   cursor(row, col);
   while (TRUE) {
      c = getch();
      switch (c) {
         case FKEY:                       /* Special function keys   */
            c = getch();
            switch (c) {
               case HOME:                 /* Go to start of string   */
                  c1 = col;
                  bindex = 0;
                  cursor(row, c1);
                  break;
do_ctrl_d:     case RARROW:               /* Move cursor 1 right      */
                  c1++;
                  cursor(row, c1);
                  bindex++;
                  break;
               case END:                  /* Go to end of string      */
                  bindex = strlen(buff);
                  c1 = col + bindex;
                  cursor(row, c1);
                  break;
```

```
do_ctrl_s:   case LARROW:              /* Move cursor 1 left       */
                c1--;
                cursor(row, c1);
                bindex--;
                break;
do_ctrl_g:   case DELETE:              /* Delete char at cursor    */
                len = strlen(buff);
                strcpy(&buff[bindex], &buff[bindex + 1]);
                buff[len] = '\0';
                cursor(row, c1);
                puts(&buff[bindex]);
                cursor(row, col + len - 1);
                putchar(' ');
                cursor(row, c1);
                break;
             case INSERT:              /* Insert char at cursor    */
                cursor(row, c1 + 1);
                puts(&buff[bindex]);
                len = strlen(&buff[bindex]);
                memmove(&buff[bindex + 1], &buff[bindex], len + 1);
                buff[bindex] = ' ';
                cursor(row, c1);
                putchar(' ');
                cursor(row, c1);
                break;
             default:
                putchar(BELL);
                break;
          }                            /* End of inner switch      */
          break;                       /* for FKEYS                */

       case NEWLINE:                    /* End of input             */
          strcpy(s, buff);
          break;
       case BACKSPACE:                  /* Backspace                */
          strcpy(&buff[bindex - 1], &buff[bindex]);
          bindex--;
          c1--;
          cursor(row, c1);
          puts(&buff[bindex]);
          len = strlen(buff);
          cursor(row, col + len);
          putchar(' ');
```

continues

Listing 9.1. continued

```
                    cursor(row, c1);
                    break;
                case CTRL_A:                    /* Move word left         */
                    if (bindex) {
                        temp = buff[bindex - 1];
                        buff[bindex - 1] = '\0';
                        ptr = strrchr(buff, ' ');
                        buff[bindex - 1] = temp;    .
                        if (ptr) {
                            bindex = ptr - buff + 1;
                        } else {
                            bindex = 0;
                        }
                    }
                    c1 = col + bindex;
                    cursor(row, c1);
                    break;
                case CTRL_D:                    /* Move letter right      */
                    goto do_ctrl_d;
                case CTRL_F:                    /* Move word right        */
                    len = strlen(&buff[bindex]);
                    ptr = memchr(&buff[bindex + 1], ' ', len);
                    if (ptr) {
                        bindex = ptr - buff + 1;
                    } else {
                        bindex = strlen(buff);
                    }
                    c1 = col + bindex;
                    cursor(row, c1);
                    break;
                case CTRL_G:                    /* Delete char (= DELETE) */
                    goto do_ctrl_g;
                case CTRL_S:                    /* Move letter left       */
                    goto do_ctrl_s;
                case CTRL_T:                    /* Delete word right      */
                    len = strlen(&buff[bindex]);
                    if (len) {
                        ptr = memchr(&buff[bindex + 1], ' ', len);
                        if (ptr) {
                            strcpy(&buff[bindex], ptr + 1);
                        } else {
```

```
                    buff[bindex] = '\0';
                    eraeol();
                    break;
                }
                if (strlen(&buff[bindex])) {
                    cursor(row, c1);
                    printf("%s", &buff[bindex]);
                    eraeol();
                    cursor(row, c1);
                }
            }
            break;
        default:                        /* ASCII key pressed        */
            cursor(row, c1);
            putchar(c);
            buff[bindex] = c;
            bindex++;
            c1++;
            break;
        }
        if (c == NEWLINE |¦ c == ESCAPE)
            break;
    }                                   /* End while (TRUE)         */
    if (c == NEWLINE) {
        strcpy(s, buff);
    }
    return c;
}
```

The geditstr() function has three arguments. The first argument is the input string's row position. Next is the string's column position. The final argument is the string character input buffer. The cursor-positioning function was discussed in Chapter 1, "Screen Functions." The third argument's use depends on the way in which you want to use the function.

The function can be used in two ways. First, you can pass the character pointer that points to an existing string. In this case, s already contains data, but you want to edit that data. The second option assumes that the character pointer s does not yet point to a valid character string, and that geditstr() will be used to fill in the string while also enabling it to be edited. The second method requires the array's first character to be the null-termination character (*s = '\0').

After program control is sent to geditstr(), the function clears the temporary storage buffer buff[] by way of a call to memset(). If the array's first character is non-null, the string passed to the function is displayed.

An infinite while loop collects the input from the keyboard by calls to getch(). Generally, the input consists of either ASCII characters to be entered into the string, or editing sequences to modify the string's existing contents. As ASCII characters are entered, they simply are written into the character array. The variable bindex keeps track of your position in the array, and c1 keeps track of your position on the screen.

Of these two input types, only editing sequences need to be discussed. If a special function key is pressed, the initial call to getch() returns a value of 0. This indicates that a special function key was read and that a second call to getch() is necessary to see which key was pressed. This is why case FKEY performs a second call to getch(). After the second call, c contains the corresponding scan code for the function key pressed by the user (see table 9.1). A second switch statement that is part of FKEY determines the specific action taken; the action can be determined by referring to the comments shown in table 9.1. (Notice that Page Up, Page Down, up arrow, and down arrow are not used in the geditstr() function. Assume that a single line of text is being edited.)

If a special function key has not been pressed, then the outermost switch statement selects the action to be taken. Again, table 9.1 shows which action occurs. Most are either ASCII characters, actions (such as BELL), or the Ctrl-key sequences (for example, Ctrl-G to delete a character). To change the key sequences or add new ones, you simply create a new macro and add it to the switch.

Using *goto* Statements

Careful readers will notice that several goto statements are used in the function. You easily can eliminate the gotos if you want to duplicate the code associated with them, or you can convolute the function's logic so that the gotos are unnecessary. Many programmers will complain about the presence of the goto statements; however, the function exemplifies a situation in which the use of goto statements makes sense. That is, the goto statements are the simplest solution to the problem.

Further, the goto statements transfer program control to code that shares multiple definitions for the same action. For example, Ctrl-G and Delete both delete the character under the cursor. But because the Delete key is a special function key, you cannot use a multiple case to cause the same section of code to execute, as in

.
.

```
case CTRL_G:
case DELETE:
    /* The appropriate code here */
```

.

This code fragment does not work because you must call `getch()` twice when the Delete key is pressed, but only once for `CTRL_G`. The `goto` statement provides a simple solution to the problem.

Terminating an Edit

The program continues to collect characters from the keyboard until one of two keystrokes is read—either the `NEWLINE` character or the `ESCAPE` character. If the `NEWLINE` character is read, the `if` statement (near the bottom of listing 9.1) transfers control out of the infinite `while` loop and copies the string from the temporary buffer `buff[]` into the pointer passed to the function (s).

If the Escape key is read, it is assumed that the user wants to abort the edit and leave s unchanged. Because all the editing in the function is done on `buff[]`, pressing Escape simply means that `buff[]` is not copied into s before the function ends. This leaves the original string held in s intact.

The `geditstr()` function uses several other functions presented in earlier chapters (such as `cursor()` and `eraeol()`); be sure that they are available at link time.

43-Line EGA-VGA Screen Mode

An MS-DOS version 4.0 command enables users to place an EGA or a VGA screen in a mode that enables them to view 43 lines at a time on the screen. Because of the EGA and VGA display adapters' higher resolution, the screen is quite readable, even with 43 lines of output displayed. Even though the function works with both EGA and VGA monitors, both types of monitors are referred to as EGA in subsequent discussions.

This section presents functions that enable you to place an EGA display in the 43-line mode even if you do not have MS-DOS 4.0. To use the 43-line mode, you first must check for the presence of an EGA video device and—assuming that an EGA is present in the system—place the screen in the 43-line mode. When the program is finished, you must reset the display to the conventional 25-line mode.

Remember that pre–MS-DOS 4.0 programs that use the 43-line mode must use direct video memory access to display data on the screen. If your programs attempt to use the BIOS services, the screen goes into the 43-line mode but still displays a maximum of 25 lines on the screen. In other words, without direct screen writes, about half of the screen is wasted. Therefore, pre-4.0 programmers should plan to use some of the techniques on direct writes to video memory that were discussed in Chapter 1, "Screen Functions."

Is There an EGA Present?—*egatest( )*

Your first task is to determine whether you have an EGA display adapter. If you do, you can use the 43-line mode. Listing 9.2 presents the code that tests for an EGA device.

***Listing 9.2.** Test for an EGA.*

```
/*****
                              egatest()

   This function determines whether an EGA system is present for
   video display.

   Argument list:    void

   Return value:     int      -1 if no EGA present; otherwise, the
                               number of 64K EGA memory blocks
                               available (0 = 64K, 1 = 128K, etc.)
*****/

#include <dos.h>

int egatest(void)
{
   union REGS ireg;
```

```
    ireg.h.ah = 0x12;
    ireg.h.al = 0x00;
    ireg.h.bl = 0x10;
    int86(0x10, &ireg, &ireg);
    if (ireg.h.bl == 0x10)
        return -1;
    else
        return ireg.h.bl;
}
```

The `egatest()` function uses function 0x12 of interrupt 0x10 to see whether an EGA is present. If the return value in `ireg.h.bl` is unchanged after the interrupt call (0x10), something other than an EGA display adapter is being used in the system, and the return value is set to −1. If the return value in `ireg.h.bl` is not equal to 0x10, the value in `ireg.h.bl` equals the number of 64K blocks being used by the EGA device, with 0 equaling one 64K block. The maximum number of blocks is three, which equals 256K of video memory.

Set EGA 43-Line Mode—*startega43( )*

If all goes well with the `egatest()` call, you can place the screen in the 43-line mode by using the code shown in listing 9.3.

Listing 9.3. *Start 43-line EGA mode.*

```
/*****

                        startega43()

    This function attempts to place an EGA screen into the 43-row
    mode. I/O in this mode requires the program to control all screen
    I/O before DOS 4.0.

    Argument list:    void

    Return value:     int      0 if an error, 1 otherwise

*****/
```

continues

Listing 9.3. continued

```c
#include <dos.h>

int startega43(void)
{
   unsigned int base;
   int mode;
   union REGS ireg;

   mode = egatest();
   if (mode < 0)                          /* No EGA present       */
      return 0;
   mode = getvmode();
   if (mode < 2 || mode > 3)
      return 0;
   ireg.x.ax = mode;                      /* Reset screen mode    */
   int86(0x10, &ireg, &ireg);
   ireg.x.ax = 0x1112;                    /* Set double dot       */
   ireg.h.bl = 0;                         /* for block load       */
   int86(0x10, &ireg, &ireg);

   poke(0x87, 0x40, peek(0x87,0x40) | 0x01);
   ireg.x.ax = 0x0100;
   ireg.h.bh = 0x00;
   ireg.x.cx = 0x0600;
   int86(0x10, &ireg, &ireg);

   base = peek(0x63, 0x40);               /* Port address for CRT */
   outportb(base, 0x14);
   outportb(base + 0x01, 0x07);
   ireg.x.ax = 0x1200;                    /* Do EGA 43            */
   ireg.h.bl = 0x20;
   int86(0x10, &ireg, &ireg);
   return 1;
}
```

The program has no function arguments and begins with a call to egatest(). If you prefer, you can move the egatest() call out of the function and call it explicitly before calling startega43(). Because it is just another detail to remember, however, I simply placed the call to egatest() in startega43().

Next, call getvmode() to be sure that you are in an 80x25 text mode. If this is not the case, an error condition returns. If the mode is either a 2 or a 3, reset the video mode to ensure that all video display's elements are properly initialized.

The next interrupt is a call to function 0x11 with AL set to 0x12. This causes the system to load the new (smaller) character set needed to display 43 lines on the screen.

The poke() call in the middle of the function at address 0x40:0x87 is necessary to preserve a screen cursor. The statement

```
poke(0x87, 0x40, peek(0x87,0x40) ¦ 0x01);
```

first returns the 16-bit value stored at 0x40:0x87, logically ORs the value with one, and then writes the value back into memory. The interrupt call to function 0x01 resets the cursor for the new character set that will be used.

The statement

```
base = peek(0x63, 0x40);
```

gets a (16-bit) word, which is the port address of the CRT controller. The following two calls to poke() initialize the controller for use in the 43-line mode. The final interrupt call to function 0x12 activates the 43-line mode.

Unless you are using MS-DOS 4.0 and already have set the screen in the 43-line mode, you must manage all screen I/O. This means that you probably will have to use writes to screen memory to display your program's output. (Program 1.1 near the end of Chapter 1, "Screen Functions," gives an example of how you can write to screen memory. A more detailed discussion is presented in Chapter 10, "Text Windows.")

If your compiler does not support peek() and poke(), you simply define a far pointer and initialize it to point to the necessary memory addresses in the BIOS data area. The following code fragment shows how this might be done.

```
unsigned far *bd;

    .

    .

bd = (unsigned *) 0x400000L;
    .
base = *(bd + 0x63);
```

These statements can be used to replace the statement

```
base = peek(0x63, 0x40);
```

A far pointer must point to the BIOS data area (bd) because it must access memory in a segment below the TPA. Although the peek() and poke() functions are not particularly elegant, they are simpler to use. You can use the peek()-poke() combination or a far pointer, however.

End EGA 43-Line Mode—*endega43()*

When your program finishes, you should restore the screen to its normal 80x25 mode, by using the code shown in listing 9.4.

Listing 9.4. *End 43-line mode.*

```
/*****
                              endega43()

    This function places the screen back to mode 3 and restores
    the cursor to a start line of 6 and an end line of 7. Note that
    peek() and poke() are assumed to work on a word (16 bits).

    Argument list:    int mode       the desired screen mode on exit
                                     from the 43-line mode.

    Return value:     void

*****/

#include <dos.h>

void endega43(int mode)
{
    union REGS ireg;

    poke(0x85, 0x40, (peek(0x85,0x40) & 0xff00) ¦ 0x000e);
    poke(0x88, 0x40, (peek(0x88,0x40) & 0xff00) ¦ 0x00f9);
    poke(0x87, 0x40, peek(0x87, 0x40) & 0xfffe);
    ireg.x.ax = mode;
    int86(0x10, &ireg, &ireg);
}
```

The first three statements restore the familiar "underscore" cursor (6 and 7 for the start-end lines). Again, a `far` pointer can be used to replace the `peek()`s and `poke()`s, as explained earlier. The final interrupt calls function 0x00 and sets the screen to `mode`. If mode is 3, for example, the screen is set to 80x25 color text.

Build a Full File Path Name— *fullpathname( )*

Sometimes you must prepend a path name to a file before it is used. In other cases you might want to save the full path name for use later. Listing 9.5 presents the `fullpathname()` function, which enables you to do this.

Listing 9.5. Build full file path name (Microsoft C).

```
/*****
                          fullpathname()

    This function uses interrupt 0x21 function 0x60 to create a full
path name for the current working directory. The argument contains
a file name found in the current working directory. On return, the
argument contains the full path for the file, including the file
name.

    Argument list:    char *filename     the file name to expand

    Return value:     int                0 if no error, 1 on error

    CAUTION: Cannot be used on pre-3.0 DOS.

*****/

#include <dos.h>
#include <string.h>

int fullpathname(char *filename)
{
    char buff[128], buff1[128];
    int flag;
```

continues

Listing 9.5. *continued*

```
union REGS regs;
struct SREGS sreg;

strcpy(buff, filename);              /* Give us a known reference */
segread(&sreg);                      /* Get segment registers      */
regs.h.ah = 0x60;
regs.x.si = (unsigned) buff;
regs.x.di = (unsigned) buff1;
sreg.ds = sreg.es = sreg.ss;
flag = intdosx(&regs, &regs, &sreg);
strcpy(filename, buff1);             /* Put pathname back          */
return (flag & 0x01);
}
```

The function expects a null-terminated string to be passed in `filename`. Copy the file name into `buff[]` to be sure that the segment registers are consistent. The call to `segread()` fills in the segment registers; a series of assignments then sets up the proper values for the pseudoregisters. The call to `indosx()` invokes interrupt 0x21, function 0x60, which causes the current directory path to be prepended to the file name pointed to by `ds:si` (`buff`).

Suppose, for example, that `filename` contains test.c and that you are working in a subdirectory named \PROJECTS\JUNK on the C drive. On return from `fullpathname()`, the file name will contain C:\PROJECTS\JUNK\TEST.C. The `indosx()` function is assumed to return the flag register, which is copied into `flag`. You logically AND `flag` with 1 to get the carry flag. If the carry flag is set, an error occurred; a value of zero means all went well.

When you are using the Turbo C compiler, the code for `fullpathname()` is somewhat different due to the availability of pseudoregisters. The Turbo C equivalent of `fullpathname()` is presented in listing 9.6.

Listing 9.6. *Build full file path name (Borland C).*

```
/*****
                        fullpathname()

    This function uses interrupt 0x21 function 0x60 to create a full
path name for the current working directory. The argument contains
a file name found in the current working directory. On return, the
argument contains the full path for the file, including the file
name.
```

```
    Argument list:     char *filename      the file name to expand

    Return value:      int                 0 if no error, 1 on error

        CAUTION: Cannot be used on pre-3.0 DOS.

*****/

#include <dos.h>
#include <string.h>

int fullpathname(char *filename)
{
   char buff[128], buff1[128];
   int flag;
   union REGS regs;
   struct SREGS sreg;

   strcpy(buff, filename);              /* Give us a known reference */
   segread(&sreg);                      /* Get segment registers     */
   regs.h.ah = 0x60;
   regs.x.si = (unsigned) buff;
   regs.x.di = (unsigned) buff1;
   _ES = _DS = (unsigned) sreg.ss;
   intdosx(&regs, &regs, &sreg);
   strcpy(filename, buff1);             /* Put pathname back         */
   return (regs.x.cflag & 0x01);
}
```

The ES and DS can be set directly using _ES and _DS. Also, the regs structure contains a member for the carry flag (cflag). You can test this directly instead of using the value returned from intdosx().

Remember that the 0x60 function call can be used only with version 3.0 or later of DOS.

Drawing smooth curves is easy, if you have enough data points. The closer together the points are, the smoother the curve becomes. It would seem to follow, therefore, that smooth curves require many data points. Well, not always. B-splines provide a way to fit a smooth curve between a rather small number of data points. The spline() function in listing 9.7 enables you to draw a smooth curve with a limited number of data points.

Listing 9.7. B-spline smoothing.

```
/*****
                              spline()

    This function calculates a B-spline curve based on the values
of x and y. The delta value enables the program to determine the
curve's smoothness; the higher the value, the smoother the curve.

    Argument list:     double *x      pointer to the x values
                       double *y      pointer to the y values
                       int n          the number of x and y values
                       int delta      sets smoothing level: 1 is minimum
                                      and n is maximum


    Return value:      void

*****/

void spline(double *x, double *y, int n, int delta)
{
   int i, j;
   double x1, x2, x3, x4, y1, y2, y3, y4, a1, a2, a3, a4, b1, b2, b3, b4;
   double step, dx, dy;

   if (delta > n || delta < 1)
      delta = n;
   for (i = 1; i < n - 1; i++) {
      x1 = *(x + i - 1); x2 = *(x + i); x3 = *(x + i + 1); x4 = *(x + i + 2);
      y1 = *(y + i - 1); y2 = *(y + i); y3 = *(y + i + 1); y4 = *(y + i + 2);
      a1 = (x1 + 4.0 * x2 + x3) * .166666667;
      b1 = (y1 + 4.0 * y2 + y3) * .166666667;
      a2 = (x3 - x1) * 0.5;
      b2 = (y3 - y1) * 0.5;
      a3 = (x1 - 2.0 * x2 + x3) * 0.5;
      b3 = (y1 - 2.0 * y2 + y3) * 0.5;
      a4 = (-x1 + 3.0 * (x2 - x3) + x4) * .166666667;
      b4 = (-y1 + 3.0 * (y2 - y3) + y4) * .166666667;
      for (j = 0; j < delta; j++) {
         step = (double) j / (double) n;
         dx = ((a4 * step + a3) * step + a2) * step + a1;
         dy = ((b4 * step + b3) * step + b2) * step + b1;
         if (i == 1) {
```

```
        moveto(dx, dy);              /* Might be _moveto()    */
    } else {
        lineto(dx, dy);              /* Might be _lineto()    */
    }
  }
 }
}
```

You construct the spline by using polynomial approximations to fill in between the measured points. The larger the number of approximations, the smoother the curve. On the other hand, the more approximations made, the longer it takes to draw the curve.

In listing 9.7, the first two arguments are the x-y coordinate pairs to be used. The third argument is the number of pairs that will be used to construct the plot. The fourth argument is the number of approximations made for each pair. The value is limited to a range between 1 and the number of pairs given (n). (Actually, at some large value of n, screen resolution will be the limiting factor.)

You might want to write a short test program to see how spline() works. One of the first things you will notice is what happens as you increase the value of delta. You also will notice that there are fewer plotted points than coordinate pairs. Therefore, if you are plotting something that needs closure (such as a circle), you must "overlap" endpoints in order for closure to occur. Finally, the code looks different than the math might suggest, for two reasons. First, Horner's Rule is used to improve computational efficiency rather than the standard polynomial form. Second, because the division operation is so costly in computational terms, multiplication is used instead. (For details on the mathematical derivation of B-splines, refer to *Fundamentals of Interactive Computer Graphics*, by J.D. Foley and A. Van Dam, Addison-Wesley, especially pages 521–523.)

Speaker Tone—*tone( )*

Sound can be a pleasant added touch to many programs. Some programs, for example, "squeak" when a menu is opened or closed. Listing 9.8 illustrates functions that make the machine generate a certain tone of a specified duration. The listing also presents a support function—called _delayset()—along with tone(). The _delayset() function defines a loop constant (constant) that is used to generate a fixed-time interval from machine to machine.

To compile the `tone()` function, you also must include `_delayset()` in the module so that the constant is available to both functions.

Listing 9.8. Generate a speaker tone (Borland C).

```
/*****
                                tone()

     This function is used to generate a tone on the speaker port. By
     calling _delayset(), the routine attempts to adjust for different
     processor speeds. This function sets an external static named
     "constant" that is used in a timing loop.

     Argument list:      int freq      the frequency of the tone
                         int time      the duration of the tone (see text)

     Return value:       void

*****/

#include <time.h>
#include <dos.h>


#define BEEPPORT      97
#define ON            79
#define TIMERMODE     182
#define FREQPORT      66
#define FREQSCALE     1190000L
#define T_MODEPORT    67

static long constant = 0L;
void _delayset(void);

void tone(int freq, int time)
{
    int i, hibyt, lobyt, port;
    long divisor, delay;
    clock_t et;

    if (constant == 0L)
        _delayset();
    if (freq == 0)
        freq = 1;
```

```
    divisor = FREQSCALE / (long) freq;
    lobyt = (int) (divisor % 256L);
    hibyt = (int) (divisor / 256L);
    outportb(T_MODEPORT, TIMERMODE);        /* NOTE: might be outp()    */
    outportb(FREQPORT, lobyt);
    outportb(FREQPORT, hibyt);
    port = inportb(BEEPPORT);               /* NOTE: might be inp()     */
    outportb(BEEPPORT, ON);
    divisor = 1L;
    delay = constant * (long) time;
    while (divisor < delay)
        divisor++;
    outportb(BEEPPORT, port);

}


/*****
                            _delayset()

    This support function should be used with the tone() function
    to set the constant for use in the tone() delay loop.

    Argument list:    void

    Return value:     void

*****/

#define SCALE  20                           /* If super fast system...  */

void _delayset(void)
{
    long i, et, interval;
    clock_t clock();

    interval = 10000L;
    for (;;) {
        i = 0L;
        et = clock();
        while (i < interval)
            i++;
```

continues

Listing 9.8. *continued*

```
    et = clock() - et;
    if (et == 0L) {                         /* If fast system, try again */
        interval *= SCALE;
        continue;
    }                                       /* If lousy resolution, try again */
    if (( ((double) et) / (double) CLK_TCK) < .5) {
        interval *= 2L;
        continue;
    }
    break;                                  /* Everything is OK         */
}
constant = (long) (((double) interval / 1000.0) /
                   (((double) et) / (double) CLK_TCK));
}
```

Note: You might need to change two function names in listing 9.8 for some compilers. Because the functions that read and write a byte to a port are not specified in the ANSI library, the compiler vendor is free to name them whatever it wants. For the Microsoft compiler, the function outportb() in listing 9.8 is called outp(). Likewise, inportb() is called inp() for Microsoft C. Your compiler probably will have equivalent functions, but you might have to search a bit to find out what they are named.

The first time tone() is called, control is passed to _delayset() to fix constant. (There is a slight delay while _delayset() executes.) Subsequent calls to tone() bypass the call to _delayset(). You might notice that the code for _delayset() attempts to get a time interval greater than one second. After that interval is determined, a constant is calculated that can be used in tone() to generate a fixed time interval. Therefore, the time argument to tone() generates a pulse that is relatively constant between machines, regardless of clock speed.

Code fragment 9.1 shows how you might generate a squeak with a rising pitch, followed by a second squeak with a falling pitch (different sounds to indicate the opening and closing of a menu, for example).

Code Fragment 9.1. *Generate a squeak tone.*

```
char buff[20];
int i, time;
```

```
printf("Enter a time value: ");
time = atoi(gets(buff));
for (i = 1; i < 10; i++) {
   tone(800 * i, time);
}
getch();
for (i = 10; i; i--) {
   tone(800 * i, time);
}
```

The tone produced will vary because the frequency (800) is multiplied by i on each pass through the loop. In the first for loop, the tone rises on each pass through the loop because i is increasing. In the second loop, the tone falls in pitch because i is decrementing. If time is set to a low value (such as 1), the result is a rising, then falling, squeak tone.

If you use the code in code fragment 9.1, try entering a value of 5 for the first run of the program. Then try reducing its value. Although some variation will occur, a value of 1 for the time variable should produce a rising, then falling, squeak.

Program to Find Function Definitions in Source Files— *funcf.c*

You probably often have compiled a program as a series of small modules and then linked them together to form the executable program. The advantage of breaking a program into smaller modules is that the "make" feature available with most compilers avoids recompilation of modules that have not been changed since the last edit. The edit and compile times thus are reduced, as is program development time.

The problem with this approach is that you tend to forget which modules contain which function definitions, and you must search for the right module when you want to edit a certain function. The function-finding program (funcf.c) generates a listing of all function definitions and the name of the file in which the function is defined. The output format is

function name   type specifier   line number   filename

A sample output might look like this:

```
fullpathname(char *filename)    int    24    fullname.c
```

All function names will be in sorted order. Note that the sort is case-sensitive. Therefore, `Myfunction()` would appear in the list before `myfunction()`.

The program is invoked with the command-line arguments

```
funcf   search_mask   table_size   [prn]
```

in which

`funcf`	is the name of the program
`search_mask`	is the type of files to be searched
`table_size`	is the approximate number of definitions to be found
`[prn]`	is the optional argument to send the output to the printer rather than the screen

The `search_mask` does support wild cards, so you can search all C source files in the current directory with a `search_mask` of "*.c". The `table_size` argument is simply your best guess of the number of function definitions to be found in the files. Unless you have a very large program, a value of 200 for `table_size` should be plenty. If a fourth argument is given, output is sent to the printer rather than to the screen, so you can generate a hard copy of the results. The program generates the results fast enough to enable you to run the program as often as needed. (In one test run on an 8MHz AT-type machine, the program read 18 source files with almost 100 function definitions and began displaying the results in less than 30 seconds.)

Program Restrictions

The program's major restriction is that you use conventional programming style when you define a function. That is, a function definition is assumed to have the following sequence:

1. A type specifier

2. A space

3. The function name

4. An opening parenthesis

5. The function prototype

The following example follows these conventions:

```
int fullpathname(char *filename)
```

The type specifier (int) is assumed to be "flush" with the screen's left side. If the function definition and prototype have more than 50 characters, they are truncated to 50 characters.

If your programming style is different from the one just described, you might have to modify the program to reflect your style. You also could modify your programming style. Otherwise, you can write a filter that produces a source file that conforms to the style conventions.

You are further restricted in that the list of type specifiers used in your source files must be present in the list held in table[]. This list also must be in sorted order, because a binary search is done on the array of pointers to char held in table[] for valid type specifiers at runtime. Note that FILE comes before char because the search is case-sensitive. If you need special type specifiers to complete the list (typedefs), simply add them at the appropriate place in table[].

The function-finding program's code is presented in program 9.1.

***Program 9.1.** Function-finding program.*

```
/*****
    PROGRAM: Function finder (funcf.c).

    This program searches C source files and displays a sorted list
    of all function definitions in each file along with the function
    type specifier, line number, and name of the file in which the
    definition appears.

    USAGE: funcf filename tablesize [prn]
           example: funcf *.c 200

                    Outputs all function definitions in *.c files
                    to the screen. The maximum number of function
                    definitions is limited to 200.

*****/
```

continues

Program 9.1. *continued*

```c
#include <stdio.h>                  /* All the include files          */
#include <alloc.h>                  /* Might also be malloc.h         */
#include <stdlib.h>
#include <string.h>
#include <dir.h>

#define NAMESIZ 13                  /* Maximum size of file name      */
#define MAXSTR  50                  /* Maximum length of function name */
#define MAXLINE 21                  /* Maximum lines on screen        */

                                    /* Prototype list                 */
int do_directory(char **command_args);

void correct_args(int num_args),
   set_output_device(int num_args),
   open_files(int num_files, int num_entries),
   show_results(void),
   sort_list(void);

                                    /* List of function type specifiers */

char *table[] = {                   /* See CAUTION in read_file()     */
   "FILE",   "char",    "double",    "int",   "long",
   "static", "struct",  "unsigned",  "void"
   };

char *tptr;                         /* Global data items              */
int room_left;
FILE *fpin, *fpout;

struct record {
   char name[MAXSTR];               /* Name of function               */
   char type[NAMESIZ];              /* Type specifier for function    */
   char file[NAMESIZ];              /* Name of C source file          */
   unsigned int line;               /* Line number of function def    */
   } list, *tbl1, *tbl2;


void main(int argc, char **argv)
{
   int i, lcompar();
```

```
    correct_args(argc);           /* Correct command line?        */
    i = do_directory(argv);       /* Get list of files in directory */
    set_output_device(argc);      /* Output to screen or printer? */
    room_left = atoi(argv[2]);    /* Allocation needed            */
    open_files(i, room_left);     /* Open and read i source files */
    sort_list();                  /* Sort function names          */
    show_results();               /* Show sorted results          */
    free(tptr);                   /* Free the allocations         */
    free(tbl1);
}


/*****
                            read_file()

    This function reads the source code from the file named fname
and searches for function definitions within that file. Matched
type specifiers and function definitions are copied into a global
structure allocation pointed to by tptr (tABLE pOINtEr).

Argument list:    char *fname       the source code file name being
                                    read

Return value:     void


    CAUTION: This function makes certain assumptions about how
function definitions appear in a source file. See text.

*****/

#define MAXBUFF 250

void read_file(char *fname)
{
    char *bptr, buff[300], buff2[300], *c, *sptr, temp[50];
    int len, compar();
    unsigned lines, nel, wide;

    wide = sizeof(table[0]);
    nel = sizeof(table) / sizeof(table[0]);
    lines = 0;
```

continues

```
printf("\nReading %s", fname);
while (fgets(buff, MAXBUFF, fpin) != NULL) {
   strcpy(buff2, buff);
   sptr = strchr(buff2, '(');   /* Look for opening paren         */
   lines++;
   if (sptr == NULL)            /* No paren; keep marching        */
      continue;
   if (buff2[0] == ' ' || buff2[0] == '\t' || buff2[0] == '\n')
      continue;
   sptr = strtok(buff, " "); /* Look for spaces                   */
                             /* If first character not white space */
   if (sptr != NULL) {       /* Now search type specifier list     */
      bptr = bsearch(&sptr, table, nel, wide, compar);
      if (bptr != NULL) {
         len = strlen(buff2);
         if (len > MAXSTR) {
            len = MAXSTR - 1; /* Chop the string if too long      */
         } else {
            len--;            /* Get rid of newline if too short...*/
         }
         buff2[len] = '\0';   /* and make it a string             */
         strncpy(temp, buff2, len);
                             /* Get a pointer to space between    */
                             /* type specifier and name           */
         c = strchr(buff2, ' ');
         while (*(c + 1) == ' ') { /* Strip space away            */
            c++;
         }
                             /* Copy function name to table       */
         strcpy(tbl1->name, c);
                             /* Now do type specifier             */
         strncpy(tbl1->type, buff2, c - buff2);

                             /* Now do source file name           */
         strncpy(tbl1->file, fname, NAMESIZ);

                             /* Finally, the line number of def   */
         tbl1->line = lines;
         room_left--;
         if (room_left <= 0) {
            cls();
            tbl1->name[0] = '\0';
```

```
                printf("\n\n          Out of memory\n");
                return;
            }
            tbl1++;                /* Ready for next one            */
        } else
            continue;
        }
    }
}
```

```
/*****
                            compar()
```

This function is used to compare type specifiers in the global table[] array with those read from the input source file. It is called by the bsearch() function as a pointer to function. Double indirection is needed because table[] is an array of pointers to char.

Argument list: char **s1   pointer to the type specifier
                                 read in the source file

                  char **s2   pointer to the type specifier
                                 found in table being searched
                                 (table[])

Return value: int   0 if a match, nonzero otherwise

```
*****/
```

```c
int compar(char **s1, char **s2)
{
   return (strcmp(*s1, *s2));
}
```

```
/*****
                            lcompar()
```

This function is called by the qsort() function as a pointer to function. It is used to sort the structure array pointed to by tptr. The sort is on function name. The actual value of each argument used in a comparison is set by the internal workings of the qsort() function.

continues

Program 9.1. *continued*

Argument list:	char **s1	first function name used in the sort comparison
	char **s2	second function name used in the sort comparison
Return value:	int	0 if a match, nonzero otherwise

```
*****/


int lcompar(char *s1, char *s2)
{
   return (strcmp(s1, s2));
}

/*****
                        open_files()
```

This function opens the files pointed to by tptr for reading. The list of files was created by the do_directory() function. The list of source files pointed to by tptr are those that match the second command-line argument for the current working directory.

Argument list:	int number	number of file names in the list
	int size	number of entries in the name table
Return value:	void	

```
*****/

void open_files(int number, int size)
{
   int j;

                              /* Allocate for function info       */
   tbl2 = tbl1 = (struct record *) calloc(size, sizeof(list));
   if (tbl1 == NULL) {
      printf("Out of table memory");
```

```
         exit(0);
   }
                              /* Open files in list for reading     */
   for (j = 0; j < number; j++) {
      if ( (fpin = fopen(tptr + (NAMESIZ * j), "r") ) == NULL) {
         printf("\n          Cannot open %s", tptr + (NAMESIZ * j));
         exit(0);
      }
      read_file(tptr + (NAMESIZ * j)); /*Read it; add to function list*/
      fclose(fpin);                 /* Free FILE pointer for reuse        */
      if (room_left <= 0)
         return;
   }
}


/*****
                        set_output_device()

    This function determines whether output will be sent to the
screen or the standard list device, which is assumed to be stdlst.
If argc is 4, output is directed to the printer. (The corresponding
argv[] does not matter.) Any other number of command-line arguments
sends output to the screen.

Argument list:     int argc        the number of command-line
                                   arguments


Return value:      void

    CAUTION: This function assumes that stdlst is the FILE pointer
for the standard list device. Other compilers might use different
names (for example, stdprn). Check stdio.h to see what is defined.

*****/

void set_output_device(int argc)
{
   if (argc == 4)
      fpout = stdprn;
   else
      fpout = stdout;
}
```

continues

Program 9.1. continued

```
/*****
                        correct_args()

    This function makes sure that at least three command-line
arguments are used with the program. More may be used, but three
are required. (Also see set_output_device()).

    Argument list:    int argc        the number of command-line
                                      arguments


    Return value:     void

*****/

void correct_args(int argc)
{
    if (argc < 3) {
        printf("Useage: FF filemask tablesize [printer]");
        exit(0);
    }
}


/*****
                        do_directory()

    This function searches the current working directory using the
string pointed to by argv[1] as the search mask (for example,
"*.c"). The third argument (argv[2]) is used to set the allocation
that holds the file names.

    Argument list:    char **argv       command-line argument vector

    Return value:     int               number of files found

    CAUTION: The findfirst() and findnext() functions are not
portable. Other compilers might use other functions. Likely
candidates for substitution are opendir() and readdir().

*****/
```

```
int do_directory(char **argv)
{
   char *bptr, buff[NAMESIZ];
   int lcompar(), empty;
   unsigned i, size;
   struct ffblk find;                        /* Use struct find_t for MSC */

   empty = findfirst(argv[1], &find, 0); /* Open the file directory    */
   size = atoi(argv[2]);
                                             /* Allocate for file names   */
   bptr = tptr = (char *) calloc(size, sizeof(buff));

   if (tptr == NULL) {
      printf("Out of filename memory");
      exit(0);
   }

   for (i = 0; i < size; i++) {        /* Copy matching file names  */
      if (!empty) {                    /* More matching files?      */
         strncpy(tptr + (NAMESIZ * i), find.ff_name, sizeof(find.ff_name));
         empty = findnext(&find);
      } else {
         break;                        /* If not, quit              */
      }
   }
   tptr = bptr;
   return i;
}

/*****

                         sort_list()

   This function sorts the list of function names into alphabetical
order using the qsort() function (UNIX System V compatible). The
function assumes that the comparison function, lcompar(), exists.

   Argument list:    void

   Return value:     void

*****/

void sort_list(void)
{
```

continues

Program 9.1. *continued*

```
        int lcompar();
        unsigned j;

        j = tbl1 - tbl2;                    /* How big is the list?        */
        tbl1 = tbl2;                        /* Point back to start of list */
        cls();
        printf("Sorting...");               /* Now sort it...              */
        qsort(tbl1, j, sizeof(list), (int (*)(const void *,
                const void *)) lcompar);
}


/*****
                            show_results()

    Function to display the sorted list of function definitions. The
    function is rather dumb (no fancy headers or printer paging), but
    it does pause when MAXLINEs of output are sent to the screen.

    Argument list:     void

    Return value:      void

*****/

void show_results(void)
{
    int count;

    count = 0;
    cls();
    while (tbl2->name[0] != '\0') {
        fprintf(fpout, "\n%-50s    %-8s  %4d  %s",
                    tbl2->name, tbl2->type, tbl2->line, tbl2->file);
        tbl2++;
        count++;                            /* Pause when needed           */
        if (count > MAXLINE && fpout == stdout) {
            printf("\n\n        Press any key to continue");
            getch();
            clrscr();
            count = 0;
        }                                   /* Space between letter groups */
```

```
        if (tbl2->name[1] != (tbl2 - 1)->name[1]) {
            fprintf(fpout, "\n");
            count++;
        }
    }
}
```

The comments that accompany the code should help you follow each function's operation in detail. There are only two nonstandard functions you might have to change—findfirst() and findnext(). The equivalent functions for Ecosoft's compiler are opendir() and readdir(). For the Microsoft compiler, the functions are _dos_findfirst() and _dos_findnext(). (These functions are discussed in greater detail in Chapter 7, "Disk and Directory Control Functions.") The other functions should be available to you from your standard library.

The program flows simply. The do_directory() function builds a list of all file names that match the second command-line argument. This list is pointed to by tptr. The list then is used by open_files() and read_file() to read the contents of files that match the command-line file mask.

The real work is done by read_file(), which searches the source file for function definitions and, after finding one, fills in the struct of type record with the information on each function definition. (The definition for record appears near the beginning of program 9.1.) When read_file() is done, tbl1 points to a list of struct records with all the function definitions, but in sequential (unsorted) order.

The call to sort_list() places the list of records in sorted order. The call to show_results() displays the sorted list on the screen or printer. The printer output results if a fourth command-line argument is given.

This program is a real time-saver. Even very large, multifile projects are processed very quickly on the new machines. In fact, this program is so fast that there is little reason to print a copy of the output. Simply rerun the program when you need to find a function definition.

Move to New Directory—*go.c*

This program is one of the first things I give to a new MS-DOS user. I use the program so often that I take it for granted. Very simply, it enables you to issue two command-line arguments that move you to any predefined subdirectory on a hard disk. Unlike batch files, the same program can handle all directory changes. This program can give your users the benefits of subdirectories, even if they don't know how to use them. You probably can appreciate this feature if you have ever tried to explain the MS-DOS subdirectory structure to a new computer user.

The go program works through an ASCII file that contains information about your frequently used subdirectories. For example, each member of my family has his or her own subdirectory; these subdirectories are named KAROL, KATIE, and JOHN. When Katie wants to write a book report, she boots the computer, types GO KATIE, and ends up in her subdirectory on drive C. To make this work, I created a data file named go.dat and made an entry that looks like this:

```
katie  c  \family\katie
```

My go.dat data file looks something like this:

```
book c \cpt\chaps
letters c \letters
test d \compiler\temp
karol c \family\karol
katie c \family\katie
john c \family\john
```

Note that each entry is separated from the next item on the line by one space, and that each line ends in a newline ('\n'). Therefore, each entry for a desired subdirectory has an entry in the following form:

```
shorthand_name drive pathname<'\n'>
```

Any text editor can be used to create the go.dat data file, and it can be changed as often as needed without recompiling the go program. The code for the go program is presented in program 9.2.

***Program 9.2.** Go to new subdirectory.*

```
/*****
   PROGRAM: Move to Subdirectory

    This program is used to move the user from the current working
   directory to a new directory.

   USAGE: go shorthand_name
          example: go katie

*****/
```

```
#include <stdio.h>
#include <stdlib.h>
#include <string.h>


#define DATAFILE  "go.dat"    /* Name of directory-info file        */
#define MAXBUFF   256

#define MATCH     0
#define FAIL      1

char buff[MAXBUFF],           /* Input buffer for file reads        */
     path[MAXBUFF],           /* Buffer for full path name          */
     drive[3];                /* Buffer for disk drive              */

                              /* Prototypes for nonstandard functions */

int search_file(FILE *fp, char *where),
    do_switch(void);

FILE *open_data_file(char *name);



void main(int argc, char **argv)
{
   int flag;
   FILE *fpin;

   if (argc != 2) {
      fprintf(stderr, "Usage: g directory-name");
      exit(0);
   }
   fpin = open_data_file(DATAFILE);     /* Open the data file       */
   flag = search_file(fpin, argv[1]);   /* Find the pseudoname      */
   fclose(fpin);                        /* You are done reading     */

   if (flag == FAIL) {
      fprintf(stderr, "\nCannot find %s in data file.\n", argv[1]);
      exit(0);
   }
```

continues

Program 9.2. *continued*

```
    flag = do_switch();                    /* Try the change        */
    if (flag != MATCH) {
        fprintf(stderr, "\nCannot find directory %s\n", path);
        exit(0);
    }

}

/*****
                        do_switch()

    This function does the work.

    Argument list:    void

    Return value:     int      0 if successful, 1 on error

*****/

int do_switch(void)
{
    int flag;

    system(drive);        /* Function to issue command to command.com */
                          /* and place you on the correct drive       */
    flag = chdir(path);   /* You should be there now                  */
    return flag;
}


/*****
                        search_file()

    This function reads the data file that holds the information
    about the directory locations, looking for a match on the string
    passed in. The format for the input file is:

            abbreviation   drive    full_pathname\n

    in which:
            abbreviation       is the abbreviation for the full path name
                   drive       is the disk drive designator for the search
```

full_pathname   is the full MS-DOS pathname desired

\n   is a newline that terminates the data for each possible directory

Argument list: FILE *fp   a FILE pointer to the open file

char *where   a string constant that is the pseudoname for the directory desired

Return value: int   0 if successful, 1 if no match

```
*****/

int search_file(FILE *fp, char *where)
{
    char *ptr, temp[MAXBUFF];
    int c, i;

    i = 0;
    while ((c = fgetc(fp)) != EOF) {
        if (c != '\n') {
            buff[i++] = (char) c;
            continue;
        }
        buff[i] = '\0';
        strcpy(temp, buff);
        ptr = strtok(temp, " ");
        if ( strcmp(ptr, where) == MATCH) {
            ptr = strtok( (char *) 0, " "); /* Get the disk drive       */
            strcpy(drive, ptr);
            strcat(drive, ":");
            ptr = strtok( (char *) 0, " "); /* Get the full path name    */
            strcpy(path, ptr);
            return MATCH;
        }
        i = 0;                              /* No match; start over      */
    }
    return FAIL;
}
```

continues

```
/*****
                            open_data_file()

     This function attempts to open the data file that holds the
information about the directory locations. It does this by
searching the PATH environment variable. The program assumes that
the data file is in the PATH directory.

     Argument list:    char *name      a string constant that is the
                                       name of the file containing the
                                       directory information

     Return value:     FILE *fp        a FILE pointer to the open file
                                       if successful. Program aborts on
                                       error.

*****/

FILE *open_data_file(char *name)
{
   char *ptr, p[MAXBUFF], temp[MAXBUFF];
   FILE *fpin;

   ptr = getenv("PATH");                     /* Find out where go.dat is   */
                                             /* NOTE: PATH must be in caps */
   strcpy(p, ptr);
   ptr = strtok(p, ";");                     /* Find first PATH            */
   while (ptr != NULL) {
      strcpy(temp, ptr);                     /* Save a copy of substring   */
      strcat(temp, "\\");                    /* Form a path and file name  */
      strcat(temp, name);
      if ( (fpin = fopen(temp, "r") ) == NULL) {
         temp[0] = '\0';                     /* Start over again           */
         ptr = strtok( (char *) 0, ";");/* Try next path             */
      } else
         break;                              /* Must have a good fpin      */
   }
```

```
    if (fpin == NULL) {
        fprintf(stderr, "\nCannot find %s on default path(s).\n", name);
        exit(0);
    }
    return fpin;
}
```

The program begins by attempting to open the ASCII data file that contains the directory information. If you examine the open_data_file() function near the end of program 9.2, you will see that getenv() is called to find the PATH environment variable's setting. If the program is to work smoothly, both the go program and its corresponding data file (go.dat) should be stored "on path." That is, if you have a subdirectory name (such as BIN or DOS) in which you store frequently used programs, this is where go.exe and go.dat should be stored. For example, suppose that go.exe and go.dat are stored in a subdirectory named BIN on drive C. Your autoexec.bat file should include a line that says

path=c:\bin

When getenv() is called with PATH as its argument, the pointer returned from the call would point to c:\bin. The path name is copied into p[]. Because there can be multiple paths, as in

path=c:\bin;c:\dos;e:;

the while loop parses the path names and attempts to open the go.dat data file in each case. If the go.dat file is on path, eventually it will be found and successfully opened by the call to fopen(). If you exhaust all path possibilities and still cannot find the data file, an error message is given and the program aborts. If go.dat is found on path, fpin becomes the FILE pointer to go.dat.

Next, search_file() is called, passing in the pseudoname for the subdirectory (such as KATIE, as in GO KATIE) and fpin. All search_file() does is read go.dat for a match on the pseudoname for the subdirectory. Each line in go.dat is read into buff[] and copied into temp[]. The call to strcmp() checks to see whether the first entry in the line (the pseudoname) matches argv[1], the pseudoname entered on the command line. If a match is found, calls to strtok() parse the rest of the line to build the drive and path name for the associated subdirectory, and MATCH is returned from the function. If no match is found in go.dat, FAIL is returned, control returns to main() where an error message is issued, and the program ends.

If a match is found, do_switch() is called. In turn, do_switch() calls system() to change the drive (system("D:")), and chdir() changes to the matching subdirectory. If the change was made successfully, do_switch() returns control to main(), and the program ends. If the subdirectory in go.dat cannot be found, an error message is given and the program ends.

When control returns to MS-DOS, the user is in the specified subdirectory. All of this happens quickly—much faster than you can type a long subdirectory path name. By the way, it helps to keep your shorthand for the subdirectory names small. This program also helps curb your urge to keep subdirectory names small. You no longer have to type them out!

Conclusion

This chapter's title suggests that the functions and programs are "leftovers." However, if you give them a try, I think you will find them very useful. After you've used the function-finding program for awhile, I think you'll wonder how you got along without it.

CHAPTER 10

Text Windows

This chapter expands on the menuing system from Chapter 4, "Menuing Systems." You will see how to write functions that provide text windows for displaying and obtaining information from the user. Because the PC market has matured and become more standardized, you can use direct video memory writes. The concepts and functions in this chapter also lay the groundwork for the material in Chapter 11, "Putting It All Together."

What Is a Text Window?

Chapter 4, "Menuing Systems," discusses both slidebar and box menuing systems. At the end of that chapter is a brief discussion of how you can save an area of the screen, write something to the screen, and then restore the screen to its original state. This chapter develops a set of functions that enable you to use this methodology in many interesting ways. Because these functions are designed for use with text characters only, they are designed to manipulate what are called *text windows*.

Although text windows cannot process any of the graphics primitives your compiler supports, you still can use the text window functions to construct some rather impressive programs. The basic theory and functions for text windows are presented in this chapter. Chapter 11 shows a complete application named SuperCopy that uses text windows for both slidebar and box menus. Unlike the menuing systems discussed in Chapter 4, the functions presented in this and the next chapter show you how to write code for pop-up menus, dialog and message boxes, and on-line help messages that can appear anywhere on the screen. When the menu or box is closed, the previous contents of the screen are restored. Text windows even can have a shadow effect.

Before you start building your own programs, however, you must understand how a text window works. After you learn the basics, you can use the primitives presented in this chapter to build more complex text windows for everything from input windows (called *dialog boxes*) to on-line help windows. Chapter 11 presents numerous examples of how functions presented earlier in this book can be combined to form new, more versatile functions.

How Text Windows Work

Normally, all interaction with the screen is sent through the I/O facilities provided by MS-DOS. With text windows, however, these resources are bypassed, and all screen I/O is done directly on video memory. The result is screen I/O that is noticeably faster than on MS-DOS facilities. The cost of this improved performance is that the video system must be 100 percent IBM compatible. For most PC-type machines, this is not a serious restriction. You should be aware, however, that some older PCs (for example, Zenith 100 and the Tandy 2000) are not IBM compatible. The remainder of this book assumes that the system is a true IBM compatible.

To use video memory directly, the first task is to determine the starting address (or *base address*) of the video memory. This task is simple, but there is one minor complication. The base address for monochrome monitors is different from that for color monitors. Monochrome monitors have a base address that starts at segment 0xb000, offset 0x0000, and color monitors use segment 0xb800, offset 0x0000. (Rather than use the words "segment" and "offset," I use the standard form of presenting segment:offset addresses. Therefore, segment 0xb800, offset 0x0000 is written as 0xb800:0000.)

Assume that you are using a color monitor and that the base address of video memory is 0xb800:0000. That address becomes the memory location for the character that appears in the upper left corner of your video display. Although that is the character's address, each character also has a second byte associated with it that tells that character's attributes. Among other things, the *attribute byte* determines the character's foreground and background colors. Therefore, even though you see only one character on the screen, a second byte of memory determines how that character is displayed. The interpretation of each bit of the attribute byte is shown in table 10.1.

Table 10.1. *Attribute byte bit interpretations.*

Bit Position	Meaning
0	Foreground attribute
1	Foreground attribute
2	Foreground attribute
3	Foreground attribute
4	Background attribute
5	Background attribute
6	Background attribute
7	Blink (0 = no blink)

As you can see from table 10.1, the first four bits are used to set the foreground attribute, the next three bits set the background attribute, and the bit at position 7 can bet set to make the character blink.

Because four bits are devoted to the foreground attribute of the character, there are 16 (that is, 2^4) possible colors that can be used. Because only three bits are available for the background attribute, only 8 (2^3) colors can be used for the background. The blink attribute is either on or off. The possible color combinations are shown in table 10.2.

Table 10.2. *Color values for attribute byte.*

	Foreground				Background	
0	Black	8	Gray	16	Black	
1	Blue	9	Light Blue	32	Blue	
2	Green	10	Light Green	48	Green	
3	Cyan	11	Light Cyan	64	Cyan	
4	Red	12	Light Red	80	Red	
5	Magenta	13	Light Magenta	96	Magenta	
6	Brown	14	Yellow	112	Brown	
7	White	15	Light White	128	White	

The numbers for the background color values shown in table 10.2 are their values when used in bit positions 4 through 6. (You can compare these values with their "unshifted" values from the `colorstr()` function in Chapter 1, "Screen Functions.")

You now know the values necessary to mix foreground and background colors. If you want to have bright white letters on a blue background, for example, the attribute byte must have a value of 47. This is the sum of the foreground color (15) plus the background color (32). In binary, you can represent this as

```
    00001111      Light White (foreground), 15 (decimal)
  + 00100000      Blue (background),         32
  -----------
    00101111      Attribute byte value       47
```

If you want the character to blink, you turn on the high bit (for example, 10101111). Using the values in table 10.2, you can form a variety of color combinations for characters on the screen.

It should be clear that each character on the screen consists of two bytes of memory: the character and its attribute byte. This looks like figure 10.1.

Fig. 10.1. The word "Test" in video memory.

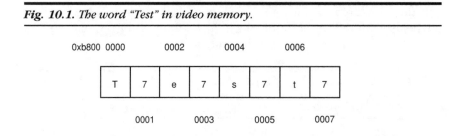

Assume that the attribute for each character is white letters on a black background. If you also assume a color monitor, the video memory starts at memory address 0xb800. Therefore, the video memory for the word "Test" is represented by figure 10.1.

If you want, you can treat each character and attribute byte as an `unsigned char`. The even memory addresses form the character, and the odd memory addresses form the attribute byte. However, you also can treat each displayed character as a single `unsigned int`. In fact, if you know that the attribute byte is the same for all characters in a certain string, it is somewhat more efficient to treat the character-attribute bytes as a single data item.

Most of the functions presented in this chapter access video memory as an `unsigned int`. If your needs are different, you can change the code to use single-byte character addressing.

Creating a Text Window

When you want to open a text window, you assume that whatever is beneath the text window needs to be saved. Therefore, the first step in creating a text window is to get a memory allocation from the operating system. After you obtain the chunk of memory, the portion of the display that will be overlaid by the text window is copied into the newly allocated memory block. Next you display the text window. As you will see, this can be as simple as displaying a message or getting input from the user.

When you are finished with the text window, you simply copy the old screen data back to video memory. This restores the screen to its original state. Finally, you free the pointer to the memory allocation that was used to hold the old screen data.

The sequence for using a text window, therefore, involves three basic steps: initializing and creating the text window; displaying the window; and closing the window. The code that performs these three steps is examined next.

Finding the Base of Video Memory—*init_video_base( )*

One of the first things you must determine is the base address of video memory. You can use the `getvmode()` function from Chapter 1, "Screen Functions," to determine the mode. If `getvmode()` returns a value of 2 or 7, then the display device cannot support color text. If the mode value is 3, color text can be used. Any other mode values cannot be used with text windows. As soon as the video mode is known, you can set the base pointer to video memory. The code is shown in listing 10.1.

Listing 10.1. *Setting the start of video memory.*

```
/*****
                          init_video_base()

    This function determines video mode and the base of video
memory. If the video mode has the proper value (i.e. 2, 3, or 7),
then the function initializes a global pointer to the start of
video memory (start_video_memory). If the Borland compiler is
used, a special function sets the segment-offset address.
Otherwise, a cast to a long pointer is used.

    Argument list:    void

    Return value:     void


    CAUTION: Some compilers might not support the (non-ANSI) far
keyword.

*****/

#include <stdio.h>
#include "win.h"



void init_video_base(void)
{
    int mode;

    mode = getvmode();                      /* From Chapter 1         */

    switch (mode) {
        case 2:
        case 7:                             /* No color text          */
            start_video_memory = (unsigned int far *) 0xb0000000L;
            break;
        case 3:                             /* Color text             */
            start_video_memory = (unsigned int far *) 0xb8000000L;
            break;
```

```
        default:
            start_video_memory = (unsigned int far *) NULL;
            break;
    }
}
```

The call to getvmode() determines the current video mode being used. A switch statement then determines whether the mode supports text windows. If mode is 3, color text is supported and the base address is set to 0xb800:0000. The global variable start_video_memory is a far pointer to an unsigned int and is defined in a new header file named win.h, shown later in this chapter. This means you can treat the character and attribute bytes as a single data item. If mode is 2 or 7, the base address is 0xb000:0000. Any other value is allowed with text windows, so the base of video memory is set to NULL.

The Borland compiler provides a special macro that enables you to set the segment and offset address to a far pointer. The MK_FP() (that is, make far pointer) macro has two arguments: the segment and offset addresses. The code is not shown in listing 10.1. However, if you want to use the macro, you can change the two assignment statements from the form

```
                        /* Most compilers */
    start_video_memory = (unsigned int far *) 0xb0000000L;
```

to

```
                        /* Borland only */
    start_video_memory = (unsigned int far *) MK_FP(0xb000,0x0000);
```

You can substitute the macro if you want, but the code works without it.

After the call to init_video_base(), start_video_memory either is a null pointer or points to the proper location for the start of video memory. Although it probably is obvious, you should check start_video_memory after the call to be sure you have a non-null memory address. A null address usually results when the display device is in some form of graphics mode. You must either exit the graphics mode and reset the display to a text mode (see setvmode() in Chapter 1, "Screen Functions") or abort the program.

Assuming that start_video_memory is non-null, you can proceed with some of the other initialization steps. Note that init_video_base() needs to be called only once in a program.

Initializing a Text Window—
init_window( )

After the base of video memory has been determined and start_video_memory has been initialized, you can create a text window. Before you do this, however, examine the information about the window you must maintain in a WINDOW structure. The members of the window structure are shown in code fragment 10.1.

***Code Fragment 10.1.** The WINDOW structure.*

```
struct WINDOW {
   char title[30];
   int num_win;
   unsigned int far *base; /* Base memory for window               */

   int x,          /* Upper left x                                 */
      y,           /* Upper left y                                 */
      wide,        /* Lower right x                                */
      deep,        /* Lower right y                                */
      border,      /* 0 = no border, 1 = single line, 2 = double line */
      wbcolor,     /* Window background color                      */
      wfcolor,     /* Window foreground color                      */
      bbcolor,     /* Border background color                      */
      bfcolor,     /* Border foreground color                      */
      mcolor,      /* Foreground message print color (back = wbcolor) */
      vscrollbar,  /* Vertical scroll bar; 0 = No, 1 = Yes         */
      hscrollbar,  /* Horizontal scroll bar; 0 = No, 1 = Yes       */
      hotspot,     /* 0 if no close button, 1 for close button     */
      shadow;      /* Does window have a shadow; 0 = No, 1 = Yes   */
};
```

The purpose of each member of the structure is fairly clear from the comments that appear in table 10.3. Some of the structure members must be filled in with specific values each time a new window is created. Other members of the structure are optional (for example, a title, scrollbars, shadow, and so on).

The members of the WINDOW structure that *must* be initialized include the following:

```
unsigned int far *base;  /* Base address for window */

int x                    /* Column position       */
int y                    /* Row position          */
int wide                 /* Window width (columns) */
int deep                 /* Window depth (rows)    */
```

Your code first must create a WINDOW structure. The following code fragment shows how this is done.

```
struct WINDOW mine;
```

After this data definition, you will have a window structure like that shown in table 10.3. Now you can use the statement

```
init_window(&mine);
```

to initialize the members of the window. The code to initialize the window is presented in listing 10.2.

Listing 10.2 *Set* WINDOW *default values.*

```
/*****

                        init_window()

    This function initializes the default settings for the members
of a WINDOW structure.

    Argument list:    struct WINDOW *w        pointer to a WINDOW
                                              structure

    Return value:     void
*****/

#include "win.h"

void init_window(struct WINDOW *w)
{

    w->x = 0;
    w->y = 0;
    w->wide = 79;
    w->deep = 24;
    w->border = 2;
```

continues

Listing 10.2. continued

```
    w->wbcolor = BBLUE;
    w->wfcolor = FLWHITE;
    w->bbcolor = BBLUE;
    w->bfcolor = FLWHITE;
    w->mcolor = FLWHITE;
    w->vscrollbar = 0;
    w->hscrollbar = 0;
    w->shadow = 1;
    w->hotspot = 0;
    w->base = NULL;
    w->title[0] = '\0';
}
```

The default values are for a window that is the same size as the entire text screen. The window background color (w->wbcolor) is set to blue (BBLUE); the window foreground color (w->wfcolor) is white; the border background color for the window (w->bbcolor) is blue; and the border foreground color (w->bfcolor) is white. Thus, the window border's background color matches the text window's background color. I think that choosing different colors for w->wbcolor and w->bbcolor makes the window look somewhat busy. You can, of course, change the default colors.

Also note that you assume that the background colors already have been shifted four bits to the left. This enables you to use symbolic color constants with values equal to those in table 10.2. (The names of the symbolic constants are shown in the win.h header file presented later in this chapter.) Because the background color values are "pre-shifted," you don't waste time doing the shifts at runtime.

The w->vscrollbar and w->hscrollbar members enable you to have vertical and horizontal scroll bars drawn on the text window. A value of 1 causes the scroll bar characters to be displayed. The default value is for no scroll bars to be shown. I find it difficult to use scroll bars with text windows. (However, both the Borland and the Microsoft compilers use them in their integrated development environment.) I can't seem to keep the mouse cursor on the scroll bar while scrolling and viewing the text. Chapter 11, "Putting It All Together," shows how to scroll the text by moving the mouse to the top or the bottom of the window. This action is much easier than using scrollbars. When you see how convenient this is, you probably will not want to use scrollbars in your programs.

The w->shadow member is set to logical True (1) if you want the window to display with a shadow. The default is for the shadow to be in effect.

The `w->hotspot` member is used to draw a small box in the upper left corner of the window if its value is 1. (The default is for no hotspot.) If active, this hotspot also has the window's *handle* value displayed within the hotspot box. The value of the handle is equal to the value held in the `num_win` structure member. This enables you to identify each window by a numeric value if you want.

If the user places the mouse cursor on the hotspot and clicks the left mouse button, subsequent window functions can sense this action. Normally, clicking on the hotspot is interpreted to mean that the user wants to close the window. You can, however, change the code so that it interprets the hotspot in another way.

The `w->base` and `w->title` are initialized to null values. The `w->title` member can be changed later to cause a title to appear at the top of the window, centered within the window border. The color used to display the title is set by the `w->mcolor` structure member. (The `w->base` structure member is explained in greater detail later in this chapter.)

Creating a Text Window— *create_w( )*

Up to now, you have defined a `WINDOW` structure variable and have initialized a certain default value for that window. Before you can open a text window, however, you must create a "safe place" to display the window. Because a text window can overlay existing information on the screen, you must copy the current screen's information using the `create_w()` function before you can safely display the text window. The primary objective of `create_w()` is to provide a place where you can store the existing contents of the screen that will be overlaid by the text window. The code is presented in listing 10.3.

Listing 10.3. *Create a text window.*

```
/*****
                        create_w()

   This function determines the memory allocation needed to create
a new window and allocates memory for it. It then copies the
existing screen data to the new memory allocation. The width and
depth always are one unit larger than required for use with a
shadow border.
```

continues

Listing 10.3. continued

```
Argument list:    int row              row position for window
                  int col              column position for window
                  int wide             width of window
                  int deep             depth of window
                  struct WINDOW *mine  pointer to a WINDOW structure

Return value:     int                  returns 0 if not enough
                                       memory for a new window; 1
                                       otherwise


    CAUTION: Some compilers might not support the (non-ANSI) far
keyword.

*****/

#include <stdlib.h>      /* NOTE: calloc() might need different header */
#include <win.h>


int create_w(int row, int col, int wide, int deep, struct WINDOW *mine)
{
    int i, j, need;
    unsigned int far *ptr, far *temp;

    mine->y = row;
    mine->x = col;
    mine->wide = wide;
    mine->deep = deep;
    need = (wide + 1) * (deep + 1); /* Figure the window size + shadow */

    mine->base = temp = (unsigned int far *) calloc(need, sizeof(unsigned));
    if (mine->base == NULL)
        return 0;                    /* Cannot get enough memory       */


    ptr = start_video_memory + (row * 80 + col);

    for (i = 0; i < deep + 1; i++) {
        for (j = 0; j < wide + 1; j++) {
```

```
            *mine->base = *ptr;
            ptr++;
            mine->base++;
        }
      ptr += 79 - wide;
    }
    mine->base = temp;
    return 1;
}
```

The function has five arguments. The first two arguments are the row and column positions for the upper left corner of the text window. Because you are using text windows, the coordinates are stated in the usual 80x24 coordinate space. The third argument is the width of the text window (in characters), and the fourth argument is the depth of the window (in screen rows). These four arguments define the outside perimeter of the text window. The fifth argument is a pointer to the WINDOW structure.

Note that these four arguments also are stored in the WINDOW structure and overwrite the default values written by init_window(). You preserve these values because they are needed to restore the previous contents of the screen.

Next you calculate the amount of memory needed to store the current contents on the screen that will be overwritten by the text window. The statement

```
need = (wide + 1) * (deep + 1);
```

actually pads the required storage with an extra row and column. This is done so that you can use a shadow effect with the window. You probably have seen this effect elsewhere. When the window opens, the right edge and bottom of the window are black, giving the impression that the window is "floating" above the screen. Any text that is in the window's shadow, however, remains readable in a light shade of gray.

After the size of the window is calculated, a call to calloc() requests sufficient storage for need bytes. If the request cannot be fulfilled, a value of 0 is returned. If the request is fulfilled, the address of the storage is copied into the base structure member. This pointer is used later to tie the original screen contents to the text window.

Note that the call to calloc() is for need bytes, each of which is of size unsigned int. This enables you to reference the character and attribute byte as a single unit. Although you could reference the memory as unsigned char, each operation on the video memory would require twice as many pointer references compared to using an unsigned int.

The statement

```
ptr = start_video_memory + (row * 80 + col);
```

determines where the first character of the text window is written. In other words, ptr points to the upper left corner of the box. The remainder of the code simply copies the existing contents of video memory (that is, character and attribute bytes) to the memory allocation pointed to by ptr. You can check the return value to see whether the window was created successfully. (The value is 1 if it was created, and zero if it wasn't.)

Another thing to note is that the code assumes a zero-based row address. That is, if row is passed as the value 3, the pointer calculation results in the corner of the window appearing at row 4 of the screen. If you want to use a one-based row address, simply subtract 1 from the value of row before it is assigned into mine->y.

Displaying a Text Window— *show_window()*

If all has gone well so far, the code has stored the previous contents of the display screen and initialized the default values for the text window. You now can display the text window. The code to do this is presented in listing 10.4.

Listing 10.4. *Show a text window.*

```
/*****
                          show_window()

    This function displays a new WINDOW. It assumes that
init_window() and create_w() have been called prior to calling this
function.

    Argument list:    struct WINDOW mine      the WINDOW to display

    Return value:     void
*****/

#include "win.h"
```

```c
void show_window(struct WINDOW mine)
{
    char buff[30];
    int i, j, len;
    unsigned int far *ptr, far *temp;
    unsigned across, letter, space, sides;
    unsigned ul, ur, ll, lr;

    temp = ptr = start_video_memory + (mine.y * 80 + mine.x);
    space = letter = (mine.bbcolor + mine.bfcolor) << 8;
    switch (mine.border) {
        case 1:                             /* Single-line            */
            across = HB;
            sides = VB;
            ul = UL; ur = UR; ll = LL; lr = LR;
            break;
        case 2:                             /* Double-line            */
            across = DHB;
            sides = DVB;
            ul = DUL; ur = DUR; ll = DLL; lr = DLR;
            break;
        case 0:                             /* No border              */
        default:
            ul = ur = ll = lr = sides = across = SPACE;
            break;
    }
    across += letter;
    sides += letter;
    *ptr++ = (letter + ul);                 /* Upper left corner      */
    for (i = 0; i < mine.wide - 2; i++) {
        *ptr++ = across;
    }
    *ptr++ = (letter + ur);                 /* Upper right corner     */

    ptr += 80 - mine.wide;                  /* Next line              */
    space = mine.wbcolor << 8;
    for (i = 0; i < mine.deep - 2; i++) { /* All rows               */
        *ptr++ = sides;
        for (j = 0; j < mine.wide - 2; j++) {
            *ptr++ = space;                 /* Clear out background    */
        }
        *ptr++ = sides;
        ptr += 80 - mine.wide;              /* Do next row            */
```

continues

Listing 10.4. continued

```
        }
        space = letter;

        *ptr++ = (letter + ll);                  /* Lower left corner      */
        for (i = 0; i < mine.wide - 2; i++) {
            *ptr++ = across;
        }
        *ptr = (letter + lr);                     /* Lower right corner     */

        if (mine.shadow) {                        /* If shadow effect wanted */
            ptr = temp + mine.wide + 80;
            letter = (FGRAY + BBLACK) << 8;
            for (i = 1; i < mine.deep; i++) {    /* Gray out right gap      */
                *ptr = letter + (*ptr & 0xff);
                ptr += 80;
            }
            ptr = temp + mine.deep * 80 + 1;
            for (i = 0; i < mine.wide; i++) {
                *ptr++ = letter + (*ptr & 0xff);
            }
        }

        if (mine.hotspot) {                       /* If window number to show */
            ptr = temp + 2;
            sprintf(buff,"%d", mine.num_win);
            len = strlen(buff);
            *ptr++ = space + '[';
            for (i = 0; i < len; i++) {
                *ptr++ = space + buff[i];
            }
            *ptr = space + ']';
        }

        if (mine.title) {                         /* If window title given   */
            space = ((mine.mcolor + mine.bbcolor) << 8);
            len = strlen(mine.title);
            len = (mine.wide - len) >> 1;
            if (len <= 0)
                return;
            ptr = temp + len;
            for (i = 0; mine.title[i]; i++) {
```

```
            *ptr++ = space + mine.title[i];
      }
   }
   space = letter;

   if (mine.vscrollbar) {                    /* Vertical scroll bar      */
      ptr = temp + 79 + mine.wide;
      *ptr = space + UARROWH;
      ptr += 80;
      *ptr = space + VSCROLLBAR;
      ptr += (mine.deep - 4) * 80;
      *ptr = space + DARROWH;
   }
   if (mine.hscrollbar) {                    /* Horizontal scroll bar    */
      ptr = temp + (mine.deep - 1) * 80 + 1;
      *ptr++ = space + LARROWH;
      *ptr++ = space + HSCROLLBAR;
      ptr += (mine.wide - 5);
      *ptr = space + RARROWH;
   }
}
```

Because the WINDOW structure contains all the necessary information, show_window() has only one argument: the WINDOW structure variable. The statement

```
temp = ptr = start_video_memory + (mine.y * 80 + mine.x);
```

initializes two pointers to the screen location of the upper left corner of the text window. Because each row on the screen has 80 characters and mine.y has been initialized to the starting row position, mine.y * 80 sets the pointer to the proper row position. Adding mine.x puts you at the proper column position. A temporary pointer (temp) also is initialized to this screen position, so you don't have to recalculate this position later in the function.

The next statement

```
space = letter = (mine.bbcolor + mine.bfcolor) << 8;
```

sets the attribute byte for the window's border. Because the Intel family stores integer data in reverse order (for example, the attribute byte, then the character), you must bit-shift the colors eight positions to the left. The result is that the attribute byte is in the high byte of the unsigned int variables space and letter.

The `switch` statement is used to set the characters used for drawing the border. The options are for a single-line border (`case 1`), a double-line border (`case 2`), or no border (`case 0` and `default`). The variables `across` and `sides` hold the proper border characters. The two statements following the `switch` add the proper attribute byte for the border characters.

The statements

```
*ptr++ = (letter + ul);       /* Upper left corner  */
for (i = 0; i < mine.wide - 2; i++) {
   *ptr++ = across;
}
*ptr++ = (letter + ur);       /* Upper right corner */
```

draw the first row of the window border. The first statement draws the upper left corner character of the border. The `for` loop draws the horizontal elements of the border, and the last statement draws the upper right corner character for the border.

The next several statements

```
ptr += 80 - mine.wide;        /* Next line          */
for (i = 0; i < mine.deep - 2; i++) {   /* All rows */
   *ptr++ = sides;
   for (j = 0; j < mine.wide - 2; j++)
      *ptr++ = space;         /* Clear out background */
   *ptr++ = sides;
   ptr += 80 - mine.wide;
}
```

draw the vertical border characters and the remainder of the window. Note that the inner `for` controlled by variable `j` is used to display nothing more than the background color of the window. (If you want to, you can use the `c_scroll()` function from Chapter 1, "Screen Functions," to scroll the window in color instead of using the `j for` loop. However, you still must perform the proper pointer arithmetic for the rest of the border drawing. The `c_scroll` function might be somewhat faster, but the method in listing 10.4 shows more clearly what the function is doing.)

The next `for` loop is used to draw the border for the bottom of the text window. It is identical to the loop used to draw the top row of the window.

Next, the `if` statement checks to see whether the window should be drawn with a shadow. If the `mine.shadow` member is nonzero, the attribute byte is changed to a gray foreground color with a black background. Because the shadow effect should preserve whatever text already exists on the screen, only the attribute byte must be changed. The first for loop shadows the right side of the window, and the second for loop shadows the row at the bottom of the text window.

The next if statement checks to see whether you elected to have a hotspot for the window. If mine.hotspot is nonzero, the hotspot is drawn over the window border. If the window is window number three, for example, the hotspot in the upper left section of the window would show

```
---[3]---
```

If the user puts the mouse cursor on the 3 and clicks the left mouse button, you can detect this action and use it to signal that the window should be closed.

The remaining if statements check to see whether the window should have a title (mine.title) and vertical (mine.vscrollbar) or horizontal (mine.hscrollbar) scrollbars displayed. If any of these WINDOW structure members is nonzero, the appropriate title or scrollbar is drawn in the text window.

When show_window() finishes, the screen displays the text window at the appropriate location on the screen. Obviously, a text window normally is used to present some form of information to the user. Instead of seeing how that is done right now, you first should examine the last window function you must call.

Closing a Text Window— *close_window( )*

When you are finished using the text window, you must call close_window(). The code for close_window() is shown in listing 10.5.

Listing 10.5. *Close a text window.*

```
/*****
                        close_window()

    This function closes a WINDOW. It first redisplays the contents
of screen memory that existed before this window was created, and
then frees the memory allocation used to store the previous display
contents.
```

continues

Listing 10.5. continued

```
    Argument list:    struct WINDOW mine        the WINDOW to display

    Return value:     void
*****/
#include "win.h"


void close_window(struct WINDOW mine)
{
    int i, j;
    unsigned int far *ptr;

    if (mine.base == NULL)
        return;

    ptr = start_video_memory + (mine.y * 80 + mine.x);
    for (i = 0; i < mine.deep + 1; i++) {              /* All rows        */
        for (j = 0; j < mine.wide + 1; j++)
            *ptr++ = *mine.base++;
        ptr += 79 - mine.wide;
    }
    free( (void *) mine.base);
}
```

This function has two primary responsibilities. First, it must restore the screen to its original state. First you initialize ptr to point to the starting screen location of the text window. Two for loops are used to copy the previously saved contents of the screen back into video memory. This has the effect of restoring the screen to its original state before displaying the text window.

The second responsibility of close_window() is to free the storage used to hold the screen's original information. As soon as you are finished using a text window, you should call close_window() immediately. This action ensures that you don't eat up more memory than is absolutely necessary.

The win.h Header File

The purpose of the win.h header file is to hold all the overhead information necessary to use text windows. Although I do not discuss all the information contained in win.h, listing 10.6 presents a partial listing of its contents. (All the items in the win.h header file are covered in this chapter or in Chapter 11, "Putting It All Together." If you want to see a full listing of the header file, you can print it from the copy stored on the disks distributed with this book.)

Listing 10.6. The win.h header file.

```
/*****

                              win.h

                     Ref. 1.0    4/14/91


     This header file contains the necessary overhead information for
  text windows.
*****/

#include <stdio.h>
#include <stdlib.h>
#include <string.h>
#include <ctype.h>
#include <dos.h>



          /*********** Data Structures and Definitions ***********/
typedef struct {
   char *prompt;          /* First line menu prompt              */
   int  plen;             /* Its length                          */
   char *desc;            /* Second line menu prompt             */
   int  dlen;             /* Its length                          */
   char letter;           /* Single letter choice option         */
   } MENU;


                        /* Structures for Chapters 10-11         */
struct WINDOW {
   char title[30];
   int num_win;
```

continues

Listing 10.6. *continued*

```
    unsigned int far *base; /* Base memory for window                 */

    int x,         /* Upper left x                                    */
       y,          /* Upper left y                                    */
       wide,       /* Lower right x                                   */
       deep,       /* Lower right y                                   */
       border,     /* 0 = no border, 1 = single line, 2 = double-line */
       wbcolor,    /* Window background color                         */
       wfcolor,    /* Window foreground color                         */
       bbcolor,    /* Border background color                         */
       bfcolor,    /* Border foreground color                         */
       mcolor,     /* Foreground message print color (back = wbcolor) */
       vscrollbar, /* Vertical scroll bar; 0 = No, 1 = Yes            */
       hscrollbar, /* Horizontal scroll bar; 0 = No, 1 = Yes          */
       hotspot,    /* 0 if no close button, 1 for close button        */
       shadow;     /* Does window have a shadow; 0 = No, 1 = Yes      */
};


struct DIALOG {

    unsigned int far *base; /* Base memory for dialog box             */

    int *locations,   /* Start of button locations; x then y         */
        *buttonlen;   /* Length of each button string                */

    int bfcolor,      /* Background input field color                */
        bmcolor,      /* Background message color                    */
        buttonnum,    /* Number of buttons in dialog box             */
        dbcolor,      /* Dialog background color                     */
        deep,         /* Dialog depth                                */
        dfcolor,      /* Dialog foreground color                     */
        ffcolor,      /* Foreground input field color                */
        fmcolor,      /* Foreground message color                    */
        shadow,       /* Does dialog have a shadow; 0 = No, 1 = Yes  */
        wide,         /* Dialog width                                */
        x,            /* Upper left x                                */
        y;            /* Upper left y                                */

};
```

```
typedef struct {
   char fname[13];          /* The file name                      */
   char use;                /* File use flag                      */
   } FILEDIR;


#ifndef MAIN
   extern
#endif
   FILEDIR *fptr;           /* Pointer to FILEDIR structure       */


#ifndef MAIN
   extern
#endif
      char *cptr,           /* Vector of single char choices      */
      old_source[128],      /* Starting directory                 */
      file_mask[128],
      file_source[128],     /* Input file path name               */
      file_dest[128];       /* Output file path name              */


#ifndef MAIN
   extern
#endif
      int delta,            /* Used for setting mouse speed       */
      increment,            /* Relative movement of marker        */
      last,                 /* The last menu choice made          */
      match_count,          /* Count of file matches              */
      menucount,            /* The number of items in the menu    */
      menulen,              /* The length of all menu choices     */
      mouse_here,           /* Is there a mouse present           */
      *nptr,                /* Pointer to menu column positions   */
      pcol,                 /* Primary column                     */
      prow;                 /* Primary row                        */


#ifndef MAIN                /* Settable color variables           */
   extern
#endif
      int main_menu_f,      /* Foreground for main menu           */
      main_menu_b,          /* Background for main menu           */
      sub_menu_f,           /* Foreground for sub menus           */
```

continues

Listing 10.6. continued

```
        sub_menu_b,          /* Background for sub menus          */
        box_f,               /* Foreground for windows           */
        box_b,               /* Background for windows           */
        box_h,               /* Background highlight for windows */
        button_b;            /* Background for window buttons    */


#ifndef MAIN                 /* Start of video memory            */
    extern
#endif
    unsigned int far *start_video_memory, hot_key_color, mkey;


                    /*********** Macros ***********/

#ifndef TRUE
    #define TRUE   1
#endif

#define UL  218              /* Graphics characters for single-  */
#define UR  191              /* line box                         */
#define LL  192
#define LR  217
#define VB  179
#define HB  196


#define DUL  201             /* Double-line box                  */
#define DUR  187
#define DLL  200
#define DLR  188
#define DVB  186
#define DHB  205


                    /* Graphics characters                       */

#define RARROWH     16       /*              right arrowhead      */
#define LARROWH     17       /*              left arrowhead       */
#define UDARROW     18       /*              up-down arrow symbol */
#define UARROWSYM   24       /*              up arrow symbol      */
#define DARROWSYM   25       /*              down arrow symbol    */
#define UARROWH     30       /*              up arrowhead symbol  */
```

```
#define DARROWH        31        /*             down arrowhead symbol */
#define LITEBOX        176       /*             light hatch area      */
#define MEDIUMBOX      177       /*             hor. background field */
#define HSCROLLFIELD   177       /*             hor. background field */
#define HEAVYBOX       176       /*             heavy hatch area      */
#define BLANK          219       /*             solid hatch area      */
#define VSCROLLBAR     219       /*             vertical scroll bar   */
#define HALFBLOCK      220       /*             half block            */
#define HALFSQUARE     223       /*             half square           */
#define CHECK          251       /*             check                 */
#define HOTSPOT        254       /*             square                */
#define HSCROLLBAR     254       /*             horizontal scroll bar */

#define SPACE          32

                         /* Macros for two-line menu bar             */

#define ifbars(x, y)    (c = (bars == 1) ? (x) : (y) )

#define ASCII_LOW      64        /* Just before uppercase letter      */
#define ASCII_HI       91        /* Just after uppercase letter       */
#define ASCII_LIMIT    128       /* Upper limit for ASCII data        */
#define EXTEND_OFF     0x100     /* Offset for extended keys           */

#define LASTCOL        63
#define LASTROW        22
#define FILENAMESIZE   15
#define MAXFLINE       5
#define MAXFILES       200
#define SCREENFULL     100

#define SCREENCOL      3
#define SCREENROW      3

#define YOUNGER        0
#define SAMEAGE        1
#define OLDER          2
#define NOT_EQUAL      3

#define LINEDOWN       0         /* For scroll line function           */
#define LINEUP         1
```

continues

Listing 10.6. *continued*

```
#define MAXWIDE     80      /* Maximum screen width-depth       */
#define MAXDEEP     24
#define MAXSTR      128
#define PATHMAX     129

#define MAXLINE     256
#define MAXITEM     50
#define EVER        ;;
#define UP          72
#define DOWN        80
#define WIDTH       80
#define ROW         5

#define LINEDOWN    0       /* For scroll functions            */
#define LINEUP      1


                            /* Color definitions               */

#define FBLACK      0       /* Foreground colors               */
#define FBLUE       1
#define FGREEN      2
#define FCYAN       3
#define FRED        4
#define FMAGENTA    5
#define FBROWN      6
#define FWHITE      7
#define FGRAY       8
#define FLBLUE      9
#define FLGREEN     10
#define FLCYAN      11
#define FLRED       12
#define FLMAGENTA   13
#define FYELLOW     14
#define FLWHITE     15

#define BBLACK      0       /* Background colors (values shifted) */
#define BBLUE       16
#define BGREEN      32
#define BCYAN       48
#define BRED        64
```

```
#define BMAGENTA     80
#define BBROWN       96
#define BWHITE      112

#define F1           59        /* Function keys                  */
#define F2           60
#define F3           61
#define F4           62
#define F5           63
#define F6           64
#define F7           65
#define F8           66
#define F9           67
#define F10          68


#define HOME    71             /* Extended key codes for keypad  */
#define UARROW  72
#define PAGEUP  73
#define LARROW  75
#define RARROW  77
#define END     79
#define DARROW  80
#define PAGEDN  81

#define OBRACKET   91          /* Open bracket                   */
#define CBRACKET   93          /* Close bracket                  */


#define LBUTTON   1            /* Define mouse buttons           */
#define RBUTTON   2
#define MBUTTON   4
/*
#define DELTA     50
*/

#define SIDEWAYS  0            /* Direction of mouse travel      */
#define UPDOWN    1
#define ANYWAY    2

#define SINGLEBAR 1            /* For box drawing                */
#define DOUBLEBAR 2
```

continues

Listing 10.6. continued

```
#define UL   218          /* Graphics characters for single-  */
#define UR   191          /* line box                         */
#define LL   192
#define LR   217
#define VB   179
#define HB   196


#define DUL  201          /* Double-line box                  */
#define DUR  187
#define DLL  200
#define DLR  188
#define DVB  186
#define DHB  205


                          /* Graphics characters              */


#define RARROWH       16     /*              right arrowhead            */
#define LARROWH       17     /*              left arrowhead             */
#define UDARROW       18     /*              up-down arrow symbol       */
#define UARROWSYM     24     /*              up arrow symbol            */
#define DARROWSYM     25     /*              down arrow symbol          */
#define UARROWH       30     /*              up arrowhead symbol        */
#define DARROWH       31     /*              down arrowhead symbol      */
#define LITEBOX       176    /*              light hatch area           */
#define MEDIUMBOX     177    /*              hor. background field      */
#define HSCROLLFIELD  177    /*              hor. background field      */
#define HEAVYBOX      176    /*              heavy hatch area           */
#define BLANK         219    /*              solid hatch area           */
#define VSCROLLBAR    219    /*              vertical scroll bar         */
#define HALFBLOCK     220    /*              half block                 */
#define HALFSQUARE    223    /*              half square                */
#define CHECK         251    /*              check                      */
#define HOTSPOT       254    /*              square                     */
#define HSCROLLBAR    254    /*              horizontal scroll bar      */


#define SPACE         32



#define ENTER      '\r'    /* This may be '\n' on some compilers   */
#define NEWLINE    '\n'
#define ESCAPE     27
```

```
#define BACKSPACE      8
#define DELETE         127
#define TAB            9
#define BELL           7           /* Terminal alarm                   */

                            /* Macros for two-line menu bar            */

#define ifbars(x, y)     (c = (bars == 1) ? (x) : (y) )

#define OPTION(a, b, c)   {a, sizeof(a) - 1, b, sizeof(b) - 1, c},
#define OPTIONEND         {0}

#define MARGIN       "  "    /* Spacing between menu items             */

/*
#define DELTA        50          /* Mickeys/menu change               */
*/

#define MAXLINE    256
#define MAXITEM    50
#define EVER       ;;
#define UP         72
#define DOWN       80
#define WIDTH      80
#define ROW        5

#define MENUCOL    1
#define MENUROW    1
#define DLINE      24              /* Description line placement       */


                            /* Function prototypes                     */

unsigned int read_key(int button),
   get_mouse_or_key(int button, int direction, int *row, int *col),
   packdate(int day, int month, int year),
   read_key_all(int *row, int *col),
   read_key_and_mouse(int *row, int *col),
   read_key_d(int button, int dir),     /* SEE LIST0414.C             */
   read_key_only(int *row, int *col);

int box_menu_start(MENU s[], int fore, int bk, int frame, int bar, int wdeep),
```

continues

Listing 10.6. continued

```
        box_select(MENU m[], int fore, int bk, int button, int limit, int marker),
        box_menu_start(MENU s[], int fore, int bk, int frame, int bars, int wdeep),
        check_paths(void),
        create_w(int y, int x, int wide, int deep, struct WINDOW *m),
        fcompare(const char *s1, const char *s2),
        get_string(int row, int col, char *m, char *buff, int field_width,
                    struct DIALOG mine, int len),
        menu_choice(MENU m[], int fore, int back, int button, int dir),
        open_file(int which),
        wbox_menu_start(int row, int col, MENU s[], int fore, int back,
                        int frame, int bars, int inverse);

long get_disk_free(char drive),
    get_disk_size(char drive);

void active(char *m, int row, int col, int fore, int back),
        cbox(int row, int col, int wide, int deep, int color, int bars),
        close_box(void),
        close_window(struct WINDOW m),
        clrwork(void),
        cursor(int row, int col),
        do_batch(void),
        do_button(int row, int col, char *prompt, int fpcolor, int bpcolor,
                    struct DIALOG active),
        do_copies(int number, int selected),
        do_copy(void),
        do_defaults(void),
        do_delete(void),
        do_mask_copy(void),
        do_read(void),
        do_read_text(int which),
        do_search(void),
        draw_box(struct WINDOW m),
        expand_slash(char *f),
        flip_file(char *fname, char use, int row, int col),
        get_date_mask(unsigned *d),
        hide_cursor(void),
        highlight(MENU m[], int row, int fore, int back),
        indicator(int fore, int marker, int limit),
        init_video_base(void),
        init_window(struct WINDOW *w),
```

```
menu_end(void),
menu_off(MENU m[], int fore, int back),
menu_on(MENU m[], int fore, int back),
menu_on_new(MENU m[], int fore, int back),
menu_start(MENU s[], int fore, int back),
mouse_cursor_on(void),
mouse_counter(int *r, int *c),
mouse_cursor_off(void),
prepare(void),
read_mouse(int *row, int *col, int *button),
redraw_window(MENU m[], int first, int fore, int limit),
restore(MENU m[], int row, int fore, int back),
restore_old_directory(void),
save_screen(int row, int col, int wide, int deep, char *s),
scroll_one_line(int direction),
set_mouse(int row, int col),
show_ascii(void),
show_binary(void),
show_files(FILEDIR *fptr, int index, int number),
show_one_line(FILEDIR *fptr, int index, int number, int row, int col),
show_window(struct WINDOW m),
small_abort(void),
wprintf(int row, int col, struct WINDOW hwnd, char *c, ...),
write_screen(int row, int col, int wide, int deep, char *s);
```

Most of the contents of the win.h header file contain structure declarations that are needed for the functions presented in this chapter and Chapter 11. (The function prototypes for the various text window functions are omitted from listing 10.6 to avoid unnecessary duplication.) You might not like some of the symbols I use (for example, VSCROLLBAR, HSCROLLBAR, and so on); feel free to change them to whatever suits your tastes.

An Example of a Text Window

Now that you know what the text window functions do, you can examine a simple program that displays a text window on the screen. The code for the sample program is presented in program 10.1.

Program 10.1. *A sample program using text windows.*

```
/*****

Sample program using text windows

*****/

#include <stdio.h>


#define MAIN 1
#define BC 1                        /* True for the Borland compiler    */
                                    /* Omit for any other compiler      */

#include "win.h"


#define MAXSCREEN   1920

void init_video_base(void);
void init_window(struct WINDOW *w);
void show_window(struct WINDOW mine);
void close_window(struct WINDOW mine);



void main(void)
{
   int i;
   unsigned int far *ptr, letter;
   struct WINDOW mine;

   init_video_base();

   if (start_video_memory == NULL) {
      printf("Display in improper mode.");
      exit(EXIT_FAILURE);
   }

   ptr = start_video_memory;

   letter = ((FLWHITE + BRED) << 8) + 'X';
```

```
    for (i = 0; i < MAXSCREEN; i++) {
        *ptr++ = letter;
    }
    getch();

    init_window(&mine);

    i = create_w(7, 25, 30, 10, &mine);
    if (i == 0) {
        printf("Could not get enough memory");
        exit(EXIT_FAILURE);
    }
    strcpy(mine.title, "This is a text window");

    show_window(mine);
    getch();

    close_window(mine);
}
```

The program begins by calling `init_video_base()` to set the base address for video memory. On return, you check to ensure that `start_video_memory` contains a valid memory address. If `start_video_memory` does not contain a valid memory address, it's probably because the display is in graphics mode. If this is the case, you issue an error message and abort the program.

If all went well with the call to `init_video_base()`, you initialize `ptr` to point to the start of the video memory. The statements

```
letter = ((FLWHITE + BRED) << 8) + 'X';
for (i = 0; i < MAXSCREEN; i++) {
    *ptr++ = letter;
}
getch();
```

prepare the program to display a screenful of X's. The variable `letter` has an attribute byte that displays the X's as bright white letters on a red background. The `for` loop then displays the X's. The call to `getch()` simply pauses the display so you can view the X's.

The call to `init_window()` fills in the default values for the window, and the call to `create_w()`

```
i = create_w(7, 25, 30, 10, &mine);
```

does the work of filling in the rest of the WINDOW structure with the proper values. The arguments say you want to put the text window at row seven, column 25, and that the window is 30 characters wide and 10 rows deep. As mentioned earlier, row seven actually is the eighth row of the screen because you are using zero-based row addressing.

The program checks the return value from create_w() to make sure that there was sufficient free memory to create the window. If the window could not be created, a short message is given and the program aborts.

Next, you copy a short string title into the mine.title[] field before actually displaying the window. If you want to change any of the default WINDOW structure values, you should do so just after the create_w() call. For example, if you do not want to use the shadow feature for the window (the default is for the shadow to be shown), the statement

```
mine.shadow = 0;
```

turns off the shadow feature. If you want to change a default setting, you must do it before calling show_window().

The call to show_window() then displays the text window. For the program presented in program 10.1, the output is shown in figure 10.2.

Fig. 10.2. Output of program 10.1.

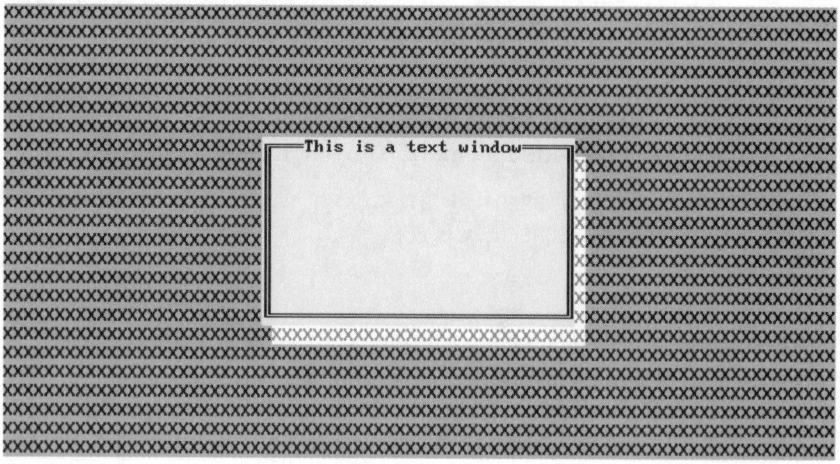

The final call to getch() pauses the screen so that you can view the window. After you press a key, the call to close_window() restores the original screen and frees the window's memory allocation.

You might want to experiment with program 10.1 to see the visual effect that the different structure members have on the window. Also, you can comment out the for loop that draws the X's and recompile the program to prove that the program does in fact restore the original screen. (One way to run this check is to do a wide directory (dir /w) on a subdirectory with many files before running the program.)

Now you'll see how to expand on the basic text window to make it more useful.

A Text Window *printf( )— wprintf( )*

The first thing you do with a text window is display some form of text in it. You could use printf(), but listing 10.7 offers an alternative.

Listing 10.7. *Displaying text in a window—*wprintf().

```
/*****

                              wprintf()

   This function works as a printf() replacement for text windows.
The first three arguments are required for the function to work
with text windows.

Argument list:    int r              row position within the
                                     window
                  int c              column position within
                                     the window
                  struct WINDOW hwnd  window to print in

  Return value:   void

*****/
```

continues

Listing 10.7. continued

```c
#include <stdarg.h>
#include "win.h"

void wprintf(int r, int c, struct WINDOW hwnd, char *control, ...)
{
    unsigned char buff[MAXSTR];
    int count, i, lines, width, deep;
    unsigned letter, hot_letter;
    unsigned int far *ptr, far *rows;
    va_list parms;

    ptr = start_video_memory;
    va_start(parms, control);
    vsprintf(buff, control, parms);

    rows = ptr = start_video_memory + ( (hwnd.y + r) * 80 + hwnd.x + 1 + c);

    letter = (hwnd.wbcolor + hwnd.mcolor) << 8;
    hot_letter = (hwnd.wbcolor + hot_key_color) << 8;
    width = hwnd.wide - 3 - c;
    deep =  hwnd.deep - 2;
    lines = count = 0;
    for (i = 0; buff[i]; i++) {
        if (buff[i] > ASCII_LOW && buff[i] < ASCII_HI) {
            *ptr++ = (buff[i] + hot_letter);
        } else {
            *ptr++ = (buff[i] + letter);
        }
        count++;
        if (count == width) {
            ptr = rows + 80;
            count = 0;
            rows = ptr;
            lines++;
            if (lines == deep)
                break;
        }
    }
}
```

Using `wprintf()` rather than a cursor-controlled `printf()` has several advantages. First, `wprintf()` automatically calculates the cursor position relative to the text window boundaries. For example, suppose that you have a text window located at row 10, column 10 and want to print something on the first line of the text window. First you calculate the proper row-column coordinates, call `cursor()`, and then call `printf()`. The code might appear as

```
cursor(11, 12);
printf("Whatever...");
```

With `wprintf()`, the call becomes

```
wprintf(1, 1, mine, "Whatever...");
```

The coordinates for the printed text are calculated relative to the window. You do not have to calculate the row-column offsets relative to the screen.

The second advantage occurs when you want to use *hotkeys* in your programs. Hotkeys usually are single keystrokes that cause some specific action to take place in the program. I tend to write menu choices so that the capitalized letter is the hotkey for the specified menu choice. For example, the representation in figure 10.3 might be a menu, with the hotkeys N, O, S, and A. The hotkeys correspond to the capital letters. With `wprintf()`, capital letters can be displayed using a "hotkey color." A global variable, `hot_key_color`, defined in win.h, can be used to hold the hotkey color. Any time `wprintf()` detects an uppercase letter, it uses the value for the hotkey color to display the capital letter.

Fig. 10.3. *A sample menu.*

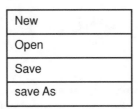

But there might be times when you want to display just plain text with no hotkey color. (Plain text, for example, might have capital letters in it.) The statements

```
temp = hot_key_color;
hot_key_color = mine.mcolor;
wprintf(1, 1, "This is a message");
        .

        .

hot_key_color = temp;
```

save the hotkey color in a temporary variable and assign the normal foreground text color into hot_key_color. When you need to restore the hotkey color, simply reassign the original hot_key_color as it was saved in the temporary variable.

Finally, wprintf() provides for automatic folding of text if the text is wider than the text window allows. Also, if the message is too long to fit in the window, it is clipped to just the text that fits in the window. Folding and clipping are done using the rather dumb Granite algorithm. If the text needs to be folded or clipped in the middle of a word, that's where it is folded or clipped. (If you implement an elegant algorithm, send it in. Perhaps I will integrate it into the next edition of this book!) In most cases, it's very simple to write the text strings to fit within the text window's specified size.

There is nothing tricky about how wprintf() works. All the conversion work to go from data into strings is done by vsprintf() and its support routines. As soon as the buffer contains the string to be displayed, the usual video memory display techniques discussed earlier in this chapter are used to write the string in the text window. You can, of course, calculate the absolute cursor addresses for the row-column positions and use cursor() and printf() if you want. But you still must contend with writing to the text window in color. Using wprintf() probably is easier.

Writing a Message Box— *alert()*

You can use the basic text window functions discussed earlier to build other functions. The alert() function can serve as a model for any function in which you need to display a message and have the user respond to it. (I refer to a text window of this form as a *message box*.) In other words, alert() can be used to create a message box in which the user must respond to a single choice. (Typically, the user will be responding to an "Ok" or a "Cancel" message.) Figure 10.4 shows an example using the alert() function to create a message box.

Fig. 10.4. Example of the alert() *function.*

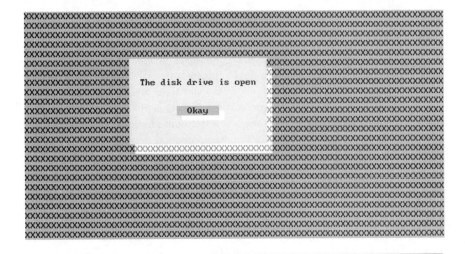

The alert() function uses two text windows, although they don't show up too well in figure 10.4. The first is the larger window on which the message is written (that is, "The disk drive is open"). The second is the *button window*, a smaller text window that holds the button message ("Okay").

The alert() function is written so that the user has three ways to close the alert message. First, the user can move the mouse cursor and click the left mouse button while the mouse cursor is on the button window. Second, the user can press a hotkey. In figure 10.4, because the letter O is capitalized in the button message ("Okay"), it is the hotkey for this message box. Finally, the user also can press the Escape key, which closes the message box.

Listing 10.8 shows the code for the alert() function.

Listing 10.8. The alert() *function.*

```
/*****
                            alert()

    This function manages a dialog box that has two basic parts: a
message string and a prompt string. The message string tells the
purpose of the dialog box, and the prompt string requires the user
to click on the prompt pushbutton. Most prompts are of the "Ok,"
"Continue," or "Cancel" variety. The system halts until the user
clicks on the pushbutton.
```

continues

Listing 10.8. continued

```
   Argument list:    int row        row position for upper left corner
                     int col        column position for upper left
                                    corner
                     char *message  message prompt
                     char *prompt   pushbutton prompt
                     int fmcolor    foreground message color
                     int bmcolor    background message color
                     int fpcolor    foreground prompt color
                     int bpcolor    background prompt color

   Return value:     int            0 if not enough memory for dialog
                                    box; 1 otherwise

*****/

#include "win.h"

#define OKDEPTH   1

int alert(int row, int col, char *message, char *prompt,
          int fmcolor, int bmcolor, int fpcolor, int bpcolor)
{
   char buff[80], prompt_hot;
   int base, deep, mlen, plen, wide;
   int coloffset, i, mrow, mcol;
   unsigned letter, select;
   struct WINDOW a;
   unsigned int far *ptr, far *rows;

   rows = ptr = start_video_memory;

   strcpy(buff, " ");   strcat(buff, prompt);   strcat(buff, "  ");
   plen = strlen(buff);
   mlen = strlen(message);

   init_window(&a);                           /* Initialized dialog     */


   wide = mlen + 4; deep = 9;       /* Set up values          */
   a.y = row;       a.x = col;
   a.wide = wide;   a.deep = deep;
```

```
      a.num_win = a.border = a.hotspot = 0;
      a.wbcolor = a.bbcolor = bmcolor;
      a.title[0] = '\0';
        for (i = 0; prompt[i]; i++) {        /* Get prompt hotkey        */
          if (isupper(prompt[i])) {
              prompt_hot = prompt[i];
          }
      }

      base = create_w(row, col, wide, deep, &a);

      if (base == 0) {
          return 0;
      }

      if (mouse_here) {
          mouse_cursor_on();
          set_mouse(row * 8, col * 7);
      }

      show_window(a);                        /* Show the message box     */

      ptr += ( (a.y + 2) * 80 + a.x + 2);    /* Show message             */
      letter = (fmcolor + bmcolor) << 8;
      while (*message) {
         *ptr++ = (*message + letter);
         message++;
      }

      coloffset = col + ((wide - plen) >> 1); /* Do pushbutton           */
      row += 5;
      ptr = rows + (row * 80 + coloffset);
      letter = (fpcolor + bpcolor) << 8;
      for (i = 0; i < plen; i++) {
         *ptr++ = (buff[i] + letter);
      }
      letter = (bmcolor + FBLACK) << 8;      /* Do shadow effect         */
      *ptr = (HALFBLOCK + letter);
      ptr += 81 - plen;
      for (i = 0; i < plen; i++)
         *ptr++ = (HALFSQUARE + letter);

      while (1) {                            /* Wait for a click         */
```

continues

Listing 10.8. continued

```
        select = read_key_all(&mrow, &mcol);
        if ( (select == ENTER && toupper(last) == prompt_hot) ¦¦
             select == ESCAPE) {
           break;
        }
        mrow = (mrow >> 3);   mcol = (mcol >> 3);
        if (select == ENTER && (mrow >= row && mrow < row + OKDEPTH) &&
             (mcol >= coloffset && mcol < coloffset + plen) ) {
           break;
        }
    }
    if (mouse_here) {
        mouse_cursor_off();
    }

    close_window(a);
    if (mouse_here) {
        mouse_cursor_on();
    }
    return 1;
}
```

The function has eight arguments, but don't let the number bother you. The arguments make sense considering what alert() is designed to do. The first two arguments are the row and column coordinates for the upper left corner of the message box. The interpretation for these two arguments is the same as for previous text windows.

The third argument is the message to be displayed in the message box. The length of the message determines the width that the message box occupies on the screen. Therefore, messages that will appear in the message box should be kept to fewer than 70 characters.

The fourth argument is the prompt string, or *button message*. It is the message that is displayed on the button used to close the window. For user consistency, this message should contain only one capital letter for use as a hotkey for the message box. If the button message is very short (for example, "Ok"), consider padding it with leading and trailing spaces before calling alert(). For example, I think the message box looks better if the button message "Ok" is expanded to " Ok ". The expanded version also makes a larger target for the user to click on the button to close the window. You might want to experiment to see what suits your tastes.

The next four arguments are the colors to be used for the message box. You can set the foreground message color (fmcolor), the background message color (bmcolor), the foreground prompt color (fpcolor), and the background prompt color (bpcolor). I prefer to set both foreground colors to bright white (FLWHITE), and to have contrasting background colors (like BBLUE and BRED).

When you are inside the function, two pointers (row and ptr) are initialized to point to the start of video memory. Note that this assumes that you have called init_video_base() before calling alert(). In most programs, alert() is called after you have called init_video_base(). If you are uncomfortable with this assumption, you can insert the call within alert(). It costs only a little code space and time to call init_video_base() a second time.

The next three statements pad the button message with two leading and trailing blank spaces. Again, this action makes the target for the mouse user somewhat larger than the prompt string itself. After the string is padded, plen and mlen are assigned the lengths of the two strings.

The call to init_window() initializes the members of the WINDOW structure. On return from init_window(), the required members are assigned the appropriate values for use with the message box. I prefer for message boxes not to have a border, hotspot, window number, or title; therefore, these members are initialized to zero. You can change them if you want.

A for loop is used to search for the capitalized letter that is used as the hotkey for the message box. The variable prompt_hot is assigned the value of the capitalized letter.

The calls to create_w() and show_window() behave the same as the text windows discussed earlier in this chapter. Between the calls, you check for the presence of a mouse and turn the mouse cursor on if a mouse is present. You also call set_mouse() to locate the mouse cursor just outside the message box.

After the call to show_window(), a while loop is used to display the message. The next dozen statements figure out where the button and its message are to be displayed. The code attempts to center the button within the limits of the message box. The button behaves much like a second, smaller text window within the message box. Although I think the button looks better when it has a shadow effect, you can remove these lines if you don't like the shadow.

At this point, all the display work for the message box is complete. An infinite while loop now is entered to wait for the user to respond to the message box. The function read_key_all() (described later in this chapter) is responsible for reading the keyboard and the mouse (if one is present). The first `if` statement checks to see whether the user pressed the hotkey or the Escape key. If the user did press one of these keys, control breaks out of the loop, the mouse cursor is turned off, and the window is closed. This causes the original screen to be restored. After the window is restored, the mouse cursor is turned on again, and control returns to the main program.

If the user did not press the Escape key or the hotkey, the code checks to see whether the user clicked on the button. The statement

```
mrow = (mrow >> 3);   mcol = (mcol >> 3);
```

converts the row and column values returned from the mouse (which correspond to pixel rows and columns) into character rows and columns. The shift-right operations on `mrow` and `mcol` is the same as dividing the values returned by `read_key_all()` by eight. This must be done to convert from the mouse coordinate system to the character-based coordinate system used in the function.

The program now checks to see whether the user clicked on the message button by way of a complex `if` statement. If the mouse was clicked on the message button, control breaks out of the `while` loop and the cleanup chores are performed. Control then passes a return value of 1 to the program.

Reading the Keyboard and the Mouse—*read_key_all()*

The actual work of selecting what the user does in the `alert()` function is performed by the `read_key_all()` function. The code for `read_key_all()` is presented in listing 10.9.

Listing 10.9. *The* `read_key_all()` *function.*

```
/*****
                          read_key_all()

    This function is designed to read both the keyboard and the
 mouse. The function draws from other functions presented in the
 text. Note that _kbhit() must be used and not the kbhit() that
 might be supplied with your compiler.
```

```
Argument list:    int *row      pointer to the row variable
                  int *col      pointer to the column variable

Return value:     int           code for the key struck
```

CAUTION: The return value is not necessarily the exact key pressed. The coding causes the following return values:

```
         Keyboard                          Mouse
Key            Return Value       Button         Return Value

Enter          ENTER             Left           ENTER
Escape         ESCAPE            Right          ESCAPE
A - z          ENTER             Movement       Direction Value
Extended       Extended Key Code
```

If an ASCII key is struck, the return value is ENTER, and a global variable named "last" equals the actual key code. If an extended key code is given, "last" equals 0.

```
*****/
#include "win.h"

unsigned int read_key_all(int *row, int *col)
{
   char press, *tptr;
   int dhm, dvm, vmove, hmove, temp, tbutton;

   hide_cursor();
                                /* Newer machines fast enough to read  */
                                /* multiple presses when user wants     */
                                /* only one. This next loop clears out  */
                                /* false presses.                       */

   if (mouse_here) {
      while (TRUE) {
         read_mouse(row, col, &tbutton);
         if (tbutton == 0)
            break;
      }
   }
   dvm = dhm = 0;
```

continues

Listing 10.9. continued

```
while (TRUE) {
    if (mouse_here) {                    /* If there is a mouse      */
        read_mouse(row, col, &tbutton);

        if (tbutton == LBUTTON) {
            return ENTER;                /* User made a choice       */
        }
        if (tbutton == RBUTTON) {
            return ESCAPE;               /* Return without choice    */
        }

                /* Could put MBUTTON code here */

        mouse_counters(&vmove, &hmove); /* Get relative movement     */
        dhm += hmove;                    /* Get horizontal movement  */
        dvm += vmove;                    /* Get vertical movement    */


        if (dhm > DELTA) {
            return RARROW;
        }
        if (dhm < -DELTA) {
            return LARROW;
        }
        if (dvm > DELTA) {
            return DARROW;
        }
        if (dvm < -DELTA) {
            return UARROW;
        }
    }
                                        /* _kbhit() changes:         */
                                        /* LIST0305.C changed to avoid */
                                        /* conflict with compilers that */
                                        /* have a kbhit() function   */
                                        /* Note leading underscore   */

    temp = _kbhit();                     /* Poll the keyboard         */

    if (temp == 0) {                     /* No key press              */
        continue;
```

```
      }
      if (temp == ENTER) {              /* Pressed Enter key?        */
         return ENTER;
      }
      if (temp == ESCAPE) {
         return ESCAPE;
      }
      if (temp < 127) {                 /* Pressed ASCII key?        */
         last = temp;
         return ENTER;
      }
      last = 0;
      return temp - EXTEND_OFF;         /* Extended keycode?         */
   }
}
```

The function begins by checking to see whether a mouse is present in the system (that is, mouse_here is nonzero). If so, a while loop is entered to clear out the mouse buttons. This might not be needed on slower machines, but on some 386 systems the code might execute fast enough to read a leftover strobe from the mouse.

The program then enters an infinite while loop. If a mouse is present, it is read by calls to read_mouse(). If a button is pressed, the row and column positions are saved, and tbutton can be checked to see which button was pressed. (The code for read_mouse() is presented in Chapter 3, "Input Functions.") If tbutton equals LBUTTON, the symbolic constant ENTER (defined in win.h) is returned. If tbutton equals RBUTTON, the symbolic constant ESCAPE is returned. Note that you can add code to check the middle button. (Some programs use the middle button to trigger on-line help.)

Although you don't use the feature in alert(), you also can detect the direction of the mouse's movement with read_key_all(). This is done by calling mouse_counters() and keeping track of what the mouse did between calls. The return values for mouse movements also are defined in win.h and are consistent with the arrow and other cursor-control keys.

If the user does not use a mouse, the code falls into the call to _kbhit(). Again, note that this is the special function presented in Chapter 3, not the kbhit() that might be supplied with your compiler. If a key is pressed, the return value is not necessarily the key pressed. If an ASCII letter is entered by the user, the return value is ENTER, and the variable last holds the key that was pressed. If the Escape key was entered, ESCAPE is returned.

If an extended key was pressed (for example, Page Up or one of the function keys), the scan code for the extended key is returned, but last is set to zero. Your program should have no conflicts between ASCII and extended key codes. Just remember that an ASCII key press always returns ENTER and sets last to the ASCII key code. An extended character returns the scan code and sets last to zero.

The program that produced the output shown in figure 10.4 is presented in program 10.2.

Program 10.2. *A sample program using* alert().

```
#define MAIN 1
#include <stdio.h>
#include "win.h"

void main(void)
{
   int i;
   unsigned int far *ptr, letter;
   struct WINDOW mine;

   init_video_base();

   if (start_video_memory == NULL) {
      printf("Display in improper mode.");
      exit(EXIT_FAILURE);
   }

   ptr = start_video_memory;

   letter = ((FLWHITE + BRED) << 8) + 'X';
   for (i = 0; i < 1920; i++) {
      *ptr++ = letter;
   }

   mouse_here = mouse_status(&i);

   alert(10, 10, "The disk drive is open", "Okay",
         FLWHITE, BRED, FLWHITE, BBLUE);
   if (mouse_here)
      mouse_cursor_off();
}
```

As in program 10.1, the program begins with a call to `init_video_base()` to set the base of video memory. The program then displays a screen of X's, with a white foreground on a red background. The call to `mouse_status()` assigns a nonzero value into `mouse_here` if a mouse is present. The program then calls `alert()` to display the message box. (Note that the program turns the mouse cursor off at the end of the program.)

Using `alert()` is not much more complicated than using a simple `printf()` and `getch()` call that typifies many programs. The message box, however, does add a touch of class to a program's appearance.

Creating Dialog Boxes

A *dialog box* is different from a message box because a dialog box is designed to obtain input data from the user. In most cases, the input is collected as a string and then converted to some other data type when necessary using a standard library conversion function (for example, `atof()`, `atoi()`). With dialog boxes, the user is presented a text window with a prompt message and an *input field* where the user types in the data that the dialog box asks for.

Typically, the user has several options during data entry using a dialog box. He or she can type in the input and then press the Enter key to accept the input. The user also can type in the data and click on an "Okay" button to accept the data. If the user does not like what was typed, he or she can click on the dialog box's "Cancel" button, and any data typed into the input field will be ignored. (If the user does type something into the input field, a dialog box usually enables simple editing of the entry using the Backspace key.) In some instances, the input field is displayed with a default value before the user types in anything. Pressing the Enter key (or clicking on the "Okay" button) means the user wants to use the default input.

Even though the dialog box presented in this section has the features just mentioned, the core of the dialog box is a series of text windows. Some complications must be addressed when working with dialog boxes, but they are not difficult problems.

The discussion of dialog boxes starts with the program itself, and then covers the support functions necessary to create the dialog box. The code for the dialog box program is presented in program 10.3.

Program 10.3. *A program using a dialog box for string input.*

```c
#include <stdio.h>
#include <stdlib.h>
#include <string.h>

#define MAIN 1
#include "win.h"


struct WINDOW mine;


void main(void)
{
   char buff[MAXSTR], m[80], button1[20], button2[20];
   int bloca[4], buttons, fw, i, row;
   unsigned int far *ptr, letter;
   struct DIALOG mine;

   init_video_base();
   if (start_video_memory == NULL) {
      printf("Wrong video mode.");
      exit(EXIT_FAILURE);
   }

   ptr = start_video_memory;
   mouse_here = mouse_status(&buttons);

   if (mouse_here) {
      mouse_cursor_on();
      set_mouse(1, 1);
   }

   letter = ( (FLWHITE + BRED) << 8) + 'X';
   for (i = 0; i < 1920; i++)
      *ptr++ = letter;


   init_dialog(&mine);
   mine.wide = 40; mine.deep = 8;
   mine.dbcolor = BBLUE;
   mine.dfcolor = FWHITE;
```

```
    if (create_d(8, 15, mine.wide, mine.deep, &mine) == 0) {
        printf("Could not create window.");
        exit(EXIT_FAILURE);
    }

    show_dialog(mine);

    strcpy(m, " Last name: ");
    strcpy(button1, "    Ok    ");
    strcpy(button2, "  Cancel  ");

    bloca[0] = 5; bloca[1] = 5;
    bloca[2] = 5; bloca[3] = 25;
    mine.locations = bloca;

    do_button(bloca[0], bloca[1], button1, FLWHITE, BRED, mine);
    do_button(bloca[2], bloca[3], button2, FLWHITE, BRED, mine);

    strcpy(buff, "Purdum");
    fw = 15;                              /* Input field width       */

    mine.fmcolor = FLWHITE; mine.bmcolor = BBLUE;
    mine.ffcolor = FLWHITE; mine.bfcolor = BRED;

    i = get_string(2, 7, m, buff, fw, mine, strlen(button1));

    if (mouse_here)
        mouse_cursor_off();
    close_dialog(mine);

    cls();
    cursor(10, 24);
    printf("buff = %s ", buff);
}
```

The program begins with a call to init_video_base() to set the start_video_memory to the base of video memory. Next, you initialize ptr to point to the video memory and check to see whether a mouse is present in the system. If a mouse is present, you turn the mouse cursor on and proceed to paint the screen with a series of white X's on a red foreground. So far, everything is the same as a text window.

The call to `init_dialog()` is used to initialize the members of a DIALOG structure. (See listing 10.10.)

Listing 10.10. *The DIALOG structure.*

```
struct DIALOG {
    char *messages,             /* Input prompt messages          */
         *buttons;              /* Button messages                */

    unsigned int far *base;     /* Base memory for dialog box      */

    int *locations,             /* Start of button locations; x then y */
        *buttonlen;             /* Length of each button string    */

    int bfcolor,                /* Background input field color    */
        bmcolor,                /* Background message color         */
        buttonnum,              /* Number of buttons in dialog box  */
        dbcolor,                /* Dialog background color          */
        deep,                   /* Dialog depth                     */
        dfcolor,                /* Dialog foreground color          */
        ffcolor,                /* Foreground input field color     */
        fmcolor,                /* Foreground message color         */
        shadow,             /* Does dialog have a shadow; 0 = No, 1 = Yes */
        wide,                   /* Dialog width                     */
        x,                      /* Upper left row                   */
        y;                      /* Upper left col                   */
};
```

The first member of the DIALOG structure, base, stores the address of the memory allocation used to store the screen contents before invoking the dialog box. It is used in the same manner as for a simple text window. The next two pointers are used to store the locations of the upper left corner of the "Okay" and "Cancel" buttons (locations), and the length of each button's string (buttonlen). The remainder of the structure members are for colors and are interpreted in much the same way as for text windows.

The members of the DIALOG structure are filled in with default values by init_dialog(). The code is shown in listing 10.11.

Listing 10.11. *The* init_dialog() *function.*

```
/*****
                            init_dialog()

    This function initializes the default settings for the members
of a DIALOG structure.

    Argument list:      struct DIALOG *d        pointer to a DIALOG
                                                structure


    Return value:       void
*****/

#include "win.h"

void init_dialog(struct DIALOG *d)
{
    d->x = 20;
    d->y = 8;
    d->wide = 40;
    d->deep = 8;
    d->dbcolor = BBLUE;
    d->dfcolor = FWHITE;
    d->shadow = 1;
    d->base = NULL;
}
```

On return from init_dialog(), several members of the structure are assigned values for use in the program. (In this example, most of them are the same as the default values. However, you always should set the width and depth of the dialog box after the call to init_dialog().)

Within the if statement is a call to create_d(). This function is virtually the same as the create_w() discussed earlier. The code is presented in listing 10.12.

Listing 10.12. *The* `create_d()` *function.*

```
/*****

                              create_d()

    This function gets the memory needed to create a dialog box. All
existing screen data is copied to the memory allocation. The width
and depth always are one unit larger than required for use with a
shadow dialog box.

    Argument list:    int row            row position for dialog box
                      int col            column position for dialog box
                      int wide           width of dialog box
                      int deep           depth of dialog box
                      struct DIALOG *d   pointer to a DIALOG structure

    Return value:     int                returns 0 if not enough
                                         memory; 1 otherwise


        CAUTION: Some compilers might not support the (non-ANSI) far
    keyword.

*****/

#include "win.h"


int create_d(int row, int col, int wide, int deep, struct DIALOG *d)
{
   int i, j, need;
   unsigned int far *ptr, far *temp;

   d->y = row;
   d->x = col;
   d->wide = wide;
   d->deep = deep;
   need = (d->wide + 1) * (d->deep + 1);

   d->base = temp = (unsigned int far *) calloc(need, sizeof(unsigned));
   if (d->base == NULL) {
      return 0;                           /* Cannot get enough memory  */
   }
```

```
    ptr = start_video_memory + (d->y * 80 + d->x);

    for (i = 0; i < d->deep + 1; i++) {    /* Copy existing screen
        */
        for (j = 0; j < d->wide + 1; j++) {
            *d->base = *ptr;
            ptr++;
            d->base++;
        }
        ptr += 79 - d->wide;
    }
    d->base = temp;
    return 1;
}
```

The function simply gets a memory allocation to store the current contents of the screen for use after the dialog box is closed. Be sure to check the return value to make sure create_d() was able to get enough memory for the screen.

If all goes well, the call to show_dialog() displays the dialog box, as shown in listing 10.13.

Listing 10.13. *The* show_dialog() *function.*

```
/*****

                            show_dialog()

    This function displays a dialog box. You must call init_dialog()
    and create_d() before calling this function.

    Argument list:    struct DIALOG d      dialog box to display

    Return value:     void
*****/

#include "win.h"

void show_dialog(struct DIALOG d)
{
```

continues

Listing 10.13. continued

```
int i, j;
unsigned int far *ptr, far *temp;
unsigned space;

temp = ptr = start_video_memory + (d.y * 80 + d.x);
space = (d.dbcolor) << 8;

for (i = 0; i < d.deep; i++) {
   for (j = 0; j < d.wide; j++) {
      *ptr++ = space;
   }
   ptr += 80 - d.wide;
}
ptr = temp + d.wide + 80;
space = (FGRAY + BBLACK) << 8;
for (i = 1; i < d.deep; i++) {          /* Gray out right gap       */
   *ptr = space + (*ptr & 0xff);
   ptr += 80;
}
ptr = temp + d.deep * 80 + 1;
for (i = 0; i < d.wide; i++) {
   *ptr++ = space + (*ptr & 0xff);
}
}
```

Again, the code is virtually the same as show_window(). All of this should look familiar to you by now. Up to this point, you have done nothing more than draw a normal text window on the screen. Now comes the new stuff.

The next three calls to strcpy() are used to initialize the strings that are displayed for the prompt message and the two buttons. I prefer to make the buttons large and of equal length to give them a balanced appearance on the screen. Padding the button strings with blanks makes them larger and easier for the user to click on.

The integer array variable bloca[] is used to hold the upper left corner coordinates for the button locations within the screen. The lvalue of bloca[] also is assigned into the mine.locations member of the DIALOG structure for later use.

The program now executes two calls to do_button(). The code for do_button() is presented in listing 10.14.

Listing 10.14. *The* do_button() *function.*

```
/*****
                            do_button()

    This function displays a prompt button at the row-column
    location passed to the function. The function assumes that the
    DIALOG structure has been activated before calling this function.

    Argument list:     int row              row position for prompt
                       int col              column position for prompt
                       char *prompt         prompt string
                       int fpcolor          foreground prompt color
                       int bpcolor          background prompt color
                       struct DIALOG active info on the dialog box

    Return value:      void

*****/

#include "win.h"


void do_button(int row, int col, char *prompt, int fpcolor, int bpcolor,
               struct DIALOG active)
{
    int plen, i;
    unsigned letter;
    unsigned int far *ptr;

    ptr = start_video_memory;

    plen = strlen(prompt);

    letter = (fpcolor + bpcolor) << 8;     /* Show message               */
    ptr += ( (active.y + row) * 80 + active.x + col);
    while (*prompt) {
        *ptr++ = (*prompt + letter);
        prompt++;
    }

    letter = (active.dbcolor + FBLACK) << 8; /* Do shadow effect         */
    *ptr = (HALFBLOCK + letter);
```

continues

```
   ptr += 80 - plen + 1;
   for (i = 0; i < plen; i++) {
      *ptr++ = (HALFSQUARE + letter);
   }
}
```

All do_button() does is display a button on the screen at the row-column coordinates passed to the function. (These coordinates are held in bloca[].) The buttons are displayed using the color arguments, and then the button string is displayed. The last part of the function simply creates a shadow effect on the buttons. If you don't like the shadow effect, you can either omit the code that draws the shadow or pass another argument that toggles the shadow code.

After the buttons are displayed, the code in program 10.3 initializes a string to my last name. This is an example of a default input string. If you do not want to use a default input string, simply set the input buffer to null (that is, buff[0] = '\0';). The variable fw is the field width for the input string, and it dictates the maximum length the input string can have. The next four statements simply set the foreground and background colors to be used in the next function call to get_string().

The purpose of get_string() is to collect input data from the user. The code is shown in listing 10.15.

Listing 10.15. *The* get_string() *function.*

```
/*****
                        get_string()

   This function displays a prompt for an input string, displays
   any default input string, and accepts input from the user. The
   programmer must send either a default or a null string in buff[].
   The row-column coordinates are relative to the dialog box, not the
   screen. The prompt and input fields can use different colors.

   Argument list:    int row              row position for prompt
                     int col              column position for prompt
                     char *m              prompt message
                     char *buff           input buffer (default or
                                          null)
                     int field_width      maximum input length
                     struct DIALOG mine   info on the dialog box
```

```
    Return value:      int                    0 if no input;
                                              1 if the default input is
                                              used; otherwise the key
                                              last pressed

*****/


#include "win.h"


int get_string(int row, int col, char *m, char *buff, int field_width,
    struct DIALOG mine, int len)
{
    char c, temp[MAXSTR];
    int count, flag, i, mrow, mcol;
    unsigned int far *ptr, far *hold;
    unsigned letter, prompt;

    ptr = start_video_memory;
    ptr += (mine.y + row) * 80 + mine.x + col;
    letter = (mine.bmcolor + mine.fmcolor) << 8;


    strcpy(temp, buff);                    /* Even if null, copy it     */

    while (*m) {                           /* Show default              */
        *ptr++ = (*m + letter);
        m++;
    }
    hold = ptr;
    letter = (FLWHITE + BBLACK) << 8;      /* Whatever you want         */
    flag = 1;

    mine.locations[1] += mine.x;
    mine.locations[3] += mine.x;

    for (count = i = 0; i < field_width; i++) { /* Show blank field     */
        if (temp[i] && flag) {
            *ptr++ = letter + temp[i];
        } else {
            flag = 0;
            *ptr++ = letter + LITEBOX;
        }
    }
```

continues

Listing 10.15. continued

```
ptr = hold;
prompt = (FLWHITE + BBLACK) << 8;      /* Whatever you like        */
while (TRUE) {
    *ptr = (*ptr & 0xff) + prompt;
    c = get_mouse_or_key(LBUTTON, ANYWAY, &mrow, &mcol);
    switch (c) {
      case LBUTTON:
          mrow = (mrow >> 3);
          mcol = (mcol >> 3);
          if (mrow == (mine.y + mine.locations[0])) {
              if (mcol >= mine.locations[1] && mcol < (mine.locations[1] + len) ) {
                  if (count) {
                      temp[count] = '\0';
                      strcpy(buff, temp);
                  }
                  return ENTER;
              } else {
                  if (mcol >= (mine.locations[3]) && mcol < (mine.locations[3] + len) ) {
                      return ESCAPE;
                  }
              }
          }
          break;

      case ENTER:
          if (count == 0 && strlen(buff) != 0) { /* Use default      */
              return 1;
          }
          temp[count] = '\0';
          strcpy(buff, temp);
          return 2;

      case RBUTTON:
      case MBUTTON:
      case ESCAPE:
          return 0;                        /* User cancelled input    */

      case BACKSPACE:
          if (count) {
              *ptr = letter + ' ';
              count--;
```

```
                        ptr--;
                        *ptr = letter + ' ';
                    }
                    break;
                case TAB:
                    return TAB;
                default:
                    if (count == 0) {
                        for (i = 0; i < field_width; i++) {
                            *ptr++ = letter + LITEBOX;
                        }
                        ptr = hold;
                    }
                if (last) {                        /* Alt key pressed?          */
                    temp[count] = '\0';
                    strcpy(buff, temp);
                    return 2;
                }
                    *ptr++ = letter + c;
                    temp[count] = c;
                    count++;
                    break;
            }
            if (count == field_width) {
                temp[count] = '\0';
                strcpy(buff, temp);
                break;
            }
        }
    }
    return c;
}
```

The get_string() begins by determining where the input will be written to the screen and assigning that address into ptr. The contents of the input buffer (buff) are copied into a temporary buffer (temp[]), and a while loop displays the buffer on the screen. This becomes the default input field. If there is no default input string, the input field is blank.

The next for loop is used to fill out the width of the input field with blank spaces. This is done to provide the user with a visual clue as to how long the input data may be. A large while loop is used to collect the input from the user. Because you must process the input differently than you have before, a new function named get_mouse_or_key() is used. This function is discussed in the next section.

The return value from get_mouse_or_key() determines what happens next by way of a switch statement. If the user clicks the left mouse button, you check to see whether the user clicked on either the "Okay" or the "Cancel" dialog buttons. If the "Okay" button was clicked, it signals the end of input. The contents of the temporary buffer are copied into buff, and the value ENTER is returned from the function. If the "Cancel" button is clicked, it signals that you want to abort the input, and the value ESCAPE is returned. Note that the content of buff is unchanged if the input is cancelled. If the Escape key or the right or middle mouse button is pressed, it is treated as a no-input situation, and 0 is returned.

If the Backspace key (BACKSPACE) is pressed, the current character in the input field is replaced with a blank space, enabling the user to change a character if desired. The Tab key actually is not processed; it simply returns the value TAB to the caller. You can, of course, add other case statements to allow for additional editing of the input field.

The default is where the input actually is processed. If the number of letters entered by the user (count) is zero, the input field is blanked out. You do this in case the user has backspaced over the entire input field. If count is nonzero, the letter collected by get_mouse_or_key() is displayed and copied into the temporary input buffer, and count is incremented. Control then breaks out of the switch.

If count is less than the field width, another iteration of the while loop is made. This continues until one of three things happens. First, if the user presses the Enter key or the left mouse button, input terminates and the new string is returned. Second, if the right or middle mouse button or the Escape key is pressed, the input is aborted and the default string is left unchanged. Third, if the user presses the Alt key and any other letter, the input is accepted. This third option causes the contents of the input buffer to be copied into buff even if no input has been entered. The function also provides a way for the user to terminate input without using a mouse or the Enter key. (The keyboard equivalent of clicking on the Cancel button is pressing the Escape key.)

Getting Input Data— *get_mouse_or_key()*

The get_mouse_or_key() function is responsible for collecting the input data from the user. The code for get_mouse_or_key() is presented in listing 10.16.

Listing 10.16. *The* get_mouse_or_key() *function.*

```
/*****

                        get_mouse_or_key()

    This function gets a keystroke or a mouse press from the
keyboard. It also decodes the keystroke.

    NOTE: This function uses the _kbhit() function discussed in
Chapter 3, "Input Functions."

    Argument list:    int button         button to check for press
                      int direction      travel direction desired
                                          0 = sideways; 1 = up-down

    Return value:     unsigned int       keystroke code

*****/



#include "win.h"



unsigned int get_mouse_or_key(int button, int direction, int *row, int *col)
{
   int press;
   int c, dhm, dvm, vmove, hmove, r, temp;

   hide_cursor();

   dvm = dhm = last = 0;
   while (TRUE) {
      if (mouse_here) {                      /* If there is a mouse      */
         read_mouse(&r, &c, &press);
         if (press) {
            *row = r;
            *col = c;
            switch (press) {      /* Could use variable button here    */
               case LBUTTON:
               case RBUTTON:
               case MBUTTON:
                  return press;
               default:
```

continues

Listing 10.16. *continued*

```
                printf("Mouse read error in get_mouse_or_key()");
                return -1;
        }
    }
    mouse_counters(&vmove, &hmove); /* Get relative movement    */
    dhm += hmove;                   /* Get horizontal movement  */
    dvm += vmove;                   /* Get vertical movement    */

    switch (direction) {
      case SIDEWAYS:                /* How about right?         */
        if (dhm > DELTA) {
            return RARROW;
        }                           /* How about left?          */
        if (dhm < -DELTA) {
            return LARROW;
        }
      case UPDOWN:                  /* How about down?          */
        if (dvm > DELTA) {
            return DARROW;
        }                           /* How about up?            */
        if (dvm < -DELTA) {
            return UARROW;
        }
      default:
        break;
    }
}

temp = _kbhit();                    /* Poll the keyboard        */
if (temp == 0) {                    /* No key press             */
    continue;
}
if (temp == ENTER) {               /* Pressed Enter key?       */
    return ENTER;
}
if (temp == ESCAPE) {
    return ESCAPE;
}
if (temp < ASCII_LIMIT) {          /* Single character?        */
    return temp;
}
```

```
        last = 1;
        return temp - EXTEND_OFF;          /* Extended keycode?        */
    }
}
```

The function is almost identical to some of the other input functions. The only difference is in the return values and the global variable last, used to detect an extended key code. (In previous input functions, last held the last ASCII character entered at the keyboard.) You must detect the extended keycode in case the user presses the Alt key to end input.

Closing a Dialog Box—
close_dialog( )

At this point in program 10.3, the user has entered the string (or accepted the default string), and control returns from get_string(). The only thing that remains is to restore the screen to its original state. This is done with the code shown in listing 10.17.

Listing 10.17. The close_dialog() *function.*

```
/*****

                           close_dialog()

     This function closes a dialog box by displaying the previous
   contents of screen memory and then freeing the memory allocation
   used to store the previous screen.

     Argument list:    struct DIALOG d        dialog box to remove

     Return value:     void
*****/

#include "win.h"

void close_dialog(struct DIALOG d)
{
    int i, j;
```

continues

Listing 10.17. continued

```
    unsigned int far *ptr;

    if (d.base == NULL)
        return;

    ptr = start_video_memory + (d.y * 80 + d.x);
    for (i = 0; i < d.deep + 1; i++) {      /* All rows              */
        for (j = 0; j < d.wide + 1; j++) {
            *ptr = *d.base;
            ptr++;
            d.base++;
        }
        ptr += 79 - d.wide;
    }
    free( (void *) d.base);
}
```

The close_dialog() uses the pointer to the storage held in the DIALOG structure to restore the screen to its original state. After the screen is restored, the storage is released to the operating system by the call to free(). At this point, control returns to main(), and program 10.3 ends. Figure 10.5 shows how the dialog box looks using the code in program 10.3.

Fig. 10.5. Dialog box from program 10.3.

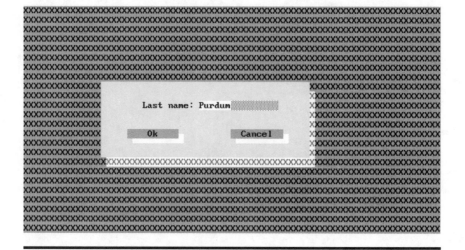

Conclusion

This chapter showed you how to create and use text windows to present new information while being able to restore the screen to its previous state. Text windows can be used for displaying messages and alerts, and for creating dialog boxes to get input from the user.

You can extend the material here to suit your needs. For example, you could collect the basic information from program 10.3 and create a dialog function that has only two buttons. Because of the way the pieces and parts are presented, you also can extend the information given in this chapter to create more complex dialog boxes (for example, a three- or four-button dialog box). With a little experimentation, you should be able to write dialog boxes to suit almost any input requirement you have.

11

Putting It All Together

The purpose of this chapter is to show how the "pieces and parts" presented in earlier chapters can be fit together into a large application. I wanted to write an application that would be useful when it was done, and an improvement on an application with which all programmers are familiar. The result is a program that I (modestly) call SuperCopy, or SC.

SC has the following features:

Normal copy and delete file functions. Both functions support a variety of options.

Copy or delete by date. Subchoices include copy or delete:

- files for a specified date
- files created earlier than a specified date
- files created later than a specified date
- all files except those with a specified file mask

Backup. The program reads files on the destination drive (for example, A:) and compares them with the files found on the source drive (for example, C:). It copies *only* files from the source drive that already exist on the destination drive.

Search for a file. Find all instances of a specified file on a hard disk and show the full path name where it is located. A 386 with a 200M hard disk can find all instances of a file in less than 5 seconds.

Display files. Both ASCII and binary (dump) can be shown. If you're not sure what's in the file, you can use the Unknown option to open and display the file and sample its contents.

Execute batch files. If you have .BAT files for copying files or other things, SC can run them for you.

Selectable colors. The user can set colors for the menus and dialog boxes. These are stored in a data file for later use. If the data file (scopy.dfl) is erased, default colors are selected automatically.

Mouse and keyboard use. Many options allow for scrolling the file list.

Other features will become apparent as you read this chapter. Perhaps the program's greatest strength is that you can add features to it very easily. In this chapter I mention several enhancements I would like to add. I'm sure you'll think of some yourself.

As you might imagine, the source code for the program is rather large—about 300K with all the support code. Because many of the functions are discussed in previous chapters, in this chapter I concentrate only on the code that ties the support functions together. Also, I add much to the win.h header file presented in Chapter 10, "Text Windows." (I warned you then that I would do this!) Rather than list almost 15K of code in this chapter, you might want simply to list the win.h header file out to a printer and keep it handy as you read through this chapter. A number of key global variables appear in win.h that are used in the new functions presented in this chapter.

An executable version of the program, SCOPY.EXE, appears on the disks included with this book. It will help you to understand the code better if you spend a half hour or so using SC. I suggest that you create a "junk" directory on your hard disk and copy some sample data files into that directory. Place a blank disk in drive A and use it to test the program's various copy features. After you've seen the program run, the program logic will have more meaning.

Operation of the Primary and Secondary Menus

Figure 11.1 shows the program in its initial state, just after it begins execution but before any options have been selected.

Fig. 11.1. Initial display screen.

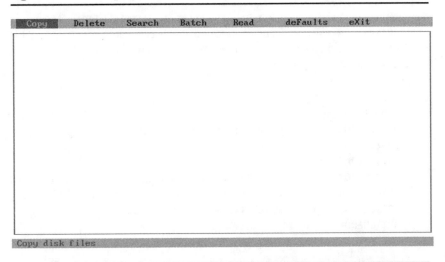

The top line of the display presents the program's *primary menu* selections. The middle of the display, referred to as the *output window*, is used to present the output produced as the options are executed. At the bottom of the display is a *description line* that presents the user with a brief statement of what the highlighted option does.

The primary menu options use the slidebar menuing system discussed in Chapter 4, "Menuing Systems." I made a few minor changes, however. The first change is that I moved the description line to the bottom of the screen. (The description line is displayed on the second line of the program examples in Chapter 4.) The primary menu options are stored in the strconts.h header file. The contents of this header file are shown in listing 11.1.

Listing 11.1. The strconts.h header file.

```
#include "win.h"


MENU menu0[] = {
    OPTION("  Copy  ", "Copy disk files", 'c')
    OPTION(" Delete ", "Erase disk files from disk", 'd')
    OPTION(" Search ", "Search for disk files", 's')
    OPTION(" Batch  ", "Create or execute a batch file", 'b')
```

continues

Listing 11.1. continued

```
        OPTION(" Read    ", "Read a text file or dump a binary file", 'r')
        OPTION(" deFaults", "User-defined default program values", 'f')
        OPTION("  eXit   ", "Exit from this program", 'x')
        OPTIONEND
    };

MENU menu1[] = {                                    /* COPY menu    */
        OPTION("Mask    ", "File search mask ", 'm')
        OPTION("Date    ", "Find with a given date", 'd')
        OPTION("All but", "Find all files except mask given", 'a')
        OPTION("Older   ", "Find files with date later than given", 'o')
        OPTION("Younger", "Find files with date earlier than given", 'y')
        OPTION("Backup ", "Match files on destination drive", 'b')
        OPTIONEND
    };

MENU menu2[] = {                                    /* ERASE menu   */
        OPTION("Mask    ", "Erase file", 'm')
        OPTION("Date    ", "Erase for given date", 'd')
        OPTION("All but", "Erase all but", 'a')
        OPTION("Older   ", "Find files with date later than given", 'o')
        OPTION("Younger", "Find files with date earlier than given", 'y')
        OPTIONEND
    };

MENU menu3[] = {                                    /* SEARCH menu  */
        OPTION("Dir    ", "Do directory", 'd')
        OPTION("File   ", "Find a file", 'f')
        OPTIONEND
    };

MENU menu4[] = {                                    /* BATCH menu   */
        OPTION("Execute", "Execute batch file", 'e')
        OPTIONEND
    };

MENU menu5[] = {                                    /* READ menu    */
        OPTION("Text   ", "Show text file", 't')
        OPTION("Binary ", "Show binary dump", 'b')
        OPTION("Unknown", "Check if text or binary file", 'u')
        OPTIONEND
```

```
    };

MENU menu6[] = {                                        /* DEFAULT menu */
    OPTION("Colors", "Set menu colors", 'c')
    OPTION("Source", "Set source drive", 's')
    OPTION("Dest. ", "Set destination drive", 'd')
    OPTION("mouse Faster", "Set mouse speed faster", 'f')
    OPTION("mouse sLower", "Set mouse speed slower", 'l')
    OPTIONEND
    };

MENU menu7[] = {                                        /* EXIT menu    */
    OPTION("eXit  ", "End this program", 'x')
    OPTIONEND
    };
```

The menu0[] MENU structure holds the primary menu options, and menu1[] through menu7[] contain the secondary menu options. The *secondary menu* options present the specific actions available for the primary menu options. Both the primary and secondary menu options can be activated with "hotkeys." On both menus, the hotkey corresponds to the uppercase letter in the menu option.

The SC menuing system uses drop-down menu boxes for the secondary menus. These drop-down secondary menus operate in conjunction with the slidebar primary menu options. That is, selecting an option from the primary menu causes the secondary menu box to appear. The code for the drop-down menu boxes is very similar to that presented in Chapter 4, except that the menu boxes use the windowing concepts discussed in Chapter 10. Therefore, you can drop a menu down without losing any data that might exist in the output window. Figure 11.2 shows how the display looks after the Copy option is selected.

Note that the description line at the bottom of the display is updated for secondary menus. The description line shown in figure 11.2 corresponds to the description field in the menu1[] MENU structure shown in listing 11.1. (In the box menuing system discussed in Chapter 4, I did not take advantage of the description field.)

Fig. 11.2. Program display after selecting the copy option.

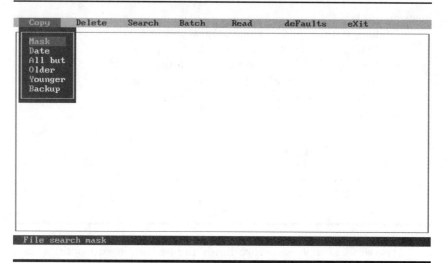

There are three ways to activate a menu selection. Both the primary and secondary menu options can be selected by using the option's hotkey, by using the arrow keys to highlight and then select the options, or by clicking the left mouse button on the highlighted option.

The Escape key can be pressed to abort a menu. If Escape is pressed when a secondary menu is active, control returns to the primary menu. If Escape is pressed when the primary menu is active, the program terminates. The user also can terminate the program by selecting the eXit option from the primary menu.

The *main( )* Program Shell

The code in the main() function is responsible for initializing the display and starting the main program loop. The code for main() is shown in listing 11.2.

Listing 11.2. The main( ) *function.*

```
/*****

                            SCOPY.EXE
                            Ver.1.0
```

```
                              7/16/91
                           Jack Purdum
                  C Programmer's Toolkit, 2nd Ed.

    This program copies, deletes, and finds disk files, and so on.

*****/


#include <stdio.h>
#include <string.h>
#include <stdlib.h>

#include <dir.h>                        /* CHANGE TO DOS.H FOR MICROSOFT C */


#include "win.h"
#include "strconts.h"                   /* Header file with menu macros    */


struct WINDOW main_screen;


/*****

                                 main()

    The main entry point for the program. No command-line
    arguments are used.

    Argument list:     void

    Return value:      void

*****/

void main(void)
{
    int i;
    unsigned int letter, temp;

    read_defaults();
    hot_key_color = FRED;
    file_source[0] = file_dest[0] = '\0';
```

continues

Listing 11.2. continued

```c
   do_main_screen();

   cursor(1, 1);
   menu_start_new(menu0, main_menu_f, main_menu_b);

   menulen = 0;
   for (i = 0; menu0[i].prompt; i++) {
      if (menu0[i].plen > menulen)          /* Maximum menu width       */
         menulen = menu0[i].plen;
   }
   menucount = i;
   cptr = (char *) calloc(menucount, sizeof(char)); /* Letter options */
   for (i = 0; i < menucount; i++) {
      cptr[i] = menu0[i].letter;            /* Single-letter choices    */
   }
   temp = last = 0;
   while (TRUE) {
      last = temp;
      cursor(1, nptr[last]);
      letter = menu_choice_new(menu0, main_menu_f, main_menu_b,
                        LBUTTON, SIDEWAYS);
      if (letter == ENTER) {
         temp = last;
      }
      if (letter == ESCAPE) {
         break;
      }
      switch (last) {                       /* Variable last is a global */
         case 0:                            /* Copy                      */
            do_copy();
            break;
         case 1:                            /* Delete                    */
            do_delete();
            break;
         case 2:                            /* Search                    */
            do_search();
            break;
         case 3:                            /* Batch                     */
            do_batch();
            break;
         case 4:                            /* Read                      */
```

```
              do_read();
              break;
          case 5:                        /* Defaults         */
              do_defaults();
         break;
          case 6:                        /* Exit             */
              break;
          default:
         break;
      }
      if (menu0[last].letter == 'x' || letter == ESCAPE)
         break;
   }
   free(cptr);
   close_window(main_screen);
   menu_end();
   write_defaults();                     /* NEW              */
   cls();
}
```

The program begins with a series of include statements. The necessary global variables and function prototypes appear in the win.h header file. Most of the #define macros are self-explanatory, except MAXFILES. This macro sets the maximum number of files that can be used with a specified option. This is because MAXFILES is used to create an array of FILEDIR structures that have the following form:

```
typedef struct {
   char fname[13];
   char use;
} FILEDIR;
```

Each file name found during a directory search is copied into a FILEDIR structure. The use member is a flag that determines whether the user has selected the file (use = 1). The value of 200 for MAXFILES is quite arbitrary, but it works fine for my development system. (I rarely have more than 100 files in a subdirectory.) When I compiled and ran the program with MAXFILES set to 600, it ran fine.

The real test of whether a higher limit for MAXFILES works is to use the Search-File option, which searches the entire disk for a certain file. Because this option uses recursion, it can use much heap space during the process. The more subdirectories you have under each directory, the more heap space that gets eaten up. If your disk system has a lot of "subdirectory depth," you might have to use realloc() to set the size of the FILEDIR structure on the fly. Try the program as it is to see whether this file limitation poses a problem for you.

Menu Colors—*read_defaults( )*

As soon as you are inside main(), the first function called is read_defaults(). The code for read_defaults() appears in listing 11.3.

Listing 11.3. *The* read_defaults() *function.*

```
/*****
                              read_defaults()

    This function reads the various colors stored in the date file
    named scopy.dfl. If scopy.dfl is opened successfully, the default
    colors stored in the file are used. If not, set_default_colors() is
    called and the default values stored there are used.

    Argument list:     void

    Return value:      void

*****/

#include "win.h"

void read_defaults(void)
{
    FILE *fpin;

    if ( (fpin = fopen("scopy.dfl", "rb")) == NULL) {
        set_default_colors();
    } else {
        fread(&main_menu_f, sizeof(int), 1, fpin);
        fread(&main_menu_b, sizeof(int), 1, fpin);
        fread(&sub_menu_f, sizeof(int), 1, fpin);
        fread(&sub_menu_b, sizeof(int), 1, fpin);
        fread(&box_f, sizeof(int), 1, fpin);
```

```
        fread(&box_b, sizeof(int), 1, fpin);
        fread(&box_h, sizeof(int), 1, fpin);
        fread(&button_b, sizeof(int), 1, fpin);
        fread(&delta, sizeof(int), 1, fpin);
    }
    fclose(fpin);
}
```

The first thing read_defaults() attempts to do is open and read the scopy.dfl data file. If you have run the program at least once in the current working directory, scopy.dfl will be found. In that situation, a series of fread() calls fills in the colors used in the program. The variable delta is used to set the mouse speed.

Set Colors—*set_default_colors( )*

If this is the first time the user has run the program in the working directory, set_default_colors() is called. The code for set_default_colors() appears in listing 11.4.

Listing 11.4. *The* set_default_colors() *function.*

```
/*****

                        set_default_colors()

    This function sets the various colors used in the program to
    their default values. On program start, the file scopy.dfl is
    opened. If the file is opened successfully, the default colors
    stored in the file are used. If not, this function is called and
    the default values stored here are used.

    Argument list:    void

    Return value:     void

*****/

#include "win.h"

void set_default_colors(void)
```

continues

Listing 11.4. continued

```
{
    main_menu_f = FBLUE;      /* Main menu foreground color   */
    main_menu_b = BCYAN;      /* Main menu background color   */
    sub_menu_f  = FBLUE;      /* Secondary foreground color   */
    sub_menu_b  = BWHITE;     /* Secondary background color   */
    box_f       = FLWHITE;    /* Window foreground color      */
    box_b       = BBLUE;      /* Window background color      */
    box_h       = BCYAN;      /* Menu highlight color         */
    button_b    = BRED;       /* Pushbutton background color  */
}
```

The comments in listing 11.4 tell you the purpose of each variable in the program. The first time you run the program, the colors shown in listing 11.4 are used if you have a color display. You can use the deFaults option from the primary menu to change the colors.

Save the Menu Colors— *write_defaults()*

When you exit the program, the call to write_defaults() is used to store the colors in the scopy.dfl file. The code for write_defaults() appears in listing 11.5.

Listing 11.5. *The* write_defaults() *function.*

```
/*****
                    write_default_colors()

    This function writes the various colors used in the program to
    the data file named scopy.dfl. If the deFault Colors options is
    used to change any of the color values, the new values are written
    to the data file.

    Argument list:    void

    Return value:     void

*****/
```

```
#include "win.h"

void write_defaults(void)
{
    FILE *fpin;

    if ( (fpin = fopen("scopy.dfl", "wb")) == NULL) {
        return;
    } else {
        fwrite(&main_menu_f, sizeof(int), 1, fpin);
        fwrite(&main_menu_b, sizeof(int), 1, fpin);
        fwrite(&sub_menu_f, sizeof(int), 1, fpin);
        fwrite(&sub_menu_b, sizeof(int), 1, fpin);
        fwrite(&box_f, sizeof(int), 1, fpin);
        fwrite(&box_b, sizeof(int), 1, fpin);
        fwrite(&box_h, sizeof(int), 1, fpin);
        fwrite(&button_b, sizeof(int), 1, fpin);
        fwrite(&delta, sizeof(int), 1, fpin);
    }
    fclose(fpin);
}
```

If the scopy.dfl file cannot be opened for writing, the program simply ignores it and returns to main(). The program does this because the default data can be used if the data file is not written. If the file is opened, the current values for the variables are saved to the file.

As you read this chapter, you will see that other color values are used in the program. For example, text in the output window always is set to FWHITE, and the text in message and dialog boxes always is set to FLWHITE (high-intensity white). The color constants can be changed to variables that the user can set. If you make such changes, simply add the new variables to the functions presented in listings 11.3 through 11.5.

An example of a variable that uses a fixed color constant is the hot_key_color variable appearing near the top of main(). (The hot_key_color variable is used to highlight the uppercase letter in the secondary menus.) You can add hot_key_color to the list of user-defined color variables and read and write them using the functions in listings 11.3 through 11.5.

After the color values are set, the program sets file_source[] and file_dest[] to null. These two global variables are used throughout the program to set the source and destination file paths. For many program options, you cannot proceed until these two variables are non-null. (Use the deFaults Source and deFaults Dest options from the primary menu to set these variables.) For safety reasons, I force these two variables to null after each program option is executed to make sure the user resets them before the next option is selected.

Draw the Main Program Screen— *do_main_screen( )*

The next function called is do_main_screen(). The code appears in listing 11.6.

Listing 11.6. The do_main_screen() *function.*

```
/*****
                        do_main_screen()

    This function displays the main window screen. It also
    determines the start of video memory, the video mode, and the
    presence or absence of a mouse, and it initializes a number of
    global variables used throughout the program.

    Argument list:    void

    Return value:     int        1 if the screen can be created; 0
                                 otherwise.

*****/

#include "win.h"

struct WINDOW main_screen;

int do_main_screen(void)
{
    int buttons, col, deep, row, swindow, wide;

    cls();

    init_video_base();
```

```
mouse_here = mouse_status(&buttons);
if (mouse_here) {
   hide_cursor();
}

init_window(&main_screen);                /* Set default values      */

                                          /* Set desired values      */
main_screen.num_win = 0; main_screen.hotspot = 0;
main_screen.shadow = 0; main_screen.border = 1;
main_screen.bbcolor = BBLACK;
main_screen.vscrollbar = 0;  main_screen.hscrollbar = 0;
main_screen.mcolor = FWHITE;
main_screen.wfcolor = main_screen.bfcolor = FGREEN;

row = 1; col = 0;
wide = 80; deep = 22;
swindow = create_w(row, col, wide, deep, &main_screen);
if (swindow == 0) {
   alert(8, 15, "    Out of Memory.   ", "Ok",
    FLWHITE, box_b, FLWHITE, button_b);
   return 0;
}
show_window(main_screen);
return 1;
}
```

The do_main_screen() screen function presents the display window and initializes a number of global variables. One of the important variables set is a pointer to screen memory. It is set by the call to init_video_base(). On return from the function call, start_video_memory points to the base address of the video RAM (that is, either 0xB000:0000 for monochrome or 0xB800:0000 for color).

After the call, a number of assignment statements set the members of the main_screen WINDOW structure to the required values. Note that I set the window's background color to black and the border color to green. This has the effect of framing the output window for the program with a green box.

You also can see that the scroll bar members are set to zero. If you use either the Borland or the Microsoft compilers in their integrated development environment, you have seen vertical scroll bars. I hate them. It's inconvenient to move the mouse over to the scrollbar and then drag it down to wherever I need to move in the text window. Also, I always manage to fall off the scroll bar in the process of dragging the mouse. In SC, if you want to scroll the output window up or down, you simply drag the mouse up or down. The output scrolls in the direction of the mouse without your having to move to the scroll bar. It is much easier to scroll the window using this approach.

The remainder of the program simply creates and displays the window using the functions discussed in Chapter 10, "Text Windows." The call to alert() shows how the box_b and button_b colors are used to set the background colors for the alert message box and its button. If the window is opened successfully, program control returns to main().

Start the Primary Menu— *menu_start_new( )*

The next call in main() is to menu_start_new(). This function is very similar to the menu_start() function discussed in Chapter 4, "Menuing Systems," but there are differences. The code for menu_start_new() is presented in listing 11.7.

Listing 11.7. *The menu_start_new( ) function.*

```
/*****
                          menu_start_new()

    This function displays the menu options on the screen using a
    two-line menuing system. The first argument is a typedef for a menu
    structure. The two lines first are cleared to the background color,
    and then the menu options are displayed.

    This function assumes that the cursor is sitting at the desired
    row-column coordinates BEFORE the function is called.

    NOTE: This function uses the colorstr() and c_scroll() functions
    discussed in Chapter 1, "Screen Functions."

    Argument list:    MENU s[]      an array of MENU structures
                      int fore      the foreground color to use
                      int back      the background color to use
```

```
      Return value:      void

*****/

#define EXTERN 1

#include "win.h"

void menu_start_new(MENU s[], int fore, int back)
{
    int buttons, i, r, c, wide;

    wide = getvcols() - 1;

    find_cursor(&prow, &pcol);                /* Find out where to put it  */

    c_scroll(prow, pcol, wide, MENUROW, 0, 6, back);
    c_scroll(DLINE, pcol, wide, MENUROW, 0, 6, back);

    last = 0;

    nptr = (int *) calloc(wide, sizeof(int));      /* Store col pos   */
    cptr = (char *) calloc(wide, sizeof(char));    /* Store letters   */

    for (menulen = i = 0; s[i].prompt; i++) {
        find_cursor(&r, &c);
        nptr[i] = c;                          /* Fill in columns         */
        cptr[i] = s[i].letter;                /* Single-letter choices   */
        colorstr(s[i].prompt, fore, back);
        colorstr(MARGIN, fore, back);
        menulen += s[i].plen;                 /* Find total menu length   */
    }
    menucount = i;                            /* Items in this menu       */
                                              /* Length of menu line      */
    menulen += (strlen(MARGIN) * (menucount - 1) );

    cursor(prow, pcol);

    if (fore > 7)                    /* See discussion of listing 11.8     */
        i = fore - 8;
    else
        i = fore;
```

continues

Listing 11.7. continued

```
    colorstr(s[last].prompt, back >> 4, i << 4);
    cursor(DLINE, pcol);
    colorstr(s[last].desc, fore, back);
    cursor(prow, pcol);
}
```

There are two minor changes in the function. First, I use a macro (DLINE) defined in win.h to relocate where the menu description line appears on the display. In the slidebar menuing system in Chapter 4, it is assumed that the description line is fixed to the second row of the display. In this version, the description line appears near the bottom of the display (that is, DLINE is set to 24).

A second change is that the background color values defined in win.h represent their "shifted" values. For example, if the background color was green, BGREEN was defined to have the value 2. Because the background colors occupy the fourth through the sixth bits of the attribute byte, the functions presented in Chapter 4 were responsible for bit-shifting background colors four positions to the left. Therefore, BGREEN was shifted to the value 32 during the function call. The functions presented in this chapter assume that BGREEN already is defined with the value 32.

You might ask, "If that's the case, then what's the purpose of the statement

```
colorstr(s[last].prompt, back >> 4, fore << 4);
```

near the bottom of listing 11.7?" Because this statement is responsible for reversing the colors for the active menu, you must shift the foreground and background colors to their proper positions in the attribute byte. In fact, with the new functions, it is only when the program must present an inverse color string that any bit-shifting takes place. In contrast, all the functions in Chapter 4 must bit-shift—*except* when highlighting. Because most strings in this program are not highlighted, the new versions presented in this chapter are more appropriate for the tasks at hand. After menu_start_new() finishes its work, program control returns to main().

Two for loops in main() determine the maximum menu length and the hotkeys for the primary menu. (The same looping code is discussed in Chapter 4.) The program then enters an infinite while loop to process the menu selections. The most important element in the while loop is the call to menu_choice_new().

Control the Primary Menu— *menu_choice_new( )*

The `menu_choice_new()` function is very similar to the `menu_choice()` function discussed in Chapter 4. There are enough differences, however, that you should examine the code here. Listing 11.8 presents the code for `menu_choice_new()`.

Listing 11.8. *The `menu_choice_new()` function.*

```
/*****
                        menu_choice_new()

    This function handles the menu display options on the screen
and returns the choice selected by the user. The user may use the
mouse, arrow keys, or capital letters to select a menu option.

    NOTE: This function uses the colorstr() and c_scroll() functions
discussed in Chapter 1, "Screen Functions."

    Argument list:    MENU s[]        an array of MENU structures
                      int fore        foreground color to use
                      int back        background color to use
                      int button      button number to signal that
                                      a choice was made
                      int direction   which way the mouse moved

    Return value:     void

*****/

#define EXTERN 1


#include "win.h"

int menu_choice_new(MENU m[], int fore, int back, int button, int direction)
{
    int delta, temp;
    unsigned int select;
```

continues

Listing 11.8. continued

```c
    while (TRUE) {
        temp = last;
        select = read_key_d(button, direction);
        if (select == ESCAPE) {
            return select;
        }
        delta = last;
        switch (select) {
            case ENTER:                     /* User selected with CRLF  */
                last = temp;
                menu_off(m, fore, back);    /* Restore to not active    */
                last = delta;
                menu_on_new(m, fore, back);
                break;

            case RARROW:                    /* Used the right arrow     */
                menu_off(m, fore, back);    /* Restore to not active    */
                if (last + 1 >= menucount)  /* Wrap menu around         */
                    last = 0;
                else                        /* Move one to the right    */
                    last++;
                menu_on_new(m, fore, back);
                break;

            case LARROW:                    /* Used the left arrow      */
                menu_off(m, fore, back);
                if (last - 1 < 0)
                    last = menucount - 1;
                else                        /* Move one to the right    */
                    last--;
                menu_on_new(m, fore, back);
                break;

            default:                        /* Don't know what it was   */
                break;
        }
        if (select == ENTER)
            break;
    }
    return select;
}
```

The `read_key_d()` function is presented in listing 4.15 in Chapter 4. It enables the user to sense the direction that the mouse moved and sense a button press as well.

The function `menu_on_new()` is the same as `menu_on()` in Chapter 4, except that I added the statements before the call to `active()`:

```
.
int i;

if (fore > 7)
   i = fore - 8;
else
   i = fore;

active(m[last].prompt, MENUROW, nptr[last], back >> 4, i << 4);
c_scroll(DLINE, 1, getvcols()-1, MENUROW, 8, 6, back);
.
```

The rest of the function is identical to the old `menu_on()`. (In the old `menu_on()`, you bit-shift all background colors at runtime.) I made this change because the foreground color might have the intensity bit on. If this value then is shifted to the background position, it is possible for the value to have bit seven, the blink bit, set. If this happens, the blink bit is turned on. The new statement sets the foreground color to the corresponding low-intensity value so that this does not happen. For example, if the foreground color is FLWHITE (a value of 15), bit shifting it four positions to the left makes the value 240 (0xf0 hex), which sets the blink bit of the attribute byte. The modification shown here prevents that.

The `menu_off_new()` function is the same as `menu_off()` in Chapter 4, except that I changed the call to `c_scroll` to

```
c_scroll(DLINE, 1, getvcols()-1, 1, 1, 6, back);
```

and added the line

```
active(m[last].desc, DLINE, pcol, fore, back);
```

I made these changes to update correctly the new description line placed at the bottom of the screen.

The return value from `menu_choice_new()` is the key returned from the call to `read_key_d()`. It tells you *which key* the user pressed. The global variable `last` tells you *where* the user was when the key was pressed. In other words, `last` contains an index number for the menu choice, and `select` is the key pressed. In listing 11.2, note that the return value from `menu_choice_new()` is assigned into `letter`. If `letter` equals ENTER, the value of last is used to select the menu option. If letter equals ESCAPE, you break out of the infinite while loop and terminate the program. Therefore, letter and last together enable you to decide what the user wants to do with the menu choice.

The switch statement in listing 11.2 is used to call the main entry points for each option shown on the primary menu. Because all the functions are very similar, I use just one of them as an example of how each entry function is written.

A Typical Entry Function— *do_copy()*

Listing 11.9 presents the code for the do_copy() entry function.

***Listing 11.9.** The do_copy() function.*

```
/*****
                              do_copy()

     This function is the main entry point for the Copy option of the
main menu.

     Argument list:    void

     Return value:     void

*****/

#include "win.h"

extern MENU menu1[];

void do_copy(void)
{
   mkey = wbox_menu_start(1, 1, menu1, hot_key_color, sub_menu_b,
                          sub_menu_f, 1, box_h);
   if (mkey == ESCAPE)
      return;
```

```
switch (last) {
    case 0:                             /* Mask              */
        do_mask_copy();
        break;
    case 1:                             /* Date              */
        do_date_copy(SAMEAGE);
        break;
    case 2:                             /* All but           */
        do_date_copy(NOT_EQUAL);
        break;
    case 3:                             /* Older             */
        do_date_copy(OLDER);
        break;
    case 4:                             /* Younger           */
        do_date_copy(YOUNGER);
        break;
    case 5:                             /* Backup            */
        do_backup();
        break;
    default:
        break;
    }
}
```

The only function presented in listing 11.9 that needs to be discussed at this time is wbox_menu_start(). This function is similar to the box_menu_start() presented in Chapter 4, but it is designed to work with text windows. If the user presses the Escape key, control returns to the primary menu.

Control a Secondary Menu— *wbox_menu_start( )*

The code for wbox_menu_start() appears in listing 11.10. The two support functions shade() and normal() also are presented in listing 11.10.

Listing 11.10. *The* wbox_menu_start() *function.*

```
/*****
                        wbox_menu_start()

    This function performs the code necessary to display the menu
box and the menu list. The first choice is highlighted
automatically. The variable "bars" determines whether single or
double lines are used for the menu box. The background color is
used only for highlighting the active menu option.

    The global variable "last" holds the menu selection.


    Argument list:      int row
                        int col
                        struct MENU m[]     array of structures that
                                            contains the menu choices
                        int fore            foreground color used
                        int back            background color
                        int frame           box color
                        int bars            flag: 1 = single bars;
                                                  2 = double bars
                        int inverse         color for background
                                            highlight


    Return value:       void

*****/



#include "win.h"



void shade(char *s, int row, int col, int fore, int back, int hot);
void normal(char *s, int row, int col, int fore, int back, int hot);



int wbox_menu_start(int row, int col, MENU s[], int fore, int back,
                    int frame, int bars, int inverse)
{
    char *mptr, *tptr;
    int count, delta, i, len, tcount, temp;
    unsigned int letter;
```

```
struct WINDOW box;

last = len = 0;
for (i = 0; s[i].prompt; i++) {
    if (s[i].plen > len)                        /* Maximum menu width */
        len = s[i].plen;
}
count = i;
mptr = (char *) calloc(count, sizeof(char)); /* Letter options     */


tptr = cptr;                                    /* Hold temporarily   */
tcount = menucount;
cptr = mptr;
menucount = count;

for (i = 0; i < count; i++) {
    mptr[i] = s[i].letter;                    /* Single-letter choices   */
}

init_window(&box);
box.hotspot = 0;
box.shadow = 1;
box.bbcolor = box.wbcolor = back;
box.wfcolor = box.bfcolor = fore;
box.mcolor = FBLUE;
box.border = bars;
create_w(row, col, len + 4, count + 2, &box);
show_window(box);
for (i = 0; s[i].prompt; i++) {
    wprintf(1 + i, 1, box, "%s", s[i].prompt);
}
last = 0;
col += 2;
shade(s[last].prompt, row + last + 1, col, fore, inverse, frame);

c_scroll(DLINE, 1, 79, 1, 1, 6, sub_menu_b);
normal(s[last].desc, DLINE - 1, 2, sub_menu_f, sub_menu_b, sub_menu_f);

while (TRUE) {
    temp = last;
    letter = read_key_d(LBUTTON, UPDOWN);
    delta = last;
```

continues

Listing 11.10. continued

```c
switch (letter) {
   case ENTER:
      last = temp;
      normal(s[last].prompt, row + last + 1, col, frame, back, fore);
      last = delta;
      shade(s[last].prompt, row + last + 1, col, fore, inverse, frame);
      break;

   case DARROW:
      last = temp;
      normal(s[last].prompt, row + last + 1, col, frame, back, fore);
      last = delta;
      if (last + 1 >= count) {
         last = 0;
      } else {
         last++;
      }
      shade(s[last].prompt, row + last + 1, col, fore, inverse, frame);
      break;

   case UARROW:
      last = temp;
      normal(s[last].prompt, row + last + 1, col, frame, back, fore);
      last = delta;
      if (last - 1 < 0) {
         last = count - 1;
      } else {
         last--;
      }
      shade(s[last].prompt, row + last + 1, col, fore, inverse, frame);
      break;
   case ESCAPE:
      break;
   default:                  /* REMOVE IN REAL CODE */
      printf("Should never get here wbox_menu_start()");
      break;
}
c_scroll(DLINE, 1, 79, 1, 1, 6, main_menu_b);
normal(s[last].desc, DLINE - 1, 2, main_menu_f, main_menu_b, main_menu_f);
if (letter == ENTER ¦¦ letter == ESCAPE)
   break;
```

```
   }
   cptr = tptr;                          /* Restore them          */
   menucount = tcount;

   close_window(box);
   free(mptr);
   return letter;
}
```

```
/*****

                          shade()
```

   This support function for wbox_menu_start() sets the foreground
and background colors for the display in inverse mode. Direct video
is used.

```
   Argument list:    char *s       pointer to string to shade
                     int row       row start position
                     int col       column start position
                     int fore      foreground color used
                     int back      background color
                     int hot       hotkey color
```

```
   Return value:     void
```

```
*****/
```

```
void shade(char *s, int row, int col, int fore, int back, int hot)
{
   unsigned int far *ptr;
   unsigned letter;

   ptr = start_video_memory + row * 80 + col;
   letter = (fore + back) << 8;
   hot = (hot + back) << 8;
   while (*s) {
      if (*s < 'a')
         *ptr++ = *s + hot;
      else
         *ptr++ = *s + letter;
      s++;
   }
}
```

continues

Listing 11.10. continued

```
/*****
                              normal()

    This support function for wbox_menu_start() sets the foreground
and background colors for normal display. Direct video is used.

    Argument list:    char *s        pointer to string to shade
                      int row        row start position
                      int col        column start position
                      int fore       foreground color used
                      int back       background color
                      int hot        hotkey color

    Return value:     void

*****/

void normal(char *s, int row, int col, int fore, int back, int hot)
{
    unsigned int far *ptr;
    unsigned letter;

    ptr = start_video_memory + row * 80 + col;
    hot = (hot + back) << 8;
    letter = (fore + back) << 8;
    while (*s) {
        if (*s < 'a')
            *ptr++ = *s + hot;
        else
            *ptr++ = *s + letter;
        s++;
    }
}
```

The wbox_menu_start() function begins with code that is almost identical to that presented in Chapter 4. For the most part, it simply finds the maximum length (len) of the secondary menu prompts and their hotkeys. The first new code begins with the call to init_window() to initialize the box menu as a window. After that call, various WINDOW structure members are set to the values you want to use in the program. Note that the message color (box_mcolor) is set to the symbolic constant FBLUE. This is another example of a color constant that could be made into a variable.

The calls to create_w() and show_window() display the box menu window. The call to wprintf() (from Chapter 10) then displays the prompts in the box menu window.

The call to shade() is responsible for highlighting the first option in the menu box. The call to c_scroll() is used to clear the description line at the bottom of the screen (DLINE). Finally, the call to normal() is used to update the message on the description line. Note that I use the background color for the secondary menu (sub_menu_b) as the background color for the description. If you make sub_menu_b a different color than main_menu_b, the new color serves as a visual clue that the message is for the secondary menu, not the primary menu.

The arguments to shade() and normal() are used to calculate the correct position in video memory for displaying the information. The two functions are identical, but I prefer to keep them separate to make more intuitive sense when they are called. The statements

```
while (*s) {
   if (*s < 'a')
      *ptr++ = *s + hot;
   else
      *ptr++ = *s + letter;
   s++;
}
```

are used to display the prompts on the screen. The if statement is used so that the hotkeys for the prompts (which always are uppercase letters) are displayed in a different color. When I call these functions, I simply use the hot_key_color variable for the last argument in the two functions.

The wbox_menu_start() function then enters an infinite while loop to get input from the user by way of a call to read_key_d(). Because you are interested only in moving up or down in the menu, the direction argument to read_key_d() is set to the macro UPDOWN, which is defined in win.h. A switch statement is used to process the various keystrokes.

Note that a default keyword is at the bottom of the switch. Typically, I leave such code in a function during development to see whether I ever reach an "unprocessed" response from the user. When I'm convinced that the function behaves as it should, I remove the default code from the program. I left it in here to show how it can be used when you test the code.

Eventually, the user enters a menu selection that sets letter to either ENTER or ESCAPE. At this point, control breaks out of the infinite while loop. The wbox_menu_start() function then calls c_scroll() to update the background color and the description on the description line. The program then closes the text window and frees the storage allocated to mptr.

On return from wbox_menu_start(), last contains the index for the menu option selected, and the return value will be either ENTER or ESCAPE. As you can see in listing 11.2, an ESCAPE terminates the program. If letter equals ENTER, last is used to select the function that corresponds to the secondary menu option selected.

If the user presses the Escape key to end the program (or if the user selects the eXit option from the primary menu), control breaks out of the infinite while loop in listing 11.2. The program then frees the storage for cptr, closes the main window, closes the menu, and writes the color values to the scopy.dfl file. At this point, the program ends.

The rest of this chapter discusses how each of the secondary menu options is written.

Copy Primary Menu Option— *do_mask_copy()*

The Copy option is the first menu option on the primary menu. Listing 11.9 showed how each secondary menu option is called. In this section, I discuss each of the secondary menu options shown in listing 11.9. I begin with the do_mask_copy() function, whose code is presented in listing 11.11.

Listing 11.11. The do_mask_copy() *function.*

```
/*****
                        do_mask_copy()

    This function provides the control for the masked copy function
of the program. Wild cards are allowed in the mask.

    Argument list:    void

    Return value:     void

*****/
```

```c
#include <stdio.h>
#include <stdlib.h>
#include <dir.h>              /* DELETE THIS FOR MICROSOFT C */
#include <dos.h>

#include "win.h"


void do_mask_copy(void)
{
   size_t number;
   int i;
   unsigned selected;


   i = check_paths();                 /* Are source-dest paths set? */
   if (i == 0) {
      clrwork();
      restore_old_directory();
      return;
   }

   i = get_filedir_alloc();           /* Get FILEDIR allocations    */
   if (i == 0) {
      clrwork();
      restore_old_directory();
      return;
   }

   i = get_file_mask();               /* Get the file mask          */
   if (i == 0) {
      clrwork();
      restore_old_directory();
      free(fptr);
      return;
   }

   if (mouse_here) {
      hide_cursor();
   }
```

continues

Listing 11.11. *continued*

```
number = do_directory(file_mask);
if (number == 0) {
    alert(5, 25, "No files matched the mask", "Ok",
        FLWHITE, box_b, FLWHITE, button_b);
    clrwork();
    restore_old_directory();
    free(fptr);
    return;
}
qsort(fptr, number, sizeof(FILEDIR), (int (*)(const void *,
        const void *))fcompare);
show_files(fptr, 0, number);
if (mouse_here) {
    hide_cursor();
}
selected = select_files(number, fptr);

clrwork();
if (selected == 0) {
    restore_old_directory();
    free(fptr);
    return;
}
do_copies(number, selected);
free(fptr);
restore_old_directory();
}
```

A number of the functions used in do_mask_copy() also are used in other modules of the SC program. I discuss these functions here, but I don't repeat the discussion when they appear in subsequent functions.

Check Path Names—*check_ paths()*

The first function called in do_mask_copy() is check_paths(). As mentioned earlier, the global variables file_source[] and file_dest[] hold the source and destination path names for all file accesses. Therefore, you must check them to ensure that they have been set before you can proceed. The code for check_paths() is presented in listing 11.12.

Listing 11.12. The check_paths() *function.*

```
/*****
                        check_paths()

    This function makes sure that file source path name
  (file_source[]) and file destination path name (file_dest[])
  have been set. Both are global variables defined in win.h.

    Argument list:   void

    Return value:    int      0 if not set; 1 otherwise

*****/

#include "win.h"

int check_paths(void)
{
    if (file_source[0] == '\0' ¦¦ file_dest[0] == '\0') {
        alert(8, 21, "Paths not set. Use deFaults Option.", "Ok",
            FLWHITE, box_b, FLWHITE, button_b);
        return 0;
    }
    return 1;
}
```

There isn't much to check_paths(), but because the check must be performed in so many places, it made sense to make it a function. If the paths are not set, the user must use the deFaults option to set the file path names.

Get a *FILEDIR* Allocation— *get_ filedir_alloc( )*

After the path names have been set, the do_mask_copy() function calls get_filedir_alloc(). Listing 11.13 presents the code for get_filedir_alloc().

Listing 11.13. *The* `get_filedir_alloc()` *function.*

```
/*****
                        get_filedir_alloc()

    This function attempts to get enough memory for an array of
    FILEDIR's of size MAXFILES.

    Argument list:    void

    Return value:     int      0 if not set; 1 otherwise

*****/

#include "win.h"

int get_filedir_alloc(void)
{
    fptr = (FILEDIR *) calloc(MAXFILES, sizeof(FILEDIR));
    if (fptr == NULL) {
        alert(8, 25, "Out of directory memory.", "Ok",
            FLWHITE, box_b, FLWHITE, button_b);
        return 0;
    }
    return 1;
}
```

Again, this function needs no comment, but note that it is called frequently throughout the program. If there is sufficient memory, the global variable `fptr` (defined in win.h) points to the allocation. Otherwise, a message is given to the user. You should be sure to free `fptr` each time you finish using it. I could have allocated a single array of FILEDIRs for use throughout the program and not worried about freeing it until the user terminated the program. However, because of the recursive function used in the search option, I was concerned that the stack might run into conflict with the heap on deeply buried subdirectories. Freeing the `fptr` storage after it is used helps to reduce the likelihood of a conflict between the heap and the stack.

Get a File Name—*get_ file_mask( )*

Assuming that you have enough memory, do_mask_copy() calls get_file_mask(). Almost every option uses this function. The code for get_file_mask() appears in listing 11.14.

Listing 11.14. *The* get_file_mask() *function.*

```
/*****
                          get_file_mask()

    This support function is used by many other functions to get a
file name or mask from the user. This is done by way of a text
window. The file mask normally is "*.*", but it may be changed with
a different argument. The global variable "file_mask" is used to
collect the input from the user.

    Argument list:     void

    Return value:      int       0 if something goes wrong;
                                 nonzero otherwise. (See
                                 get_string() for possible
                                 return values.)

*****/

#include "win.h"


int get_file_mask(void)
{
    char button1[15], button2[15], m[15];
    int bloca[4] = {5, 5, 5, 25};            /* Button coordinates      */
    int button_row, fw, i;
    struct DIALOG mine;

    init_dialog(&mine);

    mine.wide = 40; mine.deep = 8;
    mine.dfcolor = FWHITE; mine.dbcolor = box_b;

    if (create_d(8, 15, mine.wide, mine.deep, &mine) == 0) {
        alert(8, 15, "Out of Memory.", "Ok",
```

continues

Listing 11.14. continued

```
            FLWHITE, box_b, FLWHITE, button_b);
    return 0;
}

strcpy(button1, "    Ok    ");
strcpy(button2, "  Cancel  ");
strcpy(m, "File mask: ");

show_dialog(mine);

button_row = 5;                 /* Where the buttons are in the window */
mine.locations = bloca;
mine.buttonlen = &button_row;

do_button(button_row, bloca[1], button1, FLWHITE, button_b, mine);
do_button(button_row, bloca[3], button2, FLWHITE, button_b, mine);

strcpy(file_mask, "*.*");
fw = 13;                                  /* Field width for file mask */
mine.fmcolor = FLWHITE; mine.bmcolor = box_b;
mine.ffcolor = FLWHITE; mine.bfcolor = button_b;
i = get_string(2, 7, m, file_mask, fw, mine, strlen(button1));

close_dialog(mine);
return i;
}
```

Much of the code for get_file_mask() involves creating a text window as a dialog box to get an input string from the user. The variables button1[] and button2[] hold the messages that appear on the buttons, and m[] holds the prompt for the input string. Variable bloca[] is used to store the upper left corner coordinates for the two button locations within the window. The call to show_dialog() shows the dialog box, and the calls to do_button() place the buttons within the dialog box.

Think how easy it is to add three or more buttons to a window. You just add some new variables for the button strings, increase the size of bloca[] to hold the additional coordinates for the new buttons, and then call do_button() as needed.

Figure 11.3 shows how the dialog box looks when it is first displayed.

Fig. 11.3. *The* `get_file_mask()` *dialog box.*

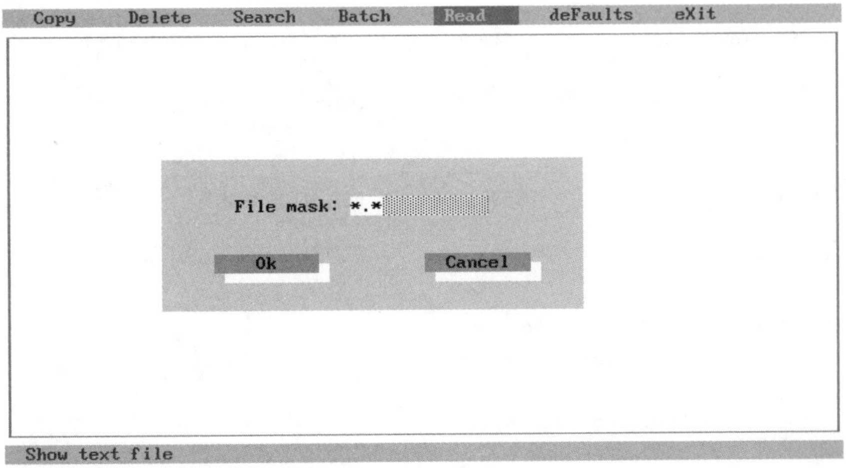

The default input string is copied into `m[]` before calling `get_string()`. (The `get_string()` function is discussed in Chapter 10, "Text Windows.") If the user presses Enter or clicks on the Ok button without typing into the input field, the default file mask (for example, "*.*") is accepted. If the user types something into the input field and presses Enter or clicks on Ok, that input becomes the file mask. The function then closes the dialog box and returns the value from `get_string()` to the calling function.

Get a File Directory—*do_directory( )*

Assuming a file mask is entered, `do_mask_copy()` calls `do_directory()` to find all files matching `file_mask[]` on the `file_source[]` path. The `do_directory()` code appears in listing 11.15.

Listing 11.15. *The* `do_directory()` *function.*

```
/*****

                        do_directory()

    This function is used to search a file directory for matches on
the file mask passed to the function.
```

continues

Listing 11.15. *continued*

```
    Argument list:      char *mask        file mask for the search

    Return value:       int               number of successful matches

*****/
#include <dir.h>      /* THIS IS DOS.H FOR MICROSOFT C */

#include "win.h"

#define ERROREND    -1
#define ALL          23

int do_directory(char *mask)
{
   char temp[129];
   int done, i, len;
   struct ffblk p;    /* CHANGE FOR MICROSOFT C */

   strcpy(temp, file_source);
   strcat(temp,"\\");
   strcat(temp, mask);

   done = findfirst(temp, &p, ALL);
   if (done == ERROREND) {
      return 0;
   }
   for (i = 0; done != ERROREND && i < MAXFILES; i++) {
      strcpy(fptr[i].fname, p.ff_name);
      len = strlen(fptr[i].fname);
      while (len < 12) {
         strcat(fptr[i].fname, " ");
         len++;
      }
      fptr[i].use = 0;
      done = findnext(&p);
   }
   return i;
}
```

When the directory search is performed, the source path name is added to the start of the file name. The function uses the findfirst() and findnext() provided with most MS-DOS compilers. (Microsoft uses the names _dos_findfirst() and _dos_findnext().) As long as the function continues to find a match on the file mask, and MAXFILES is not exceeded, the fptr pointer to the FILEDIR structure is filled in with the names of the matching files. The use member of the FILEDIR structure is set to 0 to indicate that the file has not yet been marked for use in the program. When the function ends, all matching file names have been copied into the FILEDIR structure.

Switch Directories— *restore_old_directory()*

The value returned from do_directory() is assigned into number. If the value is zero, a message is given, fptr is freed, and the previous directory is restored. The code for the restore_old_directory() function appears in listing 11.16.

Listing 11.16. *The* restore_old_directory() *function.*

```
/*****
                        restore_old_directory()

    This support function is used by many other functions to change
    the directory back to the original directory setting. Two global
    variables keep track of the original directory (old_source[]) and
    the directory being used (file_source[]).

    Argument list:    void

    Return value:     int      0 if something goes wrong;
                               nonzero otherwise.

*****/

#include "win.h"

void restore_old_directory(void)
```

continues

Listing 11.16. continued

```
{
   if (file_source[0] != old_source[0]) {     /* Change drives?      */
      change_drive(old_source[0]);
   }
   chdir(old_source);
}
```

Change Data Drives—*change_drive( )*

The change_drive() function provides a means by which you can change between disk drives. Note that the chdir() function provided with your compiler enables you to change only subdirectories. The code for change_drive() appears in listing 11.17.

Listing 11.17. The change_drive( ) function.

```
/*****

                          change_drive()

     This function is used to change the default drive used with
the copy aspects of the program. This function is used when you
need to change from drive to drive, not between subdirectories (use
chdir() for that).

   Argument list:    int drive      the drive to be changed to. It is
                                     assumed that the drive is a letter
                                     (A, B, C, and so on)

   Return value:     int            the last valid drive in the
                                     system. (Note that this is
                                     1-based, not 0-based. That is,
                                     drive A is 1, not 0.)

*****/

#include <dos.h>

int change_drive(int drive)
{
```

```
    union REGS ireg;

    ireg.h.ah = 0x0e;
    ireg.h.dl = toupper(drive) - 'A';
    intdos(&ireg, &ireg);
    return ireg.h.al;
}
```

The code contains no surprises, but the return value is somewhat inconsistent. The drive passed to the interrupt is zero-based. That is, drive A corresponds to the value 0. However, the function, a one-based value, returns the last valid drive on the system. Therefore, a single drive system returns drive A as 1.

In listing 11.16, change_drive() is called only when the first character of file_source[] and the first character of file_dest[] are not the same. The program then calls the chdir() library function to move to the appropriate subdirectory on the drive.

Sort the Files—*qsort( )* and *fcompare( )*

When control returns to do_mask_copy() after the call to do_directory(), a call to qsort() sorts the file names held in the FILEDIR array. The cast in the statement

```
qsort(fptr, number, sizeof(FILEDIR),
    (int (*)(const void *, const void *))fcompare);
```

is necessary for some compilers. (The Borland compiler gets very cranky if the cast is not expressed as shown.) The comparison function is shown in listing 11.18.

Listing 11.18. *The* fcompare() *function.*

```
/*****

                        fcompare()

    This support function is used by qsort() to compare file names.
Most program options that present lists of files present them in
sorted order.
```

continues

Listing 11.18. *continued*

```
    Argument list:    char *s1       pointer to first file name being
                                     compared
                      char *s2       pointer to second file name being
                                     compared

    Return value:     int            0 if equal; nonzero otherwise

*****/

#include <string.h>

int fcompare(const char *s1, const char *s2)
{
    return (strcmp(s1, s2));
}
```

Because similar code is discussed in Chapter 5, "Searching, Sorting, and Parsing," this code needs no explanation.

Display the Files—*show_files()* and *flip_file()*

Similar code is explained in Chapter 5. When qsort() finishes, show_files() is called to display the files. The code for show_files() is shown in listing 11.19.

Listing 11.19. *The* show_files() *function.*

```
/*****
                         show_files()

    This support function is used by several different file-listing
    functions to display a list of file names.

    Argument list:    FILEDIR *fptr      pointer to file information
                      int index          index for the starting
                                         position for the list
                      int number         number of files to show
```

```
   Return value:    void

*****/

#include "win.h"

void show_files(FILEDIR *fptr, int index, int number)
{
   int col, i, row;

   row = SCREENROW; col = SCREENCOL;

   for (i = index; i < number; i++) {
      if (col > LASTCOL) {
         row++;
         col = SCREENCOL;
      }
      if (row > LASTROW) {
         break;
      }
      flip_file(fptr[i].fname, fptr[i].use, row, col);
      col += FILENAMESIZE;
   }
}
```

The show_files() function simply displays the file names in the main output window. The symbolic constants used in the function are stored in the win.h header file. The real work of the function, however, is done by the call to flip_file(), shown in listing 11.20.

Listing 11.20. *The* flip_file() *function.*

```
/*****

                         flip_file()

   This support function is used by several different file-listing
   functions to change the display of a file name from normal to
   inverse (or color) or vice versa.

   Argument list:    char *fname      file name
                     char use         flag that sets the state of
                                      the display. 0 = normal;
                                      nonzero = inverse
```

continues

Listing 11.20. continued

```
                    int row            row position for display
                    int col            column position for display

   Return value:    void

*****/

#include "win.h"

void flip_file(char *fname, char use, int row, int col)
{
   unsigned int letter, far *ptr;

   row--; col--;                 /* Adjust for absolute screen addresses */

   if (use) {
      letter = (hot_key_color + BWHITE) << 8;
   } else {
      letter = (FWHITE + BBLACK) << 8;
   }
   ptr = start_video_memory + (row * 80) + col;
   while (*fname) {
      *ptr++ = *fname++ + letter;
   }

}
```

The flip_file() function uses direct video writes to display a file name. Note that the attributes change, depending on whether the fptr[].use member is set or not. Again, you can change the symbolic color constants to variables if you want.

When you return from show_files(), all the files are shown in the output window—or at least the first 100 are. All the files appear in the regular (noninversed) state, because all fptr[].use members are zero. Figure 11.4 shows what the screen might look like at this point in the program.

Fig. 11.4. Display after a call to show_files().

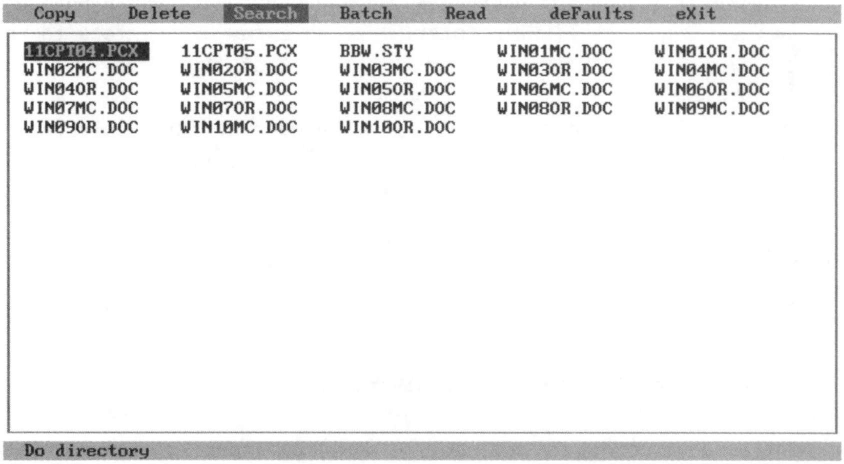

```
 Copy     Delete    Search    Batch    Read       deFaults   eXit

11CPT04.PCX    11CPT05.PCX    BBW.STY       WIN01MC.DOC    WIN01OR.DOC
WIN02MC.DOC    WIN02OR.DOC    WIN03MC.DOC   WIN03OR.DOC    WIN04MC.DOC
WIN04OR.DOC    WIN05MC.DOC    WIN05OR.DOC   WIN06MC.DOC    WIN06OR.DOC
WIN07MC.DOC    WIN07OR.DOC    WIN08MC.DOC   WIN08OR.DOC    WIN09MC.DOC
WIN09OR.DOC    WIN10MC.DOC    WIN10OR.DOC




 Do directory
```

Select a File from a List—*select_files()*

The program now calls select_files() to enable the user to select the files he or she wants to copy. The code for select_files() appears in listing 11.21. It is rather lengthy because it must provide both mouse and keyboard support.

Listing 11.21. The select_files() *function.*

```
/*****

                          select_files()


    This support function is used to select files from a previously
sorted list. Files may be selected with a mouse or the keyboard.
The left mouse button is used to select a file. When a file is
selected, it is shown in a reverse color (highlighted). If a
highlighted file is selected a second time, it reverts to a normal
display color, meaning that the file is deselected. Arrow keys,
Home, End, Page Up, and Page Down also enable you to scroll through
the list of files. The Escape key and the right mouse button abort
the selection process.
```

continues

Listing 11.21. *continued*

```
Argument list:    int number          number of files to show
                  FILEDIR fptr[]      an array of pointers to the
                                      list of files

Return value:     int                 number of files selected
                                      from the list


*****/

#include "win.h"


int select_files(int number, FILEDIR fptr[])
{
    int bottom, count, i, row, col, oldcol, oldindex, oldrow, offset;
    int mrow, mcol;
    unsigned index, letter;

    index = count = 0;

    number--;                          /* To use directly as index  */
    oldrow = row = SCREENROW;
    oldcol = col = SCREENCOL;           /* Was 3 for the mouse       */

    flip_file(fptr[0].fname, 1, row, col);
    index = offset = 0;

  while (TRUE) {
        letter = read_key_and_mouse(&mrow, &mcol);
        if (letter == ESCAPE) {

          break;
        }
        if (letter == F10) {
          number++;
          for (i = 0; i < number; i++)
             fptr[i].use = 1;
          return number;
        }
        oldindex = index;
        switch (letter) {
          case HOME:
```

```
            offset = index = 0;           /* Might need a scroll here  */
        row = SCREENROW;
        col = SCREENCOL;
        if (number > SCREENFULL) {
            show_files(fptr, offset, SCREENFULL);
            flip_file(fptr[index].fname, 1, row, col);
        } else {
            flip_file(fptr[oldindex].fname, fptr[oldindex].use, oldrow,
                      oldcol);
            flip_file(fptr[index].fname, 1, row, col);
        }
        break;

    case END:
        index = number;
        if (index > SCREENFULL) {
            offset = number % MAXFLINE;
            oldcol = col = SCREENCOL + (FILENAMESIZE * offset);
            oldrow = row = SCREENROW + 19;
            offset = (number - offset) - SCREENFULL + MAXFLINE;
            oldindex = index = number;
        } else {
            row = index / MAXFLINE + SCREENROW;
            col = (index % MAXFLINE) * FILENAMESIZE + SCREENCOL;
            flip_file(fptr[oldindex].fname, fptr[oldindex].use, oldrow,
                      oldcol);
        }
        clrwork();
        show_files(fptr, offset, number);
        flip_file(fptr[index].fname, 1, row, col);
        break;
    case PAGEUP:
if (number < SCREENFULL)
        break;
        offset -= SCREENFULL;
        if (offset < 0) {                /* Page past start of data   */
            offset = index = 0;
            row = SCREENROW; col = SCREENCOL;
        } else {
            index -= SCREENFULL;
        }
        clrwork();
        show_files(fptr, offset, number);
```

continues

Listing 11.21. continued

```
                flip_file(fptr[index].fname, 1, row, col);
                break;

        case PAGEDN:
            if (number < SCREENFULL)
                break;
            offset += SCREENFULL;
            if (offset > number ¦¦ (offset + SCREENFULL) > number) {
            /* Page past end of data                                    */
                offset = number % MAXFLINE;
                oldcol = col = SCREENCOL + (FILENAMESIZE * offset);
                oldrow = row = SCREENROW + 19;
                offset = number - SCREENFULL + offset + 1;
                oldindex = index = number;
        } else {
                index += SCREENFULL;
            }
            clrwork();
            show_files(fptr, offset, number);
            flip_file(fptr[index].fname, 1, row, col);
            break;

        case UARROW:
            if (index == 0)
                break;
            if (row > SCREENROW) {          /* Not at the top yet        */
                row--;
                index -= MAXFLINE;
                if (index < 0) {
                    index = 0;
                    offset = 0;
                }
                if (index < offset)
                    offset -= MAXFLINE;
            } else {                        /* At the top                */
                row = SCREENROW;
                if (number < SCREENFULL) {
                    offset = index = 0;
                    col = SCREENCOL;
                } else {
                    index -= MAXFLINE;
```

```
                    offset -= MAXFLINE;
                    if (index < 0 || offset < 0) {
                        index = 0;
                        offset = 0;
                        col = SCREENCOL;
            } else {

                        scroll_one_line(LINEDOWN);
                        show_one_line(fptr, offset, number, row, SCREENCOL);
                        oldrow++;
                    }
                }
            }
            flip_file(fptr[oldindex].fname, fptr[oldindex].use, oldrow,
                    oldcol);
            flip_file(fptr[index].fname, 1, row, col);
            break;
        case DARROW:
            index += MAXFLINE;
            if (number <= SCREENFULL) {  /* Less than a screenful    */
                if (index > number) {
                    index = number;
                    row = index / MAXFLINE + SCREENROW;
                    col = (index % MAXFLINE) * FILENAMESIZE + SCREENCOL;
                } else {
                    row++;
                }
            } else {                     /* More than a screenful    */
                if (row < LASTROW) {     /* Not at bottom edge       */
                    row++;
                } else {                 /* At last row              */
                    offset += MAXFLINE;
                    bottom = offset + (MAXFLINE * 19);
                    if (bottom > number) {
                        index = number;
                        col = (index % MAXFLINE) * FILENAMESIZE + SCREENCOL;
                    } else {
            scroll_one_line(LINEUP);
                        show_one_line(fptr, bottom, number, row, SCREENCOL);
                        oldrow--;
                    }
                }
            }

                                        /* Need a scroll here       */
```

continues

Listing 11.21. continued

```
            flip_file(fptr[oldindex].fname, fptr[oldindex].use, oldrow, oldcol);
            flip_file(fptr[index].fname, 1, row, col);
            break;
        case LARROW:
            col -= FILENAMESIZE;
            index--;
            if (col < SCREENCOL) {
                col = LASTCOL;
                index += MAXFLINE;
                if (index > number) {
                    index = number;
                    col = (index % MAXFLINE) * FILENAMESIZE + SCREENCOL;
                }
            }
            if (index < 0) {
                index = 0;
                col = SCREENCOL;
            }
            flip_file(fptr[oldindex].fname, fptr[oldindex].use, oldrow, oldcol);
            flip_file(fptr[index].fname, 1, row, col);
            break;
        case RARROW:
            col += FILENAMESIZE;
            index++;
            if (col > 70) {
                col = SCREENCOL;
                index -= 5;
            }
    if (index > number) {
                index = number;
                col = (index % MAXFLINE) * FILENAMESIZE + SCREENCOL;
            }
            flip_file(fptr[oldindex].fname, fptr[oldindex].use, oldrow, oldcol);
            flip_file(fptr[index].fname, 1, row, col);
            break;
        case ENTER:
            fptr[index].use = !fptr[index].use;
            if (fptr[index].use)
                count++;
            else
                count--;
```

```
            break;
        case F2:                        /* Abort option          */
            return 0;
        default:
            break;
    }
    oldrow = row;
    oldcol = col;
    }
    return count;
}
```

Note that near the top of the select_files() function you decrement the number of files (number) displayed on the screen. This enables you to directly index into the FILEDIR array. The first call to flip_file() highlights the first file on the screen. In fact, the highlighted file serves as a cursor to tell the user where he or she is in the list.

If the user presses the Enter key or clicks the left mouse button, the file remains highlighted. This also sets fptr[].use to a value of 1 (that is, the file is selected for copying). A second click on a highlighted file returns it to normal video. (The fptr[].use member is set to 0.) If the user presses the F10 key, all files are selected, even if they don't appear on the screen.

Most of the code in select_files() is necessary to maintain the proper relationship between the file display position and the fptr[] array. If the number of files exceeds 100, the display can be scrolled by moving the mouse in the direction necessary to scroll the list. The cursor keys—Home, End, Page Up, Page Down, and the arrow keys—also can be used to scroll the list. The user can move around the screen and select all or part of the files from the list. Pressing the Escape key ends the selection process.

The code uses the F2 key for an abort option. Because the F2 key causes a return value of 0 (that is, no files selected), do_mask_copy() has nothing more to do, so the do_mask_copy() option ends. Obviously, you can change the F2 and F10 keys to other values if you want.

Copy a File—*do_copies( )*

If files match the file mask and the user has selected files to be copied, the program calls to copy the selected files. The do_copies() code for do_copies() appears in listing 11.22.

Listing 11.22. *The* do_copies() *function.*

```
/*****
                            do_copies()

    This function copies the files that have been selected for
copying. The files to be copied have the fptr[i].use FILEDIR member
set to logical True.

    Argument list:    int number        number of files that match the
                                        file mask
                      int selected      number of files selected for
                                        copy by the user


    Return value:     void

*****/

#include <dir.h>      /* MAKE DOS.H FOR MICROSOFT C */

#include "win.h"

void do_copies(int number, int selected)
{
    char buff[50];
    int col, count, i, j, row, swap_flag;
    long disks, drive_storage, drive_free, space_needed;

    struct ffblk finfo;            /* CHANGE FOR MICROSOFT C */

    swap_flag = 0;
    space_needed = 0L;
    col = SCREENCOL;
    row = SCREENROW;
    for (j = i = 0; i < number; i++) {    /* Show the files          */
        cursor(row, col);
    if (fptr[i].use) {
            findfirst(fptr[i].fname, &finfo, 0);
            space_needed += finfo.ff_fsize;
            flip_file(fptr[i].fname, 1, row, col);
            j++;
            col += FILENAMESIZE;
            if (col > LASTCOL) {
```

```
                    col = SCREENCOL;
                    row++;
                }
            }
        if (row > LASTROW)
            break;
    }
    drive_storage = get_disk_size(file_dest[0]);
    drive_free = get_disk_free(file_dest[0]);

    if (space_needed > drive_free) {
        swap_flag = 1;
        if (toupper(file_dest[0]) > 'B') {
            i = two_button(5, 8, "Insufficient space. Copy what is possible?",
                "  Ok  ", "Cancel", FLWHITE, box_b, FLWHITE, button_b);
        } else {
            disks = space_needed / drive_storage;

            if (space_needed % drive_storage) {    /* If not perfect fit */
                disks++;
            }
            sprintf(buff, "No space left. Need %ld more blank disk(s).", disks);
            i = two_button(5, 12, buff, "Proceed", "Cancel ",
                FLWHITE, box_b, FLWHITE, button_b);
        }
        if (i == 2 || i == 'C') {
            clrwork();
            restore_old_directory();
            return;
        }
    }

    row = SCREENROW; col = SCREENCOL;
    for (count = i = 0; i < number; i++) {
        if (fptr[i].use) {
            findfirst(fptr[i].fname, &finfo, 0);
            space_needed -= finfo.ff_fsize;
            if (finfo.ff_fsize > space_needed && swap_flag) {
                sprintf(buff, "Insert blank disk in drive %s", file_dest);
                alert(5, 25, buff, "Ok",
                        FLWHITE, box_b, FLWHITE, button_b);
            }
            count += file_write(fptr[i].fname);
```

continues

Listing 11.22. continued

```
        flip_file(fptr[i].fname, 0, row, col);
        col += FILENAMESIZE;
        if (col > LASTCOL) {
            col = SCREENCOL;
            row++;
        }
        if (row > LASTROW) {
            clrwork();
            show_files(fptr, i + 1, number);
            row = SCREENROW; col = SCREENCOL;
        }
    }
}
if (count != selected) {
    alert(5, 25, "Copy not successful", "Ok",
        FLWHITE, box_b, FLWHITE, button_b);
    clrwork();
} else {
    if (selected) {
        alert(5, 20, "Copy completed successfully", "Ok",
            FLWHITE, box_b, FLWHITE, button_b);
        clrwork();
    }
}
}
```

If the user selects one or more files, the program calls the do_copies() function. Control enters a for loop and calls findfirst(). The purpose of these calls this time is to determine the sizes of the files. The variable space_needed keeps track of the total amount of disk space required. The program then calls get_disk_size() and get_disk_free() to determine the amount of free space left on the disk. If the destination drive does not have enough free disk space, the user is asked if he or she wants to continue. This message appears when the drive prefix is greater than B. The assumption is that drive C or higher is a hard disk.

If the drive is a floppy disk, a message is given that the user will need one or more blank disks. The user is given the opportunity to cancel the copy at this point. If he or she elects to proceed, another for loop is entered to copy the disk.

In the `for` loop, `findfirst()` is called again to subtract the file sizes from `space_needed` as the files are copied. When `space_needed` becomes negative, the user is asked to insert a blank disk in the destination drive. The copying process continues until all the files have been copied. This approach enables the user to change disks in the middle of a copy option.

Write the File—*file_write( )*

The code that actually writes the data files appears in listing 11.23.

Listing 11.23. The `file_write()` *function.*

```
/*****
                              file_write()

    This function is responsible for writing a file to the
    destination drive.

    Argument list:    char *filename     name of the file to copy

    Return value:     int                1 if successful; 0 if not

*****/

#include <stdio.h>
#include "win.h"


int file_write(char *filename)
{
    char buffi[128],buffo[128];
    int c;
    FILE *fpin, *fpout;

    strcpy(buffo, file_dest);
    strcat(buffo, filename);

    if ((fpin = fopen(filename, "rb")) == NULL) {
        sprintf(buffi, "Cannot open input file: %s", filename);
        alert(8, 15, buffi, "Ok",
            FLWHITE, box_b, FLWHITE, button_b);
```

continues

Listing 11.23. *continued*

```
    return 0;
}
if ((fpout = fopen(buffo, "wb")) == NULL) {
    sprintf(buffo, "Cannot open output file: %s", filename);
    alert(8, 15, buffo, "Ok",
        FLWHITE, box_b, FLWHITE, button_b);
    return 0;
}
while ( (c = fgetc(fpin)) != EOF) {
    fputc(c, fpout);
}
fclose(fpin);
fclose(fpout);
return 1;
}
```

Message boxes are used to inform the user if a file is not copied successfully.

Note that the code in listing 11.11 displays the files in a highlighted state after they have been selected by the user. As each file is copied by the calls to file_write(), flip_file() is called to redisplay the file in normal video mode. This gives the user a visual clue as to how the copy is progressing. If you are using a fast system with a disk cache and a few small files, this happens so quickly you might not see it. Even though fgetc() and fputc() are used for the copy, it is a fairly fast function.

Screen Support Functions

Several support functions are called at various places in listing 11.21. Most of them are used to control the display. The code for clrwork(), which simply calls scroll() to clear the output window of the display, appears in listing 11.24.

Listing 11.24. *The* clrwork() *function.*

```
/*****

                          clrwork()

This function clears the main window screen.
```

```
Argument list:    void

Return value:     void

*****/

void clrwork(void)
{
    scroll(3, 2, 76, 18, 0, 7);
}
```

A second display support function is scroll_one_line(). Its code appears in listing 11.25.

Listing 11.25. *The* scroll_one_line() *function.*

```
/*****

                          scroll_one_line()

    This function scrolls the screen one line in the direction
    specified. It normally is used to scroll a long list of files.

    Argument list:    int direction       0 = down, 1 = up

    Return value:     void

*****/

#include "win.h"

void scroll_one_line(int direction)
{
    if (direction == LINEUP)
        scroll(3, 2, 76, 18, 1, 6);
    else
        scroll(3, 2, 76, 18, 1, 7);

}
```

The last display support routine is show_one_line(). It is called when the top or the bottom of the display needs to be updated with a single entry. Listing 11.26 shows the code for show_one_line().

Listing 11.26. *The* `show_one_line()` *function.*

```
/*****
                            show_one_line()

        This function shows one line of a FILEDIR.

        Argument list:     FILEDIR *fptr        pointer to file information
                           int index            index for the starting
                                                position for the list
                           int number           number of files to show
                           int row              row position for display
                           int col              column position for display


        Return value:      void

*****/

#include "win.h"


void show_one_line(FILEDIR *fptr, int index, int number, int row, int col)
{
   int i;

   for (i = 0; i < MAXFLINE; i++) {
      if (index > number)
         break;
      flip_file(fptr[index].fname, fptr[index].use, row, col);
      index++;
      col += FILENAMESIZE;
   }
}
```

Listings 11.24 through 11.26 help manage the display screen in response to cursor keys and mouse movements. The only difficult part is keeping the first and last files displayed on the screen in sync with the index for the file. The variable `offset` is used when more than 100 files appear in the list. This variable always is adjusted so that it is the first file displayed in the upper left corner of the output window. The variable named `bottom` is set to the first file on the bottom line of the display.

The support functions discussed thus far are used in most of the secondary menu options that remain to be covered. Therefore, I concentrate only on functions that are new to the remaining menu options.

Copy by Dates—*do_date_copy( )*

The next secondary menu option is do_date_copy(). Note, however, that all but the last (that is, the backup) copy options use the do_date_copy() function. Only the argument to the function changes for the four copy options. The code for do_date_copy() appears in listing 11.27.

Listing 11.27. *The* do_date_copy() *function.*

```
/*****

                              do_date_copy()

     This function is responsible for copying files using the date
  as the controlling factor. The symbolic constants are defined in
  win.h.

     Argument list:     int test      type of date copy to perform:
                                          YOUNGER   = 0
                                          SAMEAGE   = 1
                                          OLDER     = 2
                                          NOT_EQUAL = 3


     Return value:      void

*****/

#include <stdio.h>

#include "win.h"

void do_date_copy(int test)
{
    size_t number;
    int j;
    unsigned date, selected;
```

continues

Listing 11.27. *continued*

```
number = 0;
j = check_paths();
if (j == 0) {
   clrwork();
   restore_old_directory();
   return;
}

j = get_file_mask();

if (j == 0) {
   clrwork();
   restore_old_directory();
   return;
}
j = get_filedir_alloc();
   if (j == 0) {
   clrwork();
   restore_old_directory();
   return;
}

get_date_mask(&date);
if (date == 0 || date == ESCAPE) {
   clrwork();
   restore_old_directory();
   free(fptr);
   return;
}

if (mouse_here) {
   hide_cursor();
}

number = do_date_dir(date, test);

if (number == 0) {
   alert(5, 25, "No files matched the mask", "Ok",
       FLWHITE, box_b, FLWHITE, button_b);
   free(fptr);
   return;
```

```
}
qsort(fptr, number, sizeof(FILEDIR), (int (*)(const void *,
      const void *))fcompare);
show_files(fptr, 0, number);
if (mouse_here) {
   hide_cursor();
}

selected = select_files(number, fptr);

clrwork();

if (selected) {
   do_copies(number, selected);
}
free(fptr);
restore_old_directory();
}
```

Get a Date—*get_date_mask( )*

The first function that is new is get_date_mask(). The code appears in listing 11.28.

Listing 11.28. *The* get_date_mask() *function.*

```
/*****
                        get_date_mask()

    This function presents the user with a dialog box to enter a
    date.

    Argument list:    unsigned *d      pointer to the date

    Return value:     void

*****/

#include "win.h"
```

continues

Listing 11.28. *continued*

```
void get_date_mask(unsigned *d)
{
    char button1[15], button2[15];
    char buff[20], message[34];
    int bloca[4] = {5, 15, 5, 35};         /* Button coordinates        */
    int button_row, fw, i;
    int day, month, year;
    struct DIALOG mine;

    strcpy(message, "Enter date to search (MM/DD/YY): ");
    init_dialog(&mine);
    mine.wide = 60; mine.deep = 8;
    mine.dfcolor = FWHITE; mine.dbcolor = box_b;
    if (create_d(8, 5, mine.wide, mine.deep, &mine) == 0) {
        alert(8, 15, "Out of Memory.", "Ok",
            FLWHITE, box_b, FLWHITE, button_b);
        *d = 0;
        return;
    }
    strcpy(button1, "    Ok    ");
    strcpy(button2, "  Cancel  ");

  show_dialog(mine);

    button_row = 5;                  /* Where the buttons are in the window */
    mine.locations = bloca;
    mine.buttonlen = &button_row;
    do_button(button_row, bloca[1], button1, FLWHITE, button_b, mine);
    do_button(button_row, bloca[3], button2, FLWHITE, button_b, mine);
    buff[0] = '\0';
    fw = 8;                                 /* Field width for file mask */
    mine.fmcolor = FLWHITE; mine.bmcolor = box_b;
    mine.ffcolor = FLWHITE; mine.bfcolor = button_b;
    while (TRUE) {
        i = get_string(2, 7, message, buff, fw, mine, strlen(button1));
        if (i == 0 || i == ESCAPE) {
            *d = 0;
            close_dialog(mine);
            return;
        }
        if (buff[2] == '/' && buff[5] == '/')
```

```
        break;
      alert(5, 25, "Not a valid date. Use MM/DD/YY", "Ok",
          FLWHITE, box_b, FLWHITE, button_b);
  }
  buff[5] = buff[2] = '\0';
  month = atoi(buff);
  day = atoi(&buff[3]);
  year = atoi(&buff[6]);
  *d = packdate(day, month, year);
  close_dialog(mine);
}
```

The code is very similar to that used to create the dialog box to get an input file mask, shown in listing 11.14. The differences appear after the call to get_string(). The statement

```
if (buff[2] == '/' && buff[5] == '/')
```

is a simple check to see whether the user entered the date in the proper MM/DD/YY format. In other locales, you might want to change this format check. If that check is passed, the function creates month, day, and year variables and passes them to packdate(). (The packdate() function is discussed in Chapter 6, "Time and Dates.") The return value from packdate() then is assigned into the date variable (d) passed to the function. If you are worried about not getting a valid date entered, you can use the function valid_date() as discussed in Chapter 6. Because an invalid date is not likely to show up on the disk, the check probably is not needed.

Do a Directory by Date— *do_date_dir( )*

When a date is entered, do_date_dir() is called to find the desired files. The code for do_date_dir() appears in listing 11.29.

Listing 11.29. *The do_date_dir() function.*

```
/*****

                    do_date_dir()

  This function searches the files for the date specified. It
  fills in the pointer to a FILEDIR array with the matches found.
```

continues

Listing 11.29. *continued*

```
     Argument list:     unsigned int date    a packed file date test
                        int test             flag to determine what
                                             type of test to perform.
                                             The values are:
                                               YOUNGER   = 0
                                               SAMEAGE   = 1
                                               OLDER     = 2
                                               NOT_EQUAL = 3

     Return value:      int                  number of files matched

*****/

#include <dir.h>               /* MAKE DOS.H FOR MICROSOFT C */
#include <string.h>

#include "win.h"

#define ALL           23      /* Exclude volume labels and directories */
#define ERROREND      -1

int do_date_dir(unsigned int date, int test)
{
   char mask[5];
   int count, done, flag, i, len;
   struct ffblk p;               /* CHANGE FOR MICROSOFT C */

   extern char file_mask[];

   done = findfirst(file_mask, &p, ALL);
   if (done == ERROREND) {
      return 0;
   }
   for (count = i = 0; done != ERROREND; i++) {
      flag = 0;
      switch (test) {
         case YOUNGER:                      /* Younger              */
            if (p.ff_fdate < date) {
               flag = 1;
            }
            break;
```

```
        case SAMEAGE:                   /* Same age             */
            if (p.ff_fdate == date) {
                flag = 1;
            }
            break;
        case OLDER:                     /* Older                */
            if (p.ff_fdate > date) {
                flag = 1;
            }
            break;
        case NOT_EQUAL:                 /* Unequal              */
            if (p.ff_fdate != date) {
                flag = 1;
            }
            break;

    }
    if (flag) {
        strcpy(fptr[count].fname, p.ff_name);
        len = strlen(fptr[count].fname);
        while (len < 12) {
            strcat(fptr[count].fname, " ");
            len++;
        }
        fptr[count].use = 0;
        count++;
    }
    done = findnext(&p);
}
clrwork();
return count;
}
```

Our old friends findfirst() and findnext() do most of the work. The argument named test determines which file matches are copied into the FILEDIR array pointed to by fptr. The function returns the number of files that met the date criteria by the selection process set by test.

Subsequent calls to qsort(), show_files(), and select_files() in listing 11.27 enable the user to select the files to copy. If the number of files selected is positive, do_copies() is called. (See listing 11.22.) After the files are copied, fptr is freed and the old directory is restored. Control then returns to the primary menu. All the date copy routines use the same general copy procedure for do_date_copy().

Backup Files—*do_backup( )*

The last copy routine in listing 11.9 is the do_backup() function. The code for do_backup() appears in listing 11.30.

Listing 11.30. *The do_backup() function.*

```
/*****
                              do_backup()

    This function provides the control for the backup copy function
    of the program.

    Argument list:    void

    Return value:     void

*****/

#include <stdio.h>

#include "win.h"


void do_backup(void)
{
   extern char file_mask[];
   size_t number;
   int j;
   unsigned selected;


   number = 0;

   j = check_paths();
   if (j == 0) {
      clrwork();
      restore_old_directory();
      return;
   }

   j = get_filedir_alloc();
   if (j == 0) {
```

```
        clrwork();
        restore_old_directory();
        return;
}

    j = get_file_mask();

    if (j == 0) {
        clrwork();
        restore_old_directory();
        free(fptr);
        return;
    }

    if (mouse_here) {
        hide_cursor();
    }

    if (file_source[0] != file_dest[0]) {              /* Change drives?  */
        change_drive(file_dest[0]);
    }
    chdir(file_dest);

    number = do_directory(file_mask);
    if (number == 0) {
        alert(5, 25, "No files matched the mask", "Ok",
            FLWHITE, box_b, FLWHITE, button_b);
        if (file_source[0] != file_dest[0]) {          /* Change drives?  */
            change_drive(file_source[0]);
        }
        chdir(file_source);
        free(fptr);
        return;
    }
    qsort(fptr, number, sizeof(FILEDIR), (int (*)(const void *,
        const void *))fcompare);
    show_files(fptr, 0, number);
    if (mouse_here) {
        hide_cursor();
    }
    selected = select_files(number, fptr);

    clrwork();
```

continues

Listing 11.30. continued

```
if (selected == 0) {
   restore_old_directory();
   free(fptr);
   return;
}

if (file_source[0] != file_dest[0]) {
   change_drive(file_source[0]);
}
chdir(file_source);

do_copies(number, selected);
free(fptr);
restore_old_directory();
}
```

The code is very similar to the previous copy routines, except that the directory occurs on the destination drive rather than the source drive. In other words, the file mask is applied to the destination drive and not to the source drive. After the user selects the files to copy (usually by using F10 to copy all files for a backup), the program changes back to the source directory and copies the selected files to the backup disk. With these two minor changes, the code for do_backup() is the same as the other copy options.

Delete File Control Function—*do_delete( )*

This section discusses the Delete option in the primary menu. Four secondary options are associated with Delete. Files may be deleted based on a file mask, a date, everything but a date, a file's creation later than a certain date, and a file's creation before a certain date. The shell function that controls the delete options is presented in listing 11.31.

Listing 11.31. The do_delete() *function.*

```
/*****

                        do_delete()
```

This function is the main entry point for the delete menu
option.

Argument list: void

Return value: void

```
*****/

#include "win.h"

extern MENU menu2[];

void do_delete(void)
{
   mkey = wbox_menu_start(1, 11, menu2, hot_key_color, sub_menu_b,
                       sub_menu_f, 1, box_h);
   if (mkey == ESCAPE)
      return;

   switch (last) {
      case 0:                           /* Mask          */
         do_mask_delete();
         break;
      case 1:                           /* Date          */
         do_date_delete(SAMEAGE);
         break;
      case 2:                           /* All but       */
         do_date_delete(NOT_EQUAL);
         break;
      case 3:                           /* Older         */
         do_date_delete(OLDER);
         break;
      case 4:                           /* Younger       */
         do_date_delete(YOUNGER);
         break;
      default:
         break;
   }
}
```

Delete Files—*do_mask_delete( )*

Only two functions control all the delete options. The first type of delete uses a simple file mask for the delete. The code for the first delete option, do_mask_delete( ), is shown in listing 11.32.

Listing 11.32. *The* do_mask_delete( ) *function.*

```
/*****

                          do_mask_delete()

    This function deletes files for a specified mask. The global
    variable file_mask[] is used to control the files listed for
    selection.

    Argument list:    void

    Return value:     void

*****/

#include "win.h"


void do_mask_delete(void)
{
    size_t number;
    int i;
    unsigned selected;

    number = 0;

    i = check_paths();
    if (i == 0) {
        clrwork();
        restore_old_directory();
        return;
    }

    i = get_file_mask();

    if (i == 0) {
        clrwork();
```

```
      restore_old_directory();
      return;
 }

i = get_filedir_alloc();
 if (i == 0) {
     clrwork();
     restore_old_directory();
     return;
 }

 if (mouse_here) {
     hide_cursor();
 }

 number = do_directory(file_mask);

 if (number == 0) {
     alert(5, 25, "No files matched the mask", "Ok",
         FLWHITE, box_b, FLWHITE, button_b);
     clrwork();
     restore_old_directory();
     free(fptr);
     return;
 }
 qsort(fptr, number, sizeof(FILEDIR), (int (*)(const void *, const void *))fcompare);
 show_files(fptr, 0, number);
 if (mouse_here) {
     hide_cursor();
 }

 selected = select_files(number, fptr);

 if (selected == 0) {
     clrwork();
     restore_old_directory();
     free(fptr);
     return;
 }

 clrwork();
 show_files(fptr, 0, number);
 i = two_button(12, 25, "Are you sure you want to delete them?",
```

continues

Listing 11.32. continued

```
                  "  Ok  ", "Cancel", FLWHITE, box_b, FLWHITE, button_b);

    if (i != 1) {
       clrwork();
       restore_old_directory();
       free(fptr);
       return;
    }

    if (selected) {
       do_delete_file(number, selected);
    }
    free(fptr);
    restore_old_directory();
}
```

Delete Select File—*do_delete_file( )*

All of the code in listing 11.31 should look familiar to you. The only new function is do_delete_file(), shown in listing 11.33.

Listing 11.33. The do_delete_file() function.

```
/*****
                         do_delete_file()

    This function deletes files that have been marked for deletion.
    The fptr[i].use flag is used to denote files to delete.

    Argument list:    int number      number of files that matched the
                                      mask
                      int selected    number actually selected for
                                      deletion

    Return value:     int             number of files deleted
                                      successfully

*****/
```

```c
#include "win.h"

int do_delete_file(int number, int selected)
{
    int col, count, i, row;

    row = SCREENROW; col = SCREENCOL;
    for (count = i = 0; i < number; i++) {
        if (fptr[i].use) {
            if (remove(fptr[i].fname) == 0)
                count++;
            flip_file(fptr[i].fname, 0, row, col);
            col += FILENAMESIZE;
            if (col > LASTCOL) {
                col = SCREENCOL;
                row++;
            }
        if (row > LASTROW) {
                clrwork();
                show_files(fptr, i + 1, number);
                row = SCREENROW; col = SCREENCOL;
            }
        }
    }

    if (count != selected) {
        alert(5, 25, "Not all files deleted", "Ok",
            FLWHITE, box_b, FLWHITE, button_b);
        clrwork();
    } else {
        if (selected) {
            alert(5, 20, "All files deleted successfully", "Ok",
                FLWHITE, box_b, FLWHITE, button_b);
            clrwork();
        }
    }
    return count;
}
```

The standard library function remove() is used to delete the files from the disk. If the selection process set the fptr[i].use FILEDIR member to logical True, the file is marked for deleting. As the files are deleted, count is maintained. If the number of files selected does not match the number actually deleted (for example, a read-only file), a message to that effect is given. When you run the delete option, you will note that the files are displayed first in reverse video and then in normal video as each file is deleted. This shows the user that the program is running.

Delete Files by Date— *do_date_delete( )*

All the remaining delete options are controlled by a single function: do_date_delete(). As seen in listing 11.34, much of the code for do_date_delete() is identical to listing 11.32.

Listing 11.34. *The* do_date_delete() *function.*

```
/*****

                          do_date_delete()

     This function deletes files that have been marked for deletion
     based on a date criterion.

     Argument list:    int type         type of delete to do:
                                              YOUNGER   = 0
                                              SAMEAGE   = 1
                                              OLDER     = 2
                                              NOT_EQUAL = 3

     Return value:     int              number of files deleted
                                        successfully

*****/

#include "win.h"

int do_date_delete(int type)
{
    size_t number;
    int i;
    unsigned date, selected;

    number = 0;
```

```
    i = check_paths();
    if (i == 0) {
       clrwork();
       restore_old_directory();
       return 0;
    }

    i = get_file_mask();

    if (i == 0) {
       clrwork();
       restore_old_directory();
       return 0;
}

    get_date_mask(&date);

    if (date == 0) {
       clrwork();
       restore_old_directory();
       return 0;
    }

    i = get_filedir_alloc();
    if (i == 0) {
       clrwork();
       restore_old_directory();
       return 0;
    }

    if (mouse_here) {
       hide_cursor();
    }

    switch (type) {
       case YOUNGER:
          number = do_date_dir(date, YOUNGER);
          break;
       case SAMEAGE:
          number = do_date_dir(date, SAMEAGE);
          break;
       case OLDER:
          number = do_date_dir(date, OLDER);
```

continues

Listing 11.34. continued

```
            break;
        case NOT_EQUAL:
            number = do_date_dir(date, NOT_EQUAL);
            break;
        default:
            break;
    }

    if (number == 0) {
        alert(5, 25, "No files matched the mask", "Ok",
            FLWHITE, box_b, FLWHITE, button_b);
        clrwork();
        free(fptr);
        restore_old_directory();
        return 0;
    }
    qsort(fptr, number, sizeof(FILEDIR), (int (*)(const void *, const void *))fcompare);
    show_files(fptr, 0, number);
    if (mouse_here) {
        hide_cursor();
    }

    selected = select_files(number, fptr);
    if (selected == 0) {
        clrwork();
        free(fptr);
        restore_old_directory();
        return 0;
    }

    clrwork();

    i = two_button(12, 25, "Are you sure you want to delete them?",
            "  Ok  ", "Cancel", FLWHITE, box_b, FLWHITE, button_b);

    if (i != 1) {
        clrwork();
        restore_old_directory();
        free(fptr);
        return 0;
    }
```

```
    }

    if (selected) {
        do_delete_file(number, selected);
    }
    restore_old_directory();
    free(fptr);

    return 1;
}
```

The major difference in do_date_delete() is the switch statement that controls the type of directory that is performed. Based on the type of delete being done and the file mask, the arguments to do_date_dir() determine the files that are displayed for user selection. (See listing 11.29.) The remainder of the function behaves in the same manner as do_mask_delete().

This completes the Delete option of the primary menu.

The Search Option

There are only two search options: a simple search with a file mask, and search for a specified file. The shell that controls the Search option from the primary menu is so simple it does not need to be discussed here. (You will find it on your disk, in the main() program file, Listing 11.2.)

Do Directory—*do_simple_dir( )*

The first search corresponds to a "dir /w" command to MS-DOS. The code for do_simple_dir() appears in listing 11.35.

Listing 11.35. *The do_simple_dir() function.*

```
/*****

                        do_simple_dir()

    This function does a simple directory search.

    Argument list:      void
```

continues

Listing 11.35. continued

```
    Return value:      void

*****/

#include "win.h"

extern char file_mask[];

void do_simple_dir(void)
{
    int i, number;
    char full_path[65], drive;
    char old_path[65];
    char path_name[65];


    if (file_source[0] == '\0') {
        alert(5, 25, "Source path not set. Use deFault option.", "Ok",
            FLWHITE, box_b, FLWHITE, button_b);
        clrwork();
        restore_old_directory();
        return;
    }

   i = get_file_mask();
  if (i == 0) {
        clrwork();
        restore_old_directory();
        return;
    }

    drive = (char) getcurdrive() + 'A';
    if (drive != file_source[0]) {
        change_drive(file_source[0]);
    }
    chdir(file_source);

    i = get_filedir_alloc();
    if (i == 0) {
        clrwork();
        restore_old_directory();
        return;
    }
```

```
    if (mouse_here) {
        hide_cursor();
    }

    number = do_directory(file_mask);
    if (number == 0) {
        alert(5, 25, "No files found", "Ok",
            FLWHITE, box_b, FLWHITE, button_b);
        restore_old_directory();
        free(fptr);
        return;
    }
    qsort(fptr, number, sizeof(FILEDIR), (int (*)(const void *,
        const void *))fcompare);
    show_files(fptr, 0, number);

    select_files(number, fptr);            /* Not really selecting them */

    clrwork();
    free(fptr);
    restore_old_directory();
}
```

Again, the code is almost identical to many other routines. In fact, the only difference is that you call select_files(), but do nothing after that function call. The reason for calling select_files() is that all the control logic to scroll through the list of files already is in that function. The remaining code should be old hat to you by now.

Perhaps the most useful option in the entire program is the file search command. To use this option, you set the source directory to the root of the disk drive to be searched (for example, C). Next you enter the name of the file you want to locate on the drive. The program then searches the entire disk for the file specified and displays the full path name where it finds the file. This option and the funcf.c program from Chapter 9, "Odds and Ends," make it easy to find a certain function that is hiding somewhere on the drive.

Search for a File—
do_ file_search( )

The do_file_search() control function for the file search option is presented in listing 11.36.

Listing 11.36. *The* do_file_search() *function.*

```
/*****

                           do_file_search()

      This is the entry point for the search options from the main
   menu. It is responsible for gathering the setup information for
   the file search.

      Argument list:    void

      Return value:     void

*****/

#include <string.h>
#include <dos.h>
#include <dir.h>                    /* OMIT THIS FOR MICROSOFT C */
#include <errno.h>

#include "win.h"

extern char file_mask[];
extern int match_count;


void do_file_search(void)
{
   int i;
   char full_path[65], drive;
   char old_path[65];
   char path_name[65];
   char target[13];


   if (file_source[0] =='\0') {
      alert(5, 25, "Source path not set. Use deFault option.",
      "Ok",
```

```
        FLWHITE, box_b, FLWHITE, button_b);
   clrwork();
   restore_old_directory();
   return;
}

i = get_file_mask();
if (i == 0) {
   clrwork();
   restore_old_directory();
   return;
}
i = no_wildcard_mask();
if (i == 0) {
   alert(5, 25, "No wild cards allowed in mask.", "Ok",
         FLWHITE, box_b, FLWHITE, button_b);
   clrwork();
   restore_old_directory();
   return;
}

drive = (char) getcurdrive() + 'A';
if (drive != file_source[0]) {
   change_drive(file_source[0]);
}

strcpy(full_path, file_source);
i = strlen(full_path);
switch (i) {
   case 0:
      alert(5, 25, "Source path not set. Use deFault option.", "Ok",
         FLWHITE, box_b, FLWHITE, button_b);
      clrwork();
      restore_old_directory();
      return;
   case 1:
      strcat(full_path, ":");
   case 2:
      strcat(full_path, "\\");
      break;
   default:
      if (full_path[2] != '\\') {
         alert(5, 25, "Improper source path. Use deFault option.", "Ok",
            FLWHITE, box_b, FLWHITE, button_b);
```

continues

Listing 11.36. continued

```
                clrwork();
                restore_old_directory();
                return;
            }
            break;
        }
    strcpy(old_path, full_path);

    match_count = 0;
    i = find_file(full_path, file_mask);

    if (i == 0) {
        alert(5, 25, "No files matched the mask", "Ok",
            FLWHITE, box_b, FLWHITE, button_b);
    } else {
        alert(13, 25, "No more files found", "Ok",
            FLWHITE, box_b, FLWHITE, button_b);
    }
    clrwork();
    restore_old_directory();
}
```

The program assumes that `file_source[]` is properly set before calling the function.

Check for Wild Cards—
no_wildcard_mask( )

The call to `get_file_mask()` asks the user to enter the name of the file to locate. Because a specific file must be entered, the program calls `no_wildcard_mask()`, shown in listing 11.37, to make sure the user enters a specific file name.

Listing 11.37. The `no_wildcard_mask( )` *function.*

```
/*****
                        no_wildcard_mask()
```

        This function checks the file name to make sure there are no
    wild card characters (*, ?) in the file name.

        Argument list: void   (file_mask is a global)

        Return value: int   0 if wild card found; 1 if okay

    *****/

    #include <stdio.h>
    #include <stdlib.h>
    #include <string.h>

    #include "win.h"

    int no_wildcard_mask(void)
    {
        char *ptr;
        int len;

        len = strlen(file_mask);
        ptr = memchr(file_mask, '*', len);
        if (ptr)
            return 0;
        ptr = memchr(file_mask, '?', len);
        if (ptr)
            return 0;
        return 1;
    }

The `no_wildcard_mask()` function simply checks for the presence of an asterisk or a question mark by calls to `memchr()`. If either character is found in the file name, the program issues an error message and returns control to the primary menu. Otherwise, the file source name is copied into `full_path[]`.

If the file name is unambiguous, the program enters a `switch` statement to build a full path name. The length of `full_path[]` is checked to see whether the user remembered to set it by using the deFault option from the primary menu. If the length is 0, it has not been set, and the user must reenter the file name.

If the length is 1, the user probably entered just a single drive letter. In this case, a colon is appended to the drive, and control immediately falls into case 2. In that case statement, you appended a backslash to the path name. The default case checks to see whether a longer path name has a backslash in the third character position (for example, "C:\"). If the path name is longer than two characters and the third character is not a backslash, an error message is given. If a longer, incorrect path name is given, such as "C:\this_is_a_long_path", the program simply says it cannot find a match on the file name.

Find the File—*find_ file( ) and find_ file_rec( )*

After the path name is checked and passed, the program calls find_file(), whose code is presented in listing 11.38. All the function does is convert the target file name (target[]) to uppercase letters. It then calls find_file_rec() to do all the real work.

Listing 11.38. The find_file() *function.*

```
/*****
                        find_file()

    This function converts all file names to uppercase before
calling the function that actually finds the file.

    Argument list:    char *path_name      pointer to full path name
                      char *target         pointer to file to find

    Return value:     int                  a count of matches found


*****/

#include "win.h"


int find_file(char *path_name, char *target)
{
    int i;
```

```
   for (i = 0; target[i]; i++) {
      target[i] = toupper(target[i]);
   }
   return find_file_rec(path_name, target);
}
```

The code for find_file_rec() is given in listing 11.39.

Listing 11.39. *The* find_file_rec() *function.*

```
/*****
                         find_file_rec()

      This function uses recursion to find a specified file. Note that
   this function does not allow for wild cards in the name.

      Argument list:      char *path_name      pointer to full path name
                          char *target         pointer to file to find


      Return value:       int                  a count of matches found

*****/

#include <dir.h>              /* CHANGE TO DOS.H FOR MICROSOFT C */
#include "win.h"

extern int match_count;

#define ALL       23          /* Sets all attribute bits for mask */

int find_file_rec(char *path_name, char *target)
{
   char temp_path[66];
   char temp[66];
   int done, change, i, len;
   struct ffblk p;                /* CHANGE FOR MICROSOFT C */
   unsigned int far *ptr, letter;

   strcpy(temp_path, path_name);
   len = strlen(path_name);
   if (len > 3 && path_name[len - 1] == '\\') {
```

continues

Listing 11.39. continued

```
      strcpy(temp_path, path_name);
      temp_path[len - 1] = '\0';
   }

change = chdir(temp_path);

   if (change == 0) {
      done = findfirst("*.*", &p, ALL);
      while (done == 0) {
         if ( strcmp(p.ff_name, ".") &&
               strcmp(p.ff_name, "..") &&
               p.ff_attrib == FA_DIREC) {
            strcpy(temp, path_name);
            strcat(temp, p.ff_name);
            strcat(temp, "\\");
            find_file_rec(temp, target);
         }
         if (strcmp(p.ff_name, target) == 0) {
            letter = (FWHITE + BBLACK) << 8;
            ptr = start_video_memory + 80 * (SCREENROW - 1 + match_count) + SCREENCOL + 3;
            for (i = 0; path_name[i]; i++) {
               *ptr = letter + path_name[i];
               ptr++;
            }
            for (i = 0; target[i]; i++) {
               *ptr = letter + target[i];
               ptr++;
            }
            match_count++;
         }
         done = findnext(&p);
      }
   }
   return match_count;
}
```

The function uses recursion to find the specified file. When the function begins execution, the current path name is copied into `temp_path[]`. If the user gives a path name other than just the root directory (for example, "C:\code\"), the `if` statement deletes the last slash. This is to prevent "double-slashing" the path name as recursion takes place. The program then calls chdir() to change into the directory contained in temp_path[]. The program checks the return value to present recursion on a bogus directory.

The program then calls findfirst() to begin a search of the directory. The symbolic constant ALL is #defined with the value 23. This represents the file attribute bits for all but a volume label search. Because you may find the current and parent files (for example, "." and ".."), you test explicitly for those files as well as the directory attribute. (Note that FA_DIRECT is the File Attribute for a DIRECTory for the Borland compiler. Your compiler probably has a similar macro defined for directory attributes. If not, simply define your own and set it to 0x10.) If the current file is *not* one of these types of files, the program builds a new path name by calls to strcpy() and strcat().

The program now calls itself to begin the recursion process. At each level of the call to find_file_rec(), you check the file names found for a match on the target file name you are trying to find. If a match is found, direct video addressing is used to display the full path name where the match occurred.

The program then increments match_count, which is used to find where to write the path name on the screen, and then calls findnext() to continue the process. Whenever done reaches a point where no more files exist in the directory, it returns to whatever previous level might have occurred during the process of recursion. Eventually, the code exhausts all directory entries, and the process terminates.

Because each level of recursion invokes a new set of temporary variables along the way, you might run out of stack space. The risk, however, probably is not that great. Some quick calculations suggest that you would have to use a little more than 6K of stack space for a depth of 32 sub-directories. It seems unlikely that this 6K figure would be a problem, and it seems even less likely that anyone would bury something 31 levels deep on a directory.

Execute a Batch File

Often I have a fixed set of files that I back up each day. I use a batch (BAT) file for daily backup because it is so easy to issue a single command and have it all done for me. The Batch option from the primary menu enables you to run a batch file from within the program.

The main() function calls do_batch() to execute the batch file option. However, because there is only one option, you can call the function that does the work (execute_bat()) directly. However, using a shell function lends consistency to the program, and it is easy to add any new batch-related options in the future. For example, eventually I will put a small editor in the program so that I can write or edit a BAT file from within the program.

Execute a Batch File—*execute_bat( )*

The code for the execute_bat() option appears in listing 11.40.

Listing 11.40. The execute_bat() *function.*

```
/*****
                           execute_bat()

    This function executes a BAT file. The function uses direct
video access to preserve the present state of the screen, and it
restores the screen when it is finished.

    Argument list:    void

    Return value:     void

*****/

#include <stdio.h>

#include "win.h"


void execute_bat(void)
{
    char *ptr;
    int i, j;
    unsigned int far *tptr, *vptr, *temp;

    if (file_source[0] =='\0') {
        alert(5, 25, "Source path not set. Use deFault option.", "Ok",
            FLWHITE, box_b, FLWHITE, button_b);
        clrwork();
```

```
        restore_old_directory();
        return;
    }

    j = get_file_mask();
    if (j == 0) {
        clrwork();
        restore_old_directory();
        return;
    }
ptr = (char *) memchr(file_mask, '.', strlen(file_mask));
    if (ptr) {
        j = strncmp(ptr + 1, "bat", 3);
        if (j) {
            alert(8, 21, "File must end in .bat.", "Ok",
             FLWHITE, box_b, FLWHITE, button_b);
        }
    }
    if (j ¦¦ ptr == NULL) {
        alert(8, 21, "File must end in .bat.", "Ok",
            FLWHITE, box_b, FLWHITE, button_b);
        clrwork();
        restore_old_directory();
        return;
    }
    clrwork();
    j = MAXWIDE * MAXDEEP;
    temp = vptr = (unsigned int *) calloc(j, sizeof(unsigned));
    if (vptr == NULL) {
        alert(8, 21, "Not enough memory.", "Ok",
            FLWHITE, box_b, FLWHITE, button_b);
        clrwork();
        restore_old_directory();
        return;
    }

    tptr = start_video_memory;
    for (i = 0; i < j; i++) {
        *vptr = *tptr;
        vptr++; tptr++;
    }
    system(file_mask);
    alert(8, 21, "Batch file finished.", "Ok",
```

continues

Listing 11.40. continued

```
          FLWHITE, box_b, FLWHITE, button_b);

    tptr = start_video_memory;
    vptr = temp;
    for (i = 0; i < j; i++) {
        *tptr = *vptr;
        vptr++; tptr++;
    }

    free(vptr);
    restore_old_directory();

}
```

The function performs the usual tests to make sure that the file source has been set. Next, the call to get_file_mask() gets the name of the batch file from the user. A call to memchr() checks to see that a full file name was typed in. The function then checks to see whether the file extension entered is "bat". (If you are worried that a user will use uppercase letters, you can convert the file name before performing the checks.) If either check fails, an error message is given, and control returns to the primary menu.

If the checks are passed, a call to calloc() is made to get enough memory to store the entire display screen. If there is not enough memory, an error message is given, and the option terminates. If there is enough memory, a for loop copies the screen display to the memory block.

A system() call actually executes the batch file. A message box tells the user when the batch file has terminated. After the user selects the Ok button, a for loop restores the previous state of the program display. Control then returns to the primary menu.

Read a File

The Read option of the primary menu presents three secondary options: display an ASCII text file, display a binary file, and have the program sample the file and guess whether it should be displayed in ASCII or binary format. In ASCII format, the program simply displays whatever is in the file. In binary format, the program presents the familiar hex dump of the file.

Figure 11.5 shows how a binary read is presented on the screen.

Fig. 11.5. *The output window for a binary file.*

```
 Copy     Delete     Search     Batch     Read      deFaults     eXit

   21   57 69 6E 64 6F 77 73 20   61 6E 64 20 77 69 6C 6C   Windows and will
   22   20 73 68 6F 77 20 79 6F   75 20 68 6F 77 20 74 6F    show you how to
   23   20 75 73 65 20 57 69 6E   64 6F 77 73 20 70 72 6F    use Windows pro
   24   64 75 63 74 69 76 65 6C   79 2E 20 49 66 20 79 6F   ductively. If yo
   25   75 20 61 72 65 20 72 65   61 6C 6C 79 20 65 61 67   u are really eag
   26   65 72 20 74 6F 20 74 72   79 20 6F 75 74 20 57 69   er to try out Wi
   27   6E 64 6F 77 73 2C 20 73   6B 69 70 20 74 6F 20 43   ndows, skip to C
   28   68 61 70 74 65 72 20 32   2C 20 60 60 47 65 74 74   hapter 2, ``Gett
   29   69 6E 67 20 53 74 61 72   74 65 64 20 77 69 74 68   ing Started with
   30   20 57 69 6E 64 6F 77 73   2E 27 27 20 42 65 66 6F    Windows.'' Befo
   31   72 65 20 67 6F 69 6E 67   20 74 6F 6F 20 66 61 72   re going too far
   32   20 69 6E 20 74 68 65 20   62 6F 6F 6B 2C 20 68 6F    in the book, ho
   33   77 65 76 65 72 2C 20 62   65 20 73 75 72 65 20 74   wever, be sure t
   34   6F 20 72 65 61 64 20 43   68 61 70 74 65 72 20 31   o read Chapter 1
   35   2C 20 60 60 49 6E 74 72   6F 64 75 63 74 69 6F 6E   , ``Introduction
   36   20 74 6F 20 4D 69 63 72   6F 73 6F 66 74 20 57 69    to Microsoft Wi
   37   6E 64 6F 77 73 2E 27 27   20 49 74 20 77 69 6C 6C   ndows.'' It will
   38   20 67 69 76 65 20 69 6D   70 6F 72 74 61 6E 74 20    give important
   39   69 6E 73 69 67 68 74 73   20 69 6E 74 6F 20 74 68   insights into th
   40   65 20 63 6F 6E 63 65 70   74 20 62 65 68 69 6E 64   e concept behind
```

Show binary dump

File Read Control Function—
do_read_text( )

The do_read() shell function calls do_read_text() to do the work. The argument passed from do_read() determines which option is executed. The code for do_read_text() appears in listing 11.41.

Listing 11.41. *The* do_read_text() *function.*

```
/*****

                         do_read_text()


    This function is used to display a data file. The file may be a
text, binary, or unknown file. If unknown is selected, the program
calls which_form() to make a best guess as to the file type.

    Argument list:    int which      which type of file is it:
                                      0 = ASCII
                                      1 = binary
                                      2 = unknown
```

continues

Listing 11.41. continued

```
   Return value:     void

*****/

#include <stdio.h>
#include "win.h"

#define MAXREADCHARS      76

extern char file_mask[];
FILE *fpin;
int abort_flag;

void do_read_text(int which)
{
   char buff[MAXREADCHARS + 1];
   int i;

   if (file_source[0] =='\0') {
      alert(5, 25, "Source path not set. Use deFault option.", "Ok",
           FLWHITE, box_b, FLWHITE, button_b);
      clrwork();
      restore_old_directory();
      return;
   }

   i = get_file_mask();

   if (i == 1 ¦¦ file_mask[0] == '*') {
      alert(5, 25, "Not valid file name.", "Ok",
           FLWHITE, box_b, FLWHITE, button_b);
      clrwork();
      restore_old_directory();
      return;
   }

   buff[0] = (char) getcurdrive() + 'A';
   if (buff[0] != file_source[0]) {
      change_drive(file_source[0]);
   }
   chdir(file_source);
```

```
   if (which == 0)
      i = 0;
   else
      i = 1;
   i = open_file(i);

   if (i == 0) {
      clrwork();
      restore_old_directory();
      return;
   }

   abort_flag = 0;
switch (which) {
      case 0:                    /* ASCII          */
         show_ascii();
         break;
      case 1:                    /* Binary         */
         show_binary();
         break;
      case 2:                    /* Don't know     */
         which = which_form();
         if (which == 1)
            show_ascii();
         else
            show_binary();
         break;
   }
   fclose(fpin);
   if (abort_flag == 0) {
      alert(7, 35, "End of file read", "Ok", FLWHITE, box_b, FLWHITE, button_b);
   }
   clrwork();
   restore_old_directory();

}
```

As before, the program checks to see that file_source has been set, and then gets the file name by a call to get_file_mask(). The program checks to ensure that a wild card is not used for the first character position. (If the first character is an asterisk, the user probably hit the Enter key without thinking.) The function then changes to the proper drive and subdirectory.

Open a File—*open_file()*

The variable which determines how the file is opened by the value it passes to open_file(). The code for open_file() is shown in listing 11.42.

Listing 11.42. The open_file() *function.*

```
/*****
                            open_file()

    This function is used to open a data file. The argument
  determines whether the data is read in ASCII or binary form.

    Argument list:    int which      0 = ASCII; 1 = binary

    Return value:     int            1 = file open; 0 = file not opened

*****/

#include <stdio.h>

#include "win.h"

extern FILE *fpin;


int open_file(int which)
{
   char buff[MAXREADCHARS];
   char *mode[] = {"r", "rb"};

   if ( (fpin = fopen(file_mask, mode[which])) == NULL) {
      sprintf(buff, "Cannot open input file: %s", file_mask);
      alert(8, 15, buff, "Ok",
          FLWHITE, box_b, FLWHITE, button_b);
      return 0;
   }
   return 1;
}
```

If the user selects either binary or unknown, the value passed into open_file() is 1. If the user chooses to read a text file, which equals 0. The value of which then indexes into the mode[] array to select the correct mode for opening the file. If the file cannot be opened, an error message is given and 0 is returned. If the file is opened, fpin becomes the input file pointer and 1 is returned.

What happens next is determined by the switch statement in listing 11.41. I discuss each case in the order that each appears in the switch statement.

Display an ASCII File—*show_ascii( )*

The show_ascii() function is presented in listing 11.43.

Listing 11.43. The show_ascii() *function.*

```
/*****
                              show_ascii()

     This function is used to display an ASCII data file.

     Argument list:    void

     Return value:     void


*****/

#include <stdio.h>

#include "win.h"

extern FILE *fpin;

void show_ascii(void)
{
    char buff[MAXREADCHARS + 1];
    int i, len, row, shown;
    unsigned key, letter;
    unsigned int far *ptr;



    row = SCREENROW - 1;
    ptr = start_video_memory + 80 * row + SCREENCOL - 1;
```

continues

Listing 11.43. continued

```c
    letter = (FWHITE + BBLACK) << 8;


    while (fgets(buff, MAXREADCHARS, fpin) != NULL) {
        shown = 0;
        len = strlen(buff);
        if (len == 1 || len == 0) {
            ptr += 80;
            continue;
        }
        if (buff[len - 1] == '\n') {
            buff[len - 1] = '\0';
        }
        if ( (ptr - start_video_memory) / 80 > MAXDEEP - 3) {
            key = get_mouse_or_key(LBUTTON, ANYWAY, &i, &i);
            switch (key) {
                case ESCAPE:
                    break;
                default:
                    clrwork();
                    ptr = start_video_memory + 80 * (SCREENROW - 1) + SCREENCOL - 1;
                    break;
            }
            if (key == ESCAPE) {
                small_abort();
                return;
            }
        }
        cursor(row, SCREENCOL);
        for (i = 0; buff[i]; i++) {
            if (buff[i] == TAB) {
                ptr += 2;
                shown += 2;
            } else {
                *ptr = letter + buff[i];
                ptr++;
                shown++;
            }
        }
        ptr += (80 - shown);
    }
}
```

The function begins by setting up pointers to video memory and setting the attribute byte. A while loop is used to read the file by calls to fgets(). The program reads up to a newline character or to a maximum of 76 characters (MAXREADCHARS). Because fgets() appends a null to the end of the characters read, you can treat it as though the characters read are a string. If the text ends with a newline, the newline is retained, and the null termination character is added after the newline.

If the length of the input string is 1 or 0, you read an empty line or the newline character. In both cases you don't want to display the character, but you do advance to the next display line by incrementing the video memory pointer (ptr) by 80.

The if statement

```
if ( (ptr - start_video_memory) / 80 > MAXDEEP - 3) {
```

checks to see whether you are at the bottom of the video display. If you are, a call to get_mouse_or_key() pauses the display. If key equals ESCAPE or the user clicks the right mouse button, you abort the file read. Otherwise, you reset the video memory pointer and continue to read and display the file.

To minimize the chance of "line folding," you treat any tab characters you read in a special way. Rather than expand the tab to eight characters, which is the norm, you treat them as though they were two characters. Two characters is usually enough to show where the tabs are, but reduces the chance that long lines are folded to the next line. Any other characters simply are displayed on the screen.

The variable shown is used to keep track of where you are on the display screen. That way, advancing by 80 - shown characters keeps you at the beginning of the next line. This process continues until the file is read completely, or until the user aborts the read. If the file is completely read, the program then closes the file, and control returns to the primary menu.

Abort a File Read—*small_abort( )*

If the user presses the Escape key or clicks the right mouse button, the program aborts the reading of the file. This causes the small_abort() function, presented in listing 11.44, to be called.

Listing 11.44. *The* `small_abort()` *function.*

```
/*****
                        small_abort()

     This function displays a message box if the user presses the
     Escape key to abort a file read. An external static variable
     (abort_flag) is set to true.

     Argument list:    void

     Return value:     void

*****/

#include <stdio.h>

#include "win.h"

extern FILE *fpin;
extern int abort_flag;

void small_abort(void)
{
   alert(5, 25, "File read aborted.", "Ok",
            FLWHITE, box_b, FLWHITE, button_b);
   fclose(fpin);
   clrwork();
   restore_old_directory();
   abort_flag = 1;
}
```

After the abort message is displayed, program control returns to the primary menu.

Display a Binary File—*show_binary()*

If the user elects to read a binary file, the switch statement in listing 11.41 sends control to the show_binary() function. Its code is given in listing 11.45.

Listing 11.45. *show_binary() Function.*

```
/*****
                                show_binary()

        This function is used to display a binary data file. The data is
    read in 16-byte chunks.

        Argument list:      void

        Return value:       void

*****/

#include <stdio.h>

#include "win.h"

#define BINARYSIZE    16

extern FILE *fpin;

void show_binary(void)
{
    unsigned char buff[MAXREADCHARS + 1];
    char temp[20];
    int i, len, j, row;
    unsigned count, key, letter;
    unsigned int far *ptr;


    row = SCREENROW - 1;
    ptr = start_video_memory + 80 * row + SCREENCOL - 1;
    letter = (FWHITE + BBLACK) << 8;

    count = 1;
    while ( (i = fread(buff, sizeof(char), BINARYSIZE, fpin)) != 0) {
        if ( (ptr - start_video_memory) / 80 > MAXDEEP - 3) {
            key = get_mouse_or_key(LBUTTON, ANYWAY, &i, &i);
            switch (key) {
                case ESCAPE:
                    break;
                default:
```

continues

Listing 11.45. *continued*

```
                clrwork();
                ptr = start_video_memory + 80 * (SCREENROW - 1) + SCREENCOL - 1;
                break;
            }
            if (key == ESCAPE) {
                small_abort();
                return;
            }
        }
        cursor(row, SCREENCOL);
        sprintf(temp, "%5d", count);
        for (i = 0; i < 5; i++) {
            *ptr = letter + temp[i];
            ptr++;
        }
        ptr += 2;
        for (i = 0; i < BINARYSIZE; i++) {
            if (i == 8)
                ptr++;
            sprintf(temp, "%.2X", buff[i]);
            for (j = 0; j < 2; j++) {
                *ptr = letter + temp[j];
                ptr++;
            }
            ptr++;
        }
        ptr++;
        for (i = 0; i < BINARYSIZE; i++) {
            if (isprint(buff[i]) && isascii(buff[i]))
                *ptr++ = letter + buff[i];
            else
                *ptr++ = letter + '.';
        }
        ptr += 7;
        count++;
    }
}
```

The code is very similar to show_ascii(), except when the contents are displayed on the screen. In this situation, you want to show the output in the general form of a screen dump—that is, a line number, then 16 hex characters followed by an attempt to display the 16 characters as printable ASCII characters. This formatting is accomplished using sprintf() to format the data into the desired form. If you want the output to look more like the dump.exe utility supplied with MS-DOS, you can increment count by 16 on each pass through the loop and display it as a hex number. The choice is yours.

Eventually, either the entire file is read or the user aborts the read by a call to small_abort(). In either event, the file is closed, and control returns to the primary menu.

Is It ASCII or Binary—*which_form()*

The last option in the secondary Read menu is Unknown. You can select this option when you don't know whether the file contains ASCII or binary data. The which_form() code appears in listing 11.46.

Listing 11.46. *The* which_form() *function.*

```
/*****
                              which_form()

    This function tries to determine whether a file has ASCII or
binary data. It does this by reading a small sample of the file and
counting the type of byte-data read. If half the data are non-
printing, it sets the file to binary; otherwise the data is
assumed to be ASCII. It then closes and reopens the file using
the assumed file mode.

    Argument list:    void

    Return value:     int      Assumed result: 0 = binary; 1 = ASCII

*****/

#include <stdio.h>

#include "win.h"

extern FILE *fpin;
```

continues

Listing 11.46. continued

```
int which_form(void)
{
    unsigned char buff[MAXREADCHARS];
    int c, i, unknown;

    c = 0;
    for (i = 0; i < MAXREADCHARS * 3; i++) {
        unknown = fgetc(fpin);
        if (unknown < SPACE ¦¦ unknown > DELETE) {
            c++;
        } else {
            c--;
        }
    }
    fclose(fpin);
    if (c > 0) {
        alert(5, 25, "Over 50 % is non-printable. Guess binary.", "Ok",
            FLWHITE, box_b, FLWHITE, button_b);
        open_file(1);
    } else {
        alert(5, 25, "Over 50 % is ASCII. Guess text.", "Ok",
            FLWHITE, box_b, FLWHITE, button_b);
        open_file(0);
    }
    clrwork();
    restore_old_directory();
    return (c > 0) ? 0 : 1;
}
```

All the which_form() function does is sample the contents of the file and see whether it finds more nonprinting characters than ASCII printable characters. The function reads about 200 bytes from the file and counts whether the file is a printable ASCII character. If it cannot be displayed, the count (c) is incremented. If it can be displayed, the same counter is decremented.

After the function reads the sample data, a positive count suggests a greater than 50-50 chance that it's a binary file. A negative count suggests an ASCII file. The file pointer is reset to the beginning of the file, and a message is displayed to inform the user of the results of the sample read. The program returns a 0 or 1, depending on whether the file was binary or ASCII.

When control returns to do_read_text() (shown in listing 11.41), the function calls the appropriate function based on the return value from which_form(). After the file is displayed, control returns to the primary menu.

The deFaults Options

Most of the procedures require that certain default values be set before any other option can be executed. The shell function for the default options, do_defaults(), is presented in listing 11.47.

Listing 11.47. The do_defaults() *function.*

```
/*****
                            do_defaults()

     This function is the main entry point for setting certain
  default values used throughout the program.

     Argument list:    void

     Return value:    void

*****/


#include <stdio.h>
#include <dos.h>

#include "win.h"

extern MENU menu6[];


void do_defaults(void)
{
   unsigned letter, temp, drive;

   while (TRUE) {
      last = temp;
      cursor(0, nptr[last]);
      letter = wbox_menu_start(1, 51, menu6, hot_key_color,
```

continues

Listing 11.47. *continued*

```
            sub_menu_b,
                                    sub_menu_f, 1, 0, box_h);
        if (letter == ENTER)
           temp = last;
        if (letter == ESCAPE)
           break;
        switch (last) {                    /* Variable last is a global */
           case 0:                         /* Colors                    */
              set_colors();
              break;
           case 1:                         /* Source drive              */
              get_source_drive();
              if (file_source[1] == ':') { /* A drive prefix?           */
                 drive = change_drive(file_source[0]);
                 if (drive - 1 < (int) (toupper(file_source[0]) - 'A')) {
                    alert(5, 25, "Not valid drive. Select again.", "Ok",
                       FLWHITE, box_b, FLWHITE, button_b);
                    break;
                 }
              }
              chdir(file_source);
              return;
           case 2:                         /* Destination drive         */
              get_destination_drive();
              return;
           case 3:                         /* Set mouse faster          */
              delta -= 10;
              if (delta < 10)
                 delta = 10;
              return;
           case 4:                         /* Set mouse slower          */
              delta += 10;
              if (delta > 200)
                 delta = 200;
              return;
           default:
              break;
        }
    }
}
```

The primary responsibility of the do_defaults() function is to present the secondary menu and retrieve a choice from the user. The function uses an infinite while loop to poll the keyboard and mouse for an entry. This is performed by calls to wbox_menu_start() (shown in listing 11.10). The wbox_menu_start() function returns the key that was pressed, and the global variable last contains the option selected.

The user may choose either to change the display colors (case is 0 and function set_colors() is called), set the source drive (case is 1 and function get_source_drive() is called), or set the destination drive (case is 2 and function get_destination_drive() is called). If the source drive option is selected, the source file path is checked for a drive prefix. If a drive prefix is given, a call to change_drive() is made to change to the drive. If a nonvalid drive is given, an error message is presented to the user. The call to chdir() puts the user in the proper subdirectory (if entered by the user).

No special processing for set_colors() or get_destination_drive() is needed.

Change Colors—*set_colors( )*

The set_colors() function enables the user to change the color attributes for some of the display colors. The code appears in listing 11.48.

Listing 11.48. *The* set_colors() *function.*

```
/*****
                        set_colors()

    This function is used to change the various colors used in the
program. When the program ends, any current colors in use are
written to the data named scopy.dfl.

    Argument list:    void

    Return value:    void

*****/

#include "win.h"
```

continues

Listing 11.48. *continued*

```c
#define MAXREADCHARS      76

extern MENU menu0[];

void set_default_colors(void);


static char *test_menu[] = {
   " Main menu ",
   " Sub-menus ",
   " Windows   ",
   " Highlight ",
   " Buttons   ",
   0
   };

void set_colors(void)
{
   char buff[MAXREADCHARS + 1];
   int back, c, fore, i, index, len, row;
   unsigned key;

   alert(5, 12, "'F' changes foreground, 'B' changes background.", "Ok",
           FLWHITE, box_b, FLWHITE, button_b);

   cursor(5, 10);
   colorstr(test_menu[0], main_menu_f, main_menu_b);
   cursor(7, 10);
   colorstr(test_menu[1], sub_menu_f, sub_menu_b);
   cursor(9, 10);
   colorstr(test_menu[2], box_f, box_b);
   cursor(11, 10);
   colorstr(test_menu[3], FLWHITE, box_h);
   cursor(13, 10);
   colorstr(test_menu[4], FLWHITE, button_b);
   hide_cursor();
   row = 5;
   cursor(row, 25);
   colorstr("<----", FLWHITE, BBLACK);

   index = 0;
```

```
while (TRUE) {
    key = get_mouse_or_key(LBUTTON, ANYWAY, &i, &i);
    back = fore = 0;
    switch (key) {
        case 'F':
        case 'f':
            fore = 1;
            break;
        case 'B':
        case 'b':
            back = 1;
            break;
        case ESCAPE:
            break;
        case UARROW:
            cursor(row, 25);
            colorstr("     ", FBLACK, BBLACK);
            index--;
            row -= 2;
            if (index < 0) {
                index = 3;
                row = 13;
            }
            break;
        case DARROW:
            cursor(row, 25);
            colorstr("     ", FBLACK, BBLACK);
            index++;
            row += 2;
            if (index > 4) {
                index = 0;
                row = 5;
            }
            break;
    }
    if (key == ESCAPE)
        break;
    switch (row) {
        case 5:                 /* Main menu                    */
            if (fore) {
                main_menu_f++;
                if (main_menu_f > 15)
                    main_menu_f = 0;
```

continues

Listing 11.48. continued

```
            }
        if (back) {
            main_menu_b += 16;
            if (main_menu_b > 112)
                main_menu_b = 0;
        }
        cursor(row, 10);
        colorstr(test_menu[index], main_menu_f, main_menu_b);
        cursor(row, 25);
        colorstr("<----", FLWHITE, BBLACK);
        break;
    case 7:                   /* Submenus                        */
        if (fore) {
            sub_menu_f++;
            if (sub_menu_f > 15)
                sub_menu_f = 0;
        }
        if (back) {
            sub_menu_b += 16;
            if (sub_menu_b > 112)
                sub_menu_b = 0;
        }
        cursor(row, 10);
        colorstr(test_menu[index], sub_menu_f, sub_menu_b);
        cursor(row, 25);
        colorstr("<----", FLWHITE, BBLACK);
        break;
    case 9:                   /* Windows                         */
        if (fore) {
            box_f++;
            if (box_f > 15)
                box_f = 0;
        }
        if (back) {
            box_b += 16;
            if (box_b > 112)
                box_b = 0;
        }
        cursor(row, 10);
        colorstr(test_menu[index], box_f, box_b);
        cursor(row, 25);
```

```
            colorstr("<----", FLWHITE, BBLACK);
            break;
        case 11:                 /* Highlight                        */
            if (fore)
                break;
            if (back) {
                box_h += 16;
                if (box_h > 112)
                    box_h = 0;
            }
            cursor(row, 10);
            colorstr(test_menu[index], FLWHITE, box_h);
            cursor(row, 25);
            colorstr("<----", FLWHITE, BBLACK);

            break;

        case 13:                 /* Buttons                          */
            if (fore)
                break;
            if (back) {
                button_b += 16;
                if (button_b > 112)
                    button_b = 0;
            }
            cursor(row, 10);
            colorstr(test_menu[index], FLWHITE, button_b);
            cursor(row, 25);
            colorstr("<----", FLWHITE, BBLACK);

            break;
        default:
            break;
    }
}
c_scroll(MENUROW, MENUCOL, MAXWIDE - 1, MENUROW, 0, 6, main_menu_b);
c_scroll(DLINE, MENUCOL, MAXWIDE - 1, MENUROW, 0, 6, main_menu_b);
for (menulen = i = 0; menu0[i].prompt; i++) {
    cursor(1, nptr[i]);
    colorstr(menu0[i].prompt, main_menu_f, main_menu_b);
    colorstr(MARGIN, main_menu_f, main_menu_b);
}
cursor(MENUROW, nptr[5]);
```

continues

Listing 11.48. *continued*

```
if (main_menu_f > 7) {
   i = main_menu_f - 8;
} else {
   i = main_menu_f;
}
colorstr(menu0[5].prompt, main_menu_b >> 4, i << 4);
cursor(DLINE, pcol);
colorstr(menu0[5].desc, main_menu_f, main_menu_b);
cursor(prow, pcol);

clrwork();
return;


}
```

A static array is initialized to a list of strings that are used as prompts for the function. They represent the colors that can be changed as the code is presently written. The function begins with a message box to tell the user that the F key changes the foreground colors and the B key changes the background colors.

After the user clicks on the Ok button, each of the prompts is displayed with the current color combinations. These colors are either those stored in and read from the scopy.dfl file when the program started, or any new values the user might have selected if this option was run before.

(An array of colors would make the processing of the color values in this function easier. However, using an array would compromise the readability and meaning of the color names at other places in the program. I think the extra code is well worth the readability advantages gained when variable names are used elsewhere in the program.)

After the prompts are displayed, an arrow (<----) is drawn to show the currently-active prompt. An infinite while loop calls get_mouse_or_key() to accept input from the user. The fore and back variables serve as flags for color changes. The UARROW and DARROW symbolic constants enable the user to scroll between the color prompts.

The row variable is used as the control variable for the switch statement. If the user presses the F key, the foreground color is incremented to advance the prompt color to the next value. If the B key is pressed, the background color is increased by the value 16. This is because the background colors are offset by four bits (that is, $2^4 = 16$).

After the user has made the changes desired, pressing the Escape key causes control to break out of the `while` loop. The calls to `c_scroll()`, `cursor()`, and `colorstr()` at the bottom of the function are used to update the display with the newly-selected colors.

As mentioned in several sections of this chapter, a number of new color variables can be added to those shown in listing 11.48. Simply create a new color variable, add a new prompt to the list, and add a new case to the `switch` statement. You also must modify the functions that read and write the colors to the scopy.dfl file, too.

Source and Destination Paths— *get_source_drive( )* and *get_destination_drive( )*

The `get_source_drive()` and `get_destination_drive()` functions are identical. The `get_source_drive()` function fills in the `file_source[]` array, and `get_destination_drive()` fills in the `file_dest[]` array. These two functions are presented in listings 11.49 and 11.50.

***Listing 11.49.** The `get_source_drive()` function.*

```
/*****
                          get_source_drive()

     This function is used to set the default source drive used with
     almost all aspects of the program. This function sets the global
     variable file_source[].

     Argument list:    void

     Return value:     int      1 if successful; 0 if not

*****/

#include "win.h"


int get_source_drive(void)
{
```

continues

Listing 11.49. continued

```
char button1[15], button2[15], m[20];
int bloca[4] = {5, 20, 5, 40};              /* Button coordinates        */
int fw, i;
struct DIALOG mine;

init_dialog(&mine);
mine.wide = 65; mine.deep = 8;
mine.dfcolor = FWHITE; mine.dbcolor = box_b;
if (create_d(3, 7, mine.wide, mine.deep, &mine) == 0) {
   return 0;
}
strcpy(button1, "    Ok    ");
strcpy(button2, "  Cancel  ");
strcpy(m, "Source path: ");
show_dialog(mine);
mine.locations = bloca;

do_button(bloca[0], bloca[1], button1, FLWHITE, button_b, mine);
do_button(bloca[2], bloca[3], button2, FLWHITE, button_b, mine);
getcwd(file_source, PATHMAX);
strcpy(old_source, file_source);
fw = 40;                                    /* Field width for file mask */
mine.fmcolor = FLWHITE; mine.bmcolor = box_b;
mine.ffcolor = FLWHITE; mine.bfcolor = hot_key_color;
i = get_string(2, 3, m, file_source, fw, mine, strlen(button1));
if (i == ESCAPE) {
   file_source[0] = '\0';                   /* User cancelled it         */
}
close_dialog(mine);

return 1;
}
```

Listing 11.50. The get_destination_drive() *function.*

```
/*****

                    get_destination_drive()

   This function is used to set the default destination drive used
```

with the copy options in the program. This function sets the global
variable file_dest[].

```
    Argument list:    void

    Return value:     int       1 if successful; 0 if not

*****/

#include "win.h"


int get_destination_drive(void)
{
    char button1[15], button2[15], m[20];
    int bloca[4] = {5, 20, 5, 40};           /* Button coordinates        */
    int fw, i;
    struct DIALOG mine;

    init_dialog(&mine);

    mine.wide = 65; mine.deep = 8;
    mine.dfcolor = FWHITE; mine.dbcolor = box_b;
    if (create_d(3, 7, mine.wide, mine.deep, &mine) == 0) {
        return 0;
    }
    strcpy(button1, "    Ok    ");
    strcpy(button2, "  Cancel  ");
    strcpy(m, "Destination path: ");

    show_dialog(mine);

    mine.locations = bloca;

    do_button(bloca[0], bloca[1], button1, FLWHITE, button_b, mine);
    do_button(bloca[2], bloca[3], button2, FLWHITE, button_b, mine);
    strcpy(file_dest, "A:\\");
    fw = 40;                                  /* Field width for file mask */
    mine.fmcolor = FLWHITE; mine.bmcolor = box_b;
    mine.ffcolor = FLWHITE; mine.bfcolor = hot_key_color;
    i = get_string(2, 2, m, file_dest, fw, mine, strlen(button1));
    if (i == ESCAPE) {
```

continues

Listing 11.50. continued

```
    file_dest[0] = '\0';              /* User cancelled it        */
  }
  close_dialog(mine);

  if (strlen(file_dest) > 3)
    strcat(file_dest, "\\");

  return 1;
}
```

Both functions are similar to ones shown earlier in this chapter. The only difference between listings 11.49 and 11.50 is that `file_dest[]` has a trailing backslash appended to it. This is done because the destination path name normally is used to create new files on a drive other than the currently active data drive. On the other hand, the program normally logs onto the path name held in `file_source[]`.

The eXit Option

The only remaining option is the eXit option. This option, however, has no real code. If the user selects this option or presses the Escape key, the program breaks out of the infinite `while` loop in listing 11.2. As soon as it is out of the `while` loop, the program frees `cptr`, closes the main display window, writes the color values to the scopy.dfl file, and terminates the program.

Conclusion

Although I find SC to be a useful program in its own right, its real purpose is to show you how you can fit the functions presented in this book into a rather large application. I'm sure you will find new features you want to incorporate into SC. If you do add something you think is pretty slick and want to share it with the rest of us, send it to me in care of the publisher. Perhaps it will get included in the next edition of this book.

APPENDIX A

ASCII Codes

This appendix contains the American Standard Code for Information Interchange (ASCII) codes, as well as the extended character set. The table also includes the hexadecimal and decimal representations for the ASCII character set.

Hex	Dec	Screen	Ctrl	Key	Hex	Dec	Screen	Ctrl	Key
00h	0		NUL	^@	1Ah	26	→	SUB	^Z
01h	1	☺	SOH	^A	1Bh	27	←	ESC	^[
02h	2	☻	STX	^B	1Ch	28	∟	FS	^\
03h	3	♥	ETX	^C	1Dh	29	↔	GS	^]
04h	4	♦	EOT	^D	1Eh	30	▲	RS	^^
05h	5	♣	ENQ	^E	1Fh	31	▼	US	^_
06h	6	♠	ACK	^F	20h	32			
07h	7	•	BEL	^G	21h	33	!		
08h	8	◘	BS	^H	22h	34	"		
09h	9	○	HT	^I	23h	35	#		
0Ah	10	◙	LF	^J	24h	36	$		
0Bh	11	♂	VT	^K	25h	37	%		
0Ch	12	♀	FF	^L	26h	38	&		
0Dh	13	♪	CR	^M	27h	39	'		
0Eh	14	♫	SO	^N	28h	40	(		
0Fh	15	☼	SI	^O	29h	41	)		
10h	16	►	DLE	^P	2Ah	42	*		
11h	17	◄	DC1	^Q	2Bh	43	+		
12h	18	↕	DC2	^R	2Ch	44	,		
13h	19	‼	DC3	^S	2Dh	45	-		
14h	20	¶	DC4	^T	2Eh	46	.		
15h	21	§	NAK	^U	2Fh	47	/		
16h	22	▬	SYN	^V	30h	48	0		
17h	23	↨	ETB	^W	31h	49	1		
18h	24	↑	CAN	^X	32h	50	2		
19h	25	↓	EM	^Y	33h	51	3		

Hex	Dec	Screen	Hex	Dec	Screen	Hex	Dec	Screen
34h	52	4	62h	98	b	90h	144	É
35h	53	5	63h	99	c	91h	145	æ
36h	54	6	64h	100	d	92h	146	Æ
37h	55	7	65h	101	e	93h	147	ô
38h	56	8	66h	102	f	94h	148	ö
39h	57	9	67h	103	g	95h	149	ò
3Ah	58	:	68h	104	h	96h	150	û
3Bh	59	;	69h	105	i	97h	151	ù
3Ch	60	<	6Ah	106	j	98h	152	ÿ
3Dh	61	=	6Bh	107	k	99h	153	Ö
3Eh	62	>	6Ch	108	l	9Ah	154	Ü
3Fh	63	?	6Dh	109	m	9Bh	155	¢
40h	64	@	6Eh	110	n	9Ch	156	£
41h	65	A	6Fh	111	o	9Dh	157	¥
42h	66	B	70h	112	p	9Eh	158	₧
43h	67	C	71h	113	q	9Fh	159	ƒ
44h	68	D	72h	114	r	A0h	160	á
45h	69	E	73h	115	s	A1h	161	í
46h	70	F	74h	116	t	A2h	162	ó
47h	71	G	75h	117	u	A3h	163	ú
48h	72	H	76h	118	v	A4h	164	ñ
49h	73	I	77h	119	w	A5h	165	Ñ
4Ah	74	J	78h	120	x	A6h	166	ª
4Bh	75	K	79h	121	y	A7h	167	º
4Ch	76	L	7Ah	122	z	A8h	168	¿
4Dh	77	M	7Bh	123	{	A9h	169	⌐
4Eh	78	N	7Ch	124	|	AAh	170	¬
4Fh	79	O	7Dh	125	}	ABh	171	½
50h	80	P	7Eh	126	~	ACh	172	¼
51h	81	Q	7Fh	127	Δ	ADh	173	¡
52h	82	R	80h	128	Ç	AEh	174	«
53h	83	S	81h	129	ü	AFh	175	»
54h	84	T	82h	130	é	B0h	176	░
55h	85	U	83h	131	â	B1h	177	▒
56h	86	V	84h	132	ä	B2h	178	▓
57h	87	W	85h	133	à	B3h	179	│
58h	88	X	86h	134	å	B4h	180	┤
59h	89	Y	87h	135	ç	B5h	181	╡
5Ah	90	Z	88h	136	ê	B6h	182	╢
5Bh	91	[	89h	137	ë	B7h	183	╖
5Ch	92	\	8Ah	138	è	B8h	184	╕
5Dh	93	]	8Bh	139	ï	B9h	185	╣
5Eh	94	^	8Ch	140	î	BAh	186	║
5Fh	95	_	8Dh	141	ì	BBh	187	╗
60h	96	`	8Eh	142	Ä	BCh	188	╝
61h	97	a	8Fh	143	Å	BDh	189	╜

Hex	Dec	Screen	Hex	Dec	Screen	Hex	Dec	Screen
BEh	190	⌐	D4h	212	╘	EAh	234	Ω
BFh	191	┐	D5h	213	╒	EBh	235	δ
C0h	192	└	D6h	214	╓	ECh	236	∞
C1h	193	┴	D7h	215	╫	EDh	237	φ
C2h	194	┬	D8h	216	╪	EEh	238	∈
C3h	195	├	D9h	217	┘	EFh	239	∩
C4h	196	─	DAh	218	┌	F0h	240	≡
C5h	197	┼	DBh	219	█	F1h	241	±
C6h	198	╞	DCh	220	▄	F2h	242	≥
C7h	199	╟	DDh	221	▌	F3h	243	≤
C8h	200	╚	DEh	222	▐	F4h	244	⌠
C9h	201	╔	DFh	223	▀	F5h	245	⌡
CAh	202	╩	E0h	224	α	F6h	246	÷
CBh	203	╦	E1h	225	β	F7h	247	≈
CCh	204	╠	E2h	226	Γ	F8h	248	°
CDh	205	═	E3h	227	π	F9h	249	•
CEh	206	╬	E4h	228	Σ	FAh	250	·
CFh	207	╧	E5h	229	σ	FBh	251	√
D0h	208	╨	E6h	230	μ	FCh	252	^{n}
D1h	209	╤	E7h	231	τ	FDh	253	^{2}
D2h	210	╥	E8h	232	Φ	FEh	254	■
D3h	211	╙	E9h	233	θ	FFh	255	

Index

M

T

Que Gives You The Most Comprehensive Programming Information Available!

Installation Summary

This disk contains the source and header files for the programs in *C Programmer's Toolkit,* 2nd Edition. The programs are archived in self-extracting files that can be used simply by entering the name of the corresponding chapter to unarchive. For example, to access the files in Chapter 1, enter

CHAP1

at the DOS prompt. The files in Chapter 1 will be unarchived, and you then can access them normally.

These archive files contain three types of files: listings, programs, and header files. Header files have the .H extension. Listings and programs use the following file-naming conventions:

Listings	LISTccnn.C
Programs	PROGccnn.C

Replace the characters "cc" with the chapter number, and "nn" with the listing or program number. Thus, listing 3.2 from the book is LIST0302.C on the disk.

If your computer uses 3¹/₂-inch disks . . .

Although most personal computers use 5¹/₄-inch disks to store information, some newer computers are switching to 3¹/₂-inch disks for information storage. If your computer uses 3¹/₂-inch disks, you can return this form to SAMS to obtain a 3¹/₂-inch disk to use with this book. Simply fill out the remainder of this form, and mail to:

> ***C Programmer's Toolkit,* 2nd Edition**
> Disk Exchange
> Que
> 11711 N. College Ave., Suite 140
> Carmel, IN 46032

We will then send you, free of charge, the 3¹/₂-inch version of the book software.

Name _____   Phone _____

Company _____   Title _____

Address _____

City _____   State _____ ZIP _____

Free Catalog!

Mail us this registration form today, and we'll send you a free catalog featuring Que's complete line of best-selling books.

Name of Book _____

Name _____

Title _____

Phone (   ) _____

Company _____

Address _____

City _____

State _____ ZIP _____

Please check the appropriate answers:

1. Where did you buy your Que book?
   - ☐ Bookstore (name: _____)
   - ☐ Computer store (name: _____)
   - ☐ Catalog (name: _____)
   - ☐ Direct from Que
   - ☐ Other: _____

2. How many computer books do you buy a year?
   - ☐ 1 or less
   - ☐ 2-5
   - ☐ 6-10
   - ☐ More than 10

3. How many Que books do you own?
   - ☐ 1
   - ☐ 2-5
   - ☐ 6-10
   - ☐ More than 10

4. How long have you been using this software?
   - ☐ Less than 6 months
   - ☐ 6 months to 1 year
   - ☐ 1-3 years
   - ☐ More than 3 years

5. What influenced your purchase of this Que book?
   - ☐ Personal recommendation
   - ☐ Advertisement
   - ☐ In-store display
   - ☐ Price
   - ☐ Que catalog
   - ☐ Que mailing
   - ☐ Que's reputation
   - ☐ Other: _____

6. How would you rate the overall content of the book?
   - ☐ Very good
   - ☐ Good
   - ☐ Satisfactory
   - ☐ Poor

7. What do you like *best* about this Que book?
   _____
   _____

8. What do you like *least* about this Que book?
   _____
   _____

9. Did you buy this book with your personal funds?
   - ☐ Yes   ☐ No

10. Please feel free to list any other comments you may have about this Que book.
    _____
    _____
    _____

Que

Order Your Que Books Today!

Name _____

Title _____

Company _____

City _____

State _____ ZIP _____

Phone No. (   ) _____

Method of Payment:

Check ☐   (Please enclose in envelope.)

Charge My: VISA ☐   MasterCard ☐
      American Express ☐

Charge # _____

Expiration Date _____

Order No.	Title	Qty.	Price	Total

You can **FAX** your order to **1-317-573-2583**. Or call **1-800-428-5331, ext. ORDR** to order direct.

Please add $2.50 per title for shipping and handling.

Subtotal _____

Shipping & Handling _____

Total _____

Que

BUSINESS REPLY MAIL
First Class Permit No. 9918   Indianapolis, IN

Postage will be paid by addressee

11711 N. College
Carmel, IN 46032

BUSINESS REPLY MAIL
First Class Permit No. 9918   Indianapolis, IN

Postage will be paid by addressee

11711 N. College
Carmel, IN 46032